"*Ministering to Families in Crisis*, edited by Ripley, Sells, and Chandler, is a comprehensive, biblically based, well-written, and excellent guide for nurturing the mental and emotional health of families in churches who are experiencing crises of all kinds. The editors have assembled a great group of authors who provide substantial and practical help for those ministering to such families. Highly recommended!"

Siang-Yang Tan, senior professor of clinical psychology at Fuller Theological Seminary and author of *Counseling and Psychotherapy: A Christian Perspective*

"*Ministering to Families in Crisis* is an invaluable resource for anyone involved in pastoral care or family ministry. With sensitivity and practical wisdom, this comprehensive guide addresses a wide range of challenges families may face. Each chapter is packed with practical strategies, real-life examples, and thoughtful reflections, making it an essential resource for anyone seeking to support and strengthen families in times of crisis. From establishing hope amid the pain of divorce to navigating the complexities of mental illness, LGBTQ+ issues, and domestic violence, this book covers it all, equipping ministry leaders to meet families where they are in the storms of life."

Matthew Stanford, CEO of the Hope and Healing Center and Institute in Houston, Texas

"I wish we didn't need *Ministering to Families in Crisis*, but I'm sure glad we have it. The difficult truth is that many of the families we serve are indeed hurting and in crisis. The problem is that many of us haven't been trained how to respond. Instead, we often feel afraid or paralyzed, wanting to help but not knowing how. *Ministering to Families in Crisis* provides the theologically robust and practical guidance we need to love and care for our families. All children, student, and family ministry leaders should read *Ministering to Families in Crisis* and keep it within reach."

Brian Dembowczyk, associate publisher for Thomas Nelson Bibles and author of *Family Discipleship That Works*

"*Ministering to Families in Crisis* is a timely and indispensable resource for any church committed to nurturing mental and emotional well-being. With compassion and expertise, the authors tackle complex issues affecting families today, offering practical guidance rooted in both Scripture and evidence-based approaches. This comprehensive guide equips pastors and church leaders to address a myriad of challenges—from mental illness to racial trauma—with grace and understanding. A must-read for those seeking to cultivate a community of support and healing within their congregation."

Samuel Rodriguez, lead pastor of New Season Church in Sacramento, California, and author of *Your Mess, God's Miracle*

"The family is the cornerstone of society and the bedrock of the Church. It matters more than we all know. This new resource is a welcome hands-on guide for ministry leaders to help our families navigate the complexities of the mental health disaster we are facing."

Tim Clinton, president of the American Association of Christian Counselors

MINISTERING to FAMILIES in CRISIS

The Essential Guide *for* Nurturing
Mental *and* Emotional Health

Jennifer S. Ripley, James N. Sells, and Diane J. Chandler, editors

ivp
Academic
An imprint of InterVarsity Press
Downers Grove, Illinois

InterVarsity Press
P.O. Box 1400 | Downers Grove, IL 60515-1426
ivpress.com | email@ivpress.com

©2024 by Jennifer Sulouff Ripley, James Sells, and Diane Joyce Chandler

All rights reserved. No part of this book may be reproduced in any form without written permission from InterVarsity Press.

InterVarsity Press® is the publishing division of InterVarsity Christian Fellowship/USA®. For more information, visit intervarsity.org.

All Scripture quotations, unless otherwise indicated, are taken from The Holy Bible, New International Version®, NIV®. Copyright © 1973, 1978, 1984, 2011 by Biblica, Inc.™ Used by permission of Zondervan. All rights reserved worldwide. www.zondervan.com. The "NIV" and "New International Version" are trademarks registered in the United States Patent and Trademark Office by Biblica, Inc.™

While any stories in this book are true, some names and identifying information may have been changed to protect the privacy of individuals.

The publisher cannot verify the accuracy or functionality of website URLs used in this book beyond the date of publication.

Cover design: David Fassett
Interior design: Daniel van Loon
Images: E+ / Getty Images: © THEPALMER. © marcoventuriniautieri

ISBN 978-1-5140-0042-7 (print) | ISBN 978-1-5140-0043-4 (digital)

Printed in the United States of America ∞

Library of Congress Cataloging-in-Publication Data
Names: Ripley, Jennifer S., 1972- editor. | Sells, James Nathan, 1958- editor. | Chandler, Diane J., editor.
Title: Ministering to families in crisis : the essential guide for nurturing mental and emotional health / Jennifer S. Ripley, James N. Sells, and Diane J. Chandler, editors.
Description: Downers Grove, IL : IVP Academic, [2024] | Includes bibliographical references.
Identifiers: LCCN 2024015871 (print) | LCCN 2024015872 (ebook) | ISBN 9781514000427 (print) | ISBN 9781514000434 (digital)
Subjects: LCSH: Family counseling–Religious aspects–Christianity. | Family crises. | Pastoral counseling. | BISAC: RELIGION / Christian Ministry / Counseling & Recovery | RELIGION / Christian Living / Family & Relationships
Classification: LCC BV4438 .M394 2024 (print) | LCC BV4438 (ebook) | DDC 259/.12–dc23/eng/20240523
LC record available at https://lccn.loc.gov/2024015871
LC ebook record available at https://lccn.loc.gov/2024015872

31 30 29 28 27 26 25 24 | 13 12 11 10 9 8 7 6 5 4 3 2 1

I am grateful to the Downey Church community

of Orlando and the Dees family,

who faithfully served there for 60 years, ministered to three

generations of my family, and led me to Christ as a child.

JENNIFER S. RIPLEY

To Rev. Harold E. Sells (1929–2022).

My first and best pastoral counseling instructor.

JAMES N. SELLS

To every pastor and ministry leader

who sacrificially assists God's people through troubled

waters with tenderness and grace.

DIANE J. CHANDLER

CONTENTS

Acknowledgments ix

1 ESTABLISHING HOPE AMID THE STORM OF FAMILY CRISES 1
Jennifer S. Ripley, Diane J. Chandler, and James N. Sells

2 SPIRITUAL FORMATION IN FAMILIES 12
Diane J. Chandler

3 STRATEGIES TO DISCERN MARRIAGE AND FAMILY HEALTH AND FUNCTIONING 34
Jennifer S. Ripley, John Van Epp, and J. P. De Gance

4 CARE AND SUPPORT OF FAMILIES IMPACTED BY MENTAL ILLNESS 57
Stephen Grcevich

5 LGBTQ+ ISSUES IN MARRIAGE MINISTRY 79
Mark A. Yarhouse and Anna Brose

6 MINISTERING TO FAMILIES WHEN CHILDREN COME OUT 96
Janet B. Dean, Stephen P. Stratton, and Mark A. Yarhouse

7 DOMESTIC VIOLENCE AND CHURCH MINISTRY 119
Darby A. Strickland

8 HANDLING DIVORCE AS A MINISTRY LEADER: TUTORIAL FROM A FAMILY LAWYER 143
Lynne Marie Kohm

9 FAMILIES AFFECTED BY DISABILITY 162
Ryan Wolfe

10 SCREENS, CHILDREN, AND TEENS: THE CHALLENGES ARE REAL, AND YOU CAN HELP 183
Kathy Koch

11	**ADULTS AND SCREENS: PREVENTING CRISIS THROUGH DIGITAL DISCIPLESHIP** *Arlene Pellicane*	202
12	**RACE, DISCRIMINATION, AND STRESS IN THE FAMILY** *Cassandra D. Page and Eric M. Brown*	225
13	**MINISTERING TO FAMILIES IN POVERTY AND FINANCIAL CRISIS** *Kristen Kansiewicz*	238
14	**THE CHALLENGE OF HELPING COUPLES IN CONFLICT** *David C. Olsen*	260
15	**TRAUMA IN FAMILIES: MINISTERING WHEN THE UNIMAGINABLE HAPPENS** *Fred C. Gingrich and Heather Davediuk Gingrich*	277
16	**MINISTRY TO BLENDED FAMILIES** *David P. Mikkelson and Suzanne E. Mikkelson*	299
17	**FAMILIES AND ADDICTIONS** *Megan M. Cannedy and James N. Sells*	320
18	**FAMILIES, AGING, AND CAREGIVING** *Terry D. Hargrave and Paul Flores*	342
	List of Contributors	355

ACKNOWLEDGMENTS

We want to thank doctoral student Logan Battaglini for her assistance with formatting the book and Regent University for supporting us in our long careers in this institution of higher education.

1

ESTABLISHING HOPE AMID THE STORM OF FAMILY CRISES

Jennifer S. Ripley, Diane J. Chandler, and James N. Sells

The beautiful but now stolen artwork of Rembrandt *The Storm on the Sea of Galilee* depicts a ship tossed at sea, with Jesus at the bottom of the ship just waking up. The characters in the painting have their way of trying to handle the storm. Some seem to be working extremely hard to trim the sails, manage the rigging, and keep the bow to the wind. Others are mortified and are hanging on for dear life. One appears to have tied himself to the mainsail to survive. One sits passively at the bottom of the boat while another retches over the side. Several are sitting by Jesus, pleading with anxious faces, trying to get his attention. A copy of this painting is in my (Jennifer's) home and reminds me of the quiet calm of Jesus navigating threatening storms with sailors all around him. Jesus' calm demeanor reflects how I desire to respond to family crises. We hope this book will help you find calm assurance in the storms of ministering to families.

Being a capable minister to families is like being a qualified sailor. You are skilled in sailing various storms and sea conditions. The chapters of this book take us through some of the most challenging storms of church ministry and family crises. A family minister might ask: "What am I supposed to know about this issue?" and "How do I respond to this situation with Christlike calm and confidence?" "How do I support a person or family with biblical and practical guidance?" Ministry leaders are often expected to have expertise in addressing various problems, much deeper than what ministry training or seminary provides. This book was created as a hands-on ministry resource for your digital or physical office shelf when family issues arise in ministry. Each chapter is written by a "master sailor" to help you with your family challenges.

Think back to your first days as a new ministry leader. Perhaps you stepped into the role as a young person with little experience or later in life with an excellent graduate degree. You likely started with a sense of calling from God on a new journey ministering to others. You were excited and confident that God was with you and that you could create pathways in which people could faithfully follow Jesus. Then, a problem or crisis confronted you for which you felt unprepared. A "people challenge" likely emerged early in your leadership tenure. Did you feel prepared to respond?

When families seek help for problems, many church leaders feel unprepared to respond. Perhaps their issue was related to a substance-abusing deacon, stress about a gay family member, a blended family disagreement, or maybe a relational nor'easter blew into your office with allegations of family abuse. Possibly, a family with an autistic child or adult with an anxiety disorder asked you for prayer. Maybe a family struggling with racial discrimination looked to you for wisdom, or a parent living in poverty asked for assistance with groceries and rent. These challenges overwhelm us all—even when they don't pile up before you preach your first sermon or lead your first meeting. How did you respond, and how did the situation resolve? Few in the ministry anticipate the extent of family crises that occur.

BEING COURAGEOUS IN THE STORM

Many church leaders work hard to avoid family storms in ministry. Perhaps you have been tempted to dodge "that situation" or "that family" as they approach you during Sunday services. Whether you are the church's senior pastor, youth leader, family life ministry coordinator, elder, or a dedicated Sunday school teacher, you likely hoped someone else would help that family. Everyone feels that way sometimes, even those with years of experience. Yet, just like unpredictable weather in your city, the storms of crises are unlikely to stop. Therefore, we are here to you prepare for the current or next storm. Excellent preparation can equip you to know what to do, where to go for help, and what is likely ahead as the storm continues to rock the boat.

Vincent van Gogh is credited with saying, "The fishermen know that the sea is dangerous and the storm terrible, but they have never found these dangers sufficient reason for remaining ashore." Jesus walked by the Sea of Galilee and called Peter and Andrew, asking them to become fishers for people. Similarly, church leaders like you have refused to remain ashore. The twelve disciples had no way of knowing the difficult journey ahead when they followed him. Crises and stress would become a new way of life for them.

Yet God did not leave them alone. They had the teachings of Jesus, the Scriptures, the history of Israel, the community of believers, and the Holy Spirit to guide their work. From the world's perspective, a group of followers of a rabbi who gained few possessions in their lifetime were often shipwrecked, jailed, and far from their own families seemed like failures. But God doesn't work in the way we expect. He brings beauty from ashes, gladness instead of mourning, praise instead of a faint spirit to build oaks of righteousness (Is 61:3). This is the work of church leaders at their finest when working with families in crisis.

BEING PART OF A FAMILY

No one enters the world without a family. The "family ministry" stereotype includes images of a young couple with little children. Everyone looks perfect. The images convey tranquility, order, and relational perfection, void of tension, conflict, or sorrow. The concept of family is complicated, even messy. It transcends the boundaries of the nuclear unit, extending far beyond the confines of a singular household. You have grandparents raising children, single parents, and foster families in your church. Even those who attend church alone have family members somewhere. One pastor said, "I haven't seen a 'normal, typical' family come to my church in years." Regardless of one's life journey, every individual is inherently woven into the fabric of family in ever-changing constellations, including a dynamic and expansive network that reaches across generations and embraces diverse relationships. While contemporary society often emphasizes the nuclear family structure, the true richness of familial experience lies in the extended family's expansive embrace.

While spouses and parents have unique responsibilities and roles in each other's lives, they do not always typify the depth of family influence. Grandparents play an essential role in most families and are often the source of transmission of faith.[1] Beyond blood ties, the church family is the spiritual family that contributes profoundly to the mosaic of our lives. In recognizing the depth and breadth of these connections, we unveil a broader understanding of family—one that reflects the diverse tapestry of shared experiences, collective wisdom, and enduring bonds that shape the essence of our existence. We believe these family characteristics are closer to the idea of family as laid out in Scripture and church teachings across the millennia.

RESPONDING TO THE CALL FOR COMPASSIONATE MINISTRY

Our voyage begins with a simple yet profound call to compassionate ministry. The heart of Christ's teachings lies in love and compassion. As his followers who minister in his name, we have a sacred duty to extend compassionate care to those navigating the turbulent seas of family crises. Ministering to families in their darkest hours requires more than just knowledge; it demands a spirit of empathy that mirrors the boundless love of our Savior. The authors of each chapter provide a clear, compassionate vision of the needs and struggles people face in various family crises. Whether families are facing end-of-life care, disability, conflict, or mental illness, we can improve our effectiveness with a compassionate

---

[1] Dudley Chancey and Ron Bruner, "The Transmission of Faith and Values through Generations," *Dialogismos*, 6 (2022): 36-54, www.oc.edu/uploads/images/documents/Chancey-and-Bruner-Passing-on-Faith-Dialogismos-6.2022.pdf.

understanding of the needs and dynamics at play when that particular type of storm is underway. That is an important distinction. The crisis is the storm outside the boat, threatening its safety. Too often, families turn toward one another, making the problem internal and everyone less effective. This was the disciples' response to Jesus in the boat: "Lord, save us! We're going to drown!" (Mt 8:25). Our call is to address the storm, not fight with the people who are essential for survival.

DEVELOPING FAMILIES AS THE KEY TO A THRIVING CHURCH

The need has never been greater to address families in crisis in churches everywhere. I don't need to convince you regarding the hurting of the family, which is well-documented. J. P. De Gance of Communio Ministries has made a compelling case for generational succession, passing down the faith to younger generations through intact families. There is considerable concern about declining church attendance, with weekly attendance dropping nationwide.[2] One exception, however, counters this decline in church attendance. Adults who grew up in intact families who regularly attended church and practiced their faith at home stayed in the church.[3] While less than half of young adults today enter adulthood with continuously married parents throughout childhood, 80% of people attending church today came from intact married parents across age groups.[1] That doesn't mean single parents and struggling families can't pass on the faith, but the data is stark. Therefore, anything churches can do to encourage healthy lifelong marriages and families will trickle down to create a thriving future church community through the children raised in those families. Take notice that we have not used the phrase "declining family." We prefer to use the term hurting or suffering family as it takes on the storms of society. Families get turned broadside and receive the full brunt of crashing waves. Your task is to help families get pointed into the storm, to balance the weight, and to steer it to safety.

---

[2] ChurchTrac, "The State of Church Attendance: Trends and Statistics [2023]," www.churchtrac.com/articles/the-state-of-church-attendance-trends-and-statistics-2023.

[3] John Paul De Gance, "Nationwide Study on Faith and Relationships," Communio.org, November 2023, https://communio.org/wp-content/uploads/2023/05/COMMUNIO_Survey-of-Faith-and-Relationships-1.pdf.

The chapters in this book are authored by various Christian leaders, offering expertise across multiple ministry problems. Each chapter provides a unique understanding of family issues and practical suggestions when faced with common ministry challenges.

- Do you need to fit family ministry within a larger vision of spiritual formation? Diane Chandler, associate professor of Christian formation and leadership at Regent University and an expert in spiritual formation, introduces a vision for spiritual formation within family ministry.
- Are mental health problems arising in your church? Psychiatrist and director of KEY Ministries in Ohio, Steve Grcevich, offers an excellent primer on mental health challenges experienced by families so you can sensitively and effectively support families with members who have mental health diagnoses.
- Do you hope to offer effective marriage ministries in your church? Jennifer Ripley is a professor of psychology at Regent University, John Van Epp is a psychologist who leads the Love Thinks organization, and J. P. De Gance leads the non-profit ministry Communio. Together, they describe how to understand and respond to marriages on the individual marriage level, whole-church level, and larger community level of care.
- Are families with lesbian, gay, bisexual, or transgender members bringing issues and problems to your church community? Mark Yarhouse, professor of psychology at Wheaton College, and Anne Brose, a doctoral student in psychology at Wheaton College, cast a vision for marriage ministries when LGBTQ+ issues arise in the family. In a second chapter, Janet Dean and Steve Stratton, professors of counseling at Asbury Seminary, with Mark Yarhouse, address the needs of parents who have children who identify as LGBTQ+.
- Has family violence been an issue you have had to face? In her practical chapter on domestic violence, Darby Strickland, an author and faculty member at the Christian Counseling and Education Foundation, advocates for ministry leaders to respond well to family aggression.

- Is divorce something the people in your congregation have experienced? Perhaps you could use a briefing from a Christian lawyer, Lynne Marie Kohm, a family law expert. She provides a thorough understanding of legal avenues and experiences of divorce in family law to support ministry leaders walking through divorce with a partner or family.

- If children or adults with disabilities in your church attend your church, how might you want to minister to them creatively? Ryan Wolfe, a disability ministry pastor and leader of Ability Ministry, equips churches to provide excellent ministry to those with various disabilities. His chapter will open up new ideas and avenues to meet the needs of the many people with disabilities in every church.

- How do you handle kids and teens who are always on their phones and screens at church meetings? Or do parents complain about their kids' screen use? Educational psychologist Kathy Koch, who speaks and writes on children's ministries with Celebrate Kids ministry, raises our awareness of the issues of children and teens' screen use and how to offer an effective response as a church leader.

- Maybe it's not just the kids on their screens, but the adults are also struggling with screen time, internet sex temptation, or social media problems. Writer and speaker Arlene Pellicane, host of the podcast *The Happy Home*, addresses the adult side of digital screen discipleship.

- Does your church have members who face stress from racial division and discrimination? Cassandra Page, professor of psychology at Regent University, and Eric Brown, pastor and professor of counseling at Boston University, orient us to practical ways to respond to race-based stress.

- Do family conflicts ever make their way into small groups, classes, or counseling ministries within your church community? David Olsen, director of Samaritan Counseling Center in upstate New York, provides an excellent orientation to the family systems concept of differentiation to help church leaders respond well to conflict.

- When families ask for help with the rent or electric bill, and you want to minister well to them, you will want to read the chapter from Kristen Kansiewicz, professor of counseling at Evangel University. Her chapter illuminates the needs of those struggling with poverty and effective church responses.
- Has trauma become a more common experience among those in your church community? Whether childhood abuse, military combat, witnessing the death of loved ones, or common traumas like bullying, large numbers of Americans increasingly struggle with trauma symptoms. Fred and Heather Gingrich, professors at Toccoa Falls College and former missionaries to the Philippines, share their expertise in caring for those with trauma histories.
- Are blended families part of your church community? David and Suzanne Mikkelson, counselors at Hill City Counseling in Lynchburg, Virginia, describe creative ideas to address the needs and considerations of these families. Their chapter contains ways to be more sensitive to blended families.
- Have you had church members, or even leaders, who appear to have problems with substance abuse? Jim Sells, professor of counseling education at Regent University, and Megan Cannedy, professor of counseling at Colorado Christian University, provide important information about substance abuse, the effects on family members, and how to avoid the traps that substance abuse can create in ministry.
- Do members of your church struggle with end-of-life issues and caregiving for an elderly family member? Terry Hargrave and Paul Flores, professors at Fuller Seminary, share ministry wisdom for couples and families facing the end of life and loss.

In these chapters, we explore a range of crises, the power of well-equipped ministry, and the significance of walking alongside families in crisis. Our mission is not to offer quick fixes or easy solutions but to stand as witnesses to the redemptive power of God's love. Pastoral leaders can nurture an environment where healing begins and hope is rekindled by grounding our approach in Christian principles.

RESPONDING TO FAMILY STORMS

This chapter began by describing Rembrandt's painting *The Storm on the Sea of Galilee*. Consider locating this painting online. Then, zoom in on your screen, look closely, and ponder how you have responded when faced with ministry storms. What character do you most resonate with? Rembrandt's work helps us move past our defenses to illuminate our emotional response to pain, suffering, struggle, and uncertainty. We all have ways of handling crises, and understanding our natural tendencies can help us respond more like Jesus when they arise. We might want to work too hard, passively give up, throw up, or anxiously demand Jesus rescue us. Instead, imagine that you come up next to Jesus on that boat. Ask him for what you need. Do you need him to take your hand in hard times? To smile and remind you that you are loved? To remind you that it is worth all the hardships for the ultimate reward in God's kingdom? We challenge you to ask God for what you need in the crises you will face.

As we embark on this exploration of ministering to families in crisis within the sacred context of the church, we can gather around the timeless truth that binds us—the unwavering hope found in the presence of Jesus. The irony in the story of the storm on the Sea of Galilee is that the God of the universe, who made the sea and everything in it, was sitting right there with them. The Lord over the storm was present in that very moment. Yet their faith was so small (Mt 8:26) that the disciples could hardly breathe. How comforting to know that we are not alone, whether avoiding the problem, trying desperately to solve it, pleading anxiously to God, or retching over the side of the boat. Storms are unnerving, but Jesus is King over the storm.

In difficult times, the church's job is to create a port of peace, joy, and goodness in contrast to the darkness of the world around us. In family ministry, the light and beauty of biblical family values and practices arise in stark contrast to the world around us. The world desperately needs a vision of a healthy church and home life, and Christian leaders can hold and model that vision.

HARBORING IN THE SAFETY OF THE CHURCH

In times of crisis, the church should transform into a safe harbor, a refuge where broken hearts can find solace and shattered spirits can find restoration. Just like in Rembrandt's painting, the presence of Jesus in the boat is always available to those in our congregation. We hope that your ministry can point people to the man in the boat and that they will take his hand and walk with him through their crisis. The church is a living, breathing community bound together by the shared experience of grace. Our role as ministers is to foster an environment where families feel embraced by the love of Christ, a place where the hurting can find healing and the lost can find direction.

At the core of ministry lies the recognition that we are vessels through which the divine healer, Jesus Christ, works. As we step into the lives of families in crisis, we carry the healing balm of the gospel, trusting that the Holy Spirit will guide our words and actions. Our responsibility is not to have all the answers but to point families toward the One who does.

WEIGHING ANCHOR AS YOU CONTINUE THIS JOURNEY

As we sail into the practical aspects of ministering to families in crisis, let us remember that our goal is not merely to manage the symptoms but to address the root causes of issues with the transformative power of God. As a church leader or pastor, you are already skilled in praying with parishioners, searching the Scriptures for guidance, and listening to the Holy Spirit for direction. Through Scripture, prayer, and communal support, ministers aim to facilitate a journey of healing that transcends the immediate crisis, paving the way for families to emerge stronger, more resilient, and more deeply rooted in their faith.

We hope these book chapters on relevant family issues strengthen your skill set when addressing various family problems with compassion and grace. Just like teaching pastors receive training on developing memorable messages and three-point sermons, these book chapters provide direction in navigating complex situations that affect families in your ministry context. You can think of this as a full integration of special revelation and general revelation to support your ministry. As you read these chapters and glean from the authors' wisdom, consider how you can address problems by incorporating their perspectives and proposed solutions.

In the upcoming chapters, we explore the biblical foundations of family, restoration, and the transformative power of grace. We sincerely hope this book serves as a compass, guiding you through the uncharted waters of ministering to families in crisis with wisdom, humility, and an unwavering reliance on the grace of our Lord. May the words on these pages inspire, encourage, and equip you as you answer the call to be Christ's heart, hands, and feet to families in need. Together, let us embark on this sacred voyage of ministering to families in crisis, confident that when we are with Christ, even the wind and waves will obey him.

2

SPIRITUAL FORMATION IN FAMILIES

Diane J. Chandler

We finally did it! My husband and I made our bucket-list trip to Yosemite and Sequoia National Parks in California. We hiked several trails, experienced spectacular vistas, and marveled at God's glorious creation. Needless to say, we needed to prepare beforehand for our journey, planning appropriate footwear and attire, backpacks and supplies, food and water provisions, and checking weather reports. Along the way, we consulted with park rangers, who conveyed vital park information and shared about their multi-faceted roles.

Park rangers are busy people, constantly on the move and in demand. Among their many roles, they serve as guides, safeguard park visitors and park grounds, enforce park regulations, perform emergency medical assistance, participate in search and rescue missions, and assist with wildfire control.

Like park rangers, church leaders who minister to families are in constant demand and must be prepared with essential gear for their ministry roles.[1] Their gear includes a growing relationship with the Lord, spiritual

---

[1] The terms "ministry leader," "family minister," and "church leader" are used interchangeably throughout this chapter, recognizing that family ministry is often provided by lay leaders in churches, alongside pastoral and ministry staff.

maturity, competency in applying Bible knowledge, an authentic prayer life, Spirit-led discernment, and a compassionate heart, to name a few. Family ministers must also assist others with the gear to follow Jesus well.

Sometimes, when following Jesus, however, family members on the trail encounter crises for which they are unprepared. For example, weather conditions may unexpectedly change and threaten safety. Some family members may make poor trail choices, violate warnings to stay out of restricted areas, stumble, or become injured. Others may become disoriented or lost and need rescue. Still, others may abandon the trail altogether when difficulties arise. In ministry, church leaders may find themselves responding to family crises. Family crises may include marital infidelity, a wayward child, drug or alcohol addiction, an unwelcome diagnosis, the tragic loss of a loved one, domestic violence, a family member who comes out as gay, mental illness, or financial instability.

Church leaders minister to families as spiritual trail guides, especially when crises arise. Ministry leaders must model the basics well, fueling their own spiritual practices that keep them fit and resilient as they minister to others. This chapter focuses on spiritual formation and how family ministers might better prepare to guide family members who face difficulties in life's terrain.

This chapter begins with an overview of the spiritual formation journey, then highlights the foundational role of the family in spiritual formation, followed by the crucial role family ministers play in the lives of church members. The chapter concludes by identifying family ministers' internal and external challenges and offers suggestions to address them.

THE CHRISTIAN SPIRITUAL FORMATION JOURNEY

The family minister needs to know the target destination for all who follow Jesus and the primary pathways of spiritual formation to get there. These pathways include spiritual practices, formative relationships, life circumstances and experiences, and church involvement. The final destination is Christlikeness. Becoming more like Jesus through loving obedience in word, thought, and deed is the ultimate goal of spiritual formation. The evidence of spiritual formation progress is the fruit of the Spirit—love, joy, peace, forbearance, kindness, goodness, faithfulness, gentleness, and self-control (Gal 5:22-23). These character qualities demonstrate a growing relationship with God and others. Wise is the church leader who discerns how God may be using various circumstances in a church member's life and offers comfort and support.

The combination of trails that shape us into Christlikeness is as unique as each individual. Regardless of the trail map, the Great Commandment comprises the main trailhead, our spiritual journey's entry point. We are to love the Lord with all our heart, soul, strength, and mind and love our neighbor as ourselves (Lk 10:27). Love of God and neighbor anchors the spiritual formation process. Becoming a faithful disciple follows—to fulfill the Great Commission in making other disciples (Mt 28:18-20). As we know, Christian spiritual formation is a lifelong journey comprised of peaks and valleys. Consider the journey of Jason and Isabella.

The dynamic married couple arranged a meeting with Pastor Mike. In their mid-30s, Jason and Isabella faithfully followed Jesus. They realized something was missing despite regular church attendance and small group participation. They revealed, "We desire to grow deeper in our relationship with God and one another. Could you or someone else in the church explain what is involved in spiritual formation?" How would you respond to such a question? Let's start with the basics.

What exactly is Christian spiritual formation? It is an interactive process by which God the Father fashions believers into the image of his Son, Jesus, through the empowerment of the Holy Spirit for the sake of others.[2] The spiritual formation process commences when Jesus becomes both Savior and Lord, and believers acknowledge that Jesus died for their sins and paid the price for their eternal salvation (Jn 1:12; Acts 4:12). The love and grace of God spark the spiritual formation process, as God's love in Christ invites us by faith into an intimate relationship with the Savior of our souls.

The Holy Spirit's role in spiritual formation is crucial. The Spirit is the master guide and comforter who conveys truth along life's journey. The

---

[2]For a holistic approach describing seven primary dimensions of formation, see Diane J. Chandler's *Christian Spiritual Formation: An Integrated Approach for Personal and Relational Wholeness* (Downers Grove, IL: IVP Academic, 2014), 37. These seven formation dimensions include spiritual, emotional, relational, intellectual, vocational, physical health and wellness, and resource stewardship (referring to how we steward money, possessions, time, and the earth).

Spirit works to produce Christlike character (2 Cor 3:17-18) and specializes in walking alongside God's children during challenging times. However, the spiritual formation process involves more than the Holy Spirit's initiative. The process involves our response and participation.

Certain pathways of spiritual formation are essential, beginning with balanced spiritual practices.[3] Family ministers can model and teach spiritual practices that fuel church members' spiritual formation. For example, intake of God's Word is foundational, and time in God's presence is essential for personal wholeness. There is no substitute for communion with God through consistent Bible intake, prayer, and worship, complemented by a life-giving community. When church leaders try to identify the spiritual dynamics at work in a person's life, they would do well to inquire about their spiritual practices, which is one primary indicator of spiritual health. They can also help individuals fortify their spiritual rhythms and suggest helpful resources.[4] In addition to personal spiritual practices, God uses interpersonal relationships, life experiences, and circumstances over time to shape us, including the unpleasant ones. Ministry leaders can bring perspective to church members when they experience life's challenges. Like the apostle Paul recounting how his sufferings prompted God's comfort (2 Cor 1:3-11), the family minister can sensitively remind those walking through dark valleys about God's promises to be with them through his near presence (Is 43:2; 1 Pet 5:10) and about the need to enlist the prayers of others for support (Acts 12:5). The apostle Paul provided an example of humility when he asked the Ephesians for prayer (Eph 6:19-20). We need to let church members know that it is not a sign of weakness to rally prayer during trials but rather a sign of dependence on God.

---

[3] For resources on strengthening spiritual practices, see Ruth Haley Barton, *Sacred Rhythms: Arranging Our Lives for Spiritual Transformation* (Downers Grove, IL: InterVarsity Press, 2006), 72; James Bryan Smith, *The Good and Beautiful God: Falling in Love with the God Jesus Knows* (Downers Grove, IL: InterVarsity Press, 2009), 56; and Rich Villodas, *The Deeply Formed Life: Five Transformative Values to Root Us in the Way of Jesus* (Colorado Springs, CO: WaterBrook, 2020), 94.

[4] For resources on nurturing spiritual growth in the family context, see Matt Chandler and Andy Griffin, *Family Discipleship: Leading Your Home through Time, Moments, and Milestones* (Wheaton, IL: Crossway, 2020), 110; Justin Whitmel Early, *Habits of the Household: Practicing the Story of God in Everyday Family Rhythms* (Grand Rapids, MI: Zondervan, 2021), 45; and Sarah Cowan Johnson, *Teach Your Children Well: A Step-by-Step Guide for Family Discipleship* (Downers Grove, IL: InterVarsity Press, 2022), 27.

No one prefers a path of suffering. However, suffering is life's unavoidable common denominator. C. S. Lewis observed, "Try to exclude the possibility of suffering, which the order of nature and the existence of freewills involve, and you will find that you have excluded life itself."[5] Suffering is ubiquitous and often results as a consequence of loss. And loss hurts—be it a loss of health, a relationship, a job, or the death of a loved one. Suffering presses us into God like no other conduit as we seek to make sense of it all. Suffering often prompts a unique fellowship with God, who suffered on our behalf and identifies with us through suffering (Phil 3:10). Church leaders can bring perspective to church members as they process through suffering. In other words, how do we think about God when the bottom falls out?[6] In addition to personal spiritual practices, relationships, life experiences, and circumstances, the church also provides opportunities for transformation—both proactively and reactively. Proactively, church leaders ideally model Christian character before church members and provide transformative opportunities through regular worship services, sermons, teaching and equipping sessions, recreational gatherings, other community venues, and outreach opportunities. Like park rangers who help others navigate parks, family ministers engage in personal discipleship and mentoring relationships. They provide spiritual direction and counseling to help church members navigate their journeys to remain on the trail. One such story underscores how to assist a family during a crisis.

RACHEL'S STORY: A FAMILY'S JOURNEY OF LOSS

As a teen invested in her church's youth group, Rachel evidenced a calling for crosscultural missions. Her parents had a healthy marriage, served in children's and youth ministry as volunteers, and discipled each of their four children. They encouraged Rachel to explore her life calling. After high school graduation, Rachel took a gap year to serve overseas to test the waters before considering a longer-term assignment.

After returning from this exploratory trip, Rachel became seriously ill and was hospitalized. A grim diagnosis followed. Throughout her

---

[5]C. S. Lewis, *The Problem of Pain* (New York: HarperSanFrancisco, 2001), 25.
[6]For an accessible book that addresses how to think well about God when disaster strikes, see John H. Walton and Tremper Longman III, *How to Read Job* (Downers Grove, IL: IVP Academic, 2015), 19.

month-long hospitalization, the youth pastor and key youth leaders supported Rachel, her parents, and her younger siblings. Other church members stood with the family, provided them with an emotional safety net, and offered tangible assistance such as continuous prayer, meal preparation, regular contact, and daily help. Although the church interceded in prayer with the family for a miracle, Rachel passed away.

Throughout this crisis, the family pressed into God and asked the "why" questions. Admirably, Rachel's parents retained their commitment to God and continue to serve in their church's youth ministry. Had the family not had a solid faith, this story may have been different, with a fracture in family relationships, the blame game active, and hearts turned away from God. Despite losing their daughter, the parents remain on the trail and committed to Jesus, helping others navigate grief and loss while still serving the Lord. Their other children's spiritual roots remain intertwined with their own, reinforcing the family's foundational role in spiritual formation.

THE FOUNDATIONAL ROLE OF THE FAMILY

The giant sequoia trees in California are an unspeakable sight to behold! Giant sequoias can grow upward of 300 feet (26 stories), produce 18- to 24-inch bark, and live between 2000 and 3000 years. What accounts for their stability and longevity? One would think that sequoias retain deep roots to help them withstand unfavorable conditions. Surprisingly, they lack a taproot, and their root system is between 12 to 14 feet beneath the ground, relatively shallow considering their height. But these roots reach out laterally 100 to 200 feet and occupy up to one acre of earth. Their secret? An individual sequoia tree's root system is interconnected with the root systems of other sequoias.

Sequoia trees provide a powerful picture of how the family should function—as mutually supportive of one another, helping each other to grow individually and as a family unit. When the family is functioning in this way, family members thrive. But when conditions break down, family members struggle. The family is where understanding the world begins and personal core identity develops. Regardless of family constellation, the family, for better or for worse, is the "forming center" for all formation dimensions, including the spiritual, emotional, relational, mental, and physical.[7] Healthy bonding within the family unit anchors holistic development. According to Jack and Judith Balswick, bonding in familial relationships involves (1) commitment to love and be loved, (2) grace to forgive and be forgiven, (3) empowerment to serve and be served, and (4) relational intimacy to know and be known by others.[8] Through family life, these four elements fuel trust, healthy self-esteem, and acceptance without fear of rejection. Unhealthy family dynamics undermine these four pillars and lead to conditional love, fear, isolation, faultfinding, self-centeredness, perfectionism, inappropriate control, and lack of communication. Hence, unhealthy bonding within the family leaves gaps in development. As a result, hurting family members tend to withhold unconditional love and grace, the bedrock of healthy spiritual growth and nurture.

In light of these family dynamics, family ministers also face challenges related to the variety of family constellations that reflect contemporary culture in the United States, such as traditional married heterosexual parents, unmarried heterosexual parents, married and unmarried same-sex parents, single parents, blended families, multigenerational families, families with adopted or foster children, and grandparents or other relatives raising children. Regardless of family constellation, healthy intimate relationships are the core building block for identity formation. Without quality trusting relationships, children grow up with tangible deficits. Family ministers must be aware of how family-of-origin issues affect spiritual and holistic development in children, teens, and adults.

UNDERSTANDING HUMAN ATTACHMENTS IN FAMILIES

This awareness begins with understanding how human attachments, or the lack of them, are formed and affect one's relationships over time.[9]

---

[7]Marjorie J. Thompson, *Family: The Forming Center: A Vision of the Role of Family in Spiritual Formation* (Nashville, TN: Upper Room, 1998), 19-30.
[8]Jack O. Balswick and Judith K. Balswick, *The Family: A Christian Perspective on the Contemporary Home*, 4th ed. (Grand Rapids, MI: Baker Academic, 2014), 8-18.
[9]For an overview of attachment theory, see Marjorie Lindner Gunnoe, *The Person in Psychology and Christianity: A Faith-based Critique of Five Theories of Social Development* (Downers Grove, IL: IVP Academic, 2022), chap. 6.

Psychologists have identified four main attachment styles regarding human relationships, predicated on early childhood experiences, that help frame how people process uncertainty. Based on the initial work of John Bowlby and Mary Ainsworth, who researched how babies attach to their mothers, these four attachment styles described below are thought to carry over into adulthood. The research on attachment has continued with neurobiological models that explain family relationships at three levels: biological, psychological, and social.[10] Despite previous attachment experiences, the good news for followers of Jesus is that past wounds and deficits can be healed, and people can be freed from past unhealthy patterns. These four attachment styles are:

1. **Secure attachment:** describes the ability to develop close relationships with others, evidences healthy self-esteem, is effective in communicating with others, and can appropriately regulate emotion.
2. **Anxious attachment:** describes general uncertainty within human interactions, the perspective that others are unreliable and unresponsive to personal needs, leading to low self-esteem and self-protection so as not to be hurt, often accompanied by a fear of abandonment.
3. **Avoidant attachment:** describes avoiding interaction with others, likely as a defense mechanism to fend off a sense of rejection. Rather than risk rejection, either real or perceived, those with an avoidant attachment style downplay the importance of healthy attachment to self-protect.
4. **Disorganized attachment:** describes an insecure attachment style that evidences a sense of confusion, fear, and contradictory behaviors that may appear aloof, independent, or moody.

Connecting the journey of spiritual formation to the idea of attachment is significant. The secure attachment style suggests early childhood experiences where children feel safe, accepted, valued, and understood. The anxious, avoidant, and disorganized styles possibly

---

[10] Jude Cassidy and Phillip R. Shaver, *Handbook of Attachment Theory, Research, and Clinical Applications* (New York: Guilford, 2018).

reflect inconsistent caregiving in childhood, neglect, rejection, and trauma-related experiences that result in fear of rejection or abandonment, distrust of others, and a sense of unworthiness. Ultimately, the believer longs for secure attachment with the Father and healing the disconnection with eternity, be it in anxious, avoidant, or disorganized attachment. Family ministers would do well to explore the backgrounds of family members of any age to understand the effects of past and present family fractures, dysfunction, and brokenness and how these contribute to healthy or unhealthy attachment patterns. Often, family ministers fill in relational deficits through healthy attachments.

STEVE AND JADE'S STORY: MARRIAGE ON THE BRINK

Those who come to church leaders for counsel often look for spiritual mothers and fathers to fill in past relational gaps.[11] Some look for the perfect parent, but most want someone to listen to their pain and encourage them on their journey. For example, Steve and Jade, a married couple with three children, had marital difficulties. During a meeting with Corey, the director of family ministries, Jade revealed that she uncovered Steve's pornography use. Having suspected it, she probed Steve's internet searches. She was undone and felt angry, betrayed, and minimized. Jade demanded that they seek pastoral counseling. If you were their church pastor, how would you counsel them? How might thinking about this through a spiritual formation lens inform how you would help this couple?

Corey, who counseled them, listened empathetically to the pain expressed by Steve's numerous apologies. When Corey explored Steve's spiritual practices, however, he discovered that Steve spent little time in Scripture reading or prayer. Steve confessed he was overloaded at work and stressed, leading to church avoidance. At Corey's suggestion, Steve agreed to engage in personal Bible reading and prayer, regular prayer times with Jade, and attend church. During Corey and Steve's biweekly meetings, Steve shared how the Lord spoke to him. Steve also agreed to install porn blocker software (i.e., Covenant Eyes) on his electronic devices and establish regular date nights with Jade. Jade also met with a

---

[11] See Larry Kreider, *The Cry for Spiritual Mothers and Fathers: The Next Generation Needs You to be a Spiritual Mentor* (Ventura, CA: Regal, 2014).

women's ministry leader to process her pain. Slowly, her heart softened, leading to forgiveness, as Steve began to change. Fortunately, they both agreed to meet with Corey biweekly for three months to address other issues in their marriage.

Over those three months, Corey met with Steve, helping him unravel underlying issues that fed his pornography involvement, including Steve's exposure to pornography in elementary school and his father's absence in early childhood. Steve's engaging in spiritual practices in an accountability relationship set him on a fresh trajectory. Although not a mental health professional, Corey's pastoral inclinations and willingness to walk alongside Steve jumpstarted Steve's healing and contributed to saving their marriage.

THE CRUCIAL ROLE OF FAMILY MINISTERS

The role of those in family ministries cannot be underestimated. Whether ministering to children, youth, young adults, or adults, family ministers' highest calling is to provide opportunities for transformation into Christlikeness through various facets of ministry. Specifically, all ministry initiatives and departments need to be framed with the goal of spiritual transformation in mind. Family ministers provide encouragement and guidance through these growth opportunities for those under their care.

Like seasoned trail rangers, family ministers must be aware of three main things—whom they are leading, how far along they are on their spiritual journey, and the possible terrain they may face. The key to effective family ministry is getting to know those being served—who they are as people, not just attendees of church functions. Rather than simply implementing programs, family ministries must consider the quality of the trusting relationships they nurture.

Diana Garland summarizes this well: "One of the most significant tasks of ministry with families, then, is simply being what a congregation is: a community of friends and neighbors and extended family that gathers to worship together, serve together, and support and care for one another as families."[12] She adds, "We cannot love people we do not

---

[12]Diana R. Garland, *Family Ministry: A Comprehensive Guide*, 2nd ed. (Downers Grove, IL: IVP Academic, 2012), 449.

know."[13] How true this is! As great sequoias link their roots with the root systems of other sequoias, which is true of families, the same can be said of healthy family ministries. Family ministers need to link with the people they serve. Without positive relational experiences, church members will falter in their spiritual formation and faith development. Involving people as active participants in church life and worship services strengthens the community and fuels life's purpose. An authentic church community grows as people worship Jesus, spend time together, and enjoy each other's company, resulting in spiritual formation through the Spirit's working.

Furthermore, like park rangers involved in rescue efforts, family ministers must be aware of the possible terrain of issues that family members may confront, including those identified in this book. Knowing the terrain involves both a reactive and proactive side to ministry. Dealing with family issues is the reactive side of the church minister's role. Church leaders would do well to know the kinds of problems they can reasonably address through the guidance of the Holy Spirit and their own limitations. They also need to know when drawing on the wisdom and expertise of other church leaders is wise and warranted. When issues are too severe for in-house pastoral care, ministers must refer congregants to specialized services that provide the necessary knowledge and expertise. For example, such referrals could be to reputable Christian counseling centers that specialize in trauma, medicine, or law. Every church needs to develop a referral list when outside help is required.

MAXIMIZING SPIRITUAL TRANSFORMATION IN FAMILY MINISTRIES

However, the proactive side of the pastoral role relates to thoughtful planning of all facets of ministry to maximize spiritual transformation.[14] Facets of ministry include worship services including sermons, equipping (e.g., Sunday school, youth group, adult Bible studies, life groups), prayer meetings, community building (e.g., meals together,

---

[13]Garland, *Family Ministry*, 460.
[14]For an overview of how church life and family life converge, see Garland, *Family Ministry*, chap. 13.

celebrations, camps, and recreational activities), the sacraments (e.g., baptism and Communion), healing ministries, outreach and service, and crosscultural missions.

Each ministry facet will receive varying emphases and perspectives based on a church's history and affiliation. Yet, each of these components tells God's redemptive story in some way and should contribute to nurturing family-level spiritual formation and reproducing disciples.[15] Worship services highlight the primacy of gathering to praise the living God (Ps 150:1). Singing exalts and glorifies God through psalms, hymns, and spiritual songs (Eph 5:19). Sermons declare God's Word for careful instruction and life application (2 Tim 4:2). Bible study and other equipping venues reinforce our desire to grow in grace and knowledge (2 Pet 3:18). Prayer meetings reflect our dependence on and trust in God through declaring scriptural promises, knowing that God desires the best for his children.

Community building through times together reinforces our mutual rootedness in Christ and challenges us to continue our spiritual journeys (1 Thes 5:11). Church ministers can organize church dinners for families and single adults, life groups, family outreach events, and sporting activities that fuel the fun factor.

The sacraments of baptism and Communion involve physical acts that embody the gospel. Baptism reflects Christ's death, burial, and resurrection, with which a believer identifies. The Lord's Supper reflects Christ's sacrifice on our behalf, the reality of confessed sins forgiven, and the assurance of an eternal kingdom to come. Healing ministries focus on spiritual, emotional, and relational freedom, enabling members to live as whole people. Outreach and service provide a tangible extension of the love of God to others. A church's crosscultural missions thrust authenticates Christ's commission to make disciples of all nations (Mt 28:18-20).

Regardless of church tradition, the Bible portrays the church as a holy dwelling (Eph 2:22). Those following Christ are "members of [God's] household" (Eph 2:18-19) who are to be equipped for the work of the

---

[15]Timothy Paul Jones and John David Trentham, *Practical Family Ministry: A Collection of Ideas for Your Church* (Nashville: Randall House, 2015), 20.

ministry, which is another outcome of spiritual formation (Eph 4:12). Toward that end, the goal of the church of any size, from under 100 members to megachurch-size, is to keep ministry small—in bite-sized "family-type" units, so people can authentically relate and get to know one another. Where two or three gather, Jesus is present in their midst (Mt 18:20). These family-type groups should gather in more ways and places than weekly worship services. How the church perseveres to focus on the spiritual formation of its members remains primary.

God never intended us to go it alone. Everyone—those married with children, married without children, and single adults—needs family ministry. God pictures the church as a family where people of all ages meaningfully connect. Meeting together as a church body invites the Holy Spirit to manifest Christ in our midst ("where two or three gather in my name, there am I with them," Mt 18:20). When meeting together (Heb 10:25), we strengthen each other as iron sharpens iron (Prov 27:17). Like hiking a trail solo, going through the motions of church life by oneself is both lonely and isolating. Too often, people get lost when navigating their journeys by themselves. We need each other, especially when we are on rocky ground that threatens safety—lest one fall, and there be no one to help him up (Eccles 4:10). Family ministers are there to reach out a hand to provide support and perspective to warn, encourage, and help those they serve (1 Thess 5:14).

FAMILY MINISTRIES ANNUAL ASSESSMENT

Family ministers would do well to respond to these twelve questions below on an annual basis to remain focused on their spiritual calling:

- What is the vision in your area of service for family ministry? The vision helps answer the "what" question.
- How does your family ministry vision align with the overarching vision of the church?
- What are 2-3 biblical values that undergird your family ministry area?
- What are 2-3 key goals or priorities this year that would grow and deepen your ministry area? In other words, what is your ministry strategy?

- How is your family ministry area specifically contributing to its members' spiritual formation and discipleship?
- How does family ministry promote healthy roles in families, whether the role of daughter, son, sibling, parent, cousin, or even non-biological "auntie" or "uncle" role?
- How will you convey the vision and values of your ministry area to those you serve?
- How do you train volunteers to embrace the ministry's vision, values, and goals?
- If applicable, how do you choose a teaching curriculum for your area of service (i.e., with children, youth, young adults, older adults, marriage and parenting, women, and men)?[16]
- Who has leadership potential in your ministry sphere, and who are you cultivating in leadership?
- What resources from your network of sister churches and the global church would enrich your family ministries? How could you and your ministry contribute to other churches?
- How will I evaluate my ministry (i.e., observation, verbal feedback, interview, survey)?

Giving prayer and reflection time annually to answer these above questions will assist family ministers to remain focused in providing a nurturing context where church members can grow spiritually into Christlikeness.

Family ministers can support the spiritual formation of all family members by maximizing the entire family's involvement in various facets of ministry. For example, families often segregate by age during worship services and age-specific weekly functions. Finding ways for a family unit to serve together in the church while being sensitive to incorporating single adults into these serving constellations is advisable. Serving others is a spiritual practice that contributes to Christlikeness. For example, parents can include children as greeters, children and teens can read Scripture in worship services, and children can be featured during worship. In addition,

---

[16] Age-appropriate Christian curriculum for purchase abounds at all age-levels and ministry areas. Each church should explore available resources that align with their ministry vision and values before implementing any curriculum, considering strengths and weaknesses of each.

small groups can be cross-generational, and appealing sermons can be geared toward children or teens. Whether a church favors a traditional family ministry approach, where the family separates during the church service for age-specific ministry, or a family-integrated approach, where the family attends church services together, family ministers need to be mindful that relationship building remains the key to spiritual formation.

Regardless of the ministry approach, the family needs the church. Likewise, the church needs the family. The family and the church are to work cooperatively to teach and train family members. For those with children, parents and caregivers need to know the biblically based vision of family ministries and how they can practically support the church's efforts. At the same time, family ministers must be aware that parents and caregivers may try to offload the discipleship responsibility of their children to church ministers. Nothing substitutes, however, for empowering parents to take on this primary discipling role.[17] How do spiritual formation and discipleship connect in a family context? Whereas spiritual formation is the Holy Spirit's work within a family member's life, discipleship is the human element in this process. Discipleship relates to one person walking alongside another person or group, imparting, and encouraging spiritual growth—as in parents discipling their children, grandparents discipling their grandchildren, and church ministers discipling those within families. The Holy Spirit, however, does the internal work, refining Christlike character in the faith-building process. Family ministries can provide parents and caregivers with recommended resources that maximize family members' spiritual growth and discipleship (i.e., devotionals, books, films, podcasts, websites, outings/trips, and other faith-building activities). Family ministers can also provide equipping opportunities, such as parenting and family seminars and conferences.

CORNERSTONES OF FAMILY MINISTRY

Cornerstones of family ministries relate to equipping church members to empower parents and caregivers to become spiritual leaders in their homes by discipling their children. Many attributes that frame family

---

[17]Phil Bell, *The Family Ministry Playbook for Partnering with Parents* (Nashville: Randall House, 2021), 9-18.

ministries also frame the family unit. Matt Chandler and Adam Griffin recommend four cornerstones through which parents (and churches, I might add) can live out their faith and teach their children:

1. modeling,
2. time,
3. moments,
4. milestones.[18]

First, by *modeling* personal spiritual practices, parents or caregivers demonstrate the first cornerstone—caring for their souls. Reading Scripture and praying are essential for a personal devotional life. Parents and caregivers cannot give what they do not have nor teach their children to do the same. The hope is that children will see their parents' active faith displayed.

Second, spending *time* together as a family in family devotions and worship is another cornerstone. The key is regularity with the goal of spiritual growth. Devotions need not be long to be effective, but they do need to be positive so children do not resist them. Resources abound that family ministers can recommend to parents and caregivers.[19]

The third cornerstone relates to *moments*. Family ministers can help parents frame everyday conversations to focus on God. For example, highlighting how God is working in a particular situation, asking questions that highlight godly character, affirming children when they demonstrate the fruit of the Spirit, and engaging in prayer for needy situations are ways that children learn. Moments also connect to times together for recreation and fun activities.

The fourth cornerstone relates to *milestones*. Milestones are special joyful occasions such as biological or spiritual birthdays, weddings, anniversaries, award ceremonies, graduations, promotions, vacations, mission trips, or other traditions. But milestones can also commemorate other remembrances, like the date of a spiritual or physical breakthrough,

---

[18]Chandler and Griffin, *Family Discipleship*, chaps. 2-6.
[19]For a sampling, Sally Lloyd-Jones, *Thoughts to Make Your Heart Sing: 101 Devotions about God's Great Love for You* (Grand Rapids, MI: Zonderkidz, 2021); Max Lucado, *Grace for the Moment: Family Devotional* (Nashville: Thomas Nelson, 2018); Patrick Schwenk and Ruth Schwenk, *Faith Forward Family Devotional: 100 Devotions* (Grand Rapids, MI: Zondervan, 2019).

the death of someone dear, or the end of a difficult time so that praise can be offered to honor God even through trials (cf. 2 Cor 1:3-10). These four cornerstones can also be applied to family ministry.

One church situation illustrates the power of these four cornerstones (i.e., modeling, time, moments, and milestones). As faithful church volunteers, Darryl and his wife Kim led a growing young adult ministry for several years. They mentored one of the participants, Leslie, who was raised by a single mother. Darryl and Kim often invited Leslie to their home for meals and to interact with their children. They spent *time* together reading God's Word and praying, *modeling* godly family rhythms. They enjoyed *moments* in outdoor outings and fun times together. They created *milestones* together, including birthday celebrations.

In many ways, Darryl and Kim were spiritual parents to Leslie. When Leslie's mother died after an extended illness, in grief, Leslie turned her back on God and entered into a same-sex relationship. Throughout this time, Darryl and Kim fortified their relationship with her, beckoning her back on the trail with unconditional love. Their love and stability prompted Leslie to return to the Lord and discontinue the same-sex relationship.[20] The role of the family minister remains crucial in the spiritual formation journeys of church members, although, as we have seen, it is not without its challenges.

CHALLENGES OF FAMILY MINISTRY

Family ministers often face external and internal challenges. This section identifies some of the main challenges and how to navigate them.

External challenges. Anyone who ministers in a church becomes intimately acquainted with this role's multiple challenges, which can stymie the work of the ministry. The external challenges are numerous and interrelated: (1) culture, (2) visual forces, and (3) busyness.

First, cultural forces at work discredit the Christian faith. Perceptions of Christianity as being out-of-touch, narrow-minded, judgmental, exclusionary, and discriminatory abound. Christians are often seen for what they are against rather than what they are for. The challenge for

---

[20]See chaps. 5-6 in this book for fuller discussion of LGBTQ+ issues in families.

family ministers is to remain uncompromising relative to embodying and teaching the gospel while simultaneously being authentic and relevant to those they serve. This authenticity requires a listening and learning posture and a willingness to respond sensitively to challenging questions with biblical truth in an attitude of love, wisdom, and grace (Eph 4:15). As New Testament scholar Darrell Bock suggests, cultural forces are like tectonic plates opposing each other.[21] The headwinds of cultural and political conflict have entered through the main sanctuary door. Bock adds that the church today is up against spiritual forces of darkness that work incognito. Therefore, we need to redefine the battle, as the enemy is not "flesh and blood" but spiritual forces of evil. Ministers need to develop a theology of cultural engagement on navigating counter-cultural voices, given the mission to love our neighbors and enemies while being mindful of the enemy's divisive strategies. Family ministers can respond to cultural challenges by focusing on the basics (i.e., Bible reading, prayer, fasting, worship, and service) while modeling faithful heterosexual marriage and authentic Christlike relationships.

Second, visual forces constantly vie for our attention, minds, and wallets. Social media, news outlets, sports, entertainment, and advertising ferociously compete for our attention. Incessant notifications on our mobile phones and devices poise us for internet overuse and addiction. Family ministers can help guide family members at any age to exercise discernment on the responsible use of technology to preserve personal holiness and integrity while embracing its benefits.[22]

Third, busyness is ubiquitous in most families and competes with spiritually oriented activity. Many are in chronic overdrive between family, work, school, church, and community commitments. Finding time for personal and family devotions can unintentionally become a low priority. How can ministers help family members make wise decisions about their time commitments to safeguard healthy spiritual priorities? Fundamentally, church leaders need to model balanced living before

---

[21] Darrell Bock, "We Need to Reset the Rules of Cultural Engagement," *Christianity Today* (online), October 2020, www.christianitytoday.com/pastors/2020/october-web-exclusives/we-need-to-reset-rules-of-cultural-engagement.html.

[22] See chaps. 10-11 on screens. Also see Andy Couch, *The Tech-Wise Family: Everyday Steps for Putting Technology in Its Proper Place* (Grand Rapids, MI: Baker Books, 2017).

urging others to do the same. Church leaders can encourage daily devotional time with God, engaging in a weekly sabbath, taking personal or family retreats, scheduling vacations, and the need for healthy boundaries. In addition to external challenges, family ministers also face internal challenges.

Internal challenges. Ministry leaders may be especially prone to (1) overwork and burnout, (2) codependence and transference, and (3) a sense of discouragement.

First, with multiple demands, church leaders often violate personal boundaries, given the unending pastoral task that encroaches on life balance. Consequently, anyone can push themselves beyond reasonable limits. Church and lay leaders can easily veer off the trail if left unchecked. If chronic alarm bells of isolation and depression go unchecked, they could find themselves in full-fledged burnout. They need to maintain healthy boundaries and be accountable for taking time off. Spending time with family and friends, getting enough physical exercise, enjoying God's creation outdoors, and making healthy food choices contribute to overall health.

Maintaining a spiritual and emotionally healthy lifestyle involves slowing down and facing one's shadow, as Peter Scazzero admonishes.[23] Spiritual growth for church leaders often comes through the crucible of ministry during times when pressures mount.[24] Examples of ministry pressures are predictable. A church member creates havoc in the church. A staff member needs reprimand. Church finances tumble. A personal or family health crisis arises. Each situation creates pressure that can press church leaders to their knees in prayer and humility. Establishing a prayer shield of trusted others who will cover the ministry leader in prayer is a proactive strategy for maintaining spiritual protection and health.

Second, church and lay leaders must be mindful of codependence and transference. Codependence describes the dysfunctional relationship

---

[23] Peter Scazzero, *The Emotionally Healthy Leader: How Transforming Your Inner Life Will Deeply Transform Your Church, Team, and the World* (Grand Rapids, MI: Zondervan, 2015), 51-80.

[24] Tod Bolsinger, *Tempered Resilience: How Leaders are Formed in the Crucible of Change* (Downers Grove, IL: InterVarsity Press, 2020).

whereby one person excessively depends on another, which fosters the need to be needed by the other. If church leaders feel insecure or do not properly identify this dynamic in congregants, they may become enmeshed with them, creating an ongoing cycle of unhealthy dependence. Transference is the process of projecting onto another the unmet expectations from a previous relationship. For example, congregants may expect a church leader to fulfill the role of the perfect parent they lacked in childhood. Church ministers cannot possibly meet the unmet expectations of others because of the dysfunction of their past. Knowing these possible dynamics, however, goes a long way to ensuring that church leaders do not become entangled unknowingly in unhealthy relationships. Suppose you find yourself exhausted by a church member and giving an ever-increasing amount of your time to one family while your help is consistently not good enough. In that case, it seems likely that codependence or transference may be at play in that relationship. In that situation, enlisting counsel from a peer or church leader is wise.

Third, family ministers can become discouraged when things do not go well. They need to know that despite their best efforts, not every person ministered to will be helped, pleased, or changed. Family ministers cannot solve every problem, nor should they. People may take a dangerous detour from the trail, make poor decisions, injure themselves and others, or abandon their faith altogether. Some may attack the church leader's character or become accusatory. How church leaders respond during these times is the acid test of their spiritual formation and leadership journeys.

Remaining free from offense is one of the most challenging tests in ministry and an indicator of spiritual maturity. John Bevere acknowledges that overcoming offense is "the most difficult obstacle an individual must face and overcome but is also an avenue for spiritual maturity, as difficult as this is."[25] Jesus epitomized how to deal with offense throughout his ministry, most clearly when he forgave his executioners on the cross. Receiving grace to forgive and release difficult people to God are two steps that help church leaders remain resilient—forgiving

---

[25]John Bevere, *The Bait of Satan: Living Free from the Deadly Trap of Offense*, 10th anniv. ed. (Lake Mary, FL: Strang, 2004), vii, 150-52.

those who misunderstand and criticize them, and accepting that they are in God's care when parishioners choose to walk on a contrary path.

ANDRE AND SELENA'S STORY: HEALTHY BOUNDARIES

By illustration, Pastor Andre and his wife Selena became friends with another couple in their church, Brandon and Christine. Pastor Andre and Selena regularly taught a class on marriage in the church, and Brandon was invited to become an elder at their church. Over several years, both couples enjoyed quality time together. When Brandon and Christine began experiencing marital difficulties, Christine went to Pastor Andre for help. Because of his openness and familiarity, Andre met weekly with Christine for four weeks, with Brandon's permission. Andre also invited Brandon to meet with him individually and then welcomed them to meet with him as a couple, which they did.

However, Christine repeatedly called Pastor Andre on his cell phone for counsel and reassurance, especially after an argument with Brandon. It soon became apparent. Christine had developed an ungodly attachment to Andre and transferred to Andre the father figure she never had and the husband she desired. Pastor Andre's tender heart and easy access also watered the seeds of codependence and transference. His constant overwork and fatigue contributed to his dropping his guard.

Andre's wife, Selena, had seen this problem brewing long before Andre did. When Pastor Andre awakened to these realities, the relationship between him and Christine was so enmeshed that there seemed no easy resolution. Christine admitted falling in love with Andre despite having no romantic contact. Andre became increasingly worn out and discouraged, understanding that he had contributed unwittingly to the problem. After seeking outside counsel from their pastor and recognizing that the situation was unresolvable, Andre and Selena decided to ask Brandon and Christine to seek all future counsel from another church leader and then transfer to a local sister church, which they did. Andre grew wiser through this situation and redoubled his commitment to his marriage. In other church situations, some marriages would not have survived. The internal challenges of family ministry are real. How church leaders establish appropriate guard rails to maximize spiritual, emotional, and relational health is vital for them and the churches they serve.

CONCLUSION

We began this chapter with the metaphor of a journey, describing how God fashions his children into Christ's image through the power of the Holy Spirit. This chapter also described the vital roles of the family and family ministers in contributing to the transformational process into Christlikeness of family members and how discipleship is the human dimension of the spiritual formation process. Family ministers are like park rangers and trail guides to help keep church members safely on the trail. Likewise, the chapter addressed family ministries' internal and external challenges and offered suggestions for navigating them.

As a family minister, you hold a vital role in the lives of families in your church. The Holy Spirit uses you to provide instruction, counsel, support, help, and hope to church members of all ages as they grow in Christlikeness. You encourage others—like Moses in the life of Joshua, Mordecai in the life of Esther, Elizabeth in the life of Mary, and Paul in the life of Timothy. Despite not receiving the gratitude you deserve, you have more influence in the lives of church members than you possibly know.

Be encouraged! God is with you! Stay on the trail! And as you do, others will follow you as you guide, disciple, and pray for them while trusting the Holy Spirit to nurture their spiritual formation.

3

STRATEGIES TO DISCERN MARRIAGE AND FAMILY HEALTH AND FUNCTIONING

Jennifer S. Ripley, John Van Epp, and J. P. De Gance

It was a tough day for Wendy, the family life coordinator. Two church leaders called about the Petersons and their adolescent son Adam. First, the small group leader called to say the couple fought in their small group. The conflict swamped the meeting. Then the youth pastor called to say that Adam had a bad attitude in the youth group and brought two other youths into his "I don't wanna be here" club. He was disruptive every time. No one could handle him. The mom came forward for prayer in Sunday services every week for a month. The father hadn't been seen in a long time. Wendy was about to call Mrs. Peterson. What should she say? It's evident that there was pain in the Peterson family, and she wanted to bring healing. But she was fearful that it could "blow up." She could refer the family to a counselor, but this should be where the church helps. She was not sure how.

This chapter is about three things:

1. Discerning a single-family challenge so the church ministry can effectively care for them.

2. Creating principles for churchwide relationship ministry to build family well-being.
3. Nurturing the goodness and beauty of healthy relationships through your church ministry to bless your city for those not (yet) part of your church.

The Peterson family, or families in every church and city, face many struggles. It's like their hurt leaks out and affects others. Churches help families thrive by understanding and connecting them with resources to meet their needs. Churches can help the Petersons distinguish the root of their family needs: biological, relational, spiritual, and the fusion of all three.

The needs of families in our church communities are extensive. Everyone needs help, so a church-wide ministry plan is needed to encourage healthy relationships. The Petersons are just one example of uncountable families with need. Churches can provide resources to help them and many others.

We also cast a vision for relationship ministry broadcast from your church to your neighborhood or city. Each chapter in this book targets a specific set of needs. This chapter will address broad family ministry themes essential for family ministry. We intend to prepare you for when the Petersons call again, when you have a chance to reflect on the broader ministry needs of your church community, or when you feel the loneliness and hunger for healthy relationships in the unchurched in your neighborhood.

FAMILY LEVEL DISCERNMENT: SPIRITUAL AND RELATIONAL NEEDS INTERTWINE

So, with the Peterson family, where do we start? Their need for growth and maturity in their faith is the place to begin. Their pain is uncontained. It emerges in daily life and relationships. Anger and a lack of self-control in the small group meeting are signs of emotional and spiritual immaturity. Simultaneously, their son declared his needs to the youth group and displayed an unteachable presentation, defying his leaders. The fundamental needs not met within the family become displayed outside the home. All family members contribute to forming and nurturing safe, supportive, and loving relationships. Perhaps the Petersons have never learned how to create and nurture healthy relationships, and church leaders could help them learn. Family conflict looks like a family-level problem, but it is a spiritual problem, too.

HOW TO "TRIAGE" FAMILY CARE

If you are meeting with a family member, you might consider taking a triage model, similar to an emergency room. In an ER, the charge nurse will quickly determine the level of need and where the pain comes from and then move the patient along to get the needed care.

Is it biology? One of the first questions is, "Is there a biological factor in play with this family?" Healthy relationships are affected by biological disorders such as autism, ADHD, intellectual disability, and severe mental illness. Addictions also have a vital biological component, as the body can become dependent on substances.[1] These conditions tax every family's resources, making members exhausted to address common stressors. Wendy could listen well and ask if the family is dealing with any diagnosis or suspects a diagnosis that might influence family functioning. Biological problems would need medical care, psychological care, and spiritual care. Several chapters in this book are dedicated to further exploration of disabilities, addictions, and mental illness to equip ministry leaders with information.

Is it trauma? The second question is, "Is a trauma response occurring in the home?" Some traumas are public, and a church family would be aware of things like a traumatic brain injury, homelessness, or experiences of combat in war. Other family-level traumas are often unseen, such as sexual assault, domestic violence, and infidelity. Church leaders may need training to address trauma in their congregation. Some trauma issues in your ministry may also be high-risk red flag issues, such as domestic violence, requiring consulting the church's insurance provider or lawyer, and state laws on child protective services.

Church leaders have an essential role to play in trauma care. Perhaps you were given some training on ministering to a family in the emergency room or after losing a loved one. The ministry there is spiritual comfort, prayer,

---

[1] Simone Kühn and Jürgen Gallinat, "Common Biology of Craving across Legal and Illegal Drugs—A Quantitative Meta-analysis of Cue-reactivity Brain Response," *European Journal of Neuroscience* 33, no. 7 (April 2011): 1318-26. https://doi.org/10.1111/j.1460-9568.2010.07590.x.

and engaging the community to provide practical help—similarly, invisible traumas benefit from spiritual comfort, prayer, and practical support.

The effects of trauma are experienced as avoidance, numbing, nightmares, difficulty sleeping and regulating the body, physical reactivity to slight remembrances of the traumatic experience, anxiety, and depressive symptoms.[2] Many people cope with trauma by using drugs, doing activities that numb, like binging on screens, or withdrawing from social situations (including the church community). Family, supporters, and church leaders tend to react to the symptoms and lose sight of the pain behind the presentations. It is helpful for church leaders to recognize that these behaviors may have their roots in trauma with a need for care and sometimes professional treatment. A compassionate response by church leaders is powerful in helping spiritual, psychological, and family recovery.

Is it social stress? Another question is, "Are there social factors overstressing this family?" Social stress described in this book takes the form of poverty, race-based stress, internet-based influences, or diversity-based strains like LGBTQ+ family members. Many of these stresses are difficult for family members to discuss with church leaders and may require some prompting, signaling privacy, and reassuring the church leader is safe. If the Peterson family is dealing with race-based stress, they may need their church to provide a safe community to express their anxiety. Suppose the young Adam is acting out in youth group because he struggles with negative messages he has received via social media. Most behavior is a response or reaction to previous experiences. So, what is provoking him toward disruption? In that case, he doesn't need a lecture on social media but a spiritual pathway to handling anxiety-provoking social messages. He may need mentoring with someone in the congregation who can engage that conversation well and spiritually care for him as he navigates his socially based stress. Everyone carries social stress. There are likely many leaders in your church that you could identify who could mentor, disciple, and pray with families.

Is it a spiritual struggle? Existential dread and distress are common in modern culture. This distress could happen due to external crises such as

---

[2]Julian D. Ford and Christine A. Courtois, eds., *Treating Complex Traumatic Stress Disorders in Adults: Scientific Foundations and Therapeutic Models*, 2nd ed. (New York: Guilford, 2020).

divorce, race-based conflict, deficits in character, and psychological symptoms. The effect can leave individuals, couples, or families discouraged and struggling with their sense of connection with God. Family members sometimes struggle with feeling that God has abandoned them or is unavailable to them, or that they are cursed, or have lost God's blessings. Negative religious coping or spiritual struggle involves conflicts with religious others, internal loss of faith, questioning, unnecessary guilt, and perceived distance or negative views of God. If the family member is talking about feeling punished by God, abandoned, unloved by God, that God is not strengthening them, that Satan is making them do things, or their church has abandoned them, they are in a spiritual struggle.

Some church members have deficits in character that will need spiritual discipleship and mentoring. This may be the parent with an anger problem that you witness dressing down their family in the parking lot. Or perhaps a couple of highly emotional parents have attracted much attention to their young adult son's legal trouble. Other families appear to create problems in every church they attend before moving on, leaving division and discord in their wake. Character problems often cluster in families and have an impact on family functioning. These are opportunities for spiritual care and discipleship.

Those in a spiritual struggle need their church leaders' compassionate, careful, and thoughtful spiritual care. Congregation members and leaders may need training to recognize and respond well to struggle. Like the Peterson family, you might find your church members nervous and unsure how to respond to a teen or adult withdrawing from church attendance or showing negative attitudes about God.[3] Often, when a struggle is presented, there is anxiety from those ministering to the person. The person will either go underground with their struggle or see it as confirmation that God indeed abandoned them. The best response is one of warm compassion and hospitality to those struggling with their faith so they can have relationships with caring church leaders and members. They shouldn't walk through the struggle alone. The ministry is one of presence, care, and hospitality.

---

[3]Gina M. Brelsford, Lisa A. Mondell, Tarah Raldiris, and Joshua Ramirez, "Stress and Negative Religious Coping in a Community Sample," *Journal of Psychology and Christianity* 34, no. 2 (June 2015): 141-54.

Is it a bio-psycho-social-spiritual struggle? Rarely is the only problem a biological diagnosis, a single traumatic event, or one social stressor. Often, there are multiple problems affecting multiple members of the family. When you meet with families, try not to stop asking questions when one problem is described. There are likely other related problems, and understanding the whole story will help you respond sensitively to their needs. It is helpful to try and discern how much biological, psychological, social, and spiritual factors might contribute to the family's struggle. While a church community is specially equipped to address spiritual battles, it is also an excellent venue for social support, compassionate care, and networking in the community for excellent medical and psychological treatment.

ARE WE EQUIPPED?

A good church leader has a humble awareness of their knowledge and skills in ministering to families and accurately assesses the congregation's ability to receive and care for families in pain. As new problems arise, pastoral excellence is evident in gathering information, understanding core issues, accepting guidance from others, and creating a response that heals the family and strengthens the church community. Yet, it is also essential not to try to do more than you are resourced. It's easy to assume that because we know the family, Scripture, and healthy living patterns, we know how to confront, challenge, support, encourage, admonish, and mentor a family system toward painful symptom reduction and healing. Just as we hear "Don't try this at home. . ." as a caution when watching a stunt actor conduct a dangerous maneuver, sometimes "Don't try this in your office. . ." should be heeded when there is no training and supervision. The chapter on differentiation in this book can help leaders discern the limits of their care and provide a model for understanding how family members may need to find ways to set healthy boundaries in crisis.

After learning about the factors affecting the Peterson family, Wendy may discover more about the issues uncovered in the discernment phase of care. She may wish to consult with a knowledgeable psychologist or cultural or ministry leader in her community and share her findings with leaders who minister to the family. Suppose Jesse, the father in the

Peterson family, appears to be struggling with depression. In that case, Wendy may want to offer a class on depression to the community and invite the family and their youth and/or small group leaders to attend the course. Thoughtful discussions with the Peterson family could encourage them to be in a receiving posture of ministry from the congregation and church leaders while helping them network for external care.

What are the resources available to the pastor, both internal and external? Internal resources include ongoing ministries, which might be helpful, or congregation members with relevant training. External resources are professionals or services available within the community. If a church has medical and mental health providers within the congregation or church network, they may want to create a resource from those members who can privately advise and consult on issues like the Petersons. External resources are also often needed, and a church staff keeping a resource list readily available at the front desk or similar location is essential for any church. Specialists in various aspects of care, whether medical, psychological, social, or spiritual, can support a family walking through a crisis. Many professionals care for families like the Peterson's every day. They will remind, caution, and direct you to ideas that never come to mind. Have them on your speed dial.

How do I understand my internal resources? These are willing professionals in your church who are highly competent in some areas and want to assist you "any way they can." (This can mean they try to help despite being outside their competence area, perhaps for personal or financial gain). One of a church leader's more difficult positions may be managing the boundary of a willing or enthusiastic internal resource, whether a medical or mental health provider. That provider may be limited in some aspects of care, and a church should be careful not to over-tax the provider. For example, the diagnosis of autism is complex and specialized and should not be done by a generalist. Referral to a pediatrician is often an excellent first step for biologically based disorders like autism, ADHD, and severe mental illness. Most pediatricians can refer the family to specialized local providers who can diagnose. No church leader should be alone in this process, and finding good internal and external resources is essential.

HOW DO I COLLABORATE WITH PROFESSIONALS PROVIDING CARE?

Most medical and mental health providers are glad to collaborate with church leaders to provide excellent family care. Every pastor should have a network of professionals—psychologists, counselors, social workers, couples/family therapists, addiction counselors, and psychiatrists who can be reached for consultation, referral, and support. Likewise, the family can sign a release permitting the church leader to talk with a clinical provider providing service to the family. Ethical limits restrict the clinician from discussing specific treatment details; however, they can provide insight and suggestions on how the church community can align with the family's treatment goals. The family should articulate these details to the clinician and church so that each respects the boundaries of confidentiality. Leaders like Wendy can ask if a shared phone or video meeting with their provider, even for ten minutes, might help everyone work together. The church leader wants to support the provider's work, and the church may have resources beyond what the provider can offer.

Working with professionals is an act of ministry. Rather than reinforce defenses that arise from competition with local healthcare or mental healthcare providers, think of bridgebuilding. Professional collaboration is an act of gospel care. Through an attitude of humility and gracious respect for the gifts and expertise of others, we expand the reach of the gospel while also benefiting from their competence. We do this by receiving the knowledge and skill of mental health science with the articulation of our calling. Adopting a non-anxious presence fueled by the assurance that God has blessed your calling and ministry extends the gospel's reach. By embracing a humble attitude, you draw from the expertise of others, and the church's impact and footprint are expanded. Similarly, ministers can offer expertise in spiritual care and existential issues for the clinician who is likely underequipped to address such themes. The church and the clinic have much to offer one another.

Having pressed the idea that relational ministry is essential, we turn to how to do it. This next section will discuss the implementation of a relationship education ministry based on assessing a church community's needs. We present an example of one type of ministry to help make the move from assessment to implementation clear and reachable.

CARING FOR THE WHOLE CONGREGATION

Family life pastor Mike wants to increase marriage and family ministry in the church. His wife, Carla, a marriage and family therapist, had conducted marriage intensives, and they had previously taught a marriage Sunday school class. Mike is excited about expanding his existing marriage ministries to reach more couples and also include singles, daters, and families. Where should he start?

Perhaps you have felt like Mike—needing to make decisions about marriage ministries for a church but overwhelmed by a crowded market of products. An enormous marriage ministry industrial complex seems to have too many options for the pastor or family life leader. How do you decide what resources fit your church?

One of the most common first steps taken is to evaluate the salient relationship needs of the congregation. A needs assessment can be done easily with a church survey; however, the findings may not accurately represent the struggles experienced within the relationships of those surveyed.

The reason surveys often understate problems is what researchers have called inflated positive ratings. When someone is asked about their relationship before engaging in some information about their relationship, they are prone to answer overly positively. This is why many researchers use a "retrospective pre-posttest," which allows respondents to answer the same questions they answered in the pretest again but this second time during the posttest.

In a similar way, research has found that once participants have gone through a relationship course or series, they often identify and acknowledge more problem areas that they had previously overlooked during their pretest, and, as a result, they end up adjusting *down* their pretest scores and disclosing a more accurate portrayal of their relationship struggles.

However, even without "priming the pump" with a relationship series prior to conducting a church survey, about 20% or more of a typical congregation face severe distress, infidelity, violence, and risk for divorce.[4] Churches in higher-distress neighborhoods and communities might find even higher percentages in distress.

While the 20% portion is in serious need and are willing to admit it, included in the other 80% are those who also may need help but are either unaware or unwilling to be transparent, and many others who will eventually face relationship struggles that could have been avoided if only steps of prevention had been taken earlier. Therefore, ministry is more than just crisis counseling—it must strengthen the struggling, provide prevention for the vulnerable, and promote spiritual formation and discipleship in the home.

HOW TO CHOOSE AMONG MARRIAGE MINISTRY OPTIONS

Mike understood this and decided to postpone his survey until after he provided the entire congregation with a rich growth experience that would strengthen relationships while prompting greater insight into the deficits of their dating and marriage relationships.

At first, Mike thought about planning just a sermon series on relationships to prime the pump and increase awareness of relationship concerns. The teaching pastor was interested, and this seemed like an excellent first step. He next considered a marriage mentoring program, a Sunday school class led by a local marriage counselor, a weekend marriage retreat, a marriage "book club," and a lay counseling/mentoring model. There were many options! If the many options confuse you, we hope to guide you in a set of self-reflective questions.

1. What marriage ministry is already present in my church? Although larger churches may have staff dedicated to marriage and family ministry, all churches can consider ways to infuse marriage ministry into existing ministries (e.g., kids, youth, singles, and adult

---

[4] J. P. De Gance and J. Stonestreet, *A Nationwide Study on Faith and Relationships*, 2023, https://communio.org/study. A key question frequently included in congregational surveys is the overall satisfaction of marriage: "Indicate the degree of happiness, all things considered, of your relationship." There are six options: Perfect, extremely happy, very happy, happy, a little unhappy, fairly unhappy, and extremely unhappy. Research on this question has shown that "a little unhappy" or worse predicts an increased likelihood that the couple will divorce. In Communio's surveys of over 19,000 congregants from more than 100 churches, 20% of married churchgoers report "a little unhappy" or worse. This means that one in every four couples rates their relationship in a danger zone and has an elevated risk of divorce.

small group ministries can all have regular content about biblical and healthy friendships, families, dating relationships, and marriages). This is a starting point, to make healthy relationships the mission of all ministries.

2. Where are the marriage ministry opportunities within our existing ministries? If your church is focused on Sunday school ministry, then a marriage class on Sunday morning may be the best fit for you. Small home groups may benefit from a marriage-focused discussion group type of ministry. If you already have a lay counseling or altar ministry, training ministers in caring for family needs may be ideal. That doesn't mean you can't expand into new ministries, but aligning with your current ministry style will increase impact.

3. Do you want to make marriage ministry a front porch ministry? If you're going to attract new people to your church through marriage ministry, you might need to design ministries that will be attractive to the neighborhoods around your church, which may differ from your congregation. Small churches might be best served to join with other local churches or ministries for marriage events, while moderate to larger churches host their own events.

4. Are dating, marriage, and family relationships presented clearly in doctrinal teaching? Each church should have biblical teachings on marriage and parenting. Christian teaching on marriage is often quite different from the culture, and without doctrinal teaching, the congregation may be unaware of the Christian idea of marriage.

5. Are you looking to improve struggling relationships? There is a sobering fact that all the research on marriage ministries tends to show small, short-lived effects on relationships.[5] Generally, marriage ministries are time-limited (1-8 hours) and use low-efficacy approaches to change, such as didactic teaching. Even some of the most well-designed marriage education programs have limitations.[6] If this is

---

[5] J. S. Ripley, L. Parrott, and E. L. Worthington, Jr., "An Initial Evaluation of the Parrotts' Saving Your Marriage Before It Starts (SYMBIS) Seminar: Who Benefits?," *Marriage and Family: A Christian Journal* 3:83-97.
[6] Rachel Sheffield, "Building a Happy Home: Marriage as a Tool to Strengthen Families," US Congress Joint Economics Committee, Republicans. March 4, 2022. www.jec.senate.gov/public/index

your mission, then dig deep. Marriage education may not be enough for struggling relationships needing more focused counseling and church ministry. You will likely need multiple resources for distressed couples, including pastoral care, good teaching, positive peer couples, and (often) professional counseling. Even with that, some couples will not improve much or will divorce over time. Hold onto hope and provide good care to the struggling couples within your congregation and community.

6. What are our standards for marriage content? Marriage ministry material is often quite market-driven and "packaged." If the packaging fits your needs, it might be a good match for you, but we encourage you to look past pretty websites, funny jokes, and clever analogies to ensure the material is wise. There should be a focus on relational bonds, virtues, and skills, not just entertaining stories. In an ideal ministry, the packaging would be good, and the content would be excellent. Deep dive ministry is more of a deep dive into relationship education with doctrinal teaching and educational materials for people of all ages and types of relationships.

AN EXAMPLE OF A DEEP DIVE INTERVENTION: RAM SERIES

After consulting with a relationship expert, family life pastor Mike decided to do a whole church "deep dive" into relationship education and conduct a churchwide survey on relationship health. He reviewed several high-quality resources, including Hope-Focused Couple Counseling,[7] Christian PREP education,[8] Prepare-Enrich assessment, and affiliated education.[9] Mike wanted to have a relationship sermon series that also included Christian curriculum for the adults as well as children and youth, promoting intergenerational learning and many conversations within families

---

.cfm/republicans/2022/3/building-a-happy-home-marriage-education-as-a-tool-to-strengthen-families.

[7] Hope Couple Counseling is a Christian couple counseling program that lay counselors can be trained in. www.hopecouples.com.

[8] PREP, Inc. is a relationship education program with excellent research support and a Christian version for churches. https://prepinc.com/collections/christian-material.

[9] Prepare/Enrich has relationship assessment and feedback, with optional group curriculum, and often used in churches. www.prepare-enrich.com.

after services. After careful review, his church chose the RAM Series.[10] He timed it to kick off when the church started new home groups so the groups could all engage in the material simultaneously with the sermon series.

Churches such as Mike's frequently report three outcomes that occur through conducting a churchwide relationship series. First, it is common for attendance to increase. Mike found an increase in home groups to be about 15%. This is common with relationship series, where parishioners often have pain points. Many long for help and support in their relationships.

Mike also set up a good list of local couple and family counselors for referrals. His motivation was to provide education for all and counseling referrals for the 20%+ with greater needs.

Raising a church's awareness and openness toward relationship struggles creates a second primary outcome: a much more accurate assessment when Mike surveyed the congregation's needs after conducting the churchwide relationship series. While a relationship series will improve some distressed relationships, it will also prompt those who have been denying their issues to take steps toward getting help. This outcome was confirmed by an unsolicited email sent to Mike from a director of a Christian counseling center on their marriage counseling referral list:

> Since you have started your relationship series, we have seen a marked increase in couples seeking counseling for their marriages. We have also seen individuals, who aren't married, seeking out how to evaluate with God their future relationships and current dating situations. As a therapy team, we want to come alongside your church and to give God's people good counsel in their time of need. . . . Thank you, for allowing us the privilege to do what God has ordained us as counselors to do on behalf of His Kingdom.

The third outcome that conducting this churchwide series accomplished is a marked increase in the desire for relationship content. Before the series was completed, it was common to overhear someone ask, "So, what relationship course is next!" This set the stage to introduce the

---

[10] Discussed more under the next heading, the RAM Series can be a whole-church deep dive into healthy relationship education. This series is modular, and appropriate for Protestant, Catholic, large multi-campus, or small churches. The RAM series includes six sermon/homily messages based on the RAM, and complementary video-based content for children, teens, adult singles and couples. During the sermon series, the entire church simultaneously works on building and sustaining healthy dating, marriage, friendship, and family relationships; see www.ramseries.com.

many exciting and new ways Mike's marriage ministry team planned to support singles and couples in the congregation and mobilize outreach strategies to address their community's relationship needs.

THREE TARGET AREAS FOR RELATIONSHIP HEALTH FOR YOUR CHURCH MINISTRY CARE

I (John) remember a dinner I attended with over a dozen keynote presenters at a marriage conference around fifteen years ago. I would venture to say that every one of them had used the term "healthy relationship" in their plenary, so I asked them if they would give a one-sentence definition of just what exactly a healthy relationship is. The table buzzed with endless ideas, much like a brainstorming session, but no one developed a comprehensive and succinct single-sentence definition.

So, let us take a stab at this and suggest a definition:

A healthy relationship is intentionally managing major relationship bonds with genuine relational virtues and proficient relationship skills.

Relational bonds, virtues, and skills are the three components of a mature relationship accessible in the Relational Attachment Model, or RAM Series. We wish to amplify each of these skill sets.

Components of the Relational Attachment Model (RAM). The Relationship Attachment Model (RAM)[11] can be compared to an audio mixing board with five sliders representing the five indicators of relational bonds, each having a similar range (fig. 3.1). The degree of strength of each relational bond is defined by how far the slider is moved up. However, it is common for both life and relationship experiences to cause varying degrees of fluctuation, altering the feelings of closeness within a relationship. Because the five relational bonds are also interactive, the RAM can profile specific strengths, deficits, and needed

---

[11]The Relationship Attachment Model (RAM) was developed by John Van Epp in 1985 and is the proprietary model utilized in his Love Thinks relationship courses (www.LoveThinks.com) and licensed to churches in the RAM series (www.RAMseries.com). Research has validated this theoretical model and programs based on the RAM: Morgan C. Van Epp Cutlip, "A Qualitative Examination of the Relationship Attachment Model (RAM) with Married Individuals," (PhD diss., University of Akron, 2013), https://etd.ohiolink.edu/acprod/odb_etd/ws/send_file/send?accession=akron1365099833&disposition=inline. John Van Epp and Morgan Van Epp Cutlip, "Relationship Attachment Model (RAM) Programs: PICK and LINKS," in *Evidence-based Approaches to Relationship and Marriage Education*, ed. James J. Ponzetti, Jr. (New York: Routledge, 2016), 231-52.

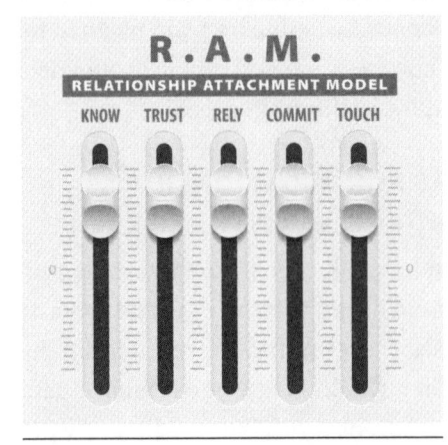

Figure 3.1. Relationship Attachment Model

growth areas of a relationship at any given period.

Understanding relationship bonds. A relationship, by definition, is a connection between two or more people. I sifted through the large body of published research and identified five major connections or relational bonds that comprise all relationships: *know, trust, rely, commit,* and *touch.* I called them relational bonds because each one, on its own, has a range that contributes to the feeling of a bond or closeness with another person. In addition, they also interact with each other, so when one increases or decreases in strength, it tends to impact the levels of the others, creating mixed and sometimes confusing feelings in the relationship.

Assessing, building, and sustaining relationships. The RAM helps to understand and assess two broad categories of relationships: the initial formation of a new relationship and the long-term sustainment of an existing relationship. First, when developing a new relationship, there are inherent risks, and the RAM provides a logical sequence for minimizing those vulnerabilities.

Relationships can grow in a "safe zone" when they are intentionally built in strength from the left side of the RAM to the right (fig. 3.2). For example, imagine a new dating relationship: What you come to *know* about your partner should set the ceiling of your trust, and your degree of *trust* should gauge how you *rely* on that person. These three areas should set the boundaries of both your *commitment* and physical/sexual interactions (*touch* can refer to sexual or non-sexual interactions depending on the nature of the relationship). It is helpful for singles of all ages to have this visual logic model to reinforce their biblical conviction of practicing boundaries in their dating relationships.

In other words, it is unsafe to trust someone significantly more than what you know about them or rely on them more than you know or trust them. It is risky to engage in sexual intimacy when the levels of your commitment, reliance, trust, and knowledge are low.

So, in a dating relationship, when the level of a relational bond exceeds any of the levels to its left, the bonds of the heart tend to override the mind's judgment, leading to a "love is blind" relationship (see fig. 3.3).[12] Similar blind spots can occur in any non-romantic relationship when these significant imbalances develop during relationship formation.

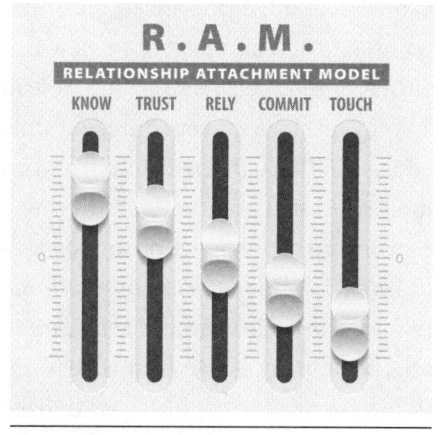

Figure 3.2. RAM safe zone

But when sustaining long-term relationships, the sequence is not nearly as important as identifying "small leaks." For instance, it is easy to imagine the birth of a baby shifting the focus from the couple's needs and wants to all the baby's demands. New babies limit conversations (lowering the "know"), create constant baby care (lowering the "rely" by replacing the meeting of personal/couple needs with baby needs), and, of course, diminish intimate touch because of the necessary recovery from birthing and the fatigue of childcare. As the old saying goes, "Sex leads to little babies, but babies lead to little sex."

Figure 3.3. RAM high-risk imbalances

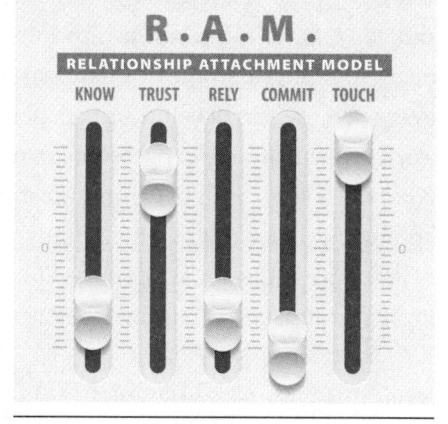

These imbalances, represented on the RAM, are normal and inevitable, yet they will impact the couple's feelings toward each other. The danger

---

[12]John Van Epp, *How to Avoid Falling in Love with a Jerk: The Foolproof Way to Follow Your Heart Without Losing Your Mind* (New York: McGraw-Hill, 2006). The *RAM Study for Singles* is a video-based small group study that leads youth or adults through the content of this book. https://ramseries.com/singles-track-sessions.

is not *becoming* imbalanced but *staying* imbalanced. When these shifts go undetected and become a new normal, a slow leak of closeness will either flatten their relationship or lead to a big blowout.[13]

Your ministry can encourage couples to engage in regular relationship education through their church and create a personal strategy to increase their relational bonds. Then, they would be much more likely to sustain a close and robust relationship over their lifetime.

Intentional formation of relational bonds, virtues, and skills. These relationship skills require *intentional formation and sustainment.* New relationships must be formed within the safe zone, and enduring relationships must be regularly revitalized. However, it is not simply the act of intentionally managing these relational bonds. Instead, it is an engagement that blends genuine *virtues* with proficient relationship *skills*, producing healthy and godly relationships. Virtues include internalized values and character qualities, like the fruit of the Spirit. Skills are behaviors or external, observable actions.

Often, pastoral care providers or relationship mentors aren't considering both the virtue and the skill. When you imagine someone highly skilled in handling relationships but lacking character and virtue, you begin to sketch a profile of a narcissist or a sociopath. The life journey of every person is to develop and deepen their virtue. The end goal of your work is to encourage congregants to navigate their relational bonds with good skills (e.g., skills of communication, conflict resolution, forgiveness, apologies, discernment, and boundaries) as well as the Christlike virtue of agape love and the fruit of the Spirit (e.g., patience, grace, generosity, loyalty, compassion, humility, perseverance).[14]

CREATING A POSITIVE IMPACT FOR COUPLES AND FAMILIES

Serving felt needs has been a common path to advancing the gospel since Jesus walked among us. The Son of God healed the lame and the blind,

---

[13] John Van Epp and M. C. Cutlip, *Becoming Better Together: The RAM Plan for Growing Together When Life is Pulling you Apart* (Washington, DC: Trinity Press: 2017).

[14] For an extensive description of skills and virtues, see chaps 8-12 in John Van Epp and J. P. De Gance, *Endgame: The Church's Strategic Move to Save Faith and Family in America* (Washington, DC: Trinity Press, 2021). https://communio.org/endgame/.

cured the sick, and fed the hungry. Today, we might address thirst by digging wells, address hunger by teaching improved agricultural techniques, or advance communities through literacy skills. These methods meet explicit gospel mandates and build trust relationships where curiosity forms.

By any measure, the collapse of healthy relationships and marriage is the felt need of the 21st century. Mother Theresa famously saw this reality. In 2004, before any awareness of an epidemic of loneliness, the little Albanian religious sister said: "In the West there is a loneliness, which I call the leprosy of the West. In many ways, it is worse than our poor in Calcutta."[15]

Researchers found that 15% of married churchgoers and at least 50% of all single churchgoers are considered lonely.[16] Nearly 66% of never-married churchgoers in their 30s were considered lonely, which was a higher rate than we found among the loneliest age group of widows. By comparison, 17% of married churchgoers in their 30s and 20% of married church-going women in this age group were also considered lonely. A Harvard study of the general population in 2021 indicated that 36% of Americans, 61% of young adults, and 51% of young mothers feel "serious loneliness."[17]

MEETING THE RELATIONAL NEEDS

The first step in considering ministry is understanding the relational needs of those around you. This is best done with a survey of the church's Sunday attendees. Then, an analysis of the community through commercially available consumer product data. Understanding your community's specific needs gives you focus to addressing the relational needs of those you serve. Every individual church should see itself as a light that displaces the darkness and attracts those in the community into it.

---

[15] Kendall Palladino, "Mother Teresa saw Loneliness as the Leprosy of the West," *The News Times*, April 17, 2004, www.newstimes.com/news/article/mother-teresa-saw-loneliness-as-leprosy-of-the-250607.php#.

[16] A score of 6-9 points on the UCLA Loneliness Index's Summary Survey places an individual into the considered lonely category.

[17] Richard Weissbourd, Milena Batanova, Virginia Lovison, and Eric Torres, "Loneliness in America: How the Pandemic Has Deepened an Epidemic of Loneliness and What We Can Do About It," Making Caring Common Project, Harvard Graduate School of Education, February 2021, https://mcc.gse.harvard.edu/reports/loneliness-in-america; "Communio at Work: Divorce Drops 24% in Jacksonville," Communio, accessed April 16, 2024, https://communio.org/jacksonville-florida-case-study/; Van Epp and De Gance, *Endgame*.

Every church has marriages struggling in the pews right now, and the singles in attendance are three to four times more likely to report being lonely and isolated than the married. Communio's model can be replicated in your church to answer important questions:

- How many married people are likely struggling in their marriage, and how many of these have young children?
- How many single people appear likely to marry in the coming months?
- How many cohabiting individuals are nearby, and how many households have single parents?
- How many women are likely to be pregnant near your church?

Whenever working to impact a community through multi-church cooperation, it is helpful to understand the breakdown of the population by religious affiliation. One free resource for insights on any city in the United States is www.City-Data.com. In Communio's work in Jacksonville, FL, Baptists and Catholics were the two largest religious populations in that region. So, their effort intentionally sought to cultivate direct partnerships with churches aligned with the Southern Baptist Convention and those in the Catholic diocese. You can leverage www.City-Data.com to analyze the religious population in any city in the country and collaborate with established church networks.

Next, Communio takes the insights from the church and city-level data to consider the community's needs. What response can your team provide? Many churches benefit from a managed service like Communio that allows the church to invite individuals from customized audiences into outreach events and ministry. However, if you have local expertise in marriage ministry, you could plan and implement marriage ministries in any church of any size.

The response in Jacksonville was to provide enrichment education ministry for marriages and ministry for the minority of couples in crisis through marriage intensives. To help the churches of Jacksonville, Communio funded a collaboration with Live the Life Ministries to provide more frequent monthly intensives. You will most likely find trained and licensed coaches and counselors who can deploy a local marriage intensive in your community. Your church might consider providing poorer couples with scholarships for intensive marriage intervention. Ultimately, if many churches within a fixed geography focus on running outreach and ministry for relationships, the health of marriages and other relationships can change citywide. Communio ultimately saw ninety-three churches participate at different levels in Jacksonville with this focus. We hope our story helps you consider how your church might reach out to your neighborhood with care for the brokenhearted and lonely people who live near you.

THREE CORE INGREDIENTS OF MARRIAGE AND FAMILY MINISTRIES

For any church to impact its surrounding community while transforming its internal relationship health, it must penetrate all facets of ministry and be seen as its primary front porch, leading souls to a real encounter with Jesus Christ. Achieving this requires a cultural shift. We suggest that the components of any cultural shift address vision, skills, and community.

You must establish the three core ingredients for an effective relationship ministry: vision, skills, and community. Vision is the first ingredient that overcomes the stigma. Vision is cast from the pulpit and then infused into every ministry within the church. Marriage enrichment ministry is accessible and supportive for all couples in a church community. Leadership must expect everyone in their church to participate in relationship enrichment ministry. Healthy marriages and relationships should magnetize those around us to Jesus. As the old hymn goes—they will know we are Christians by our love.

We offer a concrete vision you can adopt or alter for your setting. Your church might operationalize this by setting the clear expectation that everyone here invests eight hours each year in strengthening their marriage or relationship skills. Then, everyone in the church's leadership must be expected to participate in the ministry to set an example. After participating, it is so much easier to encourage others to follow.

Skills are those relationship skills that put virtues into practice. Most anyone knows to love well is to be patient and kind. Learning deep listening skills or how to have a good time out from conflict puts patience and kindness into practice. We want a church to allow individuals and couples to practice the interpersonal and intrapersonal skills that academic research says are critical to flourishing marriages and relationships.

A Christ-centered community reinforces the vision and skills. Research has indicated that couples with close friends who divorce have a 75% increase in the chances of divorce,[18] which means that cohorts of healthy marriages in congregations are a buffer in preventing divorce. In a world with high amounts of loneliness, divorce, and relationship distress, a church that can create a group of healthy marriages is a light in dark places.

Community draws a person toward faith, the ultimate purpose of the church. Faith is more likely caught than it is taught. People respond first to the emotional pull of the gospel message articulated in a relationship. It's not that sound teaching is unimportant. Instead, it is that people first connect and build trust and friendship within a community before being open to faith instruction. A healthy church community that includes many healthy marriages can be an important entry point for people who need to grow their faith.

THE MINISTRY ENGAGEMENT LADDER: HOW TO BUILD A GROWING MARRIAGE MINISTRY

The ministry engagement ladder is designed for church outreach, which ministry leaders like Mike and Wendy should consider when planning for marriage ministries. The ladder is a four-step process where a church draws nonmembers and the unchurched into their relationship ministry: (1) invitation, (2) outreach, (3) ongoing engagement, and (4) growth journey. Through this four-step process, a church actualizes the vision, skills, and community that are the core ingredients for any fruitful relationship ministry that evangelizes.

Pastor Mike and Wendy will want to examine the surrounding community before engaging in community outreach. After the community analysis phase, the church moves into the planning phase. This involves setting measurable goals around growth in Sunday attendance (the breadth goal) and the number of individuals consuming eight or

---

[18]Rose McDermott, James H. Fowler, and Nicholas A. Christakis, "Breaking Up Is Hard to Do, Unless Everyone Else Is Doing It Too: Social Network Effects on Divorce in a Longitudinal Sample," *Social Forces* 92, no. 2 (Dec 2013): 491-519, https://doi.org/10.1093/sf/sot096.

more hours of relationship skills practice (the depth goal).

When looking at the Ministry Engagement Ladder, one objective is to help your church move from thinking they are inviting people to an individual event. Instead, you are creating a vision of joining others on a relational journey. Each person is partnering with the church to be an active rather than passive agent.

The first step of that journey begins with a compelling invitation. When crafting an invitation, place yourself into the mindset of someone who is not a church member. Would I see the "offer" as something I would enjoy doing? Will I perceive that it is a valuable use of my time?

Figure 3.4. Ministry Engagement Ladder

Ministry Engagement Ladder
- 4 Growth Journey
- 3 Ongoing Engagement
- 2 Outreach
- 1 Invitation

For the outreach step, church should create a community invitation that is 85–90% fun event and 10–15% enrichment. This could be a family block party or a salsa night for couples with dance instruction and childcare. It could be a Christmas evening bonfire with Christmas carols. These events can include some enrichment or education as part of the event but are not specific. Wendy's church decided to host a monthly Parents Night, where childcare is provided. Any event with childcare tends to be a big hit.

The next step on the ladder is ongoing engagement. Consider this step to be about 70% fun and 30% enrichment. We encourage a church to insert relationship skill activities to be modeled and run by couples.

Ultimately, through outreach and ongoing engagements, the church membership forms the interlocking personal connections and friendships that are the actual glue of the Christian community. This allows the church to invite nonmembers to take the final step—the growth journey. This is where the high-dosage skills ministry lives.

Here, churches like Mike and Wendy's are challenged to think creatively about running skills-based programs. We found a significant gap in relationship satisfaction between married men and women. Women were 62% more likely to report struggling in their marriage, with the peak gap in relationship satisfaction occurring between ages 30–39. So, how can we make these growth journey experiences attractive and fun so that the average couple, particularly the married man, is open and interested in participating?

The reality is the "leprosy of the West" has a cure. That cure lives inside the local church because the local church is the actual manifestation of the body of Christ in a community. Marriage ministries are an ideal way to build community in a church.

A primary goal of relational ministry is to grow churches. An example is Fellowship of the Parks—a Fort Worth, Texas, church. Their marriage ministry is their front porch invitation to their community. Frequently, couples attend their marriage ministry for months without becoming members. Then, one day, a personal invitation prompts them to start attending services on Sunday.

Another example is St. Helen Catholic Church in Vero Beach, Florida. They applied this outreach and relationship ministry model, resulting in significant participation by the local community in their monthly marriage and relationship ministry events. This 108-year-old parish is now at all-time highs on Sunday. This model can be implemented in a local church or collaboratively with various churches in a city. We hope the principles help you as you plan your local marriage and family ministry for the coming years ahead.

When churches prioritize relationship education and enhancement within their congregations, they become a personification of hope in a world of wounded and broken relationships. Churches can then become a light to their communities and provide outreaches and resources that meet deep relational needs and open doors to share the gospel of Christ.[19] Without a doubt, relationship ministry has become the greatest avenue for evangelism for the church in the twenty-first century.

---

[19]See http://EndgameBook.org and https://communio.org/.

4

CARE AND SUPPORT OF FAMILIES IMPACTED BY MENTAL ILLNESS

Stephen Grcevich

Your church's office manager interrupts you after receiving a call from an attendee with an urgent request for assistance in dealing with a family emergency.

Steve and Rachel Wagner have been highly engaged members of your church after a job transfer led them to relocate to your community five years ago. Prior to their relocation, they served in foster care ministry for many years, during which time they adopted three children with extensive trauma histories who were placed in their home, now ages 16, 14, and 13.

Steve left work earlier in the day when his wife discovered a suicide note written by their oldest child Maria while cleaning her room. She has experienced long-standing issues with anger management, defiance toward her parents, self-injurious behavior (cutting), and several instances in the past month of sneaking out of the house late at night to meet up with young men she met online for sexual encounters.

Two months prior to the current incident, Maria overdosed on approximately twenty pills of a non-prescription antihistamine after her parents grounded her for a late-night rendezvous with a boy from a nearby community. Maria has not received any mental health treatment since seeing a counselor a year ago. The Wagners terminated treatment because they believed the counselor was undermining their efforts to parent Maria with a biblical worldview and had admonished them for being overly restrictive of her behavior.

Steve reports he and his wife, Rachel, have struggled greatly because of their daughter's mental health challenges, as they experience little or no support. Their nearest family is eight hours away, and they are unaware of the severity of Maria's behavior. They have been reluctant to share their experiences with the couples in their small group because they fear their parenting practices and devotion to the faith will be judged. They also fear Maria being labeled by other church families because they continue to hope she might discover a healthier and more mentally healthy peer group through the youth ministry.

Steve believes the challenges he and Rachel have faced raising three children with extensive trauma histories are impacting their physical and mental health and have led him to question his faith. He reports Rachel has become more distant and withdrawn over the last six months. She is struggling greatly to maintain activities of daily living and has great difficulty getting out of bed on many days. They've spent $500 on DoorDash in the past month because Rachel often complains of being too tired to shop for groceries or prepare meals. Steve no longer attends an early morning men's Bible study at the church because he has had to assume responsibility for getting the kids up and off to school. Their participation at church during the last three months has been limited to watching services online and dropping off their two younger children for several middle school ministry events. Any attempts by the Wagners in the past year to compel Maria to attend worship services or youth group culminates in a loud argument. Several arguments have resulted in Maria becoming aggressive toward Rachel, repeatedly punching and kicking her mother.

Steve has begun to question whether he can stay in his marriage. He and Rachel rarely get out to dinner, movies, concerts, or get together with other couples because their children require constant supervision when not in school. Their sexual relationship began to decline after adopting their children and deteriorated to the extent they have rarely had intercourse since the changes in Rachel's mood emerged over the last six months. More than their physical relationship, he misses the long conversations he and Rachel used to enjoy at night after their children went to bed. He fears his job performance is being negatively impacted by his increased responsibilities at home and frequently worries about his ability to provide for his family if his employers were to let him go.

Steve finds himself struggling with questions about his faith. He and his wife became involved with foster care and adoption because they shared a calling to "care for the least of these." He questions why they are now suffering despite—or because of—their obedience to their calling and wonders if God truly listens to his prayers. He doubts whether anyone at church cares about them since no one has acknowledged his absence from Bible study or their absence from weekend worship services. He finds himself lying in bed at night, wondering how much longer he can continue to live like this.

The need for churches to provide mental health support in situations like these is likely to grow as our culture's epidemic of mental illness shows no signs of slowing. Consider that 21.6% of US adults reported receiving some type of mental health treatment in 2021, including 23.2% of all adults ages 18–44 and 28.6% of all women in that age range, according to the National Health Interview Survey.[1] Nearly 20% of children and young people ages 3–17 in the United States have a mental, emotional, developmental, or behavioral disorder.[2]

Churches are often the first point of contact when a family member has an acute mental health need. Individuals and families are more likely to connect with their church in a mental health crisis than they are with a licensed psychiatrist or medical doctor. Nearly one-quarter of those

---

[1] Emily Terlizzi and Jeannine Schiller, *Mental Health Treatment Among Adults Aged 18–44: United States, 2019–2021* (Atlanta: Centers for Disease Control and Prevention, 2022), www.cdc.gov/nchs/data/databriefs/db444.pdf.

[2] US Department of Health and Human Services, "Child and Adolescent Mental Health," in *2022 National Healthcare Quality and Disparities Report* (Rockville, MD: Agency for Healthcare Research and Quality, 2022), 73–82, www.ncbi.nlm.nih.gov/books/NBK587182/pdf/Bookshelf_NBK587182.pdf.

seeking help from clergy have the most seriously impairing mental disorders. The majority are seen exclusively by clergy and not by a physician or mental health professionals.[3]

Available research suggests the church has much room for growth in its response to Christians with mental illness who turn to the church for care and support. A study of over 1,000 regular church attendees from the UK reported that while 43% experienced a mental health issue at some point in their lives, only 35% felt supported by their church regarding their mental health. Roughly 56% reported that mental health was rarely or never discussed in their churches, and 91% of church leaders surveyed reported never having received instruction on mental health in their theological training. Thirty percent of participants in a Baylor University study of 293 Christians with mental illness reported negative experiences with their church when seeking counsel or support. About 15% of adults who sought help from their church for a mental illness themselves or a family member reported a weakening of faith as a result of their interaction with their church, and for 13%, their experience ended their involvement with any church.[4]

This chapter will (1) offer ministry leaders, church staff, and volunteers a mental checklist for responding to congregants who approach the church with mental health needs, (2) present the indicators of an appropriate response to a mental health emergency or crisis, (3) provide ministry leaders with a model for determining when professional resources outside of the church are appropriate and offer strategies for connecting families with these providers, (4) examine common challenges families experience in staying engaged with a church when a family member is impacted by mental illness, and (5) introduce a process for developing a mental health outreach and inclusion strategy.

---

[3]Philip S. Wang, Patricia A. Berglund, and Ronald C. Kessler, "Patterns and Correlates of Contacting Clergy for Mental Disorders in the United States," *Health Services Research* 38, no. 2 (April 2003): 647-73, https://doi.org/10.1111/1475-6773.00138.

[4]Rachael Newham, "Mental Health Friendly Church Research," Kintsugi Hope, https://kintsugihope.com/files/mhfc/Mental%20Health%20Friendly%20Church%20Project%20Exec%20%20Summary.pdf.

RESPONSES WHEN A PERSON APPROACHES THE CHURCH WITH A MENTAL HEALTH NEED

Congregants impacted by mental illness who approach their church for support may be seeking spiritual guidance, encouragement, prayer, and support from a biblical perspective. They may want counseling for themselves or a family member or assistance in finding professional mental health care from licensed practitioners or facilities offering culturally competent mental health services supportive of their values and beliefs. They may need assistance in paying for necessary care or an advocate in dealing with legal issues, employers, schools, mental health care providers, or government bureaucracies.

During the first two decades of the twenty-first century, the bulk of research examining the frequency of clergy being sought out to provide care and assistance to persons with mental health concerns was conducted prior to the large shifts in self-reported church attendance or belief in God. Nevertheless, the clergy continue to be recognized as having an important role in serving congregants who experience mental illness and caring well for their families or caregivers.[5]

A survey conducted by the National Institute of Mental Health reported that fully one-quarter of all individuals who sought treatment for a mental health concern did so from a member of the clergy and represent a larger proportion of the population than those who sought care from a psychiatrist (17%) or a primary care physician (17%).[6]

Details of our vignette involving Mr. and Mrs. Wagner and their family illustrate the complexity of needs a pastors or church staff may encounter while providing ministry with families impacted by mental illness. Consider these circumstances:

- The Wagners' daughter, Maria, is acutely suicidal and experiencing a life-threatening mental health emergency. Connecting the family immediately with the appropriate emergency services and resources is an urgent priority.

---

[5]US Department of Health and Human Services, Center for Faith and Opportunity Initiatives, "Compassion in Action: A Guide for Faith Communities Serving People Experiencing Mental Illness and Their Caregivers," July 2020, www.hhs.gov/sites/default/files/compassion-in-action.pdf.
[6]Wang, Berglund, and Kessler, "Patterns and Correlates," 647.

- Mrs. Wagner is likely experiencing symptoms of depression sufficiently severe to impact her ability to manage tasks of daily living, including her ability to engage in worship services, small groups, and other activities offered by the church to promote healthy discipleship and spiritual growth.
- Steve may be experiencing symptoms of a mental health disorder but is acutely in need of spiritual care and support to make sense of his current situation.
- The Christian family could benefit from a variety of tangible support that is often provided by the church. These supports might include:
  - Prayer covering by trusted others who will keep a confidence.
  - Assistance with meals.
  - Respite care/support with childcare.
  - Friendship/companionship.

During an initial contact with a church member or attendee presenting with mental health concerns, a pastor or staff member might consider the following mental checklist:

- What does this person want?
- What does this person *need*?
- Do I or my church have the resources to meet this person's needs?
- How can I help them with appropriate resources our church is unable to provide?

RESPONSES WHEN A PERSON HAS A TRUE MENTAL HEALTH EMERGENCY OR CRISIS

A mental health or addiction *emergency* represents a life-threatening situation in which immediate intervention from emergency medical personnel or law enforcement is required. The immediate response for a pastor, staff member, or volunteer confronted with such an emergency in the United States is to dial 911 (or 112 within the European Union). Examples of mental health emergencies include:

- An individual who cannot be assured of safety because of suicidal thoughts, plans, behaviors, or attempts.

- Someone is threatening serious harm to themselves or others.
- Self-injury of a severity requiring medical attention.
- Severe intoxication.
- Apparent drug overdose.
- Inability to care for oneself.

When someone calls 911, typically, a dispatcher will answer the call and ask where the emergency and local law enforcement or paramedics should be sent regarding the location of the person experiencing an emergency. In some instances, a crisis intervention team will accompany law enforcement. The caller may be transferred to 988, the National Suicide and Crisis Hotline, if appropriate.

A mental health or addiction *crisis* is typically a non-life-threatening event in which immediate intervention is possible without the presence of law enforcement or emergency medical personnel. Situations considered to be mental health crises would include:

- Individuals talking about or planning suicide who aren't actively in the process of taking their lives.
- People talking about but not actively engaged in harming others.
- Excessive use of alcohol or drugs.
- Extreme symptoms of depression, anxiety, or other mental health conditions.

In situations such as these in the United States, a pastor, staff member, or volunteer should call 988, the National Suicide and Crisis Hotline. These calls are routed to over 200 state and local crisis centers with specially trained case workers familiar with the systems of care established to offer urgent mental health care and support resources in the regions and localities they serve.

When people call 988, a trained professional will answer and ask them to describe the crisis. They may ask to speak to the person experiencing the mental health crisis if someone else is calling on their behalf and assist by linking them to sources of care or dispatch a mobile intervention team to the person's immediate location. If necessary, the person in crisis will be taken to a stabilization facility. If the situation is deemed to be a true mental health emergency, the trained professional will transfer your call to 911.

In our vignette involving the Wagner family, Maria's suicide note in the context of her demonstrably poor judgment and history of suicidal behavior represents a true mental health crisis. Appropriate responses on the part of the pastor, staff member, or volunteer in response to Steve would be to provide him with information about the 988 Suicide and Crisis hotline or to call the hotline himself on the family's behalf.

CONFIDENTIALITY IN MENTAL HEALTH EMERGENCIES

Some clergy or church staff may have questions regarding confidentiality obligations when someone discloses a suicide plan in the context of a pastoral counseling relationship. The American Association of Christian Counselors and other professional associations explicitly state the duty to protect persons supersedes confidentiality when a client directly admits serious, imminent suicidal thoughts or plans; serious, imminent, and actionable plans to harm others; or has reasonable suspicion that a child, older adult, or dependent adult (regardless of age) has been abused.[7] All licensed medical and mental health professionals are obligated to breach confidentiality when such situations arise.

REFERRING OUTSIDE OF THE CHURCH WHILE OFFERING SUPPORT THROUGH THE CHURCH

Most pastors lack formal training or experience in caring for people with significant mental illness. We aren't doing our people any favors when fully a quarter of those who turn to the church for support are experiencing serious mental illness (e.g., major depression, bipolar disorder, schizophrenia), and the majority are never referred to a psychologist, counselor, or physician for care. Such conditions, when left untreated, often result in significant functional impairment at work or school, disrupt relationships with family members and friends, interfere with church engagement, and can, in some instances, be life-threatening.

---

[7] AACC Law and Ethics Committee, "AACC Code of Ethics: Y-2014 Code of Ethics," The American Association of Christian Counselors, 2014, www.aacc.net/wp-content/uploads/2020/06/AACC-Code-of-Ethics-Master-Document.pdf.

The *DSM-5* describes a mental disorder as a syndrome characterized by a clinically significant disturbance in an individual's cognition, emotion regulation, or behavior that reflects a dysfunction in the psychological, biological, or developmental processes underlying mental functioning. Mental disorders are usually associated with significant distress or disability in social, occupational, or other important activities. An acceptable or culturally approved response to a common stressor or loss, such as the death of a loved one, is not a mental disorder. Socially deviant behavior (e.g., political, religious, or sexual) and conflicts that are primarily between the individual and society are not mental disorders unless the deviance or conflict results from a dysfunction in the individual, as described above.[8]

The important part of the definition for ministry leaders is this: "significant distress or disability in social, occupational or other activities." A general rule of thumb is that when people experience a disability (i.e., significant impact to work or academic performance, family responsibilities, friendships, or the ability to engage in age-appropriate activities or commitments in the community, like church, resulting from an emotional or behavioral concern), they should be referred to a qualified mental health professional.

Some simple questions a ministry staff member might ask to get a sense of the impact a condition is having on a person's day-to-day functioning might include:

- Have you noticed any changes in how you feel physically compared to your "normal?" Sleeping? Eating? Energy? Aches and pains?
- When was the last time you had fun? Do you find yourself losing interest in things you normally enjoy?
- Is anxiety or worry getting in the way of doing things you'd like to do?
- Have you noticed a change in your ability to stay on top of your responsibilities at work or school?

---

[8] American Psychiatric Association, *Diagnostic and Statistical Manual of Mental Disorders*, 5th ed. (Washington, DC: American Psychiatric Association Publishing, 2013), 20, https://doi.org/10.1176/appi.books.9780890425596.

- Is this problem impacting your relationships with your spouse and/or other members of your family?

Using our example of the Wagner family, Maria is experiencing a true mental health emergency and requires immediate care and support. Rachel is likely experiencing depression such that her ability to care for her family and maintain her daily routines is greatly compromised. She may need referrals to both a counselor/therapist and a psychiatrist, depending on her primary care physician's willingness and/or comfort level in prescribing medication for her depression. Steve *may* be experiencing impairment related to a mental health condition, but his most pressing needs are assistance in getting his family the mental health care they need, along with spiritual care and support that his church should be able to provide.

Referral shouldn't be thought of as abandonment. Rather, it's adding resources to the team while remaining alongside an individual or family. Pastors or pastoral counselors should reassure persons they refer for professional mental health care that they will continue to be available to provide support and address their spiritual needs and concerns throughout and following their course of treatment. It's important to continue to provide spiritual and practical support even after referral to mental healthcare, just like one would if a congregant were recovering from physical illness.

The ability to assist individuals and families in accessing services from appropriate professionals and facilities is an essential component of the church's response to people in need of mental health care and support. Key to a church's capacity for connecting congregants with the help they need are the relationships staff members have with mental health professionals and facilities in the communities where the majority of their attendees live. A personal phone call from a pastor or ministry leader to a mental health clinician can be indispensable in bypassing the waiting lists typical of many mental health practices. Leaders serving in children's or student ministry should be purposeful in reaching out to mental health professionals who specialize in the treatment of youth since one in five children of school age has an identified mental health condition.[9] The

---

[9] Kathleen Ries Merikangas et al., "Lifetime Prevalence of Mental Disorders in U.S. Adolescents: Results from the National Comorbidity Survey Replication—Adolescent Supplement (NCS-A),"

American Association of Christian Counselors maintains a searchable database of counselors and clinics.[10] Medical and mental health professionals who attend the church can offer referrals based on the experiences of their patients or clients.

People turning to the church for help with a mental health crisis are often looking for recommendations for professionals they can trust who will integrate their religious beliefs into their treatment. In one study, a plurality of Americans expressed a preference for seeking care from a pastoral counselor or religious cleric. Eight in ten (81%) said they wanted their own spiritual values respected and integrated into the counseling process, and 72% said they would prefer to see a professional counselor who integrated their values and beliefs into the counseling process. The second most common reason respondents gave for not seeing a mental health professional (15%) was "fear that [their] spiritual values and beliefs may not be respected and taken seriously."[11]

Psychiatrists are the least likely of all physicians to be religious, and Christians are underrepresented among those who identify with a specific religion or denomination within the field of psychiatry. Furthermore, highly religious Protestants were the least likely of all physicians to refer patients for psychiatric care.[12] Christians are also significantly underrepresented in the fields of psychology[13] and social work.[14]

Brad Hambrick has excellent resources for helping pastors to vet Christian counselors and mental health practitioners.[15] Given the

---

Journal of the American Academy of Child and Adolescent Psychiatry 49, no. 10 (October 2010): 980-89, https://doi.org/10.1016/j.jaac.2010.05.017.
[10]See https://connect.aacc.net/?search_type=distance.
[11]Bob Boorstin and Erika Schalter, "American Association of Pastoral Counselors Samaritan Institute: Report," Greenberg Quinlan Research, Inc., November 8, 2000, http://solihten.org/affiliates/documents/GALLUPSURVEYAAPCandSISummaryfindings.pdf.
[12]Farr A. Curlin et al., "The Relationship between Psychiatry and Religion among U.S. Physicians," *Psychiatric Services* 58, no. 9 (September 2007): 1193-98, https://doi.org/10.1176/ps.2007.58.9.1193.
[13]Harold D. Delaney, William R. Miller, and Ana M. Bisonó, "Religiosity and Spirituality among Psychologists: A Survey of Clinician Members of the American Psychological Association," *Professional Psychology: Research and Practice* 38, no. 5 (October 2007): 538-46, https://doi.org/10.1037/0735-7028.38.5.538.
[14]Holly K. Oxhandler, Edward C. Polson, and W. Andrew Achenbaum, "The Religiosity and Spiritual Beliefs and Practices of Clinical Social Workers: A National Survey," *Social Work* 63, no. 1 (January 2018): 47-56, https://doi.org/10.1093/sw/swx055.
[15]Brad Hambrick, "For Pastors: How to Vet Potential Counseling Referral Sources," Bradhambrick.com, September 15, 2017, https://bradhambrick.com/vetcounselors/.

shortage of qualified professionals, pastors often need to refer to non-Christians or nominal Christians, especially for specialized mental healthcare. Parents may experience apprehension about seeking help from outside the Christian community because of concerns they'll introduce an influential person into their child's life who might be inclined to actively undermine the parents' authority, their child's sense of right and wrong, and their efforts to raise their child in accordance with the teachings of the faith. Pastors should be concerned about adult congregants receiving counsel in significant conflict with traditional Christian teaching. However, a good mental health professional of any faith background will seek to understand the individual's world and demonstrate cultural sensitivity when serving children, adults, and families of different faiths from their own.

What questions should pastors or staff members ask in developing relationships with mental health professionals outside of the faith?

- Whom do you treat? Children, adolescents, adults, couples, families?
- What conditions do you treat?
- Do you have specific areas of expertise for which you are known?
- How can the church work together with you to support individuals and families in your care?
- How do individuals and families pay for the care you provide? Are they expected to pay for services out of pocket? Do you accept insurance? If so, does that include government-funded insurance such as Medicare or Medicaid? Do you have a sliding scale for low-income individuals and families?
- What is your experience in providing culturally competent care to Christians and their families, especially when issues related to gender or sexuality are pertinent to treatment?

Churches that maintain referral lists need processes for updating the lists to ensure that licensed professionals and facilities are continuing to accept referrals and information regarding payment for services is current. One of the greatest discrepancies in responses of pastors and family members of adults with serious mental illness reported in the surveys conducted by LifeWay Research centered on the availability of current referral lists for licensed professionals and facilities. Of pastors surveyed, 70% reported their churches provided current referral lists to members or attendees, but only 28% of family members endorsed that such lists were available.[16] Ensure that resource lists are readily accessible to all ministry leaders, especially front-line staff, volunteers, and receptionists.

CHALLENGES TO CHURCH INVOLVEMENT WHEN FAMILIES ARE IMPACTED BY MENTAL ILLNESS

The church has historically considered mental health support in the context of providing counseling and pastoral care to individuals who are members or regular attenders of a local church. How might our approach to care and support be different if we considered the extent to which mental illness represents a barrier to entry into the church or a reason for "quiet quitting" the church? What if the mental health community represents a largely underserved population for evangelism and outreach?

Available research suggests the presence of mental illness in an individual or a family member is a significant impediment to church attendance. Adults who self-identified as worriers in the third wave of the Baylor Religion Survey (representing 17% of the US population) were less likely to have attended a religious service either in the past year (67% vs. 75%) or on a weekly basis (17% vs. 37%) or to consider themselves religious (19% vs. 39%) compared to non-worriers. Adults who experienced sadness or depression for ten or more days during the preceding month were less likely to have attended a religious service in the past year (61% vs. 78%), attend services weekly (15% vs. 36%), and more likely to identify as religiously non-affiliated (10% vs. 23%) compared to participants free of depressive symptoms.[17]

Sociologist Andrew Whitehead examined the impact of physical, mental health, and developmental disabilities on worship attendance

---

[16]LifeWay Research, "Study of Acute Mental Illness and Christian Faith: Research Report," 2014, https://research.lifeway.com/wp-content/uploads/2014/09/Acute-Mental-Illness-and-Christian-Faith-Research-Report-1.pdf.

[17]Kevin D. Dougherty et al., *The Values and Beliefs of the American Public: Wave III Baylor Religion Survey* (Waco, TX: Baylor University, 2011), www.baylor.edu/baylorreligionsurvey/doc.php/288938.pdf.

from data generated in each of three waves (2003, 2007, 2010–2011) of the National Survey of Children's Health (NSCH). Families of children with no disability or chronic health condition were less likely to report never attending worship services compared to the overall sample. The increase in odds of never attending worship was 84.1% for families of children with autism spectrum disorders, 72.7% for families of children with depression, 54.6% for families of children with disruptive behavioral disorders (oppositional defiant disorder or conduct disorder), 44.7% for families of children with anxiety disorders, and 19.3% for families of children with attention-deficit/hyperactivity disorder (ADHD).[18]

One hypothesis proposed to explain the underrepresentation in churches of individuals and families affected by mental illness is that attributes or traits associated with common mental health conditions represent barriers to entry into church culture insofar as they contribute to difficulties meeting expectations for how individuals will act and interact when gathered for worship services, education, fellowship, and service activities.[19] The traditional model for conceptualizing mental health ministry has involved the provision of care and support for people already part of the church. A more forward-thinking approach is to consider mental health ministry as a tool for evangelism and outreach to people who find it difficult to join the things we do at church while continuing to provide care and support to those within the church with mental health concerns. The steps we take in making our churches more welcoming to individuals and families impacted by mental illness will also improve our care for those with struggles who are already part of the church.

Thinking based on this hypothesis has resulted in a model to guide churches in developing a comprehensive mental health inclusion and support strategy. The model recognizes seven barriers to church attendance—stigma, anxiety, capacity for self-regulation, social

---

[18] Andrew L. Whitehead, "Religion and Disability: Variation in Religious Service Attendance Rates for Children with Chronic Health Conditions," *Journal for the Scientific Study of Religion* 57, no. 2 (June 2018): 377-95, https://doi.org/10.1111/jssr.12521.

[19] Stephen J. Grcevich, "Why Church Attendance is Difficult for Children with Common Mental Health Conditions and Their Families," *Journal of Psychology and Christianity* 40, no. 1 (Spring 2021): 50-60.

communication, sensory processing differences, social isolation, and past church experiences.[20]

Five characteristics of churches prepared to do mental health ministry well have been identified.[21] They include:

- Evidence of a church-wide mental health inclusion and support planning process.
- Ongoing initiatives to train staff and educate the congregation on mental health-related topics and concerns.
- Development of a mental health communication strategy.
- Provision of practical and tangible help to affected individuals and families with heartfelt needs.
- Mental health support groups.

In the remainder of this chapter, we examine how churches can expand their capacity for supporting members and attendees with mental health-related challenges while facilitating engagement for newcomers impacted by mental illness.

IMPLEMENTING A CHURCHWIDE MENTAL HEALTH OUTREACH AND INCLUSION STRATEGY

The single most important component of any plan to provide mental health support is the unequivocal support of senior leadership—in most instances, the support of the senior pastor. A reality of church life is that most congregations have far more ministry opportunities to respond to than their staffing, volunteer support, and budget can support. Initiatives that matter to the senior pastor are the ones that receive the necessary resources to succeed.

In a large church with multiple pastors and numerous ministry departments, a representative of every area of ministry should be involved in the planning process. In smaller churches where staff and volunteers

---

[20]Stephen Grcevich, *Mental Health and the Church: A Ministry Handbook for Including Children and Adults with ADHD, Anxiety, Mood Disorders, and Other Common Mental Health Conditions* (Grand Rapids, MI: Zondervan, 2018).

[21]Stephen Grcevich, "5 Marks of a Mental Health-Informed Church," The Ethics and Religious Liberty Commission of the Southern Baptist Convention, May 22, 2019, https://erlc.com /resource-library/articles/5-marks-of-a-mental-health-informed-church/.

may be responsible for multiple functions, strategizing mental health support is likely a function of the core team. As the research on church attendance in families of children with mental illness demonstrates, mental health ministry is family ministry, and each ministry department within the church may have a role in providing support.

With the Wagner family in mind, consider how many different ministries might contribute to the support they receive:

- A ministry leader or a staff member may be responsible for providing pastoral counseling.
- A student ministry representative visits the Wagner's daughter if she is admitted to an inpatient psychiatric facility for any length of time and provides guidance and support to her parents as they seek to love her unconditionally and, in so doing, draw her back into a recommitment of faith.
- An adult/discipleship minister may coach their small group leader on ways the group may support the family through their current struggles by identifying ways to sustain Steve's connection with his Bible study while his family responsibilities are expanded and supporting Mrs. Wagner.
- A care/helps minister may provide meals and other available support.

The planning process for mental health support is an ideal opportunity for engaging individuals to contribute unique gifts, talents, contacts, knowledge, or experience to the team. Mental health professionals, support staff from mental health agencies, social workers, and spiritually mature members of your congregation bring valuable perspectives to the process.

The training needs of pastors, staff, and volunteers in the provision of mental health support are as diverse as their ministry roles, the communities in which their churches are located, and the challenges their attendees present. Given the scheduling demands on leaders and volunteers, it's impossible to train them to respond to every need that may arise.

Staff who serve as the initial point of contact for individuals seeking support from the church—pastors, ministry leaders, receptionists, secretaries, and others responsible for monitoring communication systems and social media—will need training on procedures for responding to mental health crises or emergencies, including when to call 911 (the local emergency services line) or 988 (the Mental Health Crisis Hotline) and whom to notify within the church.

Church leaders responsible for resource allocation (board members, pastors, ministry leaders) will benefit from training on the mental health support needs of members, attendees, ministry staff, and communities targeted for outreach. Among the most popular trainings is Mental Health First Aid.[22] This training comprises eight hours of hands-on activities and practice, address topics such as anxiety, depression, psychosis, and addictions, and include information on local mental health resources and support groups. In addition to the adult course, a youth course is also available for adults serving the needs of 12–18-year-olds. Another frequently sought training topic by church staff is trauma-informed care,[23] since adverse childhood experiences and developmental trauma are contributing factors to mental illness in children and adults. Congregational education and awareness represent a key component of any mental health support initiative and will be discussed in the next section.

EFFECTIVE MENTAL HEALTH COMMUNICATION

What can and should ministry leaders do to assist family members in supporting loved ones with mental illness?

A survey of family members of adults with severe mental illness conducted as part of LifeWay Research's 2014 Study of Acute Mental Illness and Christian Faith found the most common response was "Talk about it openly so that the topic is not so taboo."[24] In the very same survey, nearly half of all pastors reported they "rarely" or "never" speak of mental illness during worship services. Nearly two-thirds of pastors speak of

---

[22]Jennifer Costello, Krystal Hays, and Ana M. Gamez, "Using Mental Health First Aid to Promote Mental Health in Churches," *Journal of Spirituality in Mental Health* 23, no. 4 (October 2021): 1-12, https://doi.org/10.1080/19349637.2020.1771234.

[23]Robert G. Crosby et al., "Trauma-Informed Children's Ministry: A Qualitative Descriptive Study," *Journal of Child & Adolescent Trauma* 14 (January 2021): 493-505, https://doi.org/10.1007/s40653-020-00334-w.

[24]LifeWay Research, *Study of Acute Mental Illness*, 37.

mental illness once a year or less. A follow-up survey of 1,000 Protestant pastors conducted in September 2021 noted that progress had been made, but 37% continued to report "rarely" or "never" speaking of mental illness in worship services, and an additional 16 percent who talk about it once a year.[25]

Another important finding of the 2014 study was that 55% of US adults surveyed who don't regularly attend church (and 21% of weekly church-goers) *disagreed* with the statement, "If I had a mental health issue, I believe most churches would welcome me."

How should churches approach these problems? First, an important step for any church seeking to minister to those affected by mental illness is to establish a culture that explicitly grants permission for mental health to be a topic of conversation. The stigma surrounding mental illness may be greater within the church than that present in the larger culture from widespread teaching that personal sin is a root cause of mental illness, or the persistence of incapacitating anxiety is suggestive of insufficient prayer or inadequate faith. Consider our vignette with the Wagner family. Would someone plugged into the natural support systems in your church be comfortable disclosing their needs to a small group leader, Sunday school teacher, or a fellow volunteer in a ministry where they serve?

Second, preaching on mental health-related topics brings attention to mental health and sensitizes the church to major issues that would make the church more welcoming. Cuyahoga Valley Church (CVC) kicked off its mental health initiative with a five-part sermon series on what the Bible teaches about anxiety. Upon the completion of the series, the church hosted a town meeting of sorts in which a psychologist, counselor, and pediatrician joined with members of the pastoral team to answer questions and continue the conversation.

Third, worship services may include short videos in which church members discussed their mental health struggles in the context of their faith. The founding pastor of CVC produced a short video for attendees to share through social media in which he explicitly welcomed people in

---

[25]LifeWay Research, "Pastors' Views on Mental Illness: A Survey of 1,000 Protestant Pastors," 2021, https://research.lifeway.com/wp-content/uploads/2022/08/Pastors-Sept-2021-Mental-Illness-Report.pdf.

the surrounding community with mental health challenges to visit the church and spoke openly of the impact of mental illness on his own family.

Fourth, CVC has continued to host regular events focused on mental health topics, including webinars on self-care during Covid-19, mental health during the Christmas season, and in-person gatherings for parents of middle and high schoolers on the epidemic of mental illness in youth.

Fifth, sustaining awareness of mental health concerns is easily integrated into routine ministry practices and activities. One church opened their worship service with the lead pastor welcoming visitors and praying for anyone in attendance that day suffering from depression. At a subsequent service, a deacon shared the story of how her husband's agoraphobia prevented him from attending crowded worship services and described how steps the staff took to welcome him resulted not only in his coming to church but in assuming a leadership role on the volunteer team responsible for assimilating guests.

Sixth, another consideration in a good communication strategy is maintaining awareness of the care and support resources available through the church and how resources can be accessed. Are regular attenders aware of counseling resources, referral lists, or support groups available through the church? Would someone checking out the church's website prior to attending for the first time readily be made aware of such resources? Is information about support visible in church bulletins where paper bulletins are still in use? Is information regarding support services visible and readily available at information kiosks or welcome desks?

Seventh, an effective communication strategy will combat the stigma surrounding mental illness within the church and the surrounding community, and regularly remind attendees that conversations regarding mental health struggles are actively encouraged. In addition to the ideas presented above, an easy way to combat stigma involves posting mental health information and resources consistent with the church's beliefs on its social media platforms. Attendees who share the posts with friends and neighbors are assets for changing perceptions about the church and mental health among non-believers and non-attenders in their social networks.

HELP THAT ADDRESSES IMMEDIATE NEEDS

As we discussed earlier in the chapter, the capacity of churches, individual pastors, and staff members to provide counseling to individuals, couples, and families experiencing mental illness will vary widely. When additional resources are needed, ministry leaders need to recognize their limitations and expand the care team. How can you do this?

First, churches can employ many creative approaches to provide counseling in situations where pastors or staff lack the training or experience to meet the needs of the congregation. Some hire professional counselors who make services available for a fee, at a reduced cost, or at no cost for people in need. Creative partnerships have been developed with mental health agencies to provide access to a continuum of mental health services on-site. In Tennessee and Georgia, for example, partnerships have been formed between state and local mental health departments and historically Black churches to reduce the stigma associated with mental health treatment in a historically underserved population. An innovative non-profit organization based in Colorado connects churches willing to provide free office space with licensed mental health professionals who agree to provide services at greatly reduced fees for church members and residents in the surrounding communities.[26]

Second, consider the financial costs of services. Mental health professionals are far less likely than other medical professionals to participate in insurance networks or accept reimbursement from insurance as payment in full for services.[27] What provisions could be put in place for families who need services beyond those the church offers for those lacking the financial resources to pay for needed mental health care out of pocket?

Third, consider ministries that cater to the felt needs of those affected by mental illness. An additional consideration for churches is to ask whether the same range of care and support offered to families experiencing a medical crisis is made available to families dealing with a mental health crisis. If a church offers meals to families when someone is in a

---

[26] Khesed Wellness, "Khesed Wellness—Outpatient Mental Health and Wellness," accessed April 16, 2023, www.khesedwellness.com/.

[27] Tara F. Bishop et al., "Acceptance of Insurance by Psychiatrists and the Implications for Access to Mental Health Care," *JAMA Psychiatry* 71, no. 2 (February 2014): 176, https://doi.org/10.1001/jamapsychiatry.2013.2862.

hospital or otherwise incapable of cooking or caring for themselves, would someone provide meals for the Wagners? Would the youth pastor or the pastor responsible for hospital visitation go to see the Wagners' daughter if she needs to be admitted to a psychiatric hospital? Would anyone be available to help transport the younger children to their after-school activities if the parents find themselves taking part in intensive outpatient treatment for their daughter several evenings a week?

Fourth, churches can host respite events or provide in-home respite care for families of children with autism, developmental disabilities, or severe medical disabilities because the inability to access appropriate childcare results in great strain on marital relationships. If your church provides respite, would children with mental health-related disabilities and their siblings be able to participate without feeling singled out as "different" from their peers? Would parents know the service is available and appropriate for their children?

MENTAL HEALTH SUPPORT GROUPS

For churches that place a high value on community and encourage small group ministry participation, the establishment of mental health education and support groups is often a starting point for any mental health support strategy. The availability of these groups sends a powerful message to church members and the surrounding community that anyone affected by mental illness and their families are welcome. They introduce people to the church who would never otherwise attend a weekend worship service and represent a practical and inexpensive strategy for meeting the heartfelt needs of members and marginalized people not currently part of the church.

Some churches address the need for groups by providing meeting spaces to secular organizations with established group models for education and support, such as the National Alliance on Mental Illness (NAMI), which can provide an array of educational groups, including peer and family support models. Another model involves hosting Celebrate Recovery groups,[28] a model originating in Saddleback Church

---

[28]"Mental Health," Celebrate Recovery, accessed April 16, 2023, www.celebraterecovery.com/about/ministries-of-cr/mental-health.

encompassing support for individuals in substance abuse and/or mental health recovery.

A significant development in recent years is the development of biblically based mental health group support models that are rapidly being adopted by churches in North America and beyond. The two organizations achieving the greatest impact are the Mental Health Grace Alliance and Fresh Hope.

The Mental Health Grace Alliance offers several types of Grace Groups, now offered in hundreds of churches in twenty-five countries.[29] Grace Groups are time-limited (typically 10 or 16 weeks), follow a structured curriculum, and offer models for adults (Living Grace), students (Redefine Grace), and family members (Family Grace) impacted by mental health difficulties or disorders.

Fresh Hope offers open-ended peer support group models for adults, teens, widows, and suicide survivors.[30] They afford group leaders the flexibility to address a long list of discussion topics and typically combine affected individuals and family members for at least part of each meeting.

CONCLUSION

Churches are often the first point of contact for members and attendees with mental health concerns. Pastors, staff, and any volunteers serving in positions where they are the first person to speak with someone reaching out to the church requires training on appropriate responses to mental health emergencies and crises. The presence of mental illness in an individual or family member significantly impacts the likelihood they will ever set foot in a church and the frequency of their attendance if they are connected to a church. Recognition of the challenges persons with mental health struggles face in attending worship services and maintaining their involvement at church, combined with the implementation of a mental health inclusion and support plan, prepare congregations to respond more effectively to all in need of care within the church community.

---

[29]"Welcome to Grace Academy," Mental Health Grace Alliance, accessed May 3, 2024, https://mentalhealthgracealliance.org/grace-academy.

[30]"Fresh Hope Groups," Fresh Hope for Mental Health, accessed April 16, 2023, https://freshhope.us/fh-groups/.

5

LGBTQ+ ISSUES IN MARRIAGE MINISTRY

MARK A. YARHOUSE AND ANNA BROSE

Jane and Joe sit down in your office. Joe looks anxious. Jane shares, "We need help. He needs help. I'm not sure we are going to make it. I really don't." Jane goes on to share that Joe is gay and only recently came out to her. They have been married for eight years. Jane shares that Joe had a profile on a popular gay hook-up site. Someone from Jane's work discovered Joe's profile and sent it to Jane. She says she was mortified. When she confronted Joe, he initially denied it, but has since admitted that he is gay and that the profile was a way of expressing that part of his life. He says he has not met anyone through the site and that he is willing to meet together to improve their marriage.

Rebecca and Alex have been attending your church for about three years. Alex shares in a meeting with you that he is transgender and that his gender dysphoria has been especially difficult since the birth of their second child. He occasionally cross-dresses at home after work or on the weekend. Rebecca says she doesn't like it when Alex cross-dresses, but she has gotten used to it. Alex is now saying that his attempts to decrease his distress have not been enough, and he believes that a more full-time social transition is the only way forward.

These vignettes represent ways in which marriage ministry with the LGBTQ+ (lesbian, gay, bisexual, transgender, queer, and other identities) community could present itself to you as a pastor. These reflect likely situations where pastors may feel ill-equipped to engage.

The first vignette is what we refer to as a mixed orientation couple (MOC) where one spouse is straight while the other spouse experiences same-sex attraction. The second vignette is that of a couple in which one spouse discloses that he or she is transgender or experiences gender dysphoria. Gender dysphoria refers to distress that can accompany experiences of discordant gender identity or, in other words, when a person's gender identity (as a man or a woman) does not correspond with their biological markers, such as chromosomes, gonads, and genitalia. Depending on existing coping strategies and ability to manage dysphoria, the spouse may pursue a social or medical transition.

You may read these vignettes and already feel overwhelmed by the potential complexity of pastoral needs in marriage ministry. This chapter aims to help position you to work well with couples in areas such as these. To begin, we will review important key terms to help the reader become more acquainted with sexual orientation and gender identity.

SEXUAL ORIENTATION AND IDENTITY

Sexual orientation refers to the romantic attractions a person has toward another, whether someone of the same-sex, the opposite-sex, or both sexes. Most people would describe themselves as having a heterosexual orientation, commonly known as being straight. Today, the word *homosexual* has fallen out of the vernacular, but some might have previously said that they have a homosexual orientation, if they were exclusively attracted to the same sex. Today, they might just say that they are gay, which has become an umbrella term for both sexual orientation and personal identity. Where gay refers to the attractions someone has toward someone of the same-sex, using gay as a term for one's identity means that someone includes this same-sex orientation as a way of defining oneself, and this might reflect varying degrees of affiliation within the mainstream LGBTQ+ community.

An increasing number of people identify as LGBTQ+. A recent Gallup Poll indicated that 7.1% of adults answered "yes" when asked, "Do you personally identify as lesbian, gay, bisexual, or transgender?"[1] This is a much higher percentage that has been reported in past surveys and is double what was reported in 2012. Rising percentages are segmented largely by generations, with 20.8% of Gen Z identifying as LGBTQ+ (compared to 10.5% of Millennials, 4.2% of Gen X, and 2.6% of Baby Boomers).[2]

SEXUAL ORIENTATION: IS THERE A CAUSE?

It is still unclear what causes different sexual orientations, though many theories circulate today. A common debate for many has been between what is referred to as nature versus nurture. This debate argues whether people's sexual orientation is caused by biological makeup ("nature"), such as DNA, or by how and in what setting someone was raised ("nurture"). Much research has been conducted on biological antecedents ("nature") to sexual orientation, yet no clear, singular causal theory has been sufficiently supported. In addition to the biological/nature vs. environmental/nurture debate, other theories, such as whether or how much an individual's culture and relationships have influence over his or her sexual orientation, receive varying degrees of support, with no single theory as a clear frontrunner. With something as complex as sexual orientation, biological influences may provide a push in this direction for some people, as well as environmental influences that are difficult to identify at this time.

GENDER IDENTITY

Gender refers to the emotional, psychological, and social aspects of being male or female. *Gender identity* refers to a person's experience of oneself as a man, a woman, or an alternative gender identity, such as transgender. Most people feel that their gender identity corresponds with the body they were born with. In other words, they would say their gender matches the biological markers for sex they were born with, such as chromosomes, gonads, and genitalia. These people are referred to as cisgender because *cis* means "on this side of."

---

[1] Jeffrey M. Jones, "LGBT Identification Ticks Up to 7.1%," Gallup, February 17, 2022, https://news.gallup.com/poll/389792/lgbt-identification-ticks-up.aspx.
[2] Jones, "LGBT Identification Ticks Up to 7.1%."

Transgender is an umbrella term for different ways a person experiences or expresses a gender identity that is different from what would correspond with their biological markers. Where *cis* refers to "this side of," *trans* means "the other side of." When people say they are transgender, they often mean that their gender identity (as a woman, for instance) is on "the other side" of what would normally correspond with their biological sex (as a male, in this case).

As with the word *gay*, the word *transgender* can also function merely as a descriptive of a gender identity that does not line up with biological markers. It does not necessarily tell you how someone is identifying his or her gender, just that it does not correspond with one's body as it was at birth. The use of the label transgender can also reflect greater affiliation with the mainstream LGBTQ+ community with shared assumptions, beliefs, and values about what it means to flourish as a person with an uncommon experience of gender identity. Because the identity of transgender can mean so many different things, it is usually helpful to clarify what a transgender identity means to each person.

Gender non-binary is another umbrella term for several ways in which a person may experience a gender identity outside of the two (binary) options of man or woman. Examples of gender non-binary experience include genderfluid, pangender, bi-gender, and graygender.[3] In the recent Gallup Poll, fewer than 1% of the adult population identifies as transgender. However, generational differences appear here as well, with 2.1% of Gen Z, 1.0% of Millennials, 0.5% of Gen X, and 0.1% of Baby Boomers identifying as transgender.[4]

When someone experiences their gender as something other than that which matches their biological markers, it is often referred to as gender discordance. When this is significantly distressing, it can lead to a diagnosis of *gender dysphoria*. Gender dysphoria is a disorder listed in the *Diagnostic and Statistical Manual of Mental Disorders–Fifth Edition*

---

[3]Mark A. Yarhouse and Julia A. Sadusky, *Emerging Gender Identities: Understanding the Diverse Experiences of Today's Youth* (Grand Rapids, MI: Brazos, 2020), 8-10. Genderfluid refers to a person's experience of their gender as changing or as more fluid; pangender refers to the experience of multiple genders; bi-gender refers to the experience of two genders; and graygender refers to not fully identifying with either gender in a binary.
[4]Jones, "LGBT Identification Ticks up to 7.1%."

(*DSM-5*), which is the manual of disorders widely used in the United States by medical and mental health professions. The *DSM-5* distinguishes between two presentations of gender dysphoria, which are early or late onset of gender dysphoria. Early onset refers to the presence of symptoms (i.e., distressing gender incongruence) prior to beginning puberty, while late onset refers to symptoms appearing at or after puberty.[5] In the 2015 US Transgender Survey, most transgender adults (60%) recalled experiencing gender incongruence before the age of 11, which would be considered early onset (32% ages 5 and under; 28% ages 6 to 10).[6] The remaining 40 percent of adults recalled first experiencing their gender discordance from age 11 or older (21% between ages 11 and 15; 13% between ages 16 and 20; and 6% age 21 and older).[7] It is notable that not all transgender individuals would be considered to have gender dysphoria. This is a diagnosis given only in cases of extremely distressing gender incongruence.

GENDER DYSPHORIA: IS THERE A CAUSE?

Like sexual orientation, it is unclear what causes gender dysphoria, transgender experiences, or other experiences of gender identity. A theory many specialists are drawn to today understands transgender experiences as having biological causes. Specifically, many believe there may be differences in the way the male versus female brains are structured that could suggest that transgender people have an intersex condition of the brain. *Intersex* refers to a variety of conditions where a baby is born with shared reproductive tissue of both sexes, possibly making it difficult to establish the baby as clearly male or female. Taking that same idea and applying it to transgender people, researchers propose that there may be differences in how the transgender individual's brain is structured, which may then influence how that person experiences his or her own gender. This is what researchers would call an intersex theory of the brain.

Researchers have conducted studies to test this theory by looking at areas of the brain similar to those studied with regard to sexual

---

[5]American Psychiatric Association, *Diagnostic and Statistical Manual of Mental Disorders*, 5th ed. text revision (Washington, DC: American Psychiatric Association Publishing, 2022).
[6]S. E. James et al., *The Report of the 2015 U.S. Transgender Survey* (Washington, DC: National Center for Trangender Equality, 2016).
[7]James et al., *The Report of the 2015 U.S. Transgender Survey*.

orientation. The theory of an intersex experience in the brain proposes the idea that transgender individuals have a phenotypically distinct brain (different from cisgender males and females) that has shared aspects of both male and female brains. As compelling as this theory is, it is important to note that it is predicated on the existence of distinct male and female brains, an idea that lacks evidence. In any case, scientists cannot at this time say with certainty or consensus what causes gender dysphoria or related transgender experiences.

Another common theory among society at large regarding what causes transgender experiences is that of peer influence. You may hear the phrase *social contagion* applied to the experience of transgender identities, in particular. Social contagion refers to a phenomenon discussed especially regarding eating disorders, where peer groups relay messages of acceptable body shape and size, or standards for beauty, that can be especially influential. In the past, these have contributed to the development or maintenance of eating disorders, particularly among adolescent females. Some observers of increases in the numbers of adolescent females who experience gender dysphoria have taken the idea of social contagion as understood with eating disorders and applied it to transgender self-identification. Although we believe it may be premature to use that phrase just yet, we do recognize that peer group influence can draw a person toward a phenomenon or can reinforce experiences for those who might already be seeking identity and community.

With increased social acceptance, it is not surprising to see more people identify as LGBTQ+ insofar as they feel safe and supported to do so. However, there may also be peer group influences that lead to increases as well. In some regions of the United States, for instance, there appears to be a trend toward self-identification as LGBTQ+. In other places, however, such self-identification is often associated with bullying and harassment. It will be important to gauge the atmosphere of your ministry setting and consider how people may respond to experiences of diverse sexual or gender identities. Even in some of the most socially liberal parts of the United States, churches may be places that are more socially conventional, where it may be difficult for a person to ask questions or seek resources when navigating sexual or gender identity.

So far, we have presented an introduction to the topic of sexual and gender identities and important related terms, along with prevalence rates and theories of causation. In addition to what causes a certain sexual orientation or gender identity, one may also wonder what that journey of discovery and development looks like for someone navigating these issues personally. This is what we will consider next.

SEXUAL AND GENDER IDENTITY DEVELOPMENT

When talking about sexual identity development, we often use the analogy of hiking difficult terrain. Though each person's journey is different, those navigating sexual identity often face similar developmental milestones along this hike. These commonly shared milestones can include things like their first awareness of having same-sex attractions (typically at or after puberty), initial thoughts about what sexuality means to them, whether to share this part of their life with others (often referred to as "coming out"), and whether to use identity labels such as gay in understanding oneself or describing oneself to others. Using the term *gay* to describe oneself can mean different things to different people. To some people, *gay* functions simply as an adjective or an answer to a question about sexual orientation. For others *gay* encompasses more, like being a part of a larger, mainstream LGBTQ+ community where shared beliefs, assumptions, and values contribute to a sense of human flourishing. Before assuming what people in your congregation mean when they say that they are gay, it is often useful to ask what the identity means to them and in what ways they identify with that word.

When it comes to gender identity development, less research has been conducted in the area of individual experiences. However, it is still helpful to ask about meaningful milestones along someone's personal journey. For example, you could ask about when a person first experienced gender discordance and how one's gender identity has developed over time.

PRACTICAL PASTORAL RESPONSE

We opened this chapter with two brief accounts of a spouse disclosing being either gay or transgender. How should we as pastors and ministry staff respond when learning about a couple in which a spouse has come out as gay or transgender? When sitting across from an individual or couple expressing such concerns, we recommend responding in a manner that recognizes you are not an expert in their specific situation or experience. Making a statement such as, "I feel like I am meeting you about chapter five or six of your marriage and lives. I'd like to hear more about chapters one through four," can communicate to the couple that you want to hear more about what they have already been through, while reminding yourself of your need to listen and learn.

What these statements do is give the individual or couple the opportunity to provide you with much-needed context for the present crisis. Recall that both sexual identity and gender identity develop over time. It is unlikely what they are experiencing is something new and "out of the blue." Though possible in rare instances, more often than not there is a developmental history of one's sexual and gender identity that you will want to understand and help them to understand as well.

INTERPERSONAL TRAUMA

The first two vignettes at the beginning of this chapter describe the discovery of a spouse's hidden sexual or gender identity. Discoveries such as these are often traumatic, as one finds out his or her spouse is not who he or she appeared to be. It can be jarring, to say the least. Of course, individual experiences vary considerably and are often influenced by the timing of disclosure (prior to or during the marriage) and situational stressors (i.e., whether there have been or are currently acts of infidelity or whether a spouse intends to make a medical transition). Earlier disclosure appears to be a better predictor of marital satisfaction than later disclosure for mixed orientation marriages.[8] It is better to disclose while dating, for example, than to disclose several years into the marriage. Even more challenging is an unexpected discovery, rather than an initiated disclosure, that one's spouse is a sexual minority, such as stumbling on text messages or emails or seeing pictures on social media, that leads to a confrontation at which time suspicions are confirmed.

---

[8] Jill L. Kays and Mark A. Yarhouse, "Resilient Factors in Mixed Orientation Couples: Current State of the Research," *The American Journal of Family Therapy* 38, no. 4 (June 2010): 334-43.

How might pastors and ministry staff respond to the resulting interpersonal trauma? We recommend that you listen to what has transpired and validate the range of emotions that the straight or cisgender spouse is reporting. At the same time, you will want to validate the challenges that arise for the LGBTQ+ spouse in their disclosure to their spouse of what may have been a secret held for many years. Both of them are on a journey as they begin or continue to figure out what this means for them individually and as a couple.

Consider the story of the man born blind in John 9. The disciples assume the man's blindness is because of sin, so they directly ask about the two most likely culprits as they understood it in their culture: "Who sinned, this man or his parents, that he was born blind?" The idea that a person was blind due to his own sinfulness, or the sin of his parents was a fairly common belief in that day. We are not so far removed from this way of thinking when it comes to LGBTQ+ issues. Yet ministry can get off to a better start when we recognize that the person did not choose to experience same-sex attraction or gender discordance.

A few years ago, Mark met with Ted and Janice, a couple in their late twenties.[9] Ted came with Janice for a consultation on sexual identity. At a point in the meeting, Mark discerned a misunderstanding regarding Ted's experience of same-sex attraction. Mark stopped the meeting and said, "I'm not sure what's going on, but I don't think you chose to experience same-sex attractions. It sounds like from everything you've shared that you found yourself with these attractions to the same sex when you went through puberty." Ted responded, "You've got to say that to my wife; she thinks I just chose this and that I need to choose not to have these attractions." Mark said, "I'd be happy to share my thoughts with Janice, because I think it's true. I do want to add something: I think you still have choices to make. You have choices to make about sexual behavior and about sexual identity and where you go from here." Ted exclaimed, "Don't tell Janice that!"

What this exchange illustrates is that we come into conversations with assumptions about sexual attractions and the choices a person makes.

---

[9]This case is adapted from a session with a teenager who was in conflict with his parents.

Ted didn't think he had a choice about other areas of his life because he didn't choose to have his attractions. Janice apparently thought that Ted chose to experience his same-sex attractions. Mark thought that they were both mistaken.

As a pastor, you can frame it this way: What do people have a say over? Rather than claim that people chose to experience same-sex attractions, we can recognize that they found themselves with these experiences at a young age or as they went through puberty or another developmental stage. They do have choices to make today, but to assign blame for choosing to experience their sexuality or gender as they do would be a pastoral mistake we can avoid in these initial moments of care. Additionally, they are often coming to you in a time of need, fear, and brokenness, in which it is vitally important to take a posture of compassion.

WHAT IF THEY DON'T AGREE?

Another issue that the first two vignettes raise is when the couple themselves disagree on what to do. It's one thing when a couple is on the same page about refraining from other relationships or making a transition so that they can work on their marriage. However, it is another thing if one spouse wants to do that, but the other spouse is pursuing a same-sex relationship or making a social or medical transition against the wishes of the spouse. In the latter, try to encourage the couple to clarify in their own minds the direction they would like to go. This can be done through meeting with each spouse individually or doing so together, helping them share with one another how they are doing and what things they are considering. You can help them come to a better understanding of what they are weighing, how they go about deciding among compelling alternatives, and how they will be affected by the decisions they make.

While a mental health professional has obligations to autonomy of the individuals, a church leader has obligations to both church teaching and loving pastoral care. This may be similar to other church members coming to leaders with a variety of things that are contrary to church doctrine, anything from failure to tithe to cohabitation. If the parishioner isn't aware of your church teaching, that can be communicated. If they are aware of your church teaching, then compassionate care and love have the best chance of not alienating the member in crisis. The long arc of redemption may begin with that love.

Triangulation. If the couple doesn't agree, triangulation may occur. Triangulation occurs when each spouse in a marriage is trying to get the pastor on their side against the other spouse. It is very common in couples counseling, so we would not be surprised to see it come up here. It is important to be aware of the concept of triangulation, to recognize when either spouse (or both) is attempting to get you to side with them, and to be disciplined to listen deeply and well to both spouses as they share their perspectives and resist the urge to side with one spouse or the other.

Changing beliefs. Another common point of tension is whether the couple agrees or disagrees with your church's stance on biblical sexual behavior or gender expression. Often the spouse who has disclosed his or her sexuality or gender identity no longer holds to the position of traditional church teaching. Though we should not assume this is the case, it may come up in your care for the couple, namely that one spouse's beliefs about what is morally permissible regarding same-sex relationships, or social or medical transitions have changed. In these cases, helping the couple work through what has changed and why can be helpful. This may be especially important for the future shepherding and pastoral care of both spouses, as they may be moving in different directions in terms of agreement with the church's teaching.

Belonging. An issue that arises from the second vignette concerning gender dysphoria is the issue of what it means to belong to a Christian community. Many churches, out of a desire to be missional, say that anyone and everyone is welcome. However, sometimes when everyone shows up, it raises questions of who really belongs and is welcome to stay in the community. Addressing the question, "Am I wanted here?" is a big part of ministry to the LGBTQ+ community.

More nuanced conversations that do not assume every marriage is of two heterosexual spouses would be an important consideration. Keep in mind the possibility that one spouse may be navigating questions of sexual identity or gender identity. If so, how might you word a teaching that makes room for their experience? Could you slightly change what you say in illustration to recognize that there are different experiences in marriage, so that when people in those marriages hear a story they, too, have the opportunity to see the applications of that story to their circumstances.

SPIRITUAL FORMATION

Spiritual formation for couples in these or similar situations is strongly informed by everyone's response to conflict as well as his or her personally held values and commitments to God and to their spouse. In other words, it's highly individual. For spouses in a mixed orientation marriage, the question they will be navigating is how to respond to same-sex sexuality. For the spouse who experiences same-sex attractions, decisions will include things such as: (1) should they pursue same-sex relationships?, (2) will they identify or dis-identify with the mainstream LGBTQ+ community?, and (3) how can they pursue a path that is both honest about their same-sex attractions but also considers their faith commitments and other values? For the straight spouse, questions also arise as to how they will respond to their spouse's (likely) ongoing attractions to the same sex, as well as whether they wish to grow in areas of communication and cohesion with their spouse in light of their spouse's same-sex sexuality.

Likewise, the person who is managing gender dysphoria is seeking ways to do so in keeping with their prior commitment to his or her spouse. Spiritual formation will look at how to respond to personal pain and be honest with God and with one's spouse about one's capacity to manage the distressing reality of gender dysphoria.

For the straight and cisgender spouse, discipleship largely involves learning how to respond to circumstances that feel out of one's control. This spouse will be faced with the need to turn to God and trust Him with their future and the future of a marriage that now seems drastically different from what it was. A few practical recommendations include: (1) to turn to specific passages in the Scriptures (e.g., Jn 9:1-3; Rom 8:17; Rev 21:5); (2) explore with the couple if there are a few trusted others who can pray for them, and (3) recommend some articles or books that may shine light on the issues they are facing.[10]

FOSTER RESILIENCE

How can pastors and ministry staff come alongside individuals and couples in these situations? One way is to help the couple foster resilience. Research shows that approximately half of couples who choose to stay in a marriage after a disclosure event actually do remain married.[11] What helped couples overcome the challenges of disclosure and work through conflict included (1) strong communication, (2) cohesion and commitment, and (3) negotiation and flexibility.[12]

First, communication enhanced marital relationships when it was characterized by honesty, empathy, and frequency. The couples talked frequently and openly. Interestingly, their communication did not need to be centered on sexual or gender identity to be helpful. Rather, being able to engage regularly in effective communication was itself beneficial, whether discussing everyday things or those more delicate, such as sexual or gender identity.

Second, cohesion and commitment refer to the mutual experience of love for one another and a tendency to focus on the positive. The idea of cohesion has more to do with how two people in marriage become one unit.[13] Two people together become something that did not exist prior to their marriage. This cohesive sense of "us" is unique to each couple, and couples should be encouraged to grow their own sense of unity rather

---

[10] For a recommended book for a couple in a mixed orientation marriage, see Laurie Krieg and Matt Krieg, *An Impossible Marriage: What Our Mixed-Orientation Marriage Has Taught Us About Love and the Gospel* (Downers Grove, IL: InterVarsity Press, 2020). A recommended book on the idea of "us" in a marriage, see James N. Sells and Mark A. Yarhouse, *Counseling Couples in Conflict* (Downers Grove, IL: IVP Academic, 2011). See Julia Sadusky and Mark Yarhouse's four-part series on gender dysphoria and suffering: introduction, seeking answers, sharing the burden, and continuing to seek answers. The link to begin the series is found at https://inallthings.org/introduction-to-gender-dysphoria/. For additional resources on sexual and gender identity, see the Sexual & Gender Identity Institute (www.wheaton.edu/sgi) and the Center for Faith, Sexuality and Gender (www.centerforfaith.com/).

[11] Amity Pierce Buxton, "Paths and Pitfalls: How Heterosexual Spouses Cope when their Husbands or Wives Come Out," *Journal of Couple & Relationship Therapy* 3, no. 2-3 (2004): 95-109, www.doi.org/10.1300/J398v03n02_10; and Kays and Yarhouse, "Resilient Factors," 334-43.

[12] Buxton, "Paths and Pitfalls;" 100; and Kays and Yarhouse, "Resilient Factors," 339-41.

[13] Sells and Yarhouse, *Counseling Couples in Conflict*, 48-50.

than make comparisons to others or gauge their success on media or other representations.

Third, negotiation and flexibility help the couple work together to find a new norm when faced with change. This new norm can include redefining the meaning of their marital relationship, adjusting expectations (e.g., in the area of sexual intimacy), and creating flexible relationship guidelines that work for both parties.

Additional factors that promote resilience include positive reactions of the receptive spouse during disclosure, intentional consideration of whether or not to use sexual identity and orientation labels (privately or publicly), social support from outside the marriage (whether professional help or community support), and religious coping strategies (participating in private and communal worship practices).[14] When ministering to couples, it can be beneficial to work with them to communicate honestly about their difficulties, fears, desires, and faith commitments. Help them not to discredit positive aspects of their lives and marriage while balancing the offer to feel and to share their grief and pain with one another.

Let's return to the two couples we introduced at the beginning of this chapter. Jane and Joe's marriage was in trouble, but they both wanted to work on their marriage. Joe took down his profile and used counseling to identify other ways to acknowledge the reality of his same-sex attractions but in ways that were in keeping with his values to be faithful in his marriage. His counselor used the resource *Sexual Identity & Faith: Helping Clients Achieve Congruence* and helped Joe begin by noting many stories that have been told about what it means to be gay—stories he heard growing up in his church, as well as stories he had heard from the broader culture, entertainment, and media.[15] Both of these kinds of stories were challenging to Joe. His church had said gays were an abomination, while the broader society said that gays were to be celebrated. What Joe was looking for was another way to think about himself in light of his marriage, his values, and the reality of his same-sex attractions.

---

[14]Kays and Yarhouse, "Resilient Factors," 342.
[15]Mark A. Yarhouse, *Sexual Identity and Faith: Helping Clients Achieve Congruence* (West Conshohocken, PA: The Templeton Foundation, 2019).

Counseling became a safe place for Joe to clearly articulate his values and to begin to identify a path in his behavior and identity that would be congruent to those values. Joe read a book by Greg Coles on his experience as a celibate gay Christian. He also read the book, *Costly Obedience*, which presents the experiences of people who are celibate as well as people with same-sex attraction who are married to heterosexual spouses.[16] Joe tended to use person-first language like "I am a person who experiences same-sex attraction" rather than identity-first language like "I am gay." That seemed to help de-center his sexuality from the marriage while allowing him to acknowledge his same-sex sexuality as a reality. In his service to the body of Christ, Joe began to learn that his experience navigating his faith in light of his same-sex sexuality gave him a heart for those who are sometimes overlooked in the church. He ended up engaging in ministries that some members of the church have kept at a distance, like ministry to those who are homeless. He also found that he had a certain sensitivity to others that came out in his cell group, which he co-led with Jane and another couple.

Jane was also in need of counseling. She worked through the interpersonal trauma of learning that her husband experienced same-sex attractions. She was able to work more closely with Joe on what contributed to him keeping that to himself and how she experienced that as a deception. Jane needed a place in counseling to face questions she had about who she was. She had significant insecurities related to long-established patterns in their marriage in which she could not understand why Joe seemed uninterested in "pursuing" her. This contributed to self-doubt and low self-esteem. Working through all of this took considerable time. With the new information about Joe's same-sex sexuality, several things now made more sense. She was able to face and work through dynamics that eroded her self-esteem. She was also able to forgive Joe and work with Joe eventually on ways they could strengthen their marriage through things like better and more frequent communication and activities that would enhance emotional closeness. They found a longtime friend, a confidant, in whom they could bring their experiences, just to have

---

[16]Mark A. Yarhouse and Olya Zaporozhets, *Costly Obedience: What We Can Learn from the Celibate Gay Christian Community* (Grand Rapids, MI: Zondervan, 2019).

someone outside of counseling who could listen, encourage, and pray for them.

Rebecca and Alex faced a different set of challenges. Rebecca was aware of Alex's cross-dressing behavior. She didn't like it, but it seemed like a compromise that had worked for them even though it was apparently no longer sufficient for Alex. They read through Preston Sprinkle's book *Embodied*, and the counselor used *Gender Identity and Faith* as a resource that shaped much of counseling itself.[17] It is not uncommon to think of various responses to gender dysphoria as strategies for managing the dysphoria. Alex had initially been insistent that he needed to make a full-time social transition, that the part-time management strategy he had been using was insufficient for managing his distress. What this meant was that Alex was proposing he would present as a woman at home and with extended family. He would also present as a woman at work and at church—in all areas of their lives.

What Alex learned in counseling was that most adults who experience their gender identity in this way do not make a medical transition, but that many do find ways to manage their dysphoria short of those options. Alex was willing to investigate additional management strategies that were non-medical and not quite as expansive as Alex was originally proposing. These compromises did include presenting as a woman at times, and this continued to be difficult for Rebecca and raised questions for both in terms of what God thought of Alex's experiences of gender dysphoria and some of the management strategies Alex was using.

Rebecca sought out counseling for her own response to Alex's initial request to make a full-time transition. She loved Alex, but she did not understand what had made it seem like their current compromise with his dysphoria was not enough. She had long feared that he might want to make a complete transition, and now her fears may be realized. She did work through her own experience of interpersonal trauma, which took time. She was unsure what was a reasonable response for a spouse

---

[17]Preston Sprinkle, *Embodied: Transgender Identities, the Church, and What the Bible Has to Say* (Colorado Springs, CO: David C. Cook, 2020); Mark A. Yarhouse and Julia A. Sadusky, *Gender Identity and Faith: Clinical Postures, Tools, and Case Studies for Client-Centered Care* (Downers Grove, IL: IVP Academic, 2022).

in this situation and frequently doubted herself. Rebecca would eventually forgive Alex, but Rebecca felt that his request to make a full-time transition was not something she could support at this time. She felt she needed space apart. They ended up making a short-term physical separation, which meant that they lived in different settings for about a year: Rebecca in their home with their two children and Alex in an apartment. They loved one another and they loved their children. They did not wish to pursue a divorce, so they worked out regular time to have contact with one another (including marriage counseling) and to have time with their children. This, too, was complicated, and required time to explain both to their children and to their extended family.

As Alex identified other management strategies other than making a medical or otherwise full-time social transition, they were able to work out a way to move back in together. Both Rebecca and Alex continued in their church. Rebecca was able to share her story and the challenges she faced with a few people. She would later join a parent support group for Christian parents whose children had come out to them as transgender. Although a different family dynamic, she still found another place to speak with other Christians about her journey as a spouse. She was able to take the lessons parents shared and make connections to her emotions and the decisions she was facing. It was also good to just have a place to share her journey. Alex stayed in the church as well. However, he became more peripheral to the church than Rebecca. Although Alex regularly stayed connected to a church friend who encouraged and prayed with him, his faith journey was difficult.

In closing, ministry leaders are called to care well for those they serve. Caring well for couples navigating the terrain of sexual or gender identity begins by being informed about terminology and issues marital couples face when one comes out, along with how to minister to them knowledgably with sensitivity and grace. This process begins with taking the role of a listener and a learner. We encourage you to become familiar with the resources presented in this chapter to build awareness and empathy and put you in a better position to care well for couples who are facing these unique challenges.

6

MINISTERING TO FAMILIES WHEN CHILDREN COME OUT

Janet B. Dean, Stephen P. Stratton,
and Mark A. Yarhouse

"Our son Ian told us he's gay," Tammy confesses through tears as her husband Ryan reaches over and takes her hand. Neither will look directly at me.

Ryan adds, "We've taken him to church regularly. I mean, Ian really is a Christian. How can he think this is okay?" The frustration in his voice is clear.

"Does he?" Tammy counters, "He was so afraid to share this with us. His hands were shaking. He even teared up."

"But his letter!" exclaims Ryan, "It took a lot of effort to detail all the things we've done wrong over the years. Maybe this is his way of getting back at us. He clearly blames us for failing as parents. I was too soft on him; you babied him too much."

Defending herself, Tammy looks at Ryan. "How can you blame me for this?"

"I'm not blaming you. I'm blaming us. Pastor, do you think we caused this?" Ryan looked me directly in the eye, waiting for some response.

His question is a common one for parents as they process what it means for their child to come out as gay. It's often said with a sense of regret and even shame. After some discussion, a response reflecting both their fear and the multi-faceted causation of sexual orientation can provide some immediate relief.

Tammy and Ryan, like most parents, want to find an "easy" out. Ryan suggests, "This must be a phase of some kind; maybe it's teenage rebellion and his attempt to make us angry."

Tammy looks at him, "What if it's not?" and then to me, "What will this mean for Ian? What does this road look like? What about his future?" Then she almost pleads with desperate hope, "Maybe you could work with him and help him give this up and find a nice young woman to marry."

Ryan and Tammy represent many parents who have reached out to us with similar questions over the years. They often reach out to Christian psychologists, not pastors, because they are afraid of how their pastor and church might respond.

Parents often don't know that many pastors and church leaders enter these conversations with fear themselves. Usually, they were not trained in seminary to navigate these roads, yet they know that wrong, or merely misunderstood, words and actions may cause crashes for both the family and the church, especially given our highly polarized culture. This chapter aims to help leaders for these almost inevitable conversations they will have with people in their spheres of ministry.

ROAD UNDER CONSTRUCTION

We have seen a striking cultural shift over the past twenty-plus years in both the acceptance and prevalence of gender and sexual diversity. Just consider how approval of same-sex marriage has changed. In 1996, 73% of US adults were *against* same-sex marriage; by 2023, 71% were in *support* of it.[1] There also has been a sixfold increase in the number of adults who identify as gender- and sexual-diverse individuals (GSD), with only 3.5% of those over 42 identifying as such while 21% of those 18 to 26 do the same. This is a radical reversal in the degree of societal acceptance and experience, and it is also being seen in the church.

---

[1] Justin McCarthy, "Same-Sex Marriage Support Inches Up to New High of 71%," Gallup, June 1, 2022, https://news.gallup.com/poll/393197/same-sex-marriage-support-inches-new-high.aspx.

Growing up under such disparate cultural norms, we—like Ryan, Tammy, their son Ian, and their pastor—all enter this conversation from very different perspectives. No wonder it's hard to hear, let alone tolerate, what's being said of opinions that are contrary to those we hold true. How, then, do we walk together?

THE PRECARIOUS JOURNEY

Imagine the road along which pastors and families journey alongside their GSD family members. This road leads to a place where youth can find deeper faith, greater self-acceptance, and better psychological health, even though traveling this road is challenging. This highway is fraught with potholes, cones, construction vehicles, shredded tires, and broken-down cars. Traffic is heavy and sporadic, and the storms sweep in unpredictably. The anxiety is almost too much to bear, and both parents and pastors alike are white-knuckling the steering wheel until they find the nearest off-ramp. Some will exit into theological and moral convictions, so set on what is right that they struggle to love. Others will exit into affirmation and acceptance, so determined to maintain relationships that they willingly sacrifice long-held religious values.

Unfortunately, exiting the highway, whether a parent or a pastor, means they are no longer walking with youth who are trying to navigate these tensions for themselves. Sometimes one parent veers one way, while the other chooses the opposite, causing significant conflict in the home. Sometimes the family goes a different way than their church. Whenever there is a split, the one who loses the most is the teen.

STEPPING OUT

Youth "coming out." What does it mean when a child "comes out"? Regarding sexuality, this language most often means the disclosure of non-heterosexual attractions, orientation, or identity. For example, when Ian "came out" to his parents, he shared that he was attracted to men and was gay. Young people may refer to themselves as gay, lesbian, bisexual, pansexual (i.e., attraction for both genders or other gender identities), demi-sexual (i.e., attraction only after establishing strong emotional connection), asexual (i.e., little to no attraction), or a variety of other terms.

"Coming out" also may mean revealing incongruence between one's biological sex, sex assigned at birth, or one's gender identity. Self-descriptions typically include words like transgender, gender non-conforming (i.e., gender expression different from gender role norms related to one's birth sex), or genderqueer or gender fluid (i.e., gender identity outside of the gender binary, identifying with both genders or with neither).

Such disclosure, particularly to family members, is both a difficult decision and a significant milestone in the youth's identity development process.[2] Disclosure often leads to a family crisis,[3] yet is necessary despite the bumps and hurdles lying ahead along the road, as adolescent development must occur within the context of a family system.

Deciding when and how to disclose often causes a great deal of apprehension in youth as they tend to anticipate a poor reaction from their parents. Their hesitancy increases further if they know their parents are opposed to same-sex sexual behavior and diversity in gender and sexual identity and if they have witnessed their parents responding poorly to GSD youth in the past.

Thus, teens tend to approach disclosure to their families in ways that mitigate their fear of this presumed negative response. Many wait years before sharing with their parents, often choosing to disclose to friends, siblings, mentors, or their youth pastor first, sometimes asking for advice in telling their mom and dad.[4] Disclosure may happen in a conversation, but it often is through a letter, a text, or any other means of communication. Sometimes youth approach their parents separately, revealing this to the parent with whom they are closest first, usually their mother. Sometimes a teen brings a friend along for moral support. Other times, a teen comes prepared for an argument.

Their apprehension is justifiable, as parents often react negatively to their child's initial disclosure. While some parents are able to respond

---

[2] Jeffrey L. Reed et al., "'Coming Out' to Parents in a Christian Context: A Consensual Qualitative Analysis of LGB Student Experiences," *Counseling and Values* 65, no. 1 (April 2020): 38-56, www.doi.org/10.1002/cvj.12121.

[3] Linda Freedman, "Accepting the Unacceptable: Religious Parents and Adult Gay and Lesbian Children," *Families in Society* 89, no. 2 (April 2008): 237-44, 242, www.doi.org/10.1606/1044-3894.3739.

[4] Mark A. Yarhouse et al., *Listening to Sexual Minorities: A Study of Faith and Sexual Identity on Christian College Campuses* (Downers Grove, IL: IVP Academic, 2018), 61-85.

more functionally, most struggle, even when they have some inkling prior to the disclosure. Unfortunately, the quality of a parental relationship prior to disclosure cannot accurately predict how well the disclosure will go. Family stress, timing of the disclosure, and other relational dynamics play a part in how parents receive this revelation. It is less likely to go well if their parents hold strong religious beliefs.

Just as Tammy and Ryan responded to their son, most parents tend to respond emotionally, with a broad range of emotions, such as shame, shock, grief, sadness, disappointment, disgust, and anger.[5] These emotional reactions are likely to be interpreted as anger as teens often struggle to discriminate among various emotions, assuming negative ones are anger.

According to college students who were interviewed about their disclosures of same-sex attraction to Christian parents, about 25% of the parents denied or rejected their child's disclosure, often trying to dissuade the child from believing this about themselves. Four out of ten parents made light of the disclosure, believing either this was a phase which would pass or this was chosen by their child and thus could be unchosen. About 20% of parents searched for external causes of the attraction, whether that be chemical imbalances, childhood abuse, peer influences, or even parenting mistakes. Perhaps surprisingly, only 16% of Christian college students reported their parents turning to Scripture and theology in this initial disclosure. When parents did use the Bible or theological thought, 75% of students reacted negatively.[6]

These negative parental reactions may leave a lasting negative effect on the young person. When parents respond poorly, it may color the relationship's future, as teens become less able to see later improvement in the parent-child relationship, even when parents see it. If youth interpret these parental reactions as rejection, they are likely to experience significant physical and psychological health concerns.[7]

Fortunately, only about 25% of the college students interviewed in the study mentioned above recounted the disclosure to their parents as

---

[5]Mark A. Yarhouse and Olya Zaporozhets, *When Children Come Out: A Guide for Christian Parents* (Downers Grove, IL: IVP Academic, 2022).
[6]Reed et al., "'Coming Out' to Parents," 38-56, 46.
[7]Caitlin Ryan and Rafael Diaz, *Family Acceptance Project: Intervention Guidelines and Strategies* (San Francisco: Family Acceptance Project, 2011).

wholly negative, although none reported estrangement or violence as sometimes found in other studies.[8] Another quarter of the students found the disclosure to be a good experience in which they felt loved and accepted. Half of the students described the experience in both positive and negative terms.

Pastorally, helping young people in disclosing to their parents means exploring with them different options for how to do so, particularly how options might be received. It's also important to prepare them for the broad range of responses and how these emotional reactions may not be what they seem and do not necessarily dictate the future of their relationship with their parents.

Parents "going in." Tammy and Ryan revealed they had waited a few months before seeking pastoral help. Tammy explained, "You may not know this, Pastor, but when kids come out, parents go in, especially in the church."

Many parents reported withdrawing from others after their child's initial disclosure. This may be due to the initial flood of emotions and general uncertainty about how to proceed, but often, parents are hiding due to shame, embarrassment, and even fear of rejection by others, particularly those in the church.

Shame tends to be a powerful force in the parents' affective response. Some of the first questions parents ask are "How didn't we know?" and "What did we do to cause this?" Some parents are bewildered how they had no inclination that this was true for their child. This can make them feel guilty that their child was left alone to navigate this experience for so long, particularly given that the average age of disclosure among Christian youth is seventeen. This inclination toward self-blame may highlight the parents' misunderstanding of the causes of gender and sexual identity concerns, but it also may reveal their sense of over-responsibility for their child, their sense of inadequacy as parents, or perhaps their need to maintain some control—potentially even harming the child in the effort to reassert control. This shame leaves parents alone to process complex and often overwhelming emotional reactions to this disclosure.

---

[8]Reed et al., "'Coming Out' to Parents," 38-56, 46.

FIRST LEG OF THE JOURNEY: RESPONDING TO DISCLOSURE

Pastors are often brought into the family's journey for support sometime after the disclosure has happened and the family has been disrupted by emotional reactions, discordant perspectives, and relational tensions. What this looks like for a family and how their journey moves forward will be unique for each family, and it will take time. Interestingly, after children come out, parents and their children embark on two parallel journeys. Understanding the dynamics of the journey and the needs that arise along the way help pastors to provide better pastoral care.

Youth need space and help as they learn to hold both their Christian faith and gender and sexual identity together in a way that accepts, and even honors, both. Jumping to ultimatums or dismissing identity questions most often leads to broken family relationships and significant mental health issues. Yet, if parents and pastors can create this space for youth, they most likely will maintain their ability to be part of the young person's journey. Remember, the outcome for these youth is not yet determined. How they will come to understand their gender and sexual identity, and how they will hold this together with their faith, will crystallize as they mature.

Along this way, youth will begin an attributional search for meaning, identity, and community, asking questions such as, *What does being gay or gender nonbinary mean for me? For my future? Who am I? Does this change who I am? What is my sexuality? My gender? Where do I belong? Do I still have a place in the church?* Building relationships with these youth, engaging them in these important conversations, and helping them to construct a life narrative that provides a sense of meaning, a place in community, and an integrated identity will be core components of pastoral care and Christian discipleship with them. Empathy and active listening are essential for engaging these pivotal conversations from a pastoral perspective.

Despite the difficulties associated with disclosure, youth often experience some positive outcomes. For example, many find that their anxiety lessens. They also may experience stronger self-identity, more authenticity in their relationships, and more positive relationships and social support.[9] If parents can support them to some degree, they might find that their children show increased self-acceptance and psychological stability in the long run.[10]

Parents are similarly trying to navigate this first leg of the journey, searching for what this means for them and for their child and wondering what that relationship will look like over time. In the jumble of emotions soon after disclosure, about three out of four parents feel unconditional love for their child, and nearly all of them experience some protectiveness over their child. Parents may also fear for their child's safety, imagining all the things that could go wrong like bullying, health concerns, difficult relationships, job struggles, and rejection.

While parents like Ryan and Tammy may not voice their concerns, they are often acutely aware of their potential losses within the future they had imagined, losses such as a wedding, grandkids, the passing down of a family name, and family genetics. They may also anticipate other current losses—a broken relationship with their child, conflict with their spouse about their child, and separation from their church community. This inner emotional turmoil may be exacerbated as parents attempt to reconcile their religious beliefs about sexuality and gender with their love for their child.[11] This conflict often creates confusion about the most appropriate ways to respond to the child. Parents may end up leaning into either their religion or their relationship with their child, but not both. Thus, many parents eventually will come out of hiding to seek help in resolving this unsatisfying either-or approach, just as Ryan and Tammy did, but they will be cautious in doing so.

A sound pastoral response provides a safe and confidential place for parents to process their thoughts and feelings, including spiritual counseling to alleviate shame and address questions of faith. Church leaders

---

[9]Michelle D. Vaughan and Charles A. Waehler, "Coming-out Growth: Conceptualizing and Measuring Stress-Related Growth Associated with Coming out to Others as a Sexual Minority," *Journal of Adult Development* 17, no. 2 (June 2010): 94-109, www.doi.org/10.1007/s10804-009-9084-9.

[10]Janet B. Dean et al., "The Mediating Role of Self-Acceptance in the Psychological Distress of Sexual Minority Students on Christian College Campuses," *Spirituality in Clinical Practice* 8, no. 2 (June 2021): 132-48, www.doi.org/10.1037/scp0000253.

[11]Kathryn E. Maslowe and Mark A. Yarhouse, "Christian Parental Reactions When a LGB Child Comes Out," *American Journal of Family Therapy* 43, no. 4 (August 2015): 352-63, www.doi.org/10.1080/01926187.2015.1051901.

will also want to offer comfort, reassurance, and hope as parents struggle with significant confusion, helplessness, and grief. As with youth, pastors need to be able to model how to be faithful to religious beliefs, while also creating loving relational space for parents. Pastors knowledgeable in research findings about GSD identities will be better able to answer the parents' many questions. Helping parents to structure family relationships and create a safe place for their children can ease the parental fears. Note that pastoral responses suggesting the child is the problem are likely to backfire as parents typically will want to defend their child, even if they do not voice an objection to the pastor.

Many Christian parents lean into their faith for support, finding prayer, Scripture, devotional reading, and even small groups to be particularly helpful. Spiritual activities can be fostered and shaped through pastoral support. For example, encouraging parents to pray before difficult conversations with their children may ease interactions, while instructing parents to see and love their child as God does, may shift their thoughts and feelings about their child. Contemplative prayer can be particularly helpful in teaching parents how to practice God's presence, even in reactive moments. Teaching parents how to meditate on Scripture and how to seek the Lord for the healing of those hurtful interactions with their child may also provide relief and guidance.

Some families will need help from professional counselors. Signs of significant depression and anxiety, poor functioning, family aggression, addictive patterns, and relational conflict, as well as other forms of psychological distress, indicate the church leader should refer the family to a mental health clinician. Before referring, pastors likely will want to vet clinicians to find those who are knowledgeable about and respectful of both gender and sexual identity and faith. Parents of GSD children tend to respond better when counselors share their values.

SECOND LEG OF THE JOURNEY: MAINTAINING SHIFTING RELATIONSHIPS

Given the potential for strong emotional reactions, it is no wonder that relational issues tend to arise. Just as Ryan and Tammy initially wondered if their son had chosen to come out as an act of rebellion or retaliation, many parents question what their child can and cannot choose. Parents may even believe this is some kind of willful disobedience toward them or their faith. Ian, like other GSD youth, felt rejected by his parents' strong emotional reactions, often falsely believing he'd have to deny his attractions and act like someone else to receive their love and approval. Some youth, therefore, may separate themselves from their parents as much as possible, but sometimes parents are the ones who separate from their children.

As parents attempt to carry this complex ambivalent emotional response to their child, often privately, emotions can be expressed in unexpected ways, often aimed at their partners, as Tammy and Ryan experienced. While parents may blame themselves for their child's GSD identity concerns, they may also blame their partner. Parents often reevaluate their values, relational and religious, and may come to different conclusions, such as one parent adopting a more affirmative position while the other parent leans into religious values. This polarization can appear as if one parent is siding with their child and the other is siding with their faith against the child, further straining family relationships.

Marital strain is exacerbated if parent-child triangulation occurs within the family system. Triangulation occurs when two family members (in this case a parent and the GSD child) ally against another family member instead of working together as a unit. The child is pulled into the parents' conflict, either feeling stuck in the middle or partnered with one parent while opposed to the other.[12] While some triangulation is normal, this kind of alignment can cause psychological, adjustment, and behavioral issues in the youth, or worsen already existing problems. This is particularly true when one of the family members brings God or faith into the triangulation as a way of "assigning blame, guilt, and sin through the invocation of God or claims of personal revelation."[13] Triangulation may lead to the teen emotionally cutting off one parent, the parents cutting off

---

[12]Cheryl Buehler and Deborah P. Welsh, "A Process Model of Adolescents' Triangulation into Parents' Marital Conflict: The Role of Emotional Reactivity," *Journal of Family Psychology* 23, no. 2 (April 2009): 167-80, www.doi.org/10.1037/a0014976.

[13]Chana Etengoff and Colette Daiute, "Family Members' Uses of Religion in Post–coming-out Conflicts with Their Gay Relative," *Psychology of Religion and Spirituality* 6, no. 1 (February 2014): 33-43, www.doi.org/10.1037/a0035198.supp (Supplemental).

one another, or a family member cutting off God, effectively ending relationships. Interestingly, the negative consequences of triangulation seem to occur even when parents are not being harsh or hostile to their child.

Pastors can help families overcome triangulation by bringing awareness and encouraging family members to talk directly to one another instead of talking about one another to a third party.[14] Encouraging family members to build functional relationships with each other, while instilling a sense of hopefulness grounded in reality, can help them to be less reactive and less polarized. Helping family members to grow in their own self-identity and set emotional boundaries will also reduce triangulation.[15]

Pastors also should be cautious about getting ensnared in this relational dynamic as it can end with the dissolution of the pastoral relationship with one or all parties. If pastors feel pulled to align with one family member against others, or learn they've been used as "evidence" or authority in family arguments, they need to work to step out of this triangulated position. Pastors should be careful not to side with one family member against another, always holding the entire family system as the primary focus of ministry.

SIX PRINCIPLES FOR ENGAGING WELL

Familial tensions may escalate to the point of breaking relationships, yet they don't necessarily have to do so. How can parents, like Ryan and Tammy, respond well in these conversations with Ian and even with each other? How can pastors step in to help these families? Here are six principles to help parents and pastoral caregivers navigate the many tensions that arise around family dynamics, faith beliefs, sexuality and gender identity, and related behavior through good listening and communication skills.[16]

---

[14]Anne F. Grizzle, "Family Therapy with the Faithful: Christians as Clients," in *Religion and the Family: When God Helps.*, ed. Laurel Arthur Burton (New York: Haworth, 1992), 139-62.

[15]As family members increase self-identity and set emotional boundaries, they grow in differentiation, which many family therapists see as the antidote for triangulation. Differentiation is the sense of being one's own self, with differing thoughts and feelings than others in one's relationships. It requires boundaries to determine self from others, reduces anxiety during relational conflict, and moves one to healthy interdependence in relationships.

[16]The source of the particular wording of five of these strategies is unknown, but the essence of these same approaches appears in many sources despite varied phrasing.

Listen with love. When parents and pastors listen with love, they show genuine interest in hearing the person's story—as the person experiences it, not as the listener thinks it is. This requires asking questions, perhaps to clarify what one's self-label means, what behaviors one is actually engaged in, how one holds faith and gender and sexual identity together, and then reflecting back what was said with the accompanying emotion. A good listener does not jump immediately to Scripture or theology, but rather waits to share personal beliefs and opinions for more appropriate moments. A good listener is able to hold the emotions, thoughts, and experiences of the other without feeling the need to exert control over another person.[17]

Uncover the untruths. Good listening and conversations assist families to uncover the untruths. Most people, like Tammy and Ryan, hold beliefs about GSD that they will read into relevant situations. There are numerous myths about GSDs (i.e., that they can choose their sexuality and gender, they are being willfully defiant, more prayer will change attractions, labels mean they are sexually active, and fulfillment only comes through marriage). GSD teens also may hold misbeliefs about their parents (i.e., that they are angry, will reject them, will hate them, will never understand, and are unwilling to compromise). Pastors facilitate communication, cooperation, and closeness by helping families identify and challenge these untruths.

Responding with respect. Responding with respect means holding the youth's personhood as primary regardless of what he or she might share or do. Personhood, gender, and sexual identity are not issues to be debated but rather are aspects of the self to which they have invited adults to speak. Thus, honoring the disclosure, as well as the invitation to journey with them is vital. Such honoring does not mean full agreement is necessary. However, convicted civility is. Convicted civility is the ability to give space to another even with disagreement and the ability to challenge with gentleness, truth, and confidence.[18]

---

[17]Henri J. M. Nouwen, *Bread for the Journey: A Daybook of Wisdom and Faith* (San Francisco: HarperOne, 2006), 98.

[18]Richard J. Mouw, *Uncommon Decency: Christian Civility in an Uncivil World* (Downers Grove, IL: InterVarsity Press, 2010), 11-14.

Not only is convicted civility crucial with GSD youth, but such a posture is also important in how church leaders relate to parents. Parents may have a variety of responses to their children, as will other church members who are watching from the sidelines. Pastors who respect parents' role as the parental authority in their children's lives and decisions, while also advising against rejection, aggression, and condemnation, are more likely to maintain their ability to walk with this family and speak into the youth's developmental identity process. Similarly, helping parishioners to engage with this same attitude of convicted civility transforms the church into a body of believers who can provide safety and support for this family along the way.

Support with safety. To support with safety, church leaders should consider and establish the boundaries needed to ensure physical, emotional, social, and spiritual safety without being overprotective or unrealistic. These boundaries might include developmentally appropriate dating behaviors, dress code, use of pronouns or alternate names, confidentiality, self-harm behaviors, counseling, and the like. Sometimes the boundaries in one place, like church, may be different from another place, like school. For example, disclosure may cause difficulties for the teen or the parents in their church group or in their relationship with great-grandparents, while being okay with friends. Be aware of how language contributes to a sense of safety. Derogatory or teasing language about GSD communicates hostility and lack of understanding. Commands like "stop it," "try harder," or even "pray more" suggest some kind of inadequacy in the youth, particularly because most have already tried those things unsuccessfully.

Remain in relationship. As with Ryan and Tammy, the desire to remain in relationship with their child is the primary motivation of most parents, often motivating them to address relational issues no matter how bad things get. Fortunately, family conflict does tend to resolve over time, even in families where the child was initially rejected. That is, most parents come to describe their relationship with their child as "okay," believing it would improve over time. Yarhouse and Zaporozhets found that anger and conflict in the parent-child relationship increase initially then subside, while emotional closeness, communication, engagement, authenticity, and acceptance initially declines then increases, with parents' protectiveness over their child growing over time. To facilitate this movement, pastors can teach and model how to both communicate and live out unconditional love with an unwavering commitment to the relationship (cf., 1 Cor 13:4-7). More importantly, helping families experience the free, gracious, enduring love of God (cf., Rom 8:31-39) will shape their relationships with one another.

Stay grounded in faith. As families navigate the tensions, conflicts, and uncertainties on this journey with their child, they are likely to find meaning and direction if they keep footing in faith, but this generally comes with some spiritual struggle. Through wrestling with God and faith, they often become a better parent, a better spouse, and a better person, as they grow in love, grace, and holiness. Pastors can foster this kind of spiritual transformation both in parents like Tammy and Ryan and in youth like Ian through intentional discipleship, the focus of the next leg of this journey.

THIRD LEG OF THE JOURNEY: GROWING IN FAITH

Given the emotional distress, ambiguous loss, religious challenge, and relational shifts that occur after disclosure, it is no wonder that the faith of both parents and GSD youth sometimes undergo tumultuous shifts as this journey proceeds. Most Christian parents report their faith in God grew deeper and stronger through this crisis of their child's disclosure, yet getting there often meant experiencing periods of anger, questioning, and even disbelief toward God. Some parents never return to faith.

Yarhouse and Zaporozhets describe three movements in parents' faith journey as related to their child's sexuality and gender.[19] First, early on, parents may wrestle with God, but many eventually will turn to prayer, Scripture reading, and their faith community for support. In prayer, they question, wrestle, plead, search, submit, and rest in God. Some parents turn to their churches for community and support, yet sometimes fail to find it there and seek out informal social networks or parachurch ministries. Other parents search the Scriptures for insights about the

---

[19]Yarhouse and Zaporozhets, *When Children Come Out*, 90-95.

rightness or wrongness of their beliefs about sexuality and gender as well as grace and relationships.

Second, most parents will reconsider their beliefs about gender and sexuality. While most hold traditional, orthodox Christian views, including that same-sex sexuality is a sin, about a third of them will shift these beliefs as they walk this journey with their child. Others report moving to a place of grace and acceptance in which they no longer attempt to change their child, largely because they find a way to hold the opposites of their beliefs about gender and sexuality together with a loving relationship with their child.

Third, through this journey, parents are watching how their faith community supports them and their child, and about 40% will end up moving to another church because of their discomfort and sometimes concern with this congregation's non-loving response to their family. Sometimes these observations and decisions happen even before the child "comes out" at church.

Building a congregational culture that cares for these families and helps them navigate along this journey is an important part of the ministry pastors provide to families like Ryan, Tammy, and Ian. Such an intentional church community, which will be discussed near the end of this chapter, is essential for more deliberate, personal discipleship with families. It is through discipleship that pastors walk this road with families helping them to deepen their relationships and faith alike.

HOLDING ENVIRONMENT FOR FAMILY DISCIPLESHIP

A healthy pastoral context for families is one in which family members experience being "held" during their collective journey together. If families are to arrive "safe and sound" at their destination, each member must be held well if they are to negotiate all sorts of adventurous conditions en route to being formed more into the image of Christ.

Figuratively, Christian communities hope to be "holding environments" where persons are safely engaged and securely attached to others as they navigate life. Being held within a safe and secure community is essential for any human journey but especially for persons and families navigating gender and sexual identity. Whether one is talking about the family or church contexts, this relational journey is called discipleship. German theologian Dietrich Bonhoeffer defines discipleship in relational terms.[20] For Bonhoeffer, discipleship is simply characterized as following Christ, as the first disciples followed Jesus. The disciples were relationally held by Christ, doing life together within his formational community.

Regrettably, discipleship in contemporary pastoral ministry or current Christian education can be reduced to an "informational project" only, as if head, heart, and body can be separated.[21] With GSD youth and their families, this approach can result in a diminished pastoral care that relies primarily on biblical exegesis and Christian accountability but without the relational holding environments that keep discipling healthy and effective. In info-only contexts, discipleship becomes synonymous with the life of the head and not the heart or the rest of the body.

Discipleship, like any aspect of pastoral care, attends to the whole person and encourages all disciples to attend to others holistically. For families navigating gender and sexual identity development, investing in "head discipleship" only can grow persons who grasp what is right and wrong propositionally, but they can lose the reality of being held in Christian community. Families who lose their holding environment in Christian community can also lose their ability to hold family members together. Learning to love God and by extension self and others is hindered by any approach that does not intentionally involve the whole person. Obedience to Christ, which Jesus said is the primary sign of growing love of God (Jn 14:15), can feel unsafe and insecure when conditions are not present for the whole life.

Whole-person discipleship occurs, alternatively, when families learn how to be held by Christian communities without shame. By extension, they learn how to hold other family members without shame because they are being held in the same way. They have a chance to experience and pass along love because fears are managed in securing relationships and trustworthy institutions. This whole-person discipleship is

---

[20] Dietrich Bonhoeffer, *The Cost of Discipleship* (New York: Macmillan, 1948).
[21] James K. A. Smith, *Desiring the Kingdom: Worship, Worldview, and Cultural Formation* (Grand Rapids, MI: Baker Academic, 2009), 18.

foundationally relational. Belonging is unquestioned, especially in times of threat or shame.

CHRISTIAN COMMUNITY AND FAMILY DISCIPLESHIP SPECIFICS

Ideally, whole-person discipleship becomes the context that families first experience in a Christian community and then practice at home. Christian teaching is enacted. During discipleship, tough questions are raised. Scripture is applied. Disagreements are honored. Traditions and liturgies are lived out. Differences are respected. Prayers are engaged. Love is lived out as worship of God becomes relational. Shame is actively countered with costly grace, which is Bonhoeffer's term for God's formational work in and through "life together" discipleship. All families navigate faith, sexuality, and gender development among their members, but those who are engaging in more diverse experiences especially require this whole person holding environment.

Community-based discipleship lays the relational foundation for family discipleship. Family discipleship is essential for maintaining healthy attachments that reduce fear and shame-based interactions that are so common for those navigating GSD identity development. Whole-person discipleship maintains an awareness of the quality of the holding environment when complex questions at the intersection of faith, sexuality, and gender inevitably arise. How do we hold same-sex sexuality and/or gender non-conformity in the light of faith? Where is God in all of this? Who is God in all of this? What should we expect from our faith during this experience? What does "following" look like in this context for all of us? How do we hold each other when there are so many worries and fears? What do we believe about healing? Can we tell anyone? Where does all this shame come from? We believe God loves everyone, but why don't we feel loved? How do we love one another when we cannot agree on important values and issues? These questions are rooted deeply in foundational beliefs about self, God, sin, grace, and the world. Discipling families with GSD identity experiences requires safe relational space and trustworthy pastoral facilitation for effective exploration of emotionally laden questions such as these.

Available and responsive relational engagement and pastoral facilitation happen together. One is never without the other in healthy discipleship of families or family members. "Holding environments" need both for the growth of secure relationships that mitigate shame and fear and promote views of God and others that are positive, loving, and caring. In our research we have found that the questions for families that arise at this developmental intersection are seldom settled once and for all time. Even a "coming out" event in a family, often a precipitation for family questioning, is seldom a one-time happening. Instead, it tends to be the beginning of a process in which families must decide again and again how to hold one another. Patience is foundational for discipleship with families.

Effective discipling necessitates holding families in complex moments and inviting them to follow Christ together. What are some helpful suggestions for pastoral leaders who patiently disciple families in unsettling times? The following list offers suggestions that have been gleaned through years of listening to GSD individuals and their experiences with pastoral caregiving.

1. Know Scripture and the Christian tradition but prepare for work with families navigating GSD identity concerns by seeking out resources by Christian counselors and researchers. Seek out "fellow traveler" Christians who can communicate their personal and family experiences related to gender and sexuality.

2. Be present by listening as a knowledgeable pastoral caregiver as families voice and potentially wrestle with questions and feelings. Hear and understand without judgment. Don't assume that pastoral knowledge or advice will be adequate to hold families together.

3. Help families remember the God who has held them in the past and is holding them even now. Remind families that God is not surprised by their challenges and has already been at work. He is present in every moment, whether invited or not.

4. Reassure families that it is often hard in challenging moments to "find God," even though he never leaves or forsakes. Families can become caught up in all that threatens them, forgetting that God is still "in the picture."

5. Teach families about the value of practicing the discipline of lament when in questioning periods. Lament is a prayer practice consisting of four parts: crying out to God, stating one's complaint, asking one's request, and recalling who God is.[22] Negative emotions related to God, others, and even oneself are common, and lament helps people express these in a healthy way. The ministry leader should model how to hold negative emotions, while also holding family members. Assist in normalizing negative affect, even toward God, while encouraging positive coping.
6. Remind families that this is a day-to-day process that can bring them closer to God, even when he is working in ways that they cannot see.
7. Reflect with families about how they pray with and for one another. Some family members may need to understand that prayers intended to confront behaviors or disown experience are seldom viewed as helpful. Anger and disappointment should be reserved for time alone working out these things in personal prayer.
8. Mentor family members in discursive and contemplative prayer. Both are essential for formative ministry with families during challenging times, but many remain unfamiliar with contemplative forms in contemporary Protestant communities of faith. This is unfortunate because some of the skills related to being held as well as holding oneself and others are cultivated by regular contemplative practices, which facilitate long-term acceptance of difficult situations.

Mobilize compassionate community resources that can come alongside families during difficult days. With the permission of the family, other church families or other pastoral and counseling professionals can serve as short- or longer-term support. As the experience of GSD children in Christian families has become a more common experience, local or online networks of parents supporting each other to love well may provide important ministry connections for church leaders to

---

[22]Kelly M. Kapic, *Embodied Hope: A Theological Meditation on Pain and Suffering* (Downers Grove, IL: IVP Academic, 2017), 36-38, 40.

find and utilize. Individuals negotiating development at the intersection of faith and gender and sexual identities can perceive Christian communities as cultures that are not available or responsive in securing ways. Intersectional questions are complex in any context, but faith communities are viewed as speaking for God. When discipling provides a healthy holding environment, a view of God is cultivated that promotes a secure attachment to Christ and His body—the church (Col 1:24; Eph 1:22-23) even as individuals are formed more into the image of Christ. Unfortunately, a poor holding environment invites families and family members into insecure experiences that distort who they are, who the church is, and who God is. Discipleship is never one-sided—the growth of believers impacts other believers, even those who are facilitating the discipleship. Christian communities grow in faith, as members provide the opportunity for others to see the sanctifying process of God contextualized in their lives. For this reason, the testimonies across time of families negotiating gender and sexual identity are vital for being the church in contemporary culture, although many Christian communities tend to avoid or dismiss these shared testimonies among families in their congregation. Consequently, in many Christian communities today, there exists a lack of vision and little insight into the work of God in the families of GSD individuals. Listening to GSD individuals over the years leaves one with the following conclusion. Churches are seldom viewed consistently as safe havens or secure bases for whole person discipleship. More often the perception is (true or not) that churches prefer families and their members to either keep this complicated intersection as part of a testimony of past healing or "appropriately" concealed and silent. Sadly, to the degree this perception is true, both those who need holding and those who should be doing the holding in faith communities suffer. Their view of God and his sanctifying grace is constrained and restricted without the opportunity to view the formative work of the Holy Spirit in the lives of persons and families negotiating faith, sexuality, and gender.

THE INTENTIONAL CONGREGATIONAL COMMUNITY

How then do churches become safe havens and secure bases for families on this journey? By simply being intentional. A congregational holding environment is a discipling community that is intentionally designed to be secure, relational, and formational.[23] These discipleship ingredients, when mixed together in a trinitarian theological culture, create a synergistic communal climate for identity development and meaning-making related to faith, gender, and sexuality for both parents and youth. Shaping the congregation's culture and moving them to this kind of intentional community should be one of the pastor's primary responsibilities in caring for families.

Intentionally secure. Intentionally secure communities ensure the physical, social, psychological, and spiritual safety of their members. To create a predictable and trustworthy atmosphere that reduces anxieties and fear-based ways of being with one another, congregations can minimize or remove whatever may create a sense of rejection, threat, or shame. For example, language, judgment, stereotypes, prejudice, and unnecessary boundaries that disrupt attachment-based relating should be challenged. Physical facilities and housing plans for church activities may need to be adjusted so that all may worship without feeling singled out or stigmatized. For example, can at least one restroom be designated a family or gender-neutral restroom so individuals can feel safe using the facilities? Can room assignments for summer camp be made based more on friend groups where children and parents are already comfortable with a particular GSD student rather than strictly on biological sex? Policies and procedures can be pre-established so that people don't feel like a "special case," with fairness being the goal for maintaining community. Practical caregiving, including connecting people to resources for housing, medical care, mental health, and information can be freely given as a part of the pastoral response. Finally, confidentiality and privacy are community values. Disclosures of the family's story within the church, even as a prayer request, should be the decision of the family.

Intentionally relational. Intentional, relationally secure communities are sources of hospitality, compassion, and friendship. Members know how to be present, accessible, and practice inclusion, care, appreciation,

---

[23]Janet B. Dean et al., "Becoming an Intentional Church Community: Relationships, Security, and Discipleship in Sexual Identity and Faith Development," *Christian Education Journal* 18, no. 2 (August 2021): 232-51, www.doi.org/10.1177/0739891320948882.

and encouragement in the lives of others. Walking in grace, church members value people even when their views are in tension, holding love, holiness, truth, and grace together in all they do. Friendship is one of the core values of these communities, and members are honored to share in one another's journeys.

Intentionally formational. Intentionally formational communities understand that faith development requires a relational and secure church community which grows disciples in Christlikeness across time. These communities provide space for GSD youth and their families to share their stories and patience as they "sort through the gray areas of life" within a community who loves them.[24] This sorting may be particularly tricky for GSD individuals and their families as meaning-making at the intersection of faith and sexuality/gender is more complicated than with either alone. This kind of discipleship strategy engages people where they are in their spiritual journey by explicitly and implicitly addressing faith, sexuality, and personhood to help them grow in self-acceptance and by extending grace to the self. The focus is on "whole-person," attachment-based discipleship, intentionally designed to form a certain kind of person who is developing into the image of Christ in all aspects of identity and life.

JOURNEYING IN HOLY LOVE

In many churches and families, traditional orthodox Christian beliefs about gender and sexuality are experienced as opposed to the identity and experiences of GSD youth. Many people believe holding this tension between standards and love seems impossible, although this is exactly what pastoral leaders and families are called to do. Indeed, discipleship is dependent on being able to hold fast the relational conditions for holy standards and love.

Exiting off the road to one side or the other causes us to miss truly loving these teens and families. Nazarene theologian Wynkoop illustrates this with a coin: "When holiness and love are put together, the analogy of the two sides of a coin would be closer to the truth. Neither

---

[24] Andrew P. Marin, *Us versus Us: The Untold Story of Religion and the LGBT Community* (Colorado Springs, CO: NavPress, 2016), 81.

side can be both sides at the same time. Sides are not to be equated, but the obverse side is as essential to its existence as the face. Love is the essential inner character of holiness, and holiness does not exist apart from love. That is how close they are, and in a certain sense they can be said to be the same thing."[25]

We describe this road as the Way of Holy Love, based on the theology of John Wesley.[26] As pastors model this approach of holy love, they create an atmosphere wherein healing and growth can occur, and they help parents to do the same. As parents stay on the path, living in that tension of truth and grace, along with holiness and love, they provide a stable, caring holding environment for their GSD teen to learn to hold their gender and sexuality identity together with their faith, in grace and acceptance, as they grow more and more into the image of Christ.

---

[25] Mildred Bangs Wynkoop, *A Theology of Love: The Dynamic of Wesleyanism* (Kansas City, MO: Beacon Hill, 2015), 30.
[26] Kenneth J. Collins, *The Theology of John Wesley: Holy Love and the Shape of Grace* (Nashville: Abingdon, 2007).

7

DOMESTIC VIOLENCE AND CHURCH MINISTRY

Darby A. Strickland

Andrew pleaded with his pastor for help, "I am worried about my wife. If she is not angry with me, she is riddled with anxiety and out of her mind. We struggled for months, but she was out of control last night. One minute, we were fine—the next, she shoved me against the wall. I need you to tell her to calm down and work on respecting me." The pastor asked, "What do you think is going on with her?" Andrew spent the next hour talking about all of Hannah's faults and all the ways that he felt mistreated by her. Agreeing to help, the pastor met with Hannah and asked her what had led her to be physically aggressive with Andrew. Hannah looked down, tears filled her face, and she struggled to find words. He reassured her that he wanted to help and asked what had happened. Hannah began to tell an entirely different version of events. She said that Andrew has been irritable, constantly criticizing her. That day, she had spent too much at the grocery store, so Andrew told her she could not "waste more" on the gas needed to see her parents. Andrew then blocked her and raised his fist inches from her face, so she pushed him out of the way. This was not a one-off incident. Hannah related that Andrew first physically abused her many years ago.

Andrew and Hannah's story shows the complexity of marriage counseling when aggression is part of the story. Pastors regularly encounter distressed marriages. Sometimes, what needs addressing may be apparent. For example, issues with irresponsible spending or pornography use may be obvious. Other times, with couples like Andrew and Hannah, the facets of the conflict are harder to discover, and discerning how to help may be equally difficult.

Suppose the pastor had acted on Andrew's account without first speaking separately with Hannah. In that case, he might have met with them as a couple, asking Hannah to respect Andrew more. However, time with Hannah alone revealed Andrew's history of physically abusing Hannah. The pastor learned that Andrew restricted whom Hannah could see and how often, and he would often corner her in a room, berating her for hours. A wise church leader will understand these abusive behaviors and seek to connect each spouse with wise counselors trained in addressing domestic violence to ensure safety.

This pastor was fortunate to get a pretty good picture of what was happening from Hannah. Many victims do not understand that they are enduring abuse, minimize the harm, and think of the controlling harsh behavior as normal. Some want to avoid judgment or, worse, worry that their disclosure will get back to their spouse, sparking more abuse. Victims minimize abuse for many possible reasons. Abusers may portray themselves as godly, blame the harmed party, and divert attention away from their abusive behaviors. Some abusers (usually a male, but not always) are able to obtain favorable views from fellow church members and hold leadership roles in churches but act in cruel, controlling, and abusive ways with their own family.

RECOGNIZING ABUSE IN THE CHURCH MINISTRY

Pastors are not the only ones challenged in discerning if abuse is occurring. Many people who know the couple fail to identify the presence of abuse. Several reasons account for this. First, abuse happens in secret, out of sight. As such, victims often do not understand that they are enduring abuse and, therefore, do not talk about the reality of their situation. Second, like Andrew, abusers often justify their actions, hide them, blame the harmed party, and deflect attention from their behaviors. Third, competing accounts make it hard to know who to believe. Was Andrew or Hannah providing a more accurate portrayal of events? Or was a combination of both accounts the most truthful? Fourth, the church's high view of marriage often pressures Christians to solve problems quickly, bypassing essential discoveries about the extent of abusive behavior. Fifth, abuse is not suspected because many are unaware of its prevalence.

Sometimes, church leaders have a hard time believing that the people they serve could engage in abuse. A 2018 Lifeway survey showed that more than 30% of Protestant pastors believe physical and sexual violence does not occur within their churches. Unfortunately, studies have shown that Christian women are abused roughly at the same rate as those outside the church.[1] Just under 15% of women (14.8%) and 4% of men in the United States have been injured due to intimate partner violence, including rape, physical violence, or stalking by an intimate partner.[2] The only difference is that Christian women, on average, stay three and a half years longer with an abusive partner and are more likely to return to an abusive relationship than those outside the church.[3] While men and women can both be victims of domestic abuse, "there are important differences between male violence against women and female violence against men, namely the amount, severity and impact. Women experience higher rates of repeated victimization and are much more likely to be seriously hurt or killed than male victims of domestic abuse."[4] Sadly, these statistics reveal a devastating reality about the prevalence of victims and perpetrators in churches. This chapter focuses on physical abuse that is patterned and fueled by coercive control, the most dangerous type of domestic violence. A victim who is being physically abused will most

---

[1] Kimber Huff, "Domestic Abuse: 4 Things Pastors and Churches Need to Know," *Baptist Churches of New England*, August 16, 2021, www.bcne.net/news/domestic-abuse-4-things-pastors-and-churches-need-to-know.

[2] "Domestic Violence Statistics," accessed April 23, 2024, National Domestic Violence Hotline, www.thehotline.org/stakeholders/domestic-violence-statistics.

[3] Huff, "Domestic Abuse."

[4] "Domestic Abuse Is a Gendered Crime," accessed April 23, 2024, Women's Aid, www.womensaid.org.uk/Information-support/What-is-domestic-abuse/Domestic-abuse-is-a-gendered-crime/.

likely experience several forms of abuse. Being able to identify different types of abuse is vital.

TYPES OF DOMESTIC VIOLENCE AND ABUSE

Domestic abuse takes on many forms. All forms are driven by coercive control, each using a different tactic (i.e., emotional, spiritual, financial).

1. *Physical abuse* refers to abuse that harms the body. It takes on two forms: physical and sexual. Examples include hitting, pulling hair, pinning down, throwing objects, biting, choking, refusing to provide medical care, threatening with a weapon, harming pets, and damaging personal property.

2. *Sexual abuse* includes forcing unwanted sex acts, filming without consent, controlling reproduction, relentless pursuit, injuring the partner during sex, performing a sex act on someone who is sleeping or intoxicated, and degrading comments about the spouse's performance or body.

3. *Emotional abuse* is characterized by contemptuous and harmful words or actions that disrespect the image of God in one's spouse. Nonphysical forms of abuse are more challenging to discern. While many marriages have had an occasion for contemptuous words or attempts at manipulation, abusive marriages are *characterized by* contempt and coercive control. Examples include verbal aggression, demeaning or degrading words, threats, berating the partner, creating confusion, and controlling resources like food, cars, or money. It also includes isolating, monitoring, spying on the victim, or enforcing extreme demands about the cleanliness of the home or care of the children.

4. *Spiritual abuse* is similar to emotional abuse but involves coercion of one's spouse, misusing faith, doctrine, or a leadership role to manipulate. Examples include a husband subjugating his wife by demanding submission, using headship to suppress criticism or misapplying Scripture to punish or spank a wife, dictating her clothing, food, or friendship choices, and usurping her God-given freedom (Gen 1:26; Ps 8:6).

Whether physical abuse is present, know that all types of abuse cause significant harm to a victim and must be addressed. Further, since physical abuse can start at any time in an abusive marriage, do not wait until emotional abuse becomes physical to provide protection and care.

Like many types of sinful behavior, the severity of abuse varies from mild to extreme. It is critical to be accurate and careful in assessing the types of abuse and the level of danger. You can call your local domestic violence shelter or consult a competent counselor with domestic violence experience to help you. Few ministry leaders have training in detecting domestic violence, but given time, all congregations will have incidences of domestic violence.

GOD'S CALL TO HIS CHURCH: DEFEND VICTIMS

Victims should not be left in fear and without help because the church fails to see or know how to help.[5] God is clearly on the side of the abused, as in Psalm 56. There is no specific word for domestic violence in Scripture, so many people refer to oppression in Scripture as a guide. Scripture interprets the Hebrew *'osheq* as oppression or extortion (Ezek 22:7, 12). It almost always involves a more powerful person in a hierarchical culture controlling or harming the poor, fatherless, or victims of crime for their own gain. Oppression is a helpful biblical lens to understand marriages that are coercive, exploitative, and domineering. Recently, the culture has used this word when discussing critical theory, but that is not what this chapter has in view in using this term. Further, modern English tends to interpret oppressors as evil and unredeemable. We know as Christians that no one is irredeemable. As we discuss domestic violence, we will use the terms abuser, oppressor, offender, or perpetrator.

This is a complex problem. Abusers can be dangerous, harming the people in their family in multiple ways. Those being harmed should be secured and defended by those who follow Jesus. Readers should be assured that while the road to redemption is difficult, all abusers can find

---

[5]God's care for the oppressed are expressed in Gen 16; 1 Sam 25:29, 39; Ps 146:7-9; Is 1:17; Jer 50:33-34; Zech 7:10; Lk 4:18-19.

redemption and become free of their abusive behaviors. Offenders can be redeemed, but research indicates they often (some research says usually[6]) do not follow through on repentance over the long term. Consequently, domestic violence is especially entrapping to families, and great wisdom is needed in how to respond and protect those who are being harmed.

The church can become a refuge for the violent and the victim, where they can confidently seek help and receive wise and protective counsel. Offenders face a danger of a different kind. Their sin has a stranglehold on their lives, leaving them far from the Lord. God repeatedly asks his people in Scripture to work for justice and righteousness because God cares about the vulnerable *and* the sinner. However, the Lord's heart is particularly concerned for the vulnerable. Christians are told to be people who do justice (Mic 6:8). Scripture calls God's people to confront oppression but also to provide protection and care for the vulnerable (Is 1:17). Ezekiel speaks of the watchman appointed by God, who is responsible for the safety of the lives entrusted to him (Ezek 33:6). To further highlight the Lord's priorities, Jesus uses his first words of public ministry to talk about how he came to care for the vulnerable and oppressed (Lk 4:18-19). Jesus identifies with the powerless throughout his ministry, takes up their cause, and stands against those who harm the vulnerable. This is who Christians are called to be: deliverers and protectors. The body of Christ cannot allow abuse to be unaddressed.

The church can protect the vulnerable in many ways. First, leaders can educate the church on domestic abuse and what God's Word says about it. Second, they can also care for congregants who are being abused, taking all allegations of abuse seriously and protecting victims. When domestic violence enters the church, so do the legal, ethical, psychological, and medical problems. Utilize wise resources, such as trained counselors, domestic abuse advocates, and legal and medical professionals who have experience and know how to help.

---

[6]Beth M. Costa et al. "Longitudinal Predictors of Domestic Violence Perpetration and Victimization: A Systematic Review," *Aggression and Violent Behavior* 24 (September 2015): 261-72, https://doi.org/10.1016/j.avb.2015.06.001.

DYNAMICS OF DOMESTIC VIOLENCE IN MARRIAGE

God designed marriage to be a beautiful picture of Christ's love for his bride, the church. When reflecting on how Jesus relates to his redeemed people, Jesus is seen as faithful, sacrificial, honest, accepting, honoring, caring, and serving. Abusive spouses corrupt God's design in the worst way, turning everything into its opposite. Abuse in marriage is characterized by coercive, controlling behaviors wherein one spouse seeks to dominate the other for personal advantage. Various punishments (physical, emotional, and spiritual) are used. God's opposition to oppression is clear (cf. Ex 3:7–9; Ps 9:9; Is 14:3-4; Zech 9:8).

Many people wrongly believe abuse is an anger problem, that abusers act out because they struggle with self-control. This is a dangerous misconception. Looking at examples from Scripture of people who use violence, like King Saul, Haman, or King Herod, not all perpetrators are out of control but instead use violence to try to maintain control.

When abuse occurs in a marriage, it is vital to understand if the abusive behavior benefits the offender and puts the victim at risk. Some abusers are strategic and plan their harm. Others instinctively learn that having a tantrum gets them what they want. In the case of Hannah and Andrew, after beating Hannah several years ago, Andrew only needed to put a fist in Hannah's face to get his way. The threat of violence was enough to change Hannah's behavior.

Perpetrator traits. Certain biological and mental health conditions predict perpetration, including trauma victims, childhood abuse, autism, ADHD, OCD, depression, substance abuse, brain injury, poverty, and antisocial or narcissistic personality characteristics.[7] That does not mean that everyone with those characteristics will be a perpetrator, but if you have a family with indicators of violence and these factors, then the risk is higher. Similarly, people raised in homes with domestic abuse are more likely to become perpetrators of abuse. These correlations *never* excuse abuse, but they help equip church leaders to understand what is happening in these families.

A co-occurring diagnosis is not an excuse for a perpetrator's destructive behavior. Some people with disorders might be prone to abuse

---

[7]Costa et al. "Longitudinal Predictors," 261-72.

their spouse to create the order that alleviates their anxiety. While someone might be diagnosed with a disorder, that does not account for the totality of what is occurring.

Recognize that two things can be true. First, someone can struggle with substance abuse or be diagnosed with a psychological disorder *and* perpetrate abuse. Abusive behavior should not be excused because its perpetrator struggles with other issues, but the care for them should consider these factors.

Second, people who perpetrate abuse are also made in the image of God; therefore, providing care for their whole person, not only their abuse, would be a loving approach. We want care for them that addresses their struggles, suffering, and faith. However, the risk of injury and priority of care for their victims dictates that their abusive behavior is the priority.

Coercive control. Abusive spouses who are coercively controlling often prioritize their own desires so that the primary purpose of their spouse's existence is to fulfill them. When their spouse fails to meet their rules and expectations, that spouse suffers the consequences. Here are a few of Andrew's demands: Hannah can only talk to her mom for twenty minutes every two weeks. She cannot use a debit card; she only has the cash she is allotted. Sex needs to occur daily, no matter how she feels or her other responsibilities. When Hannah could not provide Andrew with sex daily, he would wake her up at 2:00 a.m. and lecture her sometimes for hours until she gave in. Any one of these activities would be an indicator of coercion and control found in domestic violence.

Consider if the relationship has power imbalances, such as income disparity, control of assets, physical size, leverage in decision-making, disability or mental illness, and interference with outside relationships. They may take time to discover, but listen for persistent patterns that characterize a power imbalance in the relationship, which are exploited through coercion. At the same time, never dismiss single acts of violence that indicate abuse, like choking, beating, or rape.

Listen carefully. Remember Andrew cornering Hannah and her pushing past him in our example. Andrew tried to claim that Hannah was physically abusing him. However, she was reacting to being physically trapped. Research has shown that self-defense is usually the first or second motivation of women who have used violence against a spouse.[8] Was she wrong to push him? Hannah pushed Andrew because she was reacting to his threat of physical violence. We need to understand what each person's behavior accomplishes. Andrew threatens to punch Hannah to maintain control, while Hannah pushes Andrew to flee violence.

When any reports of harm or violence are reported, it is wise to consult a professional who can do a comprehensive abuse screening. We would not want to either minimize or dismiss a victim's cry for help, nor would we want to label someone as a perpetrator of abuse wrongly. Domestic abuse is both a hidden reality and a huge indictment, so it is wise to rely on others who are skilled at making careful assessments when the situation lacks clarity.

Addressing factors that might wrongly divert attention away from the abuse is essential. Alcohol and drug use are not responsible for the abuse. While a spouse might be more abusive when using substances, the abuse is still purposefully targeting one's spouse. Bancroft, an expert on domestic violence, concludes, "Abusive men are masters of excuse-making. In this respect, they are like substance abusers who believe that everyone and everything except them is responsible for their actions. When not blaming their partners, they blame stress, alcohol, childhood, children, bosses, or insecurities. More importantly, they feel entitled to make these excuses."[9] Be aware of this tendency to blame shift and stay focused on how they harm their spouse. The primary goal is to secure counseling that addresses existing violence and substance abuse.

Male victims. Male victims face different challenges. Many men are reluctant to report abuse because they are embarrassed, fear they will not be believed, or have been ridiculed by friends and family for saying they are victims of abuse. Community supports, like local shelters, are not set up to provide care for men, so they have less access to resources. Men

---

[8] Julia C. Babcock, "Distinguishing Subtypes of Mutual Violence in the Context of Self-Defense: Classifying Types of Partner Violent Couples Using a Modified Conflict Tactics Scale," *Journal of Family Violence* 34, no. 7 (October 2019): 687-96, https://doi.org/10.1007/s10896-018-0012-2.
[9] Lundy Bancroft, *Why Does He Do That?: Inside the Minds of Angry and Controlling Men* (New York: Berkley Books, 2002), 71.

fear that police will assume they are the perpetrator, so men are reluctant to engage law enforcement.

Female perpetrators are less common than males, and roughly half of female perpetrators are motivated by self-defense.[10] Though rare, you may still have a female perpetrator in your congregation.

Recidivism is high, and treatment outcomes are poor. Research on perpetrators of criminal abuse indicates several difficult realities. One is that recidivism is high, so even if the perpetrator does not intend to harm again, and even if they attend counseling, most re-engage in harm.[11] This means that when domestic violence is happening, the potential for harm is a real danger, and the chances that a perpetrator will be able to stop harming their partner/children is unsure at best. This is why living separately and safety planning are generally recommended, at least for a season of treatment.

Treatment research for patterned violence has been stubbornly resistant to good outcomes. Professional treatments over a long time (two or more years) are superior to no treatment.[12] Often, limited resources require a mixture of individual and group or team-based approaches for long-term treatment. This is why it is critical to get perpetrators in counseling before violence becomes patterned or the abuse escalates to a criminal threshold. There are resources for Christian men who are ready to take ownership of their abusive behaviors and surrender themselves fully to the Lord.[13] However, here, too, it takes a substantial amount of time for perpetrators to repent of coercion and love sacrificially. This means you cannot count on counseling to be quick and effective for a family. When you need to find treatment for an intimate partner abuser, you will need to get someone who is experienced

---

[10] Haley Boxall, Christopher Dowling, and Anthony Morgan, "Female Perpetrated Domestic Violence: Prevalence of Self-defense and Retaliatory Violence," *Trends and Issues in Crime and Criminal Justice* 584 (January 2020): 1-17.

[11] Aine Travers et al., "The Effectiveness of Interventions to Prevent Recidivism in Perpetrators of Intimate Partner Violence: A Systematic Review and Meta-Analysis," *Clinical Psychology Review* 84, no. 1 (March 2021): 101974, https://doi.org/10.1016/j.cpr.2021.101974.

[12] Travers et al., "The Effectiveness of Interventions."

[13] For Christian Resources that address male perpetrators wisely, see Chis Moles' work at www.menofpeace.org/for-men and *Caring for Families Caught in Domestic Abuse: A Guide toward Protection, Refuge, and Hope*, ed. Chris Moles (Greensboro, NC: New Growth, 2023).

and capable of working with this type of client. Everyone is different, so the best approach must be tailored to the image-bearer sitting in front of you and bring the hope of the life-transforming gospel with it.

IMPACT OF VIOLENCE ON VICTIMS

Living in fear of one's spouse has many consequences. Since people are embodied souls, abuse affects both body and soul. Victims' bodies often sound the alarm that something is off before they consciously know they are being abused. Victims tend to have panic attacks, headaches, chronic illnesses, depression, stomach problems, PTSD, insomnia, and anxiety. Hannah did not understand that Andrew waking her up at night was sexual coercion, but she began having panic attacks at bedtime. Many victims will ask for help to deal with these reactions, not the abuse itself.

Gaslighting leads to confusion. Some perpetrators gaslight their spouses for the abuse they perpetrate, saying things like, "If you weren't so stupid, I would not get angry!" "That never happened, you are delusional!" "You are being ridiculously oversensitive!" or "Look what you made me do!" These statements leave victims believing that the abuse is their fault, feeling disoriented about what happened, and questioning their memories or perceptions. Abusers need to confuse and disorient their spouses to dominate them. This confusion keeps victims from comprehending what is happening to them and confuses their communication, often causing others to question their credibility.

Spiritual abuse leads to spiritual struggle. It has been observed that some Christian victims are told by their abusive spouses that God is displeased with them for past or current sins, and thus, they believe that the abuse is part of God's punishment. If this type of spiritual abuse is present, victims tend to have trouble believing God hears their prayers and cares about their safety. They can struggle to see male authority figures as safe and different from their abuser. These factors can make pastoral encouragement difficult. Sometimes, inviting mature women leaders into conversations puts a victim at ease. Checking with victims about how the abuse impacts their relationship with the Lord and authority figures will prevent church leaders from contributing to further harm.

Abuse leads to emotional struggle. Victims will also have a variety of emotional responses. They might feel used or owned by their spouse, isolated, detached, afraid, unworthy, angry, despairing, or feel like they are losing their mind. If they have been stalked, they might wrestle with extreme fear, even paranoia, long after the abuse has ended. Some victims cope with their intense distress with destructive practices like substance abuse, self-harm, over- or under-eating, or sleeping too much. Many abusers work to isolate the family socially, leaving victims without support and struggling with loneliness. Victims might miss church meetings and avoid church invitations.

Abuse leads to health problems. Finally, domestic violence is linked to many public health issues, including physical illnesses and injuries or missed workdays. Common health problems people experience include chronic pain, hypertension, sexually transmitted infections (sometimes leading to cervical cancer or infertility), gastrointestinal problems, and sleeping and eating disorders.[14] As mentioned earlier, domestic violence can be fatal, with lethal injuries inflicted either intentionally or resulting from physical violence.

INTERVENTION STEPS AND PROCESS FOR FAMILIES OF DOMESTIC VIOLENCE

Step 1: Discern if domestic violence has occurred. Church leaders may suspect something is not quite right when a person or couple comes in for help with some of the signs listed above. The prevalence of abuse should cause church leaders to screen for abuse whenever they engage in couple counseling ministry. Abuse is typically not fully disclosed, and this makes identifying it difficult. Even when victims know they need help, they tend to be discreet, often testing the waters by offering partial information to see how the church leader responds.

Talk to potential victims alone to protect them from potential retribution. One approach is to share some concerns based on observations. Say something like, "Some of the struggles you share make me concerned

---

[14]Kavita Alejo, "Long-Term Physical and Mental Health Effects of Domestic Violence," *Themis: Research Journal of Justice Studies and Forensic Science* 2, no. 1 (May 2014): 83-84, https://doi.org/10.31979/THEMIS.2014.0205.

that someone is harming you." Alternatively, "The argument you shared with me made me concerned for you. What is it like when your spouse is angry?" Give space for them to respond. If they begin to disclose abuse, ask follow-up questions. Another approach might be equally as helpful. The conversation can start by saying, "Sadly, domestic abuse is common, so I regularly ask about it." Preferably, "Before I speak into marriages, I regularly screen for severe marital problems to ensure I am not missing anything. Can I ask you a few questions?" Most victims will struggle with thinking that their situation rises to the level of abuse, so it is better to ask questions that do not use the word *abuse*. Allow people to answer to the level of detail that makes them comfortable.

Here are a few basic screening questions:

- Have you ever been threatened or physically hurt in this relationship?
- Have you ever been an unwilling participant in a sexual act?
- Do you ever feel fearful around your spouse?
- Do you have the freedom to be yourself, make decisions, give your input, and say no to things?
- Have you ever been touched by your spouse in a way that made you uncomfortable?
- How can you tell when your spouse is angry? Be specific. What does it look like? What is said? Done?
- When discussing hard things, how is disagreement expressed (i.e., mocking, walking away, rolling eyes, hovering, or throwing things)?
- What happens when you try to share a differing opinion?
- Does your spouse ever ignore you? If so, for how long and when?
- What happens if you let him/her down?
- Do you feel pressure to do things you do not want to do? Sexually?
- Does your spouse remind you of times that you sinned against him/her? When? How?[15]

---

[15]Darby A. Strickland, "Appendices: Basic Abuse Screening Questions," in *Caring for Families Caught in Domestic Abuse: A Guide toward Protection, Refuge, and Hope*, ed. Chris Moles (Greensboro, NC: New Growth, 2023), 202-4.

As you ask these questions, resist promising that the information shared will be kept a secret. Consider the legal imperative to report child abuse or lethal danger to authorities. However, do ask: "What do you need?" "Who have you talked with?" "Can I help you get support?" "How can I pray?" Try to portray sadness instead of shock at their responses.

Remind them that God did not design marriage to be a place of domination and that they are courageous for exposing these things. Feel free to ask follow-up questions that will yield concrete stories. When there is marital conflict, the temptation is often to work on looking for a solution to the problem. Hence, lots of content questions tend to be asked. To discover abuse, questions need to be framed in such a way as to reveal how the argument or fight looks and sounds. Seek to formulate questions that expose the narrative of the abuse rather than seek to solve the problem.[16]

Do not press them for answers when victims are not ready to disclose. In fact, when questioned about a bruise, many victims will claim an accident. Simply remind them that you are here for them if they want to talk about anything or need help. You might consider talking with a knowledgeable female church leader to see if she might ask the woman to spend some time alone to listen to any concerns.

Studies show that when a Christian woman seeks help in an abusive marriage, she ordinarily consults either her pastor or a Christian woman in the congregation first. This first disclosure is critical; research consistently demonstrates that the advice of the first person a victim tells will, in considerable measure, determine her next steps.[17] Therefore, how the problem is framed at this juncture is critical. Christian victims are often told marital conflict is a submission problem or they are overreacting. It is essential to highlight the gravity of their spouse's sinful actions against them. Remember, abuse stems from a desire for control and domination. Telling victims to serve their spouse better will only feed their spouse's

---

[16]For an extensive listing of discovery questions, see Darby A. Strickland, *Is It Abuse?: A Biblical Guide to Identifying and Discovering Domestic Abuse* (Philipsburg, NJ: P&R, 2020), 144-45, 172-74, 199-204, 228-29, 245-46.

[17]Catherine Holtmann, Barbara Fisher-Townsend, and Steve McMullin, "Bibliographies on Violence and Religion," Strand Three of the MCRI Project (Religion and Domestic Violence), accessed April 23, 2024, http://religionanddiversity.ca/media/uploads/projects_and_results/biblio_and_case_law/strand_three_violence_and_religion_phase_1.pdf.

entitlements and lead victims to believe the abuse is their fault. Even if the victim's responses become more sanctified over time, the abuse will not stop without a fundamental change in the oppressor.

Step 2: Immediate care. *Address victim safety first.* When it is determined that abuse is present, the church must never lose sight of the safety of a victim. *Any* intervention or confrontation of the perpetrator can potentially increase the level of danger. Safety screening can be done by a ministry leader the victim trusts. There are apps such as "My Plan App" that are tools that provide a well-researched and effective safety assessment meant to be used by victims and their support systems.[18] A formal safety assessment and plan[19] should be conducted by a trained professional (police, domestic violence shelters, or counselors experienced with abuse). Having the victim see a counselor and involve a victim advocate is wise. Victim advocates can be located through your local shelter or a Christian ministry like Called to Peace.[20] They are experts trained to understand coercive control, assess for danger, create a safety plan, and coordinate care with the church, local resources, and social services.

Part of safety planning may involve reporting domestic violence to local authorities such as Child Protective Services or the local police. Being familiar with your state's mandated reporting law is also essential. Some states require reporting specified injuries and wounds, and others require any occurrence of domestic violence. Mandatory reporting laws for domestic violence differ from child and elder abuse. You can call your local domestic violence shelter or police station to learn about your state laws. Your church lawyer or insurance representative may also offer advice regarding legal responses. However, they tend to focus on liability, not victim care. Remember, you need to prioritize reporting abuse and victim care.

Since many abusers also physically or sexually abuse their children,[21] if there are children in the home, determine whether they are also victims

---

[18] My Plan (free app), https://myplanapp.org/.
[19] The National Domestic Violence Hotline is available 24/7 at 1-800-799-SAFE (7233), www.thehotline.org.
[20] Called to Peace Ministries, www.calledtopeace.org/.
[21] "Domestic Violence and Child Abuse," Children's Hospital of Philadelphia, Center for Violence Prevention, accessed April 22, 2024, https://violence.chop.edu/domestic-violence-and-child-abuse.

of abuse. It is no surprise that research shows if a man abuses his wife, he is more likely to abuse his children emotionally or physically.[22] Witnessing adult domestic violence is considered a type of child abuse itself, even if it does not physically harm the children.

This chapter can only alert you to potential threats but cannot address all the details involved in safety assessments and planning.[23] Involve others in your community who have experience identifying the signs of abuse. Victims cannot afford those helping to be naively optimistic or uninformed regarding safety issues. Always partner with professionals to create a safety plan.

Maintain careful confidentiality. Any information shared, even with church leaders, should not make it back to the abusive spouse. It makes the abused spouse more vulnerable to attacks and compromises their safety. For example, victims' emails and texts are typically monitored, so work from that assumption. Further, since a congregation would not generally understand or be expected to be sensitive to confidentiality concerns, it is important that domestic violence family situations not be widely discussed.

Respect a victim's pace. Not all victims will see or be honest about their level of danger. People who care for victims often have a greater sense of urgency to move a victim out of a potentially dangerous and harmful environment than the victim does. It is vital not to pressure victims. First, victims do not need another person to dictate their choices. Second, until they are ready to address the abuse firmly, victims may continue to return to the abuse, and failed interventions often only lead to increased abuse and alienation of the helper. It can take victims multiple attempts before coming forward and separating permanently. It is far better for the victim to be ready to make and enforce changes. Further, victims are often keenly aware of the consequences of addressing the abuse. Victims have to weigh things like increased threats and danger, loss of time with

---

[22]Diana Zuckerman, Jessica Becker, and Emily E. Mazurak, "Linking Spouse and Child Abuse," National Center for Health Research, accessed April 22, 2024, www.center4research.org/linking-spouse-child-abuse/.

[23]For a safety plan that addresses children, safety while the victim remains in the home, and fleeing abuse, see Strickland, *Is It Abuse?*, 307-17, or contact the National Domestic Violence Hotline (www.thehotline.org).

children, children having visitation with the abuser when they are not present to provide protection, economic hardship, and judgment from the community and family.

Some churches have wrongly emphasized that staying is better because God will use their suffering for sanctification or their abuser's conversion. Victims have been helped by hearing that even Jesus and Paul fled from danger (Lk 4:28-30; Jn 8:58-59, 11:53-54; Acts 23).

Step 3: Minister to the abused among us. Walking with the abused is a long road. Let Hebrews 13:3 inform your approach: "Remember those in prison as if you were together with them in prison, and those who are mistreated as if you yourselves were suffering." God calls his people to enter others' suffering. The members of the church can provide critical help and support, validate the presence of abuse, and assist in emergencies. Even while getting other support, pastoral involvement and care should be maintained at the same time as professional counseling. Church leaders provide spiritual care and comfort, rally community support, and showcase God's heart to them.

After addressing safety issues, here are four goals for ministry to domestic violence victims:

1. **Learn about the abuse.** As a victim gains trust and learns more about abuse, other abuses may be disclosed. The discovery of abuse should be continually revisited. This information will also be needed should the church engage in church discipline or wrestle through issues of separation and divorce.
2. **Provide support.** The church should be a refuge where victims can reveal their suffering and be in extreme distress without experiencing shame. The church can also provide an authoritative voice against aggression in the home, or any method of practical relief, like helping pay for counseling, a safe place to stay, and babysitting.
3. **Tend to their relationship with the Lord.** Abuse, especially spiritual abuse, significantly damages a victim's relationship with God. Church leaders are crucial in ministering to victims by speaking scriptural truths. Church leaders can remind the family that God's Word states that people are responsible for their sins (Mk 7:20-23)

and that God hates the sins that constitute abuse (Prov 6:16-19, Col 3:5-6).

4. ***Facilitate lament and prayer.*** Victims struggle to talk to God about the abuse because they struggle to find the words. Assist victims in locating their suffering in the pages of Scripture (Ps 55, 56, 57, 69, 88). Invite victims to see that God understands his people, even while questioning if he is tending to their cries for help (Ps 22). After all, Christ asked a similar question as he hung on the cross (Mt 27:46). Teach victims that it is good to ask God to protect them (Ps 5, 17, 64) and to pray both for our enemy's judgment (Ps 109) and redemption (Luke 6:27-28; 3:5-8, 3:12-15).

Be tender and patient in communicating these vital truths. Navigating an abusive marriage takes tremendous faith and courage. Never tire of upholding God's heart to the oppressed.

Step 4: Minister to those who have abused. Abusers are in great spiritual danger when they harm the ones God has called them to love. It is appropriate to confront their sin and limit their ability to do more damage (Gal 6:1). However, you should only engage a perpetrator with the victim's consent and after safety planning. People who use physical violence to control reflect unique idolatry and often wrestle with entrenched and habitual sin patterns. Since their goal is to maintain domination, ministering to them is difficult. Abusers tend to flee counseling, manipulate those trying to help, and perpetually shift blame. Shaping interventions that are alert to these patterns helps them see their brokenness and need to repent. Faithful pursuit of an abuser usually involves a team of church members (i.e., pastor, elder, counselor, small group leader, and deacon) willing to pursue and press in on their distorted beliefs.

With a heart darkened by so many deceptions, they usually take a long time to recognize they have a problem. Long-term, well-informed counseling specific to the person (not a one-size-fits-all type of care) will be needed.[24] It is important to help the family find experts or programs

---

[24] See Men of Peace (www.menofpeace.org/) for a biblical counseling approach, and the National Domestic Violence Hotline can provide resources from a community advocacy approach.

trained to treat domestic violators, like Batterer Intervention Prevention Programs (BIPP). (Although the word *batterer* connotes physical abuse, the term is used broadly to include all types of abuse.) Within the church, if the abuser is willing, a church might consider finding a spiritual mentor or accountability partner for the abuser in the church who is wise with more difficult situations like violence. You will want to wisely determine where abusers should and should not serve in your church. The safety of children, teens, and vulnerable members should be the priority. Regardless, inclusion in selective adult ministries can help with socialization and reduce isolation for those who are willing.

Church leadership or discipline can provide needed leverage to keep an abuser engaged in the change process. Your denominational leadership or church discipline guidelines may be useful in domestic violence. However, many abusers will not engage earnestly in the process, and even fewer will repent. Andrew's pastor, introduced in the opening vignette, took six months to lead Andrew to individual counseling, and as the counselor began to focus on his sin patterns, Andrew stopped going. While this was not the desired outcome, it provided the church with helpful information about Andrew and his commitment to his sin patterns, allowing them to counsel Hannah wisely.

Step 5: Ministering to children, who are especially vulnerable. Children are a special focus in any family where there is domestic violence. Many victims believe their children are unaware of the abuse, so they do not think they need help. Ninety percent of children report being very aware of the abuse, even if it does not happen in their presence.[25] Children experience physical, emotional, spiritual, and developmental consequences of abuse. They are also at a greater risk of being physically and sexually abused, dying by suicide, entering an abusive relationship, or perpetrating abuse.[26] Even during separation and divorce, children are often used to punish the victim. There is a significant chance the abuser will undermine parental authority, use their children as weapons

---

[25]See, for example, "Statistics," National Coalition Against Domestic Violence, accessed May 3, 2024, https://ncadv.org/statistics.
[26]Margot Shields *et al.*, "Exposure to Family Violence from Childhood to Adulthood," *BMC Public Health* 20 (November 2020): 1-15, https://doi.org/10.1186/s12889-020-09709-y.

or spies, initiate conflict at custody exchanges, neglect or abuse their children, or cause parental estrangement. Many children experience multiple traumas, leading to cumulative effects of particular concern.[27] Therefore, it is imperative to seek to minister to children affected by domestic violence.

ARE CHILDREN EXPERIENCING VIOLENCE IN THE HOME?
Sometimes, when working with a family, you discover or suspect that children are being abused. Remember that you do not need to be certain that child abuse is occurring, have evidence, or know the extent of the abuse to make a report to authorities. For a report to be made, you only need *reasonable suspicion* that child abuse is taking place. Notice that the standard is not knowledge that abuse or neglect is occurring, but only reason to believe it may be. Once you meet the threshold for reasonable suspicion, you should call your state's reporting agency, which will investigate your concerns.

Remember that child abuse is a serious sin and a crime. In many states, *failing to report* child abuse is also a crime, and pastors or family ministry leaders may be mandated reporters. Be aware of time constraints on reporting, meaning that you are responsible for knowing how long you have, from the time abuse was suspected to when you have to report it to an authority. Become familiar with your state's laws and understand which agencies you must report abuse to in your state.[28]

By law, all suspected child abuse must be reported to Child Protective Services (CPS). Reports of potential criminal abuse should be made to law enforcement, especially if there is an ongoing or immediate threat. CPS and the police serve two very different functions in our legal system. Both agencies will often advise you on what steps you could take. Further, every county or city has a local Children's Advocacy Center, and they may be able to provide guidance and support in the reporting process.

God desires to keep child safe (Mt 19:13-5, Lk 17:2). The church does not possess the training nor legal authority to assess an allegation of child abuse. Thus, you should refer the matter to the local authorities when

---
[27]Shields et al., "Exposure to Family Violence."
[28]For free training on reporting child abuse, see Church Cares (https://churchcares.com/).

you discover or suspect abuse. You may learn about abuse because the child directly discloses the abuse to you. When this happens, remember your role. If a child is making a disclosure, it is not your job to investigate or interrogate. Simply listen to the child, letting them explain what happened in their own words. Here is how to handle a disclosure of abuse.

1. Do not ask the child leading questions or ask the child for details. Doing so might increase the child's anxiety and tamper with testimony, making it harder for trained investigators later. Stick with the story the child tells you.
2. Limit questioning if the child has not already provided you with the information:
   - What happened?
   - When did it happen?
   - Where did it happen?
   - Who did it?
   - How do you know them?
3. Try to take down as many direct quotes as possible. It is wise to quickly write down what you were told after talking with the child.
4. Be supportive and compassionate. Affirm the child's bravery. Tell them they were brave for telling the truth and remind them that the abuse is not their fault. Offer to help them, but refrain from making promises you cannot keep. Do not tell the child that you will not tell anyone what he or she told you or imply that you know how things will unfold. Simply let the child know that you will do your best to support and protect him or her and that you will talk to people who can help.
5. Make a report and consider the parents. Remember, a report is not an accusation but a request to investigate a situation. If the parents in your congregation are involved, you would generally let the authorities do their work first before speaking to the parents. If the parents are not involved in your church (i.e., a stepparent is abusive and does not attend your church), then you would generally ask the parents to come in and talk with them about the child's report as

you report it. In the case of domestic abuse, it might be prudent to let the abused spouse know a report was made so that there is time to enact a safety plan. It is good to seek outside wisdom as there are many different factors to consider when involving the parents.

Pastoral care does not end once a report is made. It will be important to circle back and see what support the family needs. The discovery or disclosure of abuse will cause immense stress on the whole family. Be present by listening to, weeping with, and walking alongside them in this season of great suffering.

WHAT CAN CONGREGATIONS DO TO HELP?

We have discussed how church leaders, pastoral staff, and children's coordinators could respond to domestic violence. What about the rest of the congregation? Given the prevalence of abuse, it is a question of when, not if, domestic abuse will touch a church. As church authorities, pastors or full-time church ministers are uniquely positioned to care for the entire family affected by abuse. At the same time, they will need to prioritize and outsource other support and interventions. Utilizing outside experts and counselors can be of great help.

It is better to be prepared for a crisis than to react to one. Abuse touches on theological matters like submission, entrenched sin, repentance, separation, and divorce. Wrestling with these things at a leadership level and providing clear teaching for the congregation helps prepare the body to serve the blind sinner and the vulnerable victim in a crisis. Educating church leaders, including key women leaders, about abuse while formulating a Domestic Abuse Policy for the church will not only improve the identification of abuse but also help create church unity on a problematic issue. If your church or denomination does not have a policy or statement about domestic violence, consider forming a select committee of clergy, mental health providers, women, and a lawyer as an ideal advisory group to develop one.

During a crisis, the body of Christ can offer help in practical ways. Ensure those enlisted for direct care understand the dynamics of abuse and their role. Be creative and circumspect in providing victim care. Victims need prayer support, financial help to secure counseling or flee abuse, and help with their children and household. Since victims are often isolated, they need the community to come around them gently to provide friendship and fellowship. Many victims will not know how to tend to financial matters or have confidence in making decisions.

Churches can also work to prevent problems of abuse. Premarital counseling that screens for abuse, discusses the difference between mutual spousal submission and subjugation, teaches what healthy conflict looks like, and encourages proper expectations for sex is recommended. Talk to youth and college groups about entitlement, sex abuse, bullying, toxic jealousy, stalking, and gaslighting. Offer a vision and biblical teaching on healthy relationships. Christians need to be taught that abuse should not be tolerated and that being married does not mean enduring unrepentant and destructive behavior.

THIS IS A HEAVY BURDEN OF CARE: YOU ARE NOT ALONE

Ultimately, it is the Lord who reveals and rescues. His people are privileged to be part of the redemptive story but are finite helpers. Abuse is a problem that cannot be easily solved. It seems the enemy's tactics often include isolating families suffering from domestic violence from the love and fellowship of believers. You may find families with domestic violence exist on the outskirts of your church community or disappear once the abuse is illuminated. Reasonable offering of support from the church is expected, and being able to offer referrals for good care is helpful, but be careful not to take on the role of a rescuer.

With God's help and the church's guidance, victims can take steps to address the abuse with appropriate support. Until sufferers are ready to speak and tell more of their stories, church leaders can pray, gently pursue, and attempt to draw out victims. Yes, it is hard to wait.

The abuser's posture toward change will determine much of the outcome. However, even if repentance does not occur, be encouraged. Exposing and confronting sin, protecting adult victims and children, connecting a sufferer with the Lord, and walking with a sufferer are ways the Lord is glorified.

Caring for people who perpetrate and who are victims of domestic abuse is a weighty measure. God promises to be an ever-present help in times of trouble (Ps 46:1). In the story of Moses encouraging the Israelites of God's power and protection (Ex 17), God sent Aaron and Hur to strengthen him. The Israelites faced a mighty enemy, and Joshua engaged in his first direct battle. Moses' leadership was essential. When he grew weary, God provided Aaron and Hur to help him hold up his hands. Ministry is not a job to be done alone but can draw on a community of medical and counseling professionals, wise church leaders, and leaders of sister churches and denominational networks.

Embarking on this journey with the wisdom of those in your community who are knowledgeable, and the posture of prayer is the best way to proceed and create dependence on the Lord. Ministering in the context of deep suffering and not having clarity about what is happening and what to do is challenging. Trust that God, who is always right and just, will reveal the truth. Moreover, remember, no matter his people's suffering, he promises to be a source of comfort and refuge.

8

HANDLING DIVORCE AS A MINISTRY LEADER

Tutorial from a Family Lawyer

Lynne Marie Kohm

"Please help me protect my children from being forced to stay with their mother and the man she just ran away with. I need Christian guidance and legal protection and don't know where else to turn."

This was the despairing plea from a father of four young children.[1] His wife abandoned the family with the choir director and wanted the children to visit her in their new residence. With the sternest countenance, the husband stated, "I do not want the children to stay with them. Please help me protect them." I can still see his very serious, young face speaking slowly and quietly, conveying his objective, clearly working hard to hide formidable feelings of betrayal and a devastatingly broken heart. This father needed a guide to understand custody and visitation law for a broken family in crisis, how to protect his children, and the options for his own welfare. He also wanted to maintain an opportunity

---

[1] *Disclaimer: Nothing in this chapter is intended as legal advice; it is solely offered as informative and educational information.*

for future forgiveness and reconciliation or be prepared for divorce. These issues often arise in divorce scenarios.

Sadly, divorce among Christian families happens regularly. This $28 billion per year industry in the United States eagerly waits to help any family deconstruct not only its marriage but all the incidents of that foundation, which includes custody and visitation of children, distribution of property, support payments, and more. Divorce carries a possible financial price tag between $15,000 and $100,000 and numerous dynamic implicit costs on which no price tag can be hung.[2]

Ministry leaders are unprepared, lacking knowledge to help families like these in crisis. This chapter prepares family ministers to handle marital issues with knowledge and sensitivity. This chapter also offers guidance to help families understand and navigate the crisis of family breakdown and divorce with biblical principles and to find resources beyond the church. Empowering church leaders to serve in the crisis also encourages the exploration of alternatives to minimize complete family destruction. Ministry leaders can be prepared with the best information and perspectives to help individuals or couples approach the divorce experience in ways that reduce the collateral damage for all involved.

Couples who divorce usually either drop out of church (many never to return) or one or both separate to attend new churches—something that might be necessary due to the pain of the divorce. Ministry leaders need guidance to avoid discounting or overlooking the needs of people in troubled marriages and guard against engaging in a marital split by listening or ministering without taking sides or assuming one perspective is the whole story. While one partner may appear guiltier than the other because of infidelity or abandonment, taking sides is not what church leaders should do. Taking sides not only hurts mediation or negotiation prospects but also hurts the children, extended family, and friends of each partner. During a divorce, each partner is likely to fiercely defend his or her position as

---

[2]Chaucey Crail, "How Much Does a Divorce Cost in 2024?," *Forbes*, July 29, 2022, www.forbes.com/advisor/legal/divorce/how-much-does-divorce-cost/.

righteous. The reality is that both sides are full of deep pain, carrying serious spiritual needs.

Ministry leaders can help partners decide to continue attendance or change churches with blessings and care while maintaining care for those who leave. While theological divorce issues are best left to the church, the partners and their children (extended family and friends) need ministry guidance to make sense of the loss even if the divorce was against your church's teaching. Your role as a shepherd will include bringing perspective and facilitating spiritual formation through personal and spiritual growth amid the crisis to help those hurting strengthen their relationship with God. Spiritual practices to help them stay strong include engaging in daily devotional Scripture reading and prayer and fortifying discipleship connections. When Nathan confronted King David in taking Bathsheba and arranging the murder of Uriah, he did not desert or condemn David but allowed God to work. He told David, "The Lord has taken away your sin," while proceeding to explain the consequences of that sin (2 Sam 12:13). God is in the midst of the crisis and promises to never leave. He will comfort even in unbearable emotional pain and through the very real consequences of sin. He understands and is there.

As a church leader, you may or may not have had seminary classes or training about how to advise couples who have decided to divorce. You may likely take the position that the couple should not divorce. To divorce or not divorce does not have to be a binary decision. Ministry leaders can offer other options during counseling. This chapter addresses three main areas that will help ministry leaders integrate pragmatic legal wisdom with spiritual counseling. The first is realism about family breakdown. The second is understanding the legal options, and the third is guidance and resources for spiritual faithfulness amid family crises. Ministry leaders can help a divorcing couple access legal care, retain faith, reduce negative impact, and move toward emotional healing and spiritual health.

THE CRISIS OF DIVORCE

While the divorce rate in America has fallen since its height in 1981, around 30 percent of all first marriages end in divorce.[3] With many stressful life changes, divorce can negatively affect health in ways that resemble the bereavement process.[4] Divorce is associated with a significant increase in depressive feelings, a moderate decrease in general health, an increase in illness, and a significant decrease in life satisfaction.[5] Research on the association between death and divorce found that "the risk of early death associated with remaining separated or divorced was greater than the long-term risk conferred by being a cigarette smoker in 1960."[6] Happily, married people are believed to live longer, have lower cancer, stroke, and heart attack rates, and tend to be less stressed overall.[7] There is no understating the facts—divorce is really tough.

Christian marriages may be no different. High divorce rates in the church tend to reveal a spiritual crisis of churchgoers misunderstanding God's design for marriage permanency. Studies show, however, that couples with a vibrant religious faith are less likely to divorce and report higher marital quality.[8] Active faith translates into a lower risk of divorce.[9]

---

[3] Yerís Mayol-García, Benjamin Gurrentz, and Rose M. Kreider, "Number, Timing, and Duration of Marriages and Divorces," U.S. Census Bureau, April 2021, 14-15, www.census.gov/content/dam/Census/library/publications/2021/demo/p70-167.pdf.

[4] Matthijs Kalmijn, "The Ambiguous Link between Marriage and Health: A Dynamic Reanalysis of Loss and Gain Effects," *Social Forces* 95, no. 4 (June 2017): 1607-36, https://doi.org/10.1093/sf/sox015.

[5] Kalmijn, "The Ambiguous Link," 1624-27.

[6] David A. Sbarra and Paul J. Nietert, "Divorce and Death: Forty Years of the Charleston Heart Study," *Psychological Science* 20, no. 1 (2010): 107-13.

[7] Kalmijn, "The Ambiguous Link," 1607.

[8] Christine A. Johnson et al., *Marriage in Oklahoma: 2001 Baseline Statewide Survey on Marriage and Divorce* (Oklahoma City: Oklahoma Department of Human Services, 2002), 24-26. See also similar findings in the work of Bradley R. E. Wright, *Christians Are Hate-Filled Hypocrites... and Other Lies You've Been Told* (Bloomington, MN: Bethany House, 2010), 133; and W. Bradford Wilcox and Elizabeth Williamson, "The Cultural Contradictions of Mainline Family Ideology and Practice," in *American Religions and the Family*, ed. Don S. Browning and David A. Clairmont (New York: Columbia University Press, 2007): 50.

[9] Wilcox and Williamson, 50. "Those who say they are more religious are less likely, not more, to have already experienced divorce. Likewise, those who report more frequent attendance at religious services were significantly less likely to have been divorced." Johnson, *Marriage in Oklahoma*, 26.

Reasons for divorce vary, from finances[10] to lost attachment,[11] to children or the lack of them,[12] and to concerns related to sexuality.[13] Often, these factors reflect the heart pulling a partner away from God and the marriage. The pain and broken trust brought on by these elements drive many couples to divorce. Understanding the subliminal stressors on a marriage can help a ministry leader discuss the matter of a troubled marriage more intelligently and sensitively.[14] Understanding the law behind divorce can be equally obliging in helping couples in troubled marriages to pursue the best options for them and their circumstances.

KNOWING THE LEGAL OPTIONS OF DIVORCE: GUIDE FOR CHURCH LEADERS

We live in a divorce-friendly culture, contrary to much of our history. In earlier eras, divorce was more a matter of church oversight and rarely permitted. Marriage could end through the limited process of annulment or by judicial decree. Ministry leaders need to be aware of state laws and regulations to effectively counsel a family in crisis toward helpful resolution of complicated legal matters.

Fault-based divorce laws tend to define the outer boundaries of marital misbehavior that contemporary community standards deem tolerable. These laws allow an aggrieved spouse to terminate a marriage when the partner's misconduct is intolerable. The complaining spouse must

---

[10] See, e.g., Sharon Feiereisen, "The 12 Biggest Money-related Reasons People Get Divorced," *Business Insider*, July 7, 2019, www.businessinsider.com/divorce-money-issues-financial-relationship-couple-2019-7.

[11] Melissa McNelis and Chris Segrin, "Insecure Attachment Predicts History of Divorce, Marriage, and Current Relationship Status," *Journal of Divorce & Remarriage* 60, no. 5 (2019): 404-17, https://doi.org/10.1080/10502556.2018.1558856.

[12] Raed Abdel-Sater, "Marriage Dissolution in the United States: A Survival Analysis Approach," *Journal of Divorce & Remarriage* 63 (March 2022): 235-61, https://doi.org/10.1080/10502556.2022.2042788. See also generally Jayne E. Schooler and Thomas C. Atwood, *The Whole Life Adoption Book: Realistic Advice for Building a Healthy Adoptive Family* (Colorado Springs, CO: Nav Press, 2008); and Lynne Marie Kohm, "A Hitchhiker's Guide to ART: Implementing Self-Governed Personally Responsible Decision-Making in the Context of Artificial Reproductive Technology," *Capital University Law Review* 39 (2011): 413.

[13] See, e.g., Greg Smalley, "Pornography as Grounds for Divorce," Focus on the Family, 2020, www.focusonthefamily.com/family-qa/pornography-as-grounds-for-divorce/.

[14] See Scott Stanley, "Reasons People Give for Divorce," Institute of Family Studies, April 10, 2017, https://ifstudies.org/blog/reasons-people-give-for-divorce.

produce evidence to prove that the defendant spouse has substantially breached the core, material terms of the marital covenant.[15]

Fault divorce. These fault grounds are statutory—the legal rules on the books—and most commonly fall into the following categories, with codified particulars dependent on state jurisdiction:

- Adultery—consensual sexual intercourse with a person other than the spouse and must be generally proven by clear and convincing corroborating evidence.
- Abandonment (or desertion)—the voluntary departure of a spouse from the marital home without intention to return and without consent of the remaining spouse, generally for a length of time specified by statute.
- Abuse (or Cruelty or Inhumane Treatment)—severe, unusual, repeated mistreatment of one spouse by the other, and it may be mental or physical, dependent on the rules of the state jurisdiction where the family resides.[16]

A state's laws may also have miscellaneous possible grounds, such as habitual substance abuse/addiction, imprisonment, insanity, or felony conviction. The alleging spouse's attorney must prove these grounds, and that proof could also have a significant bearing on the distribution of property, support concerns, and custody determinations.

Defenses to divorce. Traditionally, a divorce would not be granted if a defense could be established. These defenses might include (1) provocation (being forced to act in a manner that provided fault grounds to the other party), (2) condonation (general condoning or forgiveness of the action), (3) connivance (corrupt consent to the action), (3) recrimination (committing an act of the same general nature as the grounds alleged), (4) reconciliation (forgiveness and resumption of the marital relationship), (5) collusion (spouses conspiring toward fraudulent creation or fabrication of grounds to circumvent divorce laws), and (6) insanity (mental incapacity). These defenses can be used to defend against

---

[15] Lynn D. Wardle, Mark S. Strasser, Lynne Marie Kohm, and Tanya M. Washington, *Family Law from Multiple Perspectives*, 2nd ed. (St. Paul, MN: West Academic, 2019): 675-707.
[16] Wardle, Strasser, Kohm, and Washington, *Family Law*, 705.

a cause of action for a fault-based divorce, but states that have enacted pure no-fault divorce legal schemes have tended to restrict or abolish these defenses.[17]

No-fault divorce. Though fault-based divorce rules generally served to protect victimized spouses, the effort to hear all the evidence surrounding marital fault and possible defenses was draining on the judicial system. It dramatically compromised the personal privacy of the parties, paving the way for no-fault divorce. No-fault divorce, it was hoped, would be a legal policy that would reduce the hostility surrounding family breakdown, protect children, and preserve the judicial system's integrity.[18]

A struggling marriage looking for guidance may not have any legal or biblical grounds for divorce. No-fault divorce, however, is generally available unilaterally in every state in one of three categories: (1) living separate and apart for a designated period, including refraining from sexual intercourse; (2) marital breakdown (asserting that the marriage is irretrievably broken or has irreconcilable differences); and (3) mutual consent of the parties, generally evidenced by written agreement signed by both parties.[19] The conventional wisdom was that no-fault divorce laws would not cause a rise in divorce rates but ease and foster a judicial economy. However, the opposite occurred. Statistical studies reveal that divorce rates have dramatically increased over the last fifty years since the introduction of no-fault rules.[20]

Alternatives to divorce. Generally, all these legal causes of action require litigation or a waiver of legal rights to reach a conclusion.[21] No one

---

[17] Wardle, Strasser, Kohm, and Washington, *Family Law*, 706.
[18] Lynne Marie Kohm, "On Mutual Consent to Divorce: A Debate with Two Sides to the Story," *Appalachian Journal of Law* 8, no. 35 (2008): 35, 37, https://papers.ssrn.com/sol3/papers.cfm?abstract_id=3072460.
[19] See e.g., Va. Code sec. 20-91 (9)(a). For general information, see also "Fault and No-Fault Divorce: An Overview," FindLaw, 2023, www.findlaw.com/family/divorce/an-overview-of-no-fault-and-fault-divorce-law.html.
[20] For a comprehensive review of divorce law, culture, and marriage policy, see W. Bradford Wilcox, "The Evolution of Divorce," *National Affairs* 1 (Fall 2009): 81-94, www.nationalaffairs.com/publications/detail/the-evolution-of-divorce.
[21] See e.g., again Va. Code sec. 20-91 referring to "upon application of either party," which means opening litigation with a petition, and "a decree," which refers to a court's ruling or order as a result of that litigation. Parties who cannot afford legal counsel or wish to avoid litigation are allowed by law to waive rights in the face of divorce litigation. See e.g., Va. Code sec. 20-99.1:1(A).

should ever have to waive his or her legal rights. Every individual should have legal representation to inform his or her options and to know that there are alternatives to waiving rights and litigation. These alternatives include (1) mediation, (2) legal arbitration, (3) collaborative family law, or (4) other reconciliation methods. Each of these alternatives is important to understand and counsel.

Mediation. First, church leaders should consider recommending legal mediation when talking with someone who has decided to separate or divorce. Mediation is highly recommended by family courts in the United States because it allows families to come to their own solutions rather than being told by a judge how their family will dissolve. Furthermore, mediation tends to be far less costly than litigation and can provide a path forward while constructively airing difficult hurts with healthy boundaries.[22] A popular method of dispute resolution, mediation is a process where a neutral third party, the mediator, encourages the disputants to find a mutually agreeable settlement by helping them to identify the issues, reduce misunderstandings, vent emotions, clarify priorities, find points of agreement, and explore new areas of compromise and possible solutions.[23] While mediation is a private process, and a pastor will not likely be privy to the information disclosed in the mediation, a church leader can nonetheless help by supporting the process, particularly to reduce harm.

Mediation or other alternative dispute resolution methods may be helpful to work out difficulties within the marriage while salvaging the marriage and stabilizing the family.[24] Mediation may encourage disputants to reconsider the divorce decision or allow them room to move slowly through each issue while permitting time for personal, spiritual, and psychological counseling and healing.

---

[22] Alexandra Crampton, "'We Make New Families': Findings from a Family Court Mediation Study," *Family Court Review* 60, no. 3 (2022): 391-410.
[23] See Jessica Pearson and Nancy Thoennes, "Mediating and Litigation Custody Disputes: A Longitudinal Evaluation," *Family Law Quarterly* 17 (1984): 497; and Holly A. Streeter-Schaeffer, "A Look at Court-Mandated Civil Mediation," *Drake Law Review* 49 (2001): 367.
[24] See e.g., Forrest Mosten, "Lawyer as Peacemaker: Building a Successful Law Practice Without Ever Going to Court," *Family Law Quarterly* 43 (2009): 489. Also, consider the excellent resources available at www.NoDivorceToday.org for couples who are uncertain about moving ahead with divorce and want to take a comprehensive look at their marriage before pursuing a divorce.

Arbitration. Second, legal arbitration is the resolution of a dispute by a third person, usually with special expertise, in a de-formalized setting. It is usually binding but less adversarial than traditional litigation. Attorneys outside of court or the parties can also compromise and settle their claims in private negotiation.[25] The *Model Rules of Professional Conduct* recognize that lawyers have an ethical duty to work to settle a case when it serves the best interest of their clients.[26]

Collaborative family law. Third, collaborative family law is another alternative to divorce litigation that brings parties, their lawyers, and family experts together to work out the best solutions for every individual involved. It, too, can be less costly than divorce litigation and has unique parameters that may or may not serve to limit painful damage. This type of alternative dispute resolution allows parties, with the assistance of specially trained family law attorneys, to negotiate their issues in a controlled, safe, and respectful setting using structured negotiations, various financial experts, and counselors. Under the collaboration, lawyers agree not to participate in any future litigation on behalf of the client to focus solely on settling a fair, stable, and sustainable legal agreement to dissolve the family.[27]

Reconciliation. Fourth, some states offer reconciliation or specialty courts dealing with specific issues such as substance abuse. A good family law lawyer in your state will know how to access these special legal avenues and guide a person in a family crisis through the best alternatives. A ministry leader or pastor is never expected to know how to practice law, but he or she can provide good information, helpful resources, and precious pastoral care.

Sometimes, people who need help may think the only solution to their marital problems is a complete divorce. An interview, however, may reveal

---

[25]Carrie Menkel-Meadow, "Mediation, Arbitration, and Alternative Dispute Resolution (ADR)" (research paper, International Encyclopedia of the Social and Behavioral Sciences, Elsevier Ltd. 2015, UC Irvine School of Law, 2015), https://ssrn.com/abstract=2608140.

[26]*Model Rules of Professional Conduct* (Chicago: American Bar Association, 2024), 1.2 and 1.4.

[27]See, e.g., Pauline H. Tesler, "Collaborative Family Law," *Pepperdine Dispute Resolution Law Journal* 4 (2004): 317; and Peter K. Munson, "Uniform Collaborative Law Enhances Client-Driven ADR," *Family Advocate* 39 (2017): 42. But see Margaret Drew, "Collaboration and Intention: Making the Collaborative Family Law Process Safe(r)," *Ohio State Journal on Dispute Resolution* 32 (2017): 373, discussing the dangers of Collaborative Law for those who have experienced abuse from their partners and how lawyers can identify these risks.

better alternatives than divorce. Educating the marital parties on all the various strategies available to them and the array of remedies may very well include an approach that falls short of filing for divorce tomorrow.

Separation. Separation may provide the space and safety a party needs to consider the family breakdown, and the laws of every state allow this. Every state holds strong public policy in favor of marriage, taking a most cautious attitude to divorce. Pastoral counseling is a tremendous benefit during this time. This setting is more cohesive for working toward restoration, or at least some preservation, of the family than a courtroom. A written separation agreement between the parties may be extremely helpful in setting boundaries and rebuilding trust. An attorney can draft an agreement that would protect an individual's interests, the marriage, and even a future reconciliation while leaving open the options for divorce. This may be particularly true if the client is religiously opposed to divorce but doesn't trust the spouse. A legal separation allows for time and space between the partners. For example, if one spouse is struggling with some sort of substance abuse, that time and space may allow him or her to access help to get that area under control to save the marriage and family from dissolution.[28]

Other situations may demand judicial action. For example, when a partner chooses to keep his or her income from the family, a court could order that spouse to provide maintenance for the family without pursuing a divorce. This common law action in equity for separate maintenance without divorce may be the most suitable and inexpensive solution for a marriage partner who does not want a divorce but needs support from the other partner.[29] Another option is judicial separation (called "a divorce from bed and board" in some states), which may be very appropriate for a client who is religiously opposed to divorce. This judicial

---

[28]Lynne Marie Kohm, "Understanding and Encouraging Realistic Reconciliation in an Age of Divorce," *Virginia Bar Association Journal* 32 (June 2006): 8, https://papers.ssrn.com/sol3/papers.cfm?abstract_id=1949256.

[29]Virginia Code § 20-107.1 (iv) allows for a separate maintenance action: "Upon entry of a decree providing . . . (iv) for separate maintenance, the court may make such further decree as it shall deem expedient concerning the maintenance and support of the spouses." All the provisions, restrictions, and factors found in this statute apply to separate maintenance actions. An article on this cause of action can be found at Ronald R. Tweel, and Elizabeth P. Coughter, "When is Separate Maintenance Applicable?," *Virginia Lawyer Magazine* 1 (2012): 48.

action declares the parties legally separated but still legally married and responsible for marital support obligations.[30] The court's judgment replaces any potential agreement between the parties. Still, this remedy also allows individuals to contemplate whether divorce is the best strategy, particularly considering any faith convictions.

Annulment. An annulment can be an alternative to divorce. Grounds for annulment vary by state but may include an invalid license or marriage ceremony, entering a marriage before the dissolution of an earlier marriage of one of the parties, a marriage with someone too closely related, or some sort of fraud in the marriage. These remedies are defined by state law and may be preferable for a client under certain circumstances.

MAKING A DIFFERENCE THROUGH MINISTRY

Once a ministry leader is aware of the deeper issues and the individuals' options, he or she can make a tremendous difference in listening to problems, spotting the real issues, sharing information, and availing the family of legal options accessible to them. Priceless Spirit-filled and Spirit-directed assistance could make all the difference.

Picking up the pieces of divorce is never easy. The personal consequences of divorce are often greater than clients initially comprehend. Marital disruption can precipitate intense and complicated emotional responses from rejection to anger, instability, helplessness, and even loss of identity. These detrimental consequences can lead to mental health, social, physical, and career and vocational problems, as well as a host of incidental consequences.[31]

For example, it is common for parties to underestimate the challenges associated with post-separation parenting. The instability created by separation can be one of the many harmful effects of divorce on children. Separation and divorce disrupt and change a child's relationship with each parent, causing the child to experience uncertainty. Keenly needed are efforts to spare children the negative effects of divorce. Attempts to

---

[30] See, e.g., Va. Code §20-95, "Grounds for Divorce from Bed and Board."
[31] See generally Kalmijn. See also Richard E. Lucas, "Time Does Not Heal All Wounds: A Longitudinal Study of Reaction and Adaptation to Divorce," *Psychological Science* 16 (2005): 945; and Linda J. Waite and Maggie Gallagher, *The Case For Marriage* (New York: Broadway Books, 2000) discussing the benefits of marriage.

bring a restorative approach to family dissolution and parenting can be extremely helpful in sparing children from the trauma of full-on divorce. Pastors and church leaders can work to respect the needs of families organizing new family priorities amid shared custody arrangements. Ministry leaders can be supportive and compassionately help parents as they negotiate shared custody and church activities for their children.

Additionally, divorce is an economic disaster for most families. No one fares well financially—especially women. The "feminization of poverty" refers to the disproportionality of women in poverty, much of which has resulted from divorce.[32] Generally, women and children may suffer more severe financial loss in a divorce and typically experience economic consequences associated with divorce. Reductions in available income, a lower standard of living, and inferior housing are the start of those outcomes. Women may experience stress, depression, changes in social life and status, fewer funds for recreation and leisure, deprivation of retirement hopes and benefits, difficulties in improving their economic position, and possible gender discrimination in employment. Health benefits and medical insurance may be uncertain after divorce as well.

Furthermore, these economic costs do not consider the emotional, social, spiritual, mental, or physical health costs involved in any family breakdown or dissolution. All this can begin even before litigation commences, and ministry leaders can be a practical support for divorcing families with financial needs. While your church may not engage in "casserole sign up" for a parent who is newly separated or divorced, it is wise to consider whether meals, benevolence, and practical help, like church members arranging rides for children to youth meetings, may be important supports for a family in economic and relational crisis.

Remember, divorce is a $28 billion per year industry; its costs can be outrageous,[33] even while it may be necessary to remedy the harm to an aggrieved spouse. The phenomenon of unilateral no-fault divorce (where

---

[32]See Patrick Parkinson, *Family Law and the Indissolubility of Parenthood* (Cambridge: Cambridge University Press, 2011): 208; and Sara McLanahan and Erin L. Kelley, "The Feminization of Poverty, Past and Future," in *Handbook on the Sociology of Gender*, ed. Janet Saltzman Chafetz (New York: Springer, 2006), 127.
[33]Crail, "How Much."

a party may obtain a divorce regardless of whether the other party wants to divorce or reconcile) without a cause of action (even if a petitioner is a victim of his or her spouse's adultery) does not provide a legal remedy for an aggrieved spouse. Especially in the face of no satisfactory legal remedy, he or she needs spiritual remedies that only God can provide.

In addition to the actual financial cost of the divorce, parties may experience a loss of earning capacity and assets. Specifically, the assets of the parties' marriage are subject to equitable distribution, where the court splits the assets according to its discretion and will assign or award spousal support depending on the parties' circumstances. The timeline for a divorce is never quick but can drag on for years, taking a toll on the parties in uncontemplated ways.

MINISTRY OPPORTUNITIES

When the emotional toll of marital discord manifests or explodes, an opportunity exists for sharing a theology of suffering (theodicy) and spiritual care for all family members. As mentioned earlier, health consequences for both parties have been documented by researchers, showing that divorce can not only make one sick but can even lead to early death.[34] Finally, couples may not realize the consequences of divorce on their social circles, friendships, and even their church community. The forfeiture of friends and extended family is sadly unavoidable. While this social loss is inevitable, ministry leaders must rally around church families when people need it most and offer Spirit-led counseling.

A significant contribution ministry leaders can make in preparing for divorce intervention is learning how to respond to a spouse experiencing frequent and persistent frustration and conflict. Support programs like DivorceCare can provide specific spiritual support to people going through a divorce.[35] Even if a church does not have resources to provide a DivorceCare group in their church, connecting with a local group is commonly available. Christian marriage seminars, conferences, and

---

[34] Susannah Cahalan, "How a Divorce can Make you Sick and Even Lead to Early Death," *New York Post*, February 12, 2022, https://nypost.com/2022/02/12/how-a-divorce-can-make-you-sick-and-even-lead-to-early-death/.
[35] DivorceCare, www.divorcecare.org.

retreats might also be helpful as they serve as proactive offerings to strengthen marriages.

Churches may need to be creative in ministering to family members going through a divorce, as the demands of single-parenting and decreased funds often cause practical barriers to engaging in church programs. Programs like single-sex ministry groups in the evening with childcare provided can make the church more accessible to single parents who desperately need support through a divorce. How a church allocates resources can create barriers or open pathways for spiritual care and formation for struggling families.

In pastoral care, couples often come to pastors or counselors and are so argumentative that even the one offering support may begin to think that divorce is the best option. Every pastor should know this could happen, particularly if working with couples who have already decided to divorce. Even in this context, however, the pastoral wisdom, compassion, and knowledge offered here can go a long way in defusing even the most persistent conflict. Ministry leaders can help the parties begin to understand the incidental effects their arguing and poor decision-making will have on their health and their children. Especially when the stakes of divorce and separation are on the table, pastors or church counselors need to avoid taking sides in the decision. Church leaders can support and care for each party as they decide their future. Pastors can share church teachings on divorce with deep compassion. No happy person seeks a divorce, and respecting the pain and struggle of parishioners communicates genuine empathy that can contribute to spouses' spiritual formation.

PROTECTING CHILDREN

As mentioned earlier, child welfare in divorce is critically important. Parents, church leaders, and counselors can benefit from understanding basic legal rules surrounding custody and visitation, some of the most difficult decisions that courts must make in family law cases. When parents cannot agree about custody or visitation, they ask the state to make these decisions through litigation. The legal standard is to determine what is in the child's best interest, but the judge often has little to no chance to get to know the child or what is best for him or her.[36] Furthermore, the parents may forget their role as protectors and guardians of their children because they may be so wrapped up in their grief and pain. A ministry leader or counselor who can remind parents to put their children above their needs can change the world.

The roots of traditional legal concepts regarding children and their custody begin from antiquity with Jewish tradition, Greco-Roman mores, and early Christianity. These ancient codes agreed that children deserved protection, as a hint of a divine reflection. However, children's value has waxed and waned over the centuries. Roman law placed children under the ownership of their father, affording them low social status and high vulnerability, the truth of which is still powerfully captured today in cultures that commonly practice infanticide and exposing children. In contrast, Jewish and Christian values vigorously opposed these tenets, holding children as a blessing deserving of care and protection.[37] All fifty states have adopted some form of the best interest of the child standard in child custody determinations. When parents separate, children's interests are determined by the state rather than the parents.

The costs of divorce to children are nothing short of significant and generally stay with them throughout their lifetimes.[38] If parents do not handle their divorce with sensitivity, awareness, and cooperation from both parties, the consequences of their actions can severely impact their children.[39] Divorce outcomes include increased instability for a child and can affect a child's physical health and mental health. Children of divorce face educational challenges, from diminished learning capacity to poor behavior outcomes and fewer college opportunities.[40] This results in the

---

[36]See Lynne Marie Kohm, "Tracing the Foundations of the Best Interests of the Child Standard in American Jurisprudence," *Journal of Law and Family Studies* 10 (2008): 337, 341-55, http://ssrn.com/abstract=1957143.

[37]Kohm, "Tracing," 341-55.

[38]Leah Cameron, "The Possible Negative Emotional and Psychological Consequences in Children of Divorce," *ESSAI* 6, article 15 (March 2008): 25-30, https://dc.cod.edu/essai/vol6/iss1/15. See for example, Virginia State Bar, "Spare the Child," Vimeo, November 19, 2010, https://vimeo.com/16997474, an instructional video detailing the accounts of adult children of divorce, and experts who work to help parents spare their children of the harms of divorce.

[39]Cameron, "Possible Negative Emotional and Psychological Consequences."

[40]"Effects of Divorce on Children's Education," Marriage and Religious Research Institute, 2022, www.marripedia.org/effects_of_divorce_on_children_s_education.

forfeit of human capital, the notion that an investment in children yields social good for both them and society.[41] Supporting cooperative and respectful parenting of any divorced adults in your church reaps huge dividends in their children's lives.

SPIRITUAL FAITHFULNESS AND FAMILY RESTORATION

The best strategy for assisting a family in the divorce crisis is to begin with empathy and then move to providing basic information. Educating the parties about the realities of the process, the pillage of the legal rules, and their progression, along with the challenging negative outcomes, can go a long way in drawing back the racehorse of divorce from the track. Providing a roadmap for the crisis allows a ministry leader or counselor to work from a strategy that offers the best support and makes the best referrals. Some excellent resources have already been offered in the footnotes of this chapter, but every leader should create a list of resources as a handout for those counseled. This list should include, for example, Hope and Healing from DivorceCare Ministry,[42] "Understanding Realistic Reconciliation in an Age of Divorce,"[43] and "Lawyer as Peacemaker."[44]

Christian teaching on divorce varies by church denomination and local church history. Still, if a church has not resolved its stance, the book *Divorce and Remarriage in the Church* is a respected theological review of divorce for church leaders.[45] Preventative resources include Dr. Gary Chapman's *Hope for the Separated: Wounded Marriages Can Be Healed*, which offers post-separation or divorce encouragement and helps individuals in crisis make better decisions.[46]

Healing is needed for those who experience divorce. Focus on the Family's *When Happily Ever After Shatters: Seeing God in the Midst of*

---

[41]For a better understanding of this concept and how it relates to marriage and marital stability see Kathleen E. Akers and Lynne Marie Kohm, "Solving Millennial Marriage Evolution," *University of Baltimore Law Review* 48 (2018): 1, https://papers.ssrn.com/sol3/papers.cfm?abstract_id=3293263.
[42]"Hope and Healing," DivorceCare, www.divorcecare.org.
[43]Kohm, "Understanding and Encouraging Realistic Reconciliation."
[44]Mosten, "Lawyer as Peacemaker."
[45]David Instone-Brewer, *Divorce and Remarriage in the Church* (Downers Grove, IL: InterVarsity Press, 2003).
[46]Gary Chapman, *Hope for the Separated: Wounded Marriages Can Be Healed* (Chicago: Moody, 2005).

Divorce & Single Parenting offers authentic direction for honoring God through a broken marriage.[47] *When I Do Becomes I Don't: Practical Steps During Separation and Divorce* helps through the grief,[48] and *A Woman's Guide to Healing the Heartbreak of Divorce* offers authentic pain care whether one is facing divorce or grieving a past marriage and guidance to begin the healing process by forgiving, problem-solving, communicating, and setting new priorities and boundaries.[49] Finally, *Moving Forward* by divorce recovery pioneer Jim Smoke is a devotional guide to finding hope and peace during the divorce.[50]

For parents in custody disputes, an excellent educational resource used by courts and mediators throughout the country is *Spare the Child*, an instructional video from the Virginia State Bar Family Law Board of Governors detailing the accounts of adult children of divorce and those of family law experts who work to help parents spare their children from the harms of divorce.[51] Other states may have state-specific resources for child custody issues. *Family Restoration* is a blog contending that family breakdown in American culture opens up incredible opportunities for the body of Christ to propose new hope to a struggling world, particularly in family life.[52] The realities of divorce and family breakdown allow us to understand the desperate need for ministry leaders to serve as healers of human conflict. Understanding the law can be a valuable asset in the arsenal of tools working toward family restoration.

Finally, as a ministry leader, have your list of Christian attorneys ready for referral to struggling individuals and families. This list should include the names and contact information of at least three lawyers to whom you, as a pastor or counselor, would refer a church member. Speak with the recommended lawyers personally before placing their names on your

---

[47] Susan Birdseye, *When Happily Ever After Shatters: Seeing God in the Midst of Divorce & Single Parenting*, (Colorado Springs, CO: Focus on the Family, 2015).
[48] Laura Petherbride, *When I Do Becomes I Don't: Practical Steps During Separation and Divorce* (Colorado Springs, CO: David C. Cook, 2008).
[49] Rose Sweet, *A Woman's Guide to Healing the Heartbreak of Divorce* (Hurst, TX: Tyndale, 2000).
[50] Jim Smoke, *Moving Forward* (Nashville: Thomas Nelson, 1995).
[51] Virginia State Bar, *Spare the Child*, directed by Stuart Holt (2010), www.vsb.org/site/sections/family/spare-the-child/.
[52] *Family Restoration* (blog), Regent University School of Law, https://regentfamilyrestoration.blogspot.com/p/about.html.

preferred referral list. No pastor or ministry leader can serve simultaneously as an individual's legal guide and counselor but rather should use the information in this chapter to spot issues, identify the problems, and offer guidance soaked in wisdom to make the best referral if necessary. Finding like-minded Christian lawyers includes local churches, local Christian law school alumni directories, and the Christian Legal Society (CLS).

Furthermore, some state chapters of CLS also offer attorney referral lists based on the area of practice. This list will be one of your most priceless resources when working with couples in marital crisis. As you do the work of ministry, this strategy allows you to bring alongside your guidance a lawyer to help the family in crisis from a biblical worldview.

CONCLUSION

I can still see that young father working hard to hide formidable feelings of betrayal and a broken heart. Even amid his emotional trauma, he wanted to avoid litigation and public airing of their family crisis to protect their children. He needed empathy, information, and Spirit-filled guidance. We worked to develop a custody and visitation agreement that kept the children safe from having to stay overnight with their mom in her new residence, settling the decision-making between the parents on behalf of the children. This allowed them to move forward, providing some control and comfort for my client but leaving a pathway for the wayward spouse to return, should she so decide. This remedy kept the matter out of court and protected the welfare of the children. His pastor provided spiritual support and direction and helped him find me to guide him through the legal decisions.

The end of their story is unknown to me. This scenario, however, alerted me to the very tangible realities of unfaithfulness in marriages within the church. It also exposed a parent's concerns about the potential risk to children who could be subject to non-custodial adult caregivers. Like-minded guides focused on the ultimate Healer and Reconciler made all the difference to a family in crisis by offering them Spirit-filled guidance through the toughest part of the crisis.

Ministry leaders can take a toxic and volatile crisis like this and turn it into an opportunity for God to work. Being prepared with the legal knowledge and resources to help in a meaningful way is priceless. Ignoring divorce and family breakdown is not an option for ministry leaders. Rather, authentic guidance is needed to help families understand and navigate the crisis of divorce and family breakdown, to help them find resources beyond the church, and encourage them to be empowered by their faith amid the crisis. Finally, ministry leaders help marital partners explore divorce alternatives to mitigate and avert complete family destruction. Leading and serving in this way can authentically make a positive difference to those counseled and their families for generations to come.

9

FAMILIES AFFECTED BY DISABILITY

Ryan Wolfe

"Pastor Ryan, Pastor Ryan!" cries out a children's ministry volunteer running after the senior pastor on Sunday morning between services. The pastor turns to greet her, but before he gets a word out, the visibly shaken volunteer blurts out, "We have a problem!" The pastor's mind races as he considers the many variables. He tries not to assume the worst. "Take a deep breath. Everything is going to be okay." He says this, half reminding himself, too, before continuing. "Now, what is going on?" The volunteer gathers herself as much as possible and says, "We have a new child today. His parents said he is on the autism spectrum. I don't know what we did wrong, but he is having a meltdown. We don't know what to do!"

The pastor is usually good on his feet handling unknown situations, but this time, he finds himself at a loss for words. Staring back at his volunteer, he opens his mouth to speak, but no words come out. Most senior pastors would not know what to do because few understand autism. Seminaries do not offer courses in "Sunday School Crises."

Families with disabilities and special needs create unique opportunities for churches. According to the Centers for Disease Control (CDC),

26% of adults in the United States have some form of disability.[1] How the pastor, the congregation, and the church campus greet and include individuals and families affected by disability will determine whether they attend and remain in the church.

Let's rewind to the scenario above at the point the frantic volunteer runs down the senior pastor and see how the interaction could have gone differently, picking up with the volunteer laying out the perceived problem.

The volunteer gathers herself as much as possible and says, "We have a new child today. His parents said he is on the autism spectrum. I don't know what we did wrong, but he is having a meltdown. We don't know what to do!"

The senior pastor calmly responds, "It is going to be okay. We may not have all the answers right now, but we will figure it out together. Here is what is important. The child and his family must know they are loved and welcome here. God loves everyone, and Jesus made a way for all people to find a place of belonging in God's family. We will do the same for this child and his family no matter what it takes. Now go and find the family and let them know how happy we are they are here. Ask them to help us as we figure this out together."

Now, that is a better response! Pastors and churches can have the confidence to respond this way when they have a heart for inclusion that matches the great love of God. This chapter aims to give pastors and churches the tools necessary to respond in confidence when, not if, a similar situation arises. In fact, after implementing strategies from this chapter, the goal would be that no church would find themselves in a state of crisis.

FACTS ON DISABILITY IN THE UNITED STATES

People often only think of disability within the framework of what is commonly recognized as the international symbol of disability, the sign with an icon of a person using a wheelchair set against a blue background. A Danish design student, Susanne Koefoed, created this design over fifty

---

[1] "Disability Impacts All of Us," CDC, accessed July 5, 2023, www.cdc.gov/ncbddd/disabilityandhealth/infographic-disability-impacts-all.html.

years ago.[2] However, not all people with disabilities use wheelchairs. It is common not to see a single wheelchair in a Sunday service at any church. One could falsely conclude that people with disabilities were not present. This, however, could not be further from the truth.

As mentioned, the CDC estimates 26% of US adults have some form of disability. With an estimated population of 332 million in 2022,[3] roughly 66 million people live with disabilities. Of that 66 million, only three million are wheelchair users.[4] That leaves 95.5% of the population with disabilities as non-wheelchair users. Eighty percent of those with disabilities have what are referred to as invisible disabilities, or disabilities that go unnoticed at first glance.[5]

People affected by disability are the largest minority group in the United States and the world. People affected by disability are in a mission field that does not require travel to reach them with the gospel. Disability does not discriminate based on gender, race, religion, geography, or socioeconomics. It is also the only minority group that has open enrollment. At any point in life, someone can go from being able-bodied to becoming permanently disabled because of a traumatic event or illness. If anyone lives long enough, they will inevitably join this people group.

While people with disabilities are common in each community, there is one place they are missing—the local church. Recent studies disclosed that 57% of adults without disabilities attend church monthly compared to 45% of adults with a disability.[6] That is a significant gap in attendance. According to Mike Dobes of Joni and Friends, part of the gap can be

---

[2] Sarah Dawood, "Why the Wheelchair Symbol Should be Rethought to Include 'Invisible Disabilities,'" *Design Week*, August 1, 2018, www.designweek.co.uk/issues/30-july-5-august-2018/why-the-wheelchair-symbol-should-be-rethought-to-include-invisible-disabilities/.
[3] "U.S. Population Estimated at 332,403,650 on Jan. 1, 2022," US Department of Commerce, January 6, 2022, www.commerce.gov/news/blog/2022/01/us-population-estimated-332403650-jan-1-2022.
[4] "Wheelchairs in the United States," Karman Healthcare, January 20, 2021, www.karmanhealthcare.com/wheelchairs-in-the-united-states/.
[5] "Invisible Disabilities: 80% of Disabled People Are Concerned!," Inclusive City Maker, August 6, 2021, www.inclusivecitymaker.com/invisible-disabilities-80-of-disabled-people-are-concerned/.
[6] Erik W. Carter, "A Place of Belonging: Research at the Intersection of Faith and Disability," *Review and Expositor* 113, no. 2 (2016): 167-80.

attributed to 80-85% of churches having no disability ministry programming or outreach.[7]

Reaching the disabled community is truly the epitome of Jesus' words when he speaks about how there are so few workers in a plentiful harvest. "When he saw the crowds, he had compassion on them, because they were harassed and helpless, like sheep without a shepherd. Then he said to his disciples, 'The harvest is plentiful but the workers are few. Ask the Lord of the harvest, therefore, to send out workers into his harvest field" (Mt 9:36-38). Sharing the gospel and reaching the unbelievers who are disabled and those who are disengaged from the church should be a ministry goal of every church.

Beyond the prevalence of disability and the vast opportunities to share the gospel being a reason for congregational engagement, churches need to be a voice of hope and an advocate for their disability communities. The work of disability ministry is the ministry of the gospel. The upside-down kingdom of God prioritizes that the last be first. The special care Jesus showed individuals with disabilities should also be mirrored and prioritized in churches.

There is abundant evidence to support this gospel priority. Children with disabilities are three times more likely to be abused and neglected than children without disabilities.[8] The divorce rate for families with children with all different forms of disabilities is as high as 85-87% compared to the general population divorce rate being around 50%.[9] The previous statistics speak to children with disabilities and their families who have embraced life. Now consider that it is estimated that between 60-90% of children diagnosed with Down syndrome are aborted in the United States, compared to 18% of all other pregnancies that end in abortion.[10]

---

[7]Sarah Eekhoff Zylstra, "Let No Special Needs Hinder the Spread of the Gospel," *The Gospel Coalition*, September 2, 2014, www.thegospelcoalition.org/article/let-no-special-need-hinder-the-spread-of-the-gospel/.

[8]Lori A. Legan et al., "Maltreatment of Children with Disabilities," *Pediatrics* 147, no. 5 (May 2021), https://publications.aap.org/pediatrics/article/147/5/e2021050920/180813/Maltreatment-of-Children-With-Disabilities.

[9]Annette Hines, "Divorce and Estate Planning for Parents of Special Needs Children," Special Needs Law Group of Massachusetts, September 3, 2020, https://specialneeds-law.com/divorce-and-estate-planning-for-parents-of-special-needs-children/.

[10]"Down Syndrome and Social Capital: Assessing the Costs of Selective Abortion," Joint Economic Committee Republicans, March 18, 2022, www.jec.senate.gov/public/index.cfm

Living with a disability or supporting a loved one with a disability can be difficult. The church has an incredible opportunity to bring hope to a hurting world while obeying God's calling. "Speak up for those who cannot speak for themselves; ensure justice for those being crushed" (Prov 31:8 NLT).

Where should pastors and churches begin when presented with the prospect of ministering to individuals and families affected by disabilities? They should expand their general understanding of disability and how to engage those affected by disability. Pastors and churches do not need to be experts to minister to individuals and families affected by disabilities effectively. They just need to be able to find the answers to the different scenarios they encounter. Below is a 10,000-foot view of disabilities and tips for effectively ministering to people in each disability category.

DISABILITY DEFINITIONS AND QUICK TIPS

Martin Luther King Jr. once said, "People fail to get along with each other because they fear each other. They fear each other because they don't know each other. They don't know each other because they have not properly communicated with each other."[11] People fear what they do not know. Fear separates, distorts, and discourages. Fear of perceived differences is among the greatest barriers to meaningful inclusion and belonging. His idea also applies to groups with and without disabilities. Understanding disabilities and the fact that all people are more alike than different should go a long way toward lifting fear and creating pathways to inclusion and belonging.

What is a disability? A disability is any condition of the body or mind that makes it more difficult for the person with the condition to do certain activities and interact with others.[12] Disabilities can be lifelong, progressive, or temporary. There are six general types of disabilities: physical, visual, hearing, mental health, developmental, and learning

---

/republicans/2022/3/down-syndrome-and-social-capital-assessing-the-costs-of-selective-abortion.

[11] Martin Luther King Jr., "Advice for Living," in *The Papers of Martin Luther King, Jr.*, vol. 4, *Symbol of the Movement January 1957—December 1958*, ed. Susan Carson et. al. (Berkeley: University of California Press, 2000), 401.

[12] "Disability and Health Overview," CDC, September 16, 2020, www.cdc.gov/ncbddd/disabilityandhealth/disability.html.

disabilities. It is important to note that many congregants live with impairments that have either gone undiagnosed or do not fully meet the legal qualifications for disability. Removing barriers by making accommodations benefits everyone, whether formally diagnosed or not.

Tips when ministering to people with physical disabilities. Physical disabilities include any physical limitation that can inhibit the physical function of one or more limbs of a person.[13] They can be temporary, progressive, or permanent. Common physical disabilities include multiple sclerosis, muscular dystrophy, chronic arthritis, cerebral palsy, spina bifida, spinal cord injury, fibromyalgia, and myalgic encephalomyelitis (formerly called chronic fatigue syndrome).

Quick tips for meaningful inclusion of people with physical disabilities include (but are not limited to) ample handicap parking, curb cuts, ramps, automatic doors, elevators, wheelchair-accessible seating in multiple areas of the worship center, ADA-accessible bathroom stalls, and a universal-sized changing table. Well-trained ushers and deaconate ministers can be key to providing personal assistance to people with physical disabilities at church events.

Tips when ministering to people with visual disabilities. Visual disabilities or impairments include any kind of vision loss. Being diagnosed as legally blind describes someone with 10% or less of normal vision. Only 10% of people with visual disabilities are totally blind, meaning that 90% of people are visually impaired.[14]

Quick tips for meaningful inclusion of people with visual disabilities include offering braille signage, well-lit pathways to worship center seating, large print Bibles, large print hymnals, magnifying devices, using large text sizes on screens with fewer words, and using dark backgrounds and light-colored text.

Tips when ministering to people with hearing disabilities. Hearing disabilities are defined as any person who cannot hear as well as someone with normal hearing. The term deaf refers to someone who has severe

---

[13] "Physical Disabilities," Center for Disability Sports, Health and Wellness, Rutgers School of Arts and Sciences, accessed July 5, 2023, https://kines.rutgers.edu/dshw/disabilities/physical/1060-physical-disabilities.
[14] Trish Robichaud, "6 General Types of Disabilities," Changing Paces, February 1, 2011, https://changingpaces.com/6-general-types-of-disabilities/.

to profound hearing loss. Hard of hearing or hearing impaired describes someone with limited hearing in one or both ears who uses their residual hearing and speech to communicate.[15] The World Health Organization estimates that in 2050, one in every ten people will have disabling hearing loss.[16]

Quick tips for meaningful inclusion of people with hearing disabilities include sign language interpretation, real-time captioning for speakers, closed captions for videos, hearing amplifiers, FM systems, qualified note-takers, printed service notes, and available scripts for sermons or other teachings.

Tips when ministering to people with mental health disabilities. Mental health disabilities, like physical disabilities, take many different forms and modes of treatment. Mental health disabilities fall into six categories: thought disorders such as schizophrenia; mood disorders like depression; anxiety disorders, which include obsessive-compulsive disorders, panic disorders, and phobias; eating disorders; personality disorders; and organic brain disorders like Alzheimer's, stroke, and dementia.[17] The World Health Organization reported a 25% increase in the prevalence of anxiety and depression one year removed from the onset of the Covid-19 pandemic. Young people and women were the people groups most dramatically affected.[18] Of all types of disabilities, people with mental health disabilities will likely be the church's largest source of encounters and opportunities for extending hope in the coming years.

Quick tips for meaningful inclusion of people with mental health disabilities include offering support groups, referrals to professional counseling, financial assistance for counseling, ample seating options or online worship for people with social anxieties, forming community partnerships with mental health organizations, and providing routine,

---

[15] Robichaud, "6 General Types of Disabilities."
[16] "Deafness and Hearing Loss," World Health Organization, February 2, 2024, www.who.int/news-room/fact-sheets/detail/deafness-and-hearing-loss.
[17] Robichaud, "6 General Types of Disabilities."
[18] "COVID-19 Pandemic Triggers 25% Increase in Prevalence of Anxiety and Depression Worldwide," World Health Organization, March 2, 2022, www.who.int/news/item/02-03-2022-covid-19-pandemic-triggers-25-increase-in-prevalence-of-anxiety-and-depression-worldwide.

sound biblical teaching on depression and anxiety. A must-have resource that will help your church welcome and serve those with mental health diagnoses is the book *Mental Health and the Church* by Dr. Stephen Grcevich, who also authored a chapter in this book that might be helpful.

Tips when ministering to people with developmental disabilities. Developmental disabilities are a group of conditions describing an impairment in physical, learning, language, or behavior areas. Intellectual disabilities are permanent and affect day-to-day functioning.[19] The most common developmental disabilities are autism, Down syndrome, fragile X syndrome, fetal alcohol syndrome, and Prader-Willi syndrome.[20] People with developmental disabilities typically experience difficulties with daily activities such as communication, socialization, and independent living. A recent Lifeway Research study conducted by Andrew Whitehead found that children with autism are almost twice as likely never to attend church.[21] Their research also found that children with autism are often viewed as a problem in the church. This results from volunteers not being familiar with autism, not having a plan, or not being equipped to identify triggers to behaviors within the church environment.

Quick tips for meaningful inclusion of people with developmental disabilities include having a thorough intake process, meeting with families before programming, training for volunteers, a buddy ministry, developmentally appropriate curriculum, visual schedules, social stories, sensory bags, noise-canceling headphones, communication devices, and a sensory or quiet room made available. A must-have resource to help your church meaningfully include individuals with autism is the book *Autism and Your Church* by J. Barbara Newman.

Tips when ministering to people with learning disabilities. Learning disabilities affect a person's ability to understand, use spoken or written language, do mathematical calculations, coordinate movements, or

---

[19]"Facts About Developmental Disabilities," CDC, April 27, 2022, www.cdc.gov/ncbddd/develop mentaldisabilities/facts.html.
[20]"4 Types of Intellectual Disabilities," Enable Me. Accessed May 30, 2024, https://www.enableme .ke/en/article/4-types-of-intellectual-disabilities-1534.
[21]Bob Smietana, "Few Churches Are Autism Friendly," Lifeway Research, July 30, 2018, https:// research.lifeway.com/2018/07/30/few-churches-are-autism-friendly/.

direct attention. Research shows that 8–10% of children under eighteen have a learning disability.[22] Having a learning disability does not mean that a person is not capable of learning. It means that they learn differently. Dyslexia is the most common learning disability. Attention deficit hyperactivity disorder (ADHD) often gets lumped into this category, but it is not considered a learning disability because although it affects learning, it is a mental health diagnosis. Mental health diagnoses like ADHD can lead to spiritual impairment[23] when mental health symptoms interfere with spiritual goals and strivings.

Quick tips for meaningful inclusion of people with learning disabilities include using accessible language, avoiding jargon, going at a slower pace, clarifying that you understand and are understood, including various types of learning material such as audio versions, and remembering that everyone is unique. Getting to know each individual will promote the best possible scenario for success.

After expanding a knowledge base of general disabilities and how to engage those affected by disability, pastors and churches must build a firm foundation of truth from God's Word about disability.

BUILDING A FIRM FOUNDATION: A BIBLICAL THEOLOGY OF DISABILITY

Jesus taught his followers, "Therefore everyone who hears these words of mine and puts them into practice is like a wise man who built his house on the rock. The rain came down, the streams rose, and the winds blew and beat against that house; yet it did not fall, because it had its foundation on the rock" (Mt 7:24-25). Short- and long-term success will be determined by the foundation that the church has established around its theology of disability. God is not silent on the topic of disability. The church shouldn't be silent, either. When churches have a proper understanding of the theology of disability, it will help them to navigate the rocky moments and pave their way for success.

---

[22]"Learning Disabilities," National Institute of Neurological Disorders and Stroke, November 28, 2023, www.ninds.nih.gov/health-information/disorders/learning-disabilities.

[23]William Hathaway and Russell Barkley, "Self-regulation, ADHD, and Child Religiousness," *Journal of Psychology and Christianity* 22, no. 2 (January 2003): 101.

The following biblical truths will confront lies that are widely believed about disability.

Truth #1: Disabled people are not a mistake. The world teaches a lie that disability is ugly, undesirable, a mistake, shameful, and something that should be ignored or eliminated if at all possible. God has a different view of disability. Disability is not a mistake because God makes no mistakes. Scripture teaches that all people are created in God's image, wonderfully—on purpose for a purpose. There are no exceptions for people with disabilities. This truth begins in the very first chapter of the Bible when God says, "Let us make mankind in our image, in our likeness" (Gen 1:26). All people, including people with disabilities, are created in the *imago Dei* and are image bearers of the Creator.

God is intimately and actively involved in creation, constantly working for healing in a fallen world where disease, injury, and illness are common. "For you created my inmost being; you knit me together in my mother's womb. I praise you because I am fearfully and wonderfully made; your works are wonderful, I know that full well" (Ps 139:13-14). Nowhere in Psalm 139 does it say that only babies who are born healthy and without perceived complications or flaws are wonderfully made.

A second lie is assumed in the world, and many in the church believe that people born with disabilities are genetic mistakes or are marred by sin. Psychologists have coined the term "metaphysical model of disability," signifying the mistaken presumption that morally upright people will be rewarded with health while immoral behavior will be punished.[24] The implication is that people with disabilities are being punished for immoral acts. A careful look at a heated conversation between Moses and the Lord gives a very different idea. "Moses said to the LORD, 'Pardon your servant, Lord. I have never been eloquent, neither in the past nor since you have spoken to your servant. I am slow of speech and tongue.' The LORD said to him, 'Who gave human beings their mouths? Who makes them deaf or mute? Who gives them sight or makes them blind? Is it not I, the Lord? Now go; I will help you speak and will teach you what to say'" (Ex 4:10-12). Undeniably, the Lord claims to be the author

---

[24]Bernard Dan, "The Metaphysical Model of Disability: Is This a Just World?" *Developmental Medicine and Child Neurology* 63, no. 3 (March 2021): 240. https://doi.org/10.1111/dmcn.14775.

of disability in these verses. This is a hard truth for many to accept, but there is hope. The Lord promises to be with Moses and to intercede on his behalf. So, whether God creates disability or allows it later in life, it is not without hope or purpose.

But what about people who become disabled later in life? This may be due to a work accident, willful sin, or the actions of others. Take, for example, a drunk driver driving 100 mph doses off and goes left of center, causing an accident that leaves innocent people disabled for life. The fallen world involves sin, mistakes, illness, and disability. None of this happens outside of the knowledge of God. While this can challenge one's understanding and faith, God is faithful, and His grace is sufficient for all.

Jesus changed the entire worldview and theology of disability for his disciples in one sentence. "As he went along, he saw a man blind from birth. His disciples asked him, 'Rabbi, who sinned, this man or his parents, that he was born blind?' 'Neither this man nor his parents sinned,' said Jesus, 'but this happened so that the works of God might be displayed in him'" (Jn 9:1-3). In this mic drop moment for Jesus, he puts a stake in the ground, confirming that people with disabilities are given a divine purpose by God that only they can fulfill. There is great power in knowing that all people were created on purpose for a purpose. Believing and teaching this theological truth about disability empowers people with disabilities and their loved ones and sets them free from the lies that they are a mistake, giving them hope and a purpose.

Truth #2: The suffering of disability engages grace. The world teaches that those affected by disability should be avoided and, in turn, left to suffer alone. The world does not believe that there is any redeeming value to disability.

People with disabilities need to know that they are not alone. God is with them. "For we do not have a high priest who is unable to empathize with our weaknesses" (Heb 4:15). God more than empathizes with people with disabilities—He promises to be with them and to provide for them.

The apostle Paul is our example of weakness becoming a strength in his discourse with the Lord surrounding the "thorn in his flesh" (2 Cor 12:7). Many believe that Paul suffered from a disabling condition.

"But he said to me, 'My grace is sufficient for you, for my power is made perfect in weakness.' Therefore, I will boast all the more gladly about my weaknesses, so that Christ's power may rest on me" (v. 9). The Lord promised to give Paul what he needed. For Paul, it was not necessarily what he wanted, but it served the divine purpose that God had for him. God will also give people what they need and promises his power will be shown throughout their lives despite their difficulties.

Finally, having an eternal perspective brings comfort to people who struggle with disabilities. Paul gives the following powerful reminder, "I consider that our present sufferings are not worth comparing with the glory that will be revealed in us" (Rom 8:18). While this life involves suffering, in glory, there will be no struggles, no pain, no confusion, and no doubts.

Truth #3: All means all. The world and many churches believe a lie that people with intellectual and developmental disabilities either do not need to accept Jesus as their Savior or are unable to do so because of cognitive limitations. People falsely believe that God will give them a free pass into heaven. There is no basis for a free pass in the Bible, as there are no asterisks in the Bible for people with IQ scores below 70. "All have sinned and fall short of the glory of God" (Rom 3:23). All means all. No exceptions.

If everyone has sinned, then everyone needs Jesus. Thankfully, God sent Jesus for all people, not just those the world would say can understand. "For God so loved the world that he gave his one and only Son, that whoever believes in him shall not perish but have eternal life" (Jn 3:16). While age and cognitive disabilities can create differentials in capacity to understand the complexities of theology or the consequences of sin, all people have fallen into sin in this world and need Jesus to redeem them.

The capacity for understanding God and his love for humanity has been made clear from the moment of creation. "For since the creation of the world God's invisible qualities—his eternal power and divine nature—have been clearly seen, being understood from what has been made, so that people are without excuse" (Rom 1:20). If all people have a capacity for understanding God's love, then the church must reach out to all people with the saving gospel message. It is not our place to judge one's level of understanding. God has that part covered.

Truth #4: Jesus commands churches to include the disability community. The world excludes and discriminates against people with disabilities. Over the years, churches have followed suit, consciously or subconsciously, believing in the lies the world has told. This, however, is contrary to what God desires for the local church.

This desire of God for the inclusion of people with disabilities can be seen from cover to cover in the Bible. Maybe the most beautiful story in the Old Testament is that of David and Mephibosheth in 2 Samuel 9. This story richly foreshadows Jesus and his desire to include people with disabilities. David seeks out Mephibosheth, who was disabled from a very young age due to a childhood accident. In any other ancient culture, his disability would have excluded him from being able to sit at the king's table. David does otherwise: "Mephibosheth lived in Jerusalem, because he always ate at the king's table; he was lame in both feet" (2 Sam 9:13). Mephibosheth was never healed of his disability, which did not matter to David. David understood Mephibosheth's worth to God because of who he was and the promise that he had made.

A few Sabbaths before going to the cross, Jesus gave a final teaching about who belongs in God's family. This command for meaningful inclusion was not just a future declaration but one with immediate urgency. In Luke 14, Jesus makes this clear no fewer than three times, most notably as part of the parable of the great banquet. "The servant came back and reported this to his master. Then the owner of the house became angry and ordered his servant, 'Go out quickly into the streets and alleys of the town and bring in the poor, the crippled, the blind, and the lame'" (Lk 14:21). To not actively include people with disabilities in the church is to disobey a command of Jesus directly.

Other than being disobedient to Jesus, there are other consequences to not including people with disabilities in the church. The apostle Paul speaks about the body of Christ, "On the contrary, those parts of the body that seem to be weaker are indispensable" (1 Cor 12:22). Who would qualify better for the description "seem to be weaker" than people with disabilities? Paul states that the body of Christ—the church—is incomplete without them. The church is missing body parts and not functioning as God designed if people with disabilities are not present and actively using their gifts. The word *indispensable* is key to understanding the importance of people with disabilities to the church. Indispensable means something you cannot do without or something of the highest important. God's view of people with disabilities should not be a shocker because God's view of the kingdom has always been upside down in the eyes of the world.

After building a general knowledge based on disability, how to engage those with disabilities, and settling a firm foundation on the truth in God's Word, we are ready to dive in! Below are practical steps to formalizing an inclusive culture, disability ministry programming, and outreach.

WISDOM FOR THE PASTOR AND CHURCH'S FIRST INTERACTIONS

Naeen Callaway wisely exhorts: "Sometimes the smallest step in the right direction ends up being the biggest step of your life. Tip Toe if you must, but take a step."[25] Pastors can feel overwhelmed by the thought of ministering to individuals and families affected by disability if they have no experience in that area. There is good news! Leaders do not need to be an expert to be able to make a difference. They just have to have the heart and the willingness to take that first small step and risk opening the door for new relationships. Individuals and families affected by disability eagerly await to meet their pastor partway.

Understandably, the saying "people do not care what you know until they know that you care" is very real for individuals and families affected by disability. Once they know that the pastor genuinely cares, they will have an ally for life. But beware! Those with disabilities can easily sniff out a phony. The church has hurt many people affected by disability, and so they come apprehensively if they come at all. It is not uncommon for a new family at your church to have been asked to leave multiple churches before they show up at your church.

---

[25]"Naeem Callaway," Quozio, accessed on July 5, 2023, https://quozio.com/quote/1149a66f/1025/sometimes-the-smallest-step-in-the-right-direction-ends-up.

Because the church has hurt many, pastors need to extend grace. Because of history, some initial interactions may be bumpy. Pastors should avoid jumping to conclusions and seek to know the individual and the family. Being patient and making time to interact is crucial in extending grace. Sometimes, the best thing a leader can do is just listen. Drawing close in the presence of pain is life-giving.

Whether hurt was experienced at the current church or a former one, a pastor extending apologies and a humble attitude can make a world of difference. Apologies from a pastor who represents the offending church congregation can release people from the pain of the past and open the door for acceptance and meaningful belonging.

After communicating care, extending grace, and offering apologies, pastors should seek wisdom. This wisdom goes beyond general disability awareness and the theology of disability. This wisdom can only be found in and through relationships. The source of this unique wisdom is from the individuals and families affected by disability themselves. Each individual and family is unique. Don't be afraid to ask questions. Getting to know them, their story, their hurts, their needs, their hopes, and their dreams will unveil a great source of wisdom to the pastor.

FIRST STEPS FOR PASTORS AND CHURCHES

You have been made aware of the need to reach and include people affected by disability and their families. Now you are ready to act! If you are unsure where to start, don't stress. Each church, regardless of size, has the same starting point. It doesn't matter if you are a church of twenty or twenty thousand people. Want to know where your starting point is? Here you go. *Start with who you have.* That is it. If you have one person with a disability in your church, you have a viable disability ministry. Start with them. How? Take the following steps.

Step 1: Build a team. Warning! You cannot go at this alone. Part of starting with who you have is developing a leadership team from people within your church and community. This group of key volunteers will champion this ministry effort. Your disability ministry will only be as successful as the team you assemble. Ask, "Who in my church is going to be a champion for disability ministry?" Gather a list of names of parents, staff leaders, individuals affected by disability, and anyone connected to your local disability community who will likely have long-term buy-in for your ministry. Share your heart, dream, and reason for starting a disability ministry in your church.

After your team is assembled, commit to praying and growing together. Study what the Bible says about disability, disability facts, disability etiquette, strategies for engagement, and local statistics.

Step 2: Start with who you have. Why start with who you have? Because people in your congregation affected by disability will forgive you when you make mistakes. That is okay! It is better to fine-tune your disability ministry efforts with your people before rolling out the red carpet to your community. Individuals from your community may not be as forgiving, and word spreads fast—good or bad.

Don't forget you have a congregation full of people with disabilities already. Remember, according to the CDC, 26% of all the adults in your congregation are personally affected by disability. Likely most of your congregation has family affected by disability which means more than half of your congregation's families would benefit from your intentional efforts to meaningfully include people with disabilities in your church.

So how do you identify who is who without offending people? Pray. Begin to build awareness in your congregation by showing disability awareness videos and having conversations. Preach a sermon or a series of sermons on the topic of disability in the Bible. Do a church survey. Find people who work in the field of disability within your congregation. If you need help with any of these steps, there are excellent disability ministry organizations that have great free resources for you. For example, check out Ability Ministry's resource page online.[26]

Step 3: Find your unique starting point. After you identify who you have, find a starting point for your disability ministry efforts. It will be revealed as you get to know the needs of the individuals affected by disability in your congregation. Have an informational meeting. Invite all who have an interest. Share your heart. Ask people what their needs are, what their hopes and dreams are, what they wish the church could do for

---

[26] Ability Ministry, Resources, accessed April 26, 2024, https://abilityministry.com/resources/.

their family, and how they can contribute to the church as well. As your people share, the Holy Spirit will reveal a unique starting point for your church. There may be several themes that will surface. Pray and decide where to begin. Start small and meet one need at a time. There will be a pull to do several initiatives at once. Do not overpromise. Tackle one thing at a time with excellence.

Common starting points for disability ministry programming in churches include buddy systems for children and youth ministry, parent support groups, respite events for families, the creation of a sensory room, Sunday school classes for adults with intellectual and developmental disabilities, and monthly social events to provide opportunities for friendship and socialization.

Step 4: Study your church campus. When you begin meeting internal needs, you will next want to investigate the physical structure of your church facility. The building presents a message to your congregants with disabilities and prospective people from your community about what your church believes about those with disabilities. Hopefully, the message it gives lines up with your heart. If you want to know the message it sends, fill out a Church Campus Accessibility Checklist offered by Ability Ministry. You can download it today.[27] As you work on the checklist, identify accessibility barriers, and commit to correcting them over time.

Step 5: Engage your community. Once you have built your team, started meeting internal needs, and corrected accessibility barriers, you are ready to take your efforts to your community. Identify needs in your community and meet them one by one. Be a blessing—no strings attached! As you build relationships in your community, people will learn that your church cares and trust will be built over time. As people attend your church, get to know them. Identify needs and expand programming based on the needs of those who are coming. Not every church can do everything, but every church can do something.

For detailed help on how to start a disability ministry from square one, Ability Ministry provides a free step-by-step guide on its website,

---

[27] Ability Ministry, Disability Ministry Church Campus Accessibility Checklist, accessed April 26, 2024, https://abilityministry.com/product/disability-ministry-church-campus-accessibility-checklist/.

AbilityMinistry.com. Select the "I want to start a disability ministry option"[28] online and hit the ground running!

INDIVIDUAL AND FAMILY FEEDBACK

Tim Grover says in his book *Relentless: From Good to Great to Unstoppable* that "the only difference between 'feedback' and 'criticism' is the way you hear it."[29] If pastors are going to be successful in reaching families affected by disability, they must be willing to hear both. Unstoppable churches are not only able to hear feedback and criticism from families, but they seek it out to grow and become better from it.

The following section gives feedback from real families affected by disability that were surveyed in preparation for this chapter. May these words grant wisdom to you the reader as you seek to build an inclusive and welcoming environment at your churches.

What are practical ways churches can make families feel welcome?

- "Smile at our kids and acknowledge them."
- "Talk to our children even if they can't talk back."
- "Don't be afraid to offer to help, but don't help without asking first."
- "Knowing there was a safe place for our children where volunteers were both background checked and trained meant the world to us. We could relax knowing our kids would be okay while we worshiped together as a couple."
- "Volunteers met us in the parking lot knowing that I could not push both a stroller and a wheelchair."
- "We felt welcomed when we saw that the volunteers and staff were willing to listen, learn, and be flexible with the needs of our family."
- "We felt welcomed when the church interacted with us outside of the church walls. That let us know that they really cared about us."
- "The church sent us cards, small gifts, and brought meals during the many surgeries and procedures she endured."

---

[28] Ability Ministry, Start Here, accessed April 26, 2024, https://abilityministry.com/start-here/.
[29] Tim S. Grover, *Relentless: From Good to Great to Unstoppable* (New York: Scribner, 2014), xvii.

What are common pitfalls to avoid when interacting with families?

- "Don't stare at us. We already feel uncomfortable. That makes things worse."
- "Churches are often afraid to ask questions. Don't be afraid!"
- "All children and families with disabilities are different. Don't assume. Get to know each person and family."
- "Don't promise more than you are able to do. It is always better to under-promise and over-deliver."
- "Parents of children with disabilities cringe when someone says, 'God only gives these special needs children to people He knows can handle it.'"
- "Never say you are praying for the healing of our child unless you know that is what we are praying for too."

What are the greatest needs of families in your congregation?

- "I need to know that my son will be safe when I drop him off at church."
- "We need respite even if it is just for a few hours once a month. You don't know how hard it is to be on the clock around the clock."
- "Providing social events for our children outside of Sunday mornings. We want our child to have friends, be invited to birthday parties, and have the same experiences that every other child naturally has because they have friendships."
- "Check in on families outside of Sunday morning. Being a parent of a special needs child is difficult and sometimes very lonely. Just ask if we are okay or if there is anything you can do to help."
- "Having a parent support group would be amazing! I would love to be mentored by someone who has already gone through what I am going through right now."
- "What will happen to my child when I am not around to care for him? Having someone help my family figure out how to plan for the future is a huge need of ours."

What encouraging words can you offer to pastors who are reading this book?

- "Don't hesitate to start a disability ministry. There are so many families like mine in every community that needs to know that the church cares about them and that they are not alone."
- "Maybe your church can't afford to remodel your building, but you can start with a small set of sensory toys and build on that. It doesn't cost you anything to be compassionate and understanding."
- "Do what you can until you can do more."
- "Special needs families are willing to travel to be a part of a church that allows them to come as a family."
- "Pastors that take on this challenge will receive many more blessings than they could ever give."
- "Please be willing to get in the mess. Sometimes taking care of special needs children or individuals is messy. Remember that God was willing to send his son Jesus into our mess to save us. It is always worth it."
- "Give the cup of cold water. Special needs families are so thirsty for what every other family is thirsty for, Jesus. They may in fact be thirstier than others."
- "Don't do this ministry because you want to do something nice for people. Do it because you want people to be part of the identity of your church just like you would want from anyone else."

FINALLY

Napolean Hill stated, "Do not wait. The time will never be 'just right.' Start where you stand, work whatever tools you may have at your command, and better tools will be found as you go along."[30]

Jesus urged the religious leaders of his day to "go out quickly into the streets and alleys of the town and bring in the poor, the crippled, the blind and the lame" (Lk 14:21). The time is now for pastors and churches to reach and include individuals and families affected by disabilities.

---

[30]Napoleon Hill, *Think and Grow Rich* (New York: Jeremy P. Tarcher, 2007), 116.

Don't wait! Start with who you have. Identify needs. Meet those needs. Grow from there. As you seek to be a blessing to your disability community, God will bless you and give you exactly what you need along the way.

Let's close out this chapter the way it started, with the scenario of the frantic volunteer seeking the senior pastor for help. Now imagine with me how it would have played out differently if the church did the work laid out in the chapter.

"Pastor Ryan, Pastor Ryan!" cries out a children's ministry volunteer running after the senior pastor in the hallway on Sunday morning between services. The pastor turns to greet her with a smile and a hello, but before he gets a word out, the volunteer blurts out, "We had something amazing happen today!"

"Really? What happened?" The pastor responds, eager to know what transpired.

The elated volunteer says, "We had a new family come today. They were nervous because it was their first time, and they explained that they'd had some difficult experiences in previous churches because their child is on the autism spectrum. We told them not to worry and that they are welcome here. We told them that God loves everyone, and Jesus made a way for us to find belonging in God's family, so we are going to do the same. We are going to work together and make this a great experience for everyone."

"Wow! That is amazing. How did things end up going?" The pastor responds.

The volunteer says, "They went great. We took time to get to know the child and had the family fill out all the important paperwork. We then buddied up our new friend with one of our trained volunteers for the morning. The parents were surprised when they came to pick up their child that the child did not want to leave."

This too can be your experience when engaging with individuals and families affected by disability. All it takes is a little work and a heart that desires inclusion and belonging for all people. You got this!

10

SCREENS, CHILDREN, AND TEENS

The Challenges Are Real, and You Can Help

Kathy Koch

Once upon a time, there were Walkmans and earphones, which was the end of civilization. Some predicted it would happen because youth would no longer interact. Everyone would be in their sound bubble. It didn't happen. But technology continues to change and to change us. Changes in the church are noticeable, too.

Churches both embrace and are cautious toward technology. They use websites, Facebook pages, text alerts, and email blasts for announcements, prayer requests, and encouragement. People can watch services online and stay connected from all over the world. Bible apps make it easy for people always to have a Bible.

There is a dark side to technology, also. Phones can be distracting. Kids might exchange pornographic images as if they were as harmless as baseball cards. Social media "challenges" can result in severe physical and mental health problems. Thus, parents may feel at a loss as to how to manage technology in a safe way for their families.

Challenges at home regarding technology can also find their way into your church. Parents often seek senior and youth pastors for guidance in helping them manage technology, which they may see as destroying their families. Discouragement is close at hand when parents can't effectively protect their families from harm. They see character changes, mood flips, and compulsion-like attachments to phones, gaming, and videos . . . and maybe these issues are interconnected. So, they meet with you to discuss their frustrations and concerns. You can help them connect the dots and the dotcoms.

WHAT HAVE YOU HEARD? IDENTIFYING ISSUES FROM OUR OBSERVATIONS

Possibly, you have met with parents because of problems associated with technology. Familiar comments include statements like:

- "We don't want to give our kids phones yet, but many in the youth group have them. Pastor Jim likes to communicate through texting and Instagram, so what can we do?"
- "My son and daughter saw porn by mistake. I feel horrible. What should I do?"
- "I can't get my kids to come out of their rooms. They binge-watch YouTube videos all night. Their grades are slipping, and we're not connected much anymore. How can I get them to care?"
- "We want our kids to come to us with questions, but they use Siri all the time instead."
- "Our son says he learns so much from people he follows on social media that he doesn't need our input."

Pastors and staff have questions, too. One asked, "So many of my students are distracted by their phones, and they distract others as well. It happens more often on Sundays than on Wednesdays. It's so frustrating! We talk about self-control and respect, but they succumb to the temptation to multitask. They seem to get bored so quickly now! I'm tempted to change the policy to no phones at all. What do you think?"

What about this question? "Can we do anything to encourage more youth and adults to use paper Bibles rather than phone apps? Especially youth, they don't focus and concentrate well when using their phones. I'm concerned because they're dishonoring the Word of God and not treating it or God with the respect they deserve."

There is much to understand if we respond to parents with wisdom, discretion, and direction and equip them to expand their discernment, compassion, and practicality. Let's start with the brain.

WHAT MUST YOU KNOW? TECHNOLOGY AND THE BRAIN

The use of technology affects children's brains at all ages. Because children's and teens' brains are not fully developed, screens have more significant and longer-lasting power over them than adults.[1] Young brains become "wired" for technology, and they may expect much in the world to behave like technology does. For example, they may always expect and prefer large amounts of stimuli and everything and everyone to be quick-paced. Brain-wiring is how habits form quickly, and expectations are learned, even unintentionally. For example, Choudhury and McKinney state that "Internet use exacerbates existing natural cognitive deficits and proneness for instant gratification and risk orientation in adolescents, impairing social and reasoning abilities by stunting the development of the prefrontal cortex."[2] Teen girls report they can't stop using social media even when they realize it's not good for their mental health.[3]

Repetition is powerful. For example, I've asked young people if they planned to "x" out of a game but chose "play again" even though they didn't mean to. Many admit they've done it. I've done it! When actions

---

[1] Kathy Koch, *Screens and Teens: Connecting with Our Kids in a Wireless World* (Chicago: Moody, 2015), 31-36; Doug Smith, *[Un]intentional: How Screens Secretly Shape Your Desires and How You Can Break Free* (Grand Rapids, MI: Credo House, 2021), 11-26; and Cory Turner, "10 Things to Know about How Social Media Affects Teens' Brains," NPR, February 16, 2023, www.npr.org/2023/02/16/1157180971/10-things-to-know-about-how-social-media-affects-teens-brains.
[2] Suparna Choudhury and Kelly A. McKinney, "Digital Media, the Developing Brain and the Interpretive Plasticity of Neuroplasticity," *Transcultural Psychiatry* 50, no. 2 (April 2013): 192-215, https://doi.org/10.1177/1363461512474623.
[3] Derek Thompson, "Social Media is Attention Alcohol," *The Atlantic*, September 17, 2021, www.theatlantic.com/ideas/archive/2021/09/social-media-attention-alcohol-booze-instagram-twitter/620101/; and Georgia Wells, Jeff Horwitz, and Deepa Seetharaman, "Facebook Knows Instagram Is Toxic for Teen Girls, Company Documents Show," *Wall Street Journal*, September 14, 2021, www.wsj.com/articles/facebook-knows-instagram-is-toxic-for-teen-girls-company-documents-show-11631620739.

are repeated over time, it's easy to keep doing them. Adrenaline is real, and online media forms habits that are difficult to break.

If you drive home from church the same way every time, I imagine you can almost turn onto your street without thought. Going a different way feels unnatural and requires effort. Patterns are set. This is how children are with screens. Using screens is natural, easy, and becomes very intuitive. For them, doing other things takes more effort and may feel uncomfortable or unnatural, and they may push back and resist.

Not only does frequent screen use cause comfort and desire, but screen use can be harmfully captivating. Children can become addicted to the adrenaline that surges when they get a like, win a game, enjoy a song, or get a message from a friend. Teens become so used to having devices in their hands that they miss them when they aren't there. When disconnected from their phones, they feel disconnected from their friends, society, and life in general. The phenomenon called phantom vibration syndrome can occur, which is a false perception that a device is vibrating.[4] The devices have become children's electronic pacifiers or security blankets.

Among the reasons to warn against tech addiction in children is evidence that those who develop addictions to screens now are much more susceptible to developing other addictions in the future. Research suggests that 90% of addictions have roots in the teen years.[5] Other reasons include missing activities that are much more beneficial for their development.[6] These include playing games with siblings and peers, exploring the outside world, reading, listening to music with others, talking with friends, and completing homework. These are not merely activities. While children and teens engage with others, they can problem-solve, create, find adventure, and develop negotiating skills. With diverse experiences, brains develop

---

[4]Margaret Rouse, "Phantom Vibration Syndrome," Techopedia, May 11, 2015, www.techopedia.com/definition/31221/phantom-vibration-syndrome.
[5]The National Center on Addiction and Substance Abuse (CASA) at Columbia University, "National Study Reveals: Origins of an Epidemic, Teen Substance Use America's #1 Public Health Problem," PR Newswire, June 29, 2011, www.prnewswire.com/news-releases/national-study-reveals-origins-of-an-epidemic-teen-substance-use-americas-1-public-health-problem-124690008.html.
[6]Mitch Prinstein, "Protecting Our Children Online" (written testimony, U.S. Senate Committee on Judiciary, 2023), 17, www.judiciary.senate.gov/imo/media/doc/2023-02-14%20-%20Testimony%20-%20Prinstein.pdf.

for more than technology use in the future. Confidence, autonomy, and self-reliance are formed. The ability to give and take with others grows. Hard things become more natural and easier to do.

Overuse or problematic use of technology contributes to unhealthy behaviors. These include overeating, irregular or deprived sleep, behavioral problems, weakened academic performance, violence, and less time spent playing and being outside.[7] Too much time on screens, coupled with less time for healthy activities, contributes to the stress, anxiety, and suicidal ideation that you may have to deal with in family and church settings.[8]

The American Academy of Child & Adolescent Psychiatry recommends time limits on children's social media usage to enhance overall development.[9] To help parents decide what's best for their families, you can encourage them to create a Family Media Plan. Focus on the Family also produces an excellent guide. These age recommendations will serve you well.[10]

- For children under eighteen months, avoid screen-based media except video chatting.
- For children eighteen to twenty-four months, watch only high-quality programming with adults for no more than one hour per week.
- For children two to five years old, limit screen time to one hour per day of high-quality programming, and often watch it with children.

---

[7]Jill Christensen, "Children and Screen Time: How Much Is Too Much?," Mayo Clinic Health System, May 28, 2021, www.mayoclinichealthsystem.org/hometown-health/speaking-of-health/children-and-screen-time.

[8]Allison Aubrey, "How to Help Young People Limit Screen Time—and Feel Better about How They Look," NPR, February 26, 2023, www.npr.org/sections/health-shots/2023/02/26/1159099629/teens-social-media-body-image; Jonathan Haidt, "The Dangerous Experiment on Teen Girls," *The Atlantic*, November 21, 2021, www.theatlantic.com/ideas/archive/2021/11/facebooks-dangerous-experiment-teen-girls/620767/; and TechDetox Mom, "Always on: Technology, Stress and Anxiety," TechDetox Box, November 20, 2023, www.techdetoxbox.com/screen-time-problems/always-on/.

[9]"Screen Time and Children," American Academy of Child & Adolescent Psychiatry, February 2020, www.aacap.org/AACAP/Families_and_Youth/Facts_for_Families/FFF-Guide/Children-And-Watching-TV-054.aspx.

[10]Rachel Ehmke, "Media Guidelines for Kids of All Ages," Child Mind Institute, November 20, 2023, https://childmind.org/article/media-guidelines-for-kids-of-all-ages/; and Mary Alvord, "Digital Guidelines: Promoting Healthy Technology Use for Children," American Psychological Association, December 12, 2019, www.apa.org/topics/social-media-internet/technology-use-children.

- For children six and up, establish consistent limits on how much time is spent using media and the types of media used. Continue to interact with children so you can help them interpret what they see—model appropriate technology use. Protect bedtime and create media-free spaces like bedrooms, the dinner table, and the car unless you're on long trips. Encourage other activities.

WHAT MUST YOU KNOW? TECHNOLOGY AND THE HEART

Technology doesn't just change children's brains; it changes their hearts. Of course, I don't mean that it causes physical changes as it does to the brain. I mean alterations to what children think is good and right and what is harmful and wrong. Changes to their attitudes, actions, and decisions can spring from the amount of technology they use and what they do with it. Let's consider a few of the most important "heart changes." They include bullying and online harassment, doubts about God, others, and self, and accepting lies and deceptions without questioning.

Internet bullying and harassment are a big deal. The internet is impersonal. It is a fertile environment to exert power, revenge, and retaliation. Young users often have no filter and little realization of the effects and consequences of their actions. As leaders, if you and the parents in your ministry don't deal with bullying issues well, young people will believe they can continue, and their behavior will very likely escalate to more serious levels. Online bullying *is* a serious issue. If you become aware that it is going on, intervene and do what you can to stop it. Mitch Prinstein concluded: "Brain scans of adults and youths reveal that online harassment activates the same regions of the brain that respond to physical pain and trigger a cascade of reactions that replicate physical assault and create physical and mental health damage."[11]

Maybe parents have asked how to respond to their children's doubts about God. Lonely internet searches about God can lead children down pathways that draw them away from God. It is painful and even scary for them to see their children waver in their faith and question whether they want to be followers of Jesus. Yet, as you know, it's not uncommon for

---

[11] Prinstein, "Protecting Our Children Online," 12.

adolescents to ask questions because they need to find their way to faith. Church ministry in late elementary and early middle school years can prepare parents for this reality. By identifying subtle and bold lies children may be exposed to online, ministry leaders can teach corresponding truths to help children recognize and reject these lies. Such teaching doesn't guarantee children will follow their parents' faith or recommended cautions, but offering trusted adults to help children understand and evaluate messages and platforms is part of good ministry leadership.

You might have wondered if some behavioral issues and doubts stem from technology. Maybe you haven't been confident enough to bring this up to parents. What I share below will help you frame future discussions.

When I teach parents about the lies children believe, they're relieved and concerned.[12] They're relieved because the lies reveal that children's defiant, argumentative behaviors and other challenges may not be due to poor parenting. Technology is often a primary culprit. I'm not leaving parents or children totally off the hook. The amount of tech use and what children and teens do with technology must be considered.

I've already pointed out that children can become *physically* addicted to the adrenaline that technology use causes. As a result, they want more of that same rush and joy. This is why it's hard for them to put their phones down and fully concentrate without thinking about what they might miss.[13] Since we are exploring issues of technology and the heart, let me suggest the metaphor that individuals can become *emotionally* attached to lies they find compelling. In my decades of interacting with thousands of children, parents, and ministers about what destructive beliefs drive us and our culture, I have identified four common lies about personhood rooted in technology. They deal with self-centeredness, happiness, options, and authority. Living out these addictive falsehoods as though they were true is a source of concern; they may feel emotionally satisfying, but they intertwine with the physical addiction cycle and become barriers to personal and emotional growth.

---

[12] Koch, *Screens and Teens*, 83-88, 103-05, 137-38, 163-64, 181-82.
[13] Maria T. Maza et al., "Association of Habitual Checking Behaviors on Social Media with Longitudinal Functional Brain Development," *JAMA Pediatrics* 177, no. 2 (January 3, 2023): 160-67, https://doi.org/10.1001/jamapediatrics.2022.4924.

FOUR LIES TECHNOLOGY TEACHES CHILDREN

Lie #1: I am the center of my own universe. Technology can cause children to believe, "I am the center of my own universe." Children may believe this because of the convenience of their phones, the ease of posting pictures, getting reactions to their videos and posts on social media, and the freedom to watch and listen to whatever they want. All this attention amplifies the sense of a world integrated around self, where all things connect with and come to or from me. Also, parents may consistently put children first and act as if the world revolves around them, reinforcing this self-centered perception.

Children's hearts can turn toward pride, entitlement, and anger if they believe this lie. This belief can also cause loneliness because they elevate their importance over others, which causes them to think they don't need anyone. If children know God, believing this lie negatively affects their relationship with Him. They begin to think He serves them. If they haven't yet trusted Christ as Savior and Lord and they believe this lie, God seems unnecessary.

Today's youth may struggle with boredom more than their parents did at their age. But boredom is a fact of life, and the misbelief that we can or should avoid boredom at all costs will cost something. Ministry leaders can equip and encourage parents to help their children navigate boredom, given that life is more than novelty, fun, and entertainment. Leaders might also advise young people on ways to use their free time constructively, such as developing hobbies, playing an instrument, engaging in sports, spending time outdoors, learning, and serving others.

When children get their eyes off themselves, they can recognize there's a whole God-created universe worth living in. Now, they may be willing to serve others, which is one of the best ways for children and teens to discover more about themselves and the world they are *part* of—not the *center* of. Serving can be challenging for them at first, so they may resist. They may initially serve because it makes them feel important. Changes in their attitudes and character will likely happen when parents and church staff engage children in conversations during and after serving. Sharing relevant Scripture such as Mark 10:45 (Jesus came to serve), Luke 22:26 (leaders serve), and Galatians 5:13 (serve through love) is also wise.

Lie #2: I deserve to be happy all the time. If you reflect on your experiences with children, you'll realize many of them think, "I deserve to be happy all the time." Because technology is new, convenient, immediate, easy, personal, and entertaining, they've learned to prioritize happiness. Many would like the world to behave as tech does—with a happy-clappy marketing style of immediate gratification. Young parents also may believe this "I deserve to be happy" lie. They may feed into it by giving in to their children's complaining, even when it's not in their children's best interest.

Believing happiness is their right orients children's hearts to entitlement, similar to the first lie. If parents complain to you about their children's lack of gratitude, talk with them about these first two lies. And, because working hard doesn't make young people happy, you may also hear about laziness and children who give up quickly and complain about chores and expectations. Also, children may be depressed and angry when they don't feel happy. However, being happy all the time isn't realistic or satisfying.

How do children relate to God? They may not bother praying because they believe it's God's job to make them happy and keep them happy. They just expect it. If they do pray, they may sound demanding and pray only for themselves. They can be quickly disappointed and angry if God doesn't give them what they believe they need or deserve.

Children who believe this lie need help processing hard emotions. It's dangerous for them to stuff down emotions like grief, fear, loss, shame, and embarrassment so they can stay happy. If parents tell you their children aren't talking to them, their closed hearts may be the reason.

A second recommendation is to teach children and teens that challenges have a purpose. Share God's reasons from Romans 5:3-5: "Not only so, but we also glory in our sufferings, because we know that suffering produces perseverance; perseverance, character; and character, hope. And hope does not put us to shame, because God's love has been poured out into our hearts through the Holy Spirit, who has been given to us." Talk about how your character matured and your faith deepened because God allowed you to experience some hard times. Inspire youth to see the big picture of life so they will try new things and risk not being happy. Challenges will strengthen them to handle the realities of life. Remind them they can make a difference if they serve and take risks. Heroes like Daniel, Esther, and Mary were young and inexperienced. You can point to how these biblical characters surmounted challenges without appearing triumphal. They trusted God. Inspire children, youth, and their parents to believe God has purposes for them so they can be wise and courageous now. If they consistently do a U-turn when they see challenges up ahead, they'll turn out immature and unhappy.

Lie #3: I must have choices. The third lie is "I must have choices." When I teach this to teens and children, they agree they don't like being told what to do and having no options. Many thank me for pointing out the root of their dissatisfaction and negative behaviors. It's not hard to see why they believe it. How many apps, shows, movies, songs, brands, coffees, and other products are available? Millions! The drop-down menu effect from all platforms and devices contributes to this lie, too. Parents also believe this lie and come to expect their children to suggest options. Many parents give in and change their plans to make their children happy because they're tired of the fight.

Much has been written about the effects of an instant culture. No example is more apparent than pizza! You used to have to bake your own, and then pizza restaurants became the thing. Then someone thought of pizza delivery. Now you can have any meal delivered. That's not all! Groceries are delivered, too. None of this is wrong, but those who are older know that choice is a privilege. Young people think it's their right. Yet, research indicates that the more choices people have, the more unhappy they are![14] The cereal aisle in the grocery store is an unhappiness zone! This seems counterintuitive, but when many options are offered and considered, people can worry that they missed out on the best option, which reduces their happiness and contentment.

This lie, "I must have choices," is a definite reason children struggle to stay focused. They'd rather multitask than stay bored, rather do something easy than something hard. Their experiences with all the games,

---

[14]Nathan Cheek et al., "Is Having Too Many Choices (Versus Too Few) Really the Greater Problem for Consumers?," *Behavioral Scientist*, October 3, 2022, https://behavioralscientist.org/is-having-too-many-choices-versus-too-few-really-the-greater-problem-for-consumers/.

videos, products, and shows make having dozens of choices natural for them. They know they have many choices available at their fingertips. To help, youth pastors can explain the goals of focus and teach that clearing away distractions is an important Christian discipline. They can start by having everyone put their phones in a basket when they enter the room. They can encourage youth to use paper Bibles in services, not the Bible app on their phones. The temptation to respond to the alerts and to multitask is strong. Children are perfectly capable of not having a phone in their hands at all times. We encourage them to mature when we prove they can survive without their phones 24/7. This anti-establishment or "rebel" approach to tech can appeal to teens.

Other effects of this lie are similar and, in some cases, identical to the first two lies. Children who believe they must have choices aren't content and complain, argue, and struggle with obedience. They need options, but they're overwhelmed by them all. They need to stay happy at the center of their universe and don't know what choice will cater to them. Hence, they may struggle to decide whom to date, what to do after high school, and whether to trust Christ as their Savior. Teens who believe this "I must have choices" lie may deny Christ because they want to keep their options open. For example, a high school graduate I spoke with chose not to trust Christ at an event because he said he might have better options at college. I'm unsure what options he was considering, but he couldn't commit to Jesus.

Students who follow this lie can also resist God because they mistake "I am the way and the truth and the life" (Jn 14:6) as a limitation. We must remind teens that God doesn't force anyone to believe. Choices abound within God's protective boundaries!

We must teach children to make decisions using standards other than happiness as a baseline. A sermon series on decision-making may be in order. This way, everyone benefits, and teens learn from you how to use Scripture and God's principles when making decisions. Reinforce wise standards that are biblical, healthy, others-focused, and mature that can inform decisions that align with family values.

Parents and perhaps staff may share with you issues regarding their disobedient children. Their children may talk back, be disrespectful, and not follow through on commitments. When I teach teens and young adults that the choice lie and the happiness lie cause at least some of their argumentative, disagreeable behavior, they realize they've been immature. Most want to change. This will take time because they've developed habits of presenting options, disagreeing with what their parents want them to do, and debating at the drop of a hat. They will appreciate knowing they're not bad kids. Instead, technology is training them how to behave, which can be controlled.

Children will stop debating with their parents when parents make their "yes" a "yes" and their "no" a "no" and choose not to debate their children. Help parents learn why and how to stand up to their children assertively, wisely, and in developmentally appropriate ways while humbly listening to understand. They need encouragement and confidence to be in control, which counters the fourth lie.

Lie #4: I am my own authority. Children who believe the first three lies usually believe the fourth, "I am my own authority." They must believe they are their own authority if they want to be at the center of their universe, happy always, and free to make choices. If they allow parents or pastors to tell them what to do, all three desires are at risk.

This dangerous lie is one of Satan's more convincing lies—that we can be masters of our own destiny. Of course, everyone worships or follows something or someone. People may not follow Jesus but will follow social influencers, media stars, or friends. Unknowingly, they will put themselves under their authority as they follow them. Hopefully, children and teens in your church follow you and their parents, in addition to God.

Busy and absent parents may cause children to believe they must be responsible for themselves. This is also true if their parents are available but don't answer their questions or don't answer them truthfully. The same is true for pastors. Young people may decide whether or not they can trust you and other leaders to lead them based on your availability and ability to answer their questions.

Children will turn to ChatGPT, Siri, Alexa, Echo, and Google if parents and other authority figures aren't available. These online sources are always available. However, as I wrote earlier, it is important to remember that these devices and platforms are programmed by people who do not have a biblical worldview. They're probably harmless when wondering what other movies an actress starred in. But, for example, children could be harmed if they rely on these tools for answering questions about God, the meaning of life, and sexual ethics.

There are other reasons children believe they can be their own authority. They're aware of authority failures because of social media announcements they see and conversations they overhear. When leaders fail, they may conclude that leaders aren't trustworthy or necessary. Another key truth driving this lie is that there are no clear standards for right and wrong, good and evil, and true and false. Experts can disagree, and young people may be raised by parents who don't agree about essential principles. Disagreements among Christians and church attendees are especially damaging. All of this makes trusting leaders difficult for children.

Perhaps you're already thinking about the ramifications of this "I am my own authority" lie. As with other lies, children may be prideful, angry, and argumentative. Without biblically informed boundaries, teens are at risk of a weakened faith and life witness. Also, I'm concerned and saddened that although children are often overwhelmed when making decisions independently, they frequently reject input and instruction from others. They could make foolish and dangerous decisions because they have limited knowledge and experience.

To help children learn to trust God-given authority, their parents, pastors, and teachers must tell the truth, admit when they've made mistakes, apologize, and ask to be forgiven when they've sinned against children. They can also introduce their children to others who can be positive role models. It's beneficial for someone to explain how to process disappointments and how to discern when to trust again.

Again, encourage parents to stop arguing with their children. Empower and equip them to stand their ground without fear or anxiety. Help them enjoy their role as parents, leaving friendship for something that develops when their children are older. If they continually argue and debate and give in to their children, children can react badly and believe they are their own authority.

It's easy for children to treat God like any other authority if they don't see parents and others vital to them relating to God differently. Encourage parents to demonstrate with their choices and behavior that

God is their authority. Children need to see parents using Scripture on more than Sundays and pray more often than at meals. They must see them relate well with their pastors as their shepherds here on earth. Parents can also explain why they put themselves under God's authority. They should never assume children will figure it out.

These four lies described above (i.e., I am the center of my own universe, I deserve to be happy all the time, I must have choices, and I am my own authority) cause major character issues and can challenge relationships. They also can contribute to crises of faith. Trying to live up to these four lies is also a significant cause of digital stress, characterized by four things: connection overload, the fear of missing out, the need to be constantly available, and approval anxiety.[15]

WHAT MUST YOU KNOW? THE ISSUE OF PORNOGRAPHY

There are many screen-based negatives we need to know about and discuss. I recommend children understand that many things are off-limits, not only porn. These include people using guns for violence, violent movies, movies with ratings older than the children's ages, drugs, glamorizing alcohol, and any abuse featured in films, pictures, shows, games, and whoever they follow on social media. Making porn the one big no-no can cause more problems. Curiosity about porn will increase. Young people likely will not come to you as a ministry leader if they see porn because you've presented it as the most terrible thing. They may fear your reaction.

This chapter does not have space to cover all of these significant issues. But it would be irresponsible not to address the crucial topic of pornography. Let's get specific. Wise pastors understand it's not "if" children will see porn but "when." Porn is so common today that even young children are being exposed.[16] For instance, at the time of this writing, 93% of boys

---

[15] Elizabeth A. Nick et al., "Adolescent Digital Stress: Frequencies, Correlates, and Longitudinal Association with Depressive Symptoms," *Journal of Adolescent Health* 70, no. 2 (February 2022): 336-39, https://doi.org/10.1016/j.jadohealth.2021.08.025; and Ric G. Steele, Jeffrey A. Hall, and Jennifer L. Christofferson, "Conceptualizing Digital Stress in Adolescents and Young Adults: Toward the Development of an Empirically Based Model," *Clinical Child and Family Psychology Review* 23, no. 1 (2020): 15-26, https://doi.org/10.1007/s10567-019-00300-5.

[16] Matt Fradd, "10 Shocking Stats about Teens and Pornography (2024)," Covenant Eyes, January 2, 2024, www.covenanteyes.com/2015/04/10/10-shocking-stats-about-teens-and-pornography/; "Internet Statistics," GuardChild, April 26, 2024, www.guardchild.com/statistics/.

and 62% of girls are exposed to internet porn before 18, with 70% of children 7–18 years old having accidentally encountered online pornography, often while searching the web while doing homework. Research shows that 69% of teen boys and 55% of teen girls have seen porn showing same-sex intercourse.

As a church leader, how you and your parents respond to the news that children have seen porn is critical. Stay calm, avoid accusations, and reassure them that you'll help them. Also, children respond to their emotions before gathering information. Be quiet and feel their pain. Listen to their story and then get essential details. You may want to ask how their body responded to let them know what happened is normal and outside their control.[17] Feeling something when viewing porn does not make them terrible people. You may want to ask if they are remembering or replaying images they've seen so you can assure them that this isn't the same as viewing porn or sinning again. Ask them if they have questions that they want to ask you. Let them know you'll be available and that you expect to have many conversations about this and not a one-and-done discussion.

Emphasize the future and not the past in these conversations. Judging and talking about the past is necessary, but do it so the future is positively affected. Believe and teach that the past can inform us, but it shouldn't control us. Talk about whether the children sinned. Help them know there's a difference between accidentally seeing porn, having a friend show it to them, and searching it out. Talk about forgiveness if sin is relevant. Let them hear you pray for them.

Demonstrating unconditional love is easiest when ministry leaders and parents prepare for how children may disappoint or concern them. Preparation allows them to be proactive instead of reactive when something does happen. For example, practice and role-play potential conversations that your ministry staff and parents might have with children. This kind of preparation will make clear and calm communication more likely, which will help children feel safe.[18]

---

[17] Stacey Dittman, "The 8 Best Questions to Ask When Your Child Has Seen Porn," Defend Young Minds, July 24, 2018, www.defendyoungminds.com/post/8-questions-ask-child-has-seen-porn.
[18] Kathy Koch, *Resilient Kids: Helping Children Embrace Life with Confidence* (Chicago: Moody, 2022), 87-121; Bob Waliszewski, *Plugged-in Parenting* (Carol Stream, IL: Tyndale, 2011), 107-9.

You can also assist parents by offering education and anonymous question-and-answer opportunities about pornography to help them. Many believing parents ask me questions about how to parent, such as "What difference should my faith make? How will the church affect me? How will I parent differently from how my parents raised me?" Helping parents navigate their parenting role regarding pornography will encourage them. Addressing sensitive topics of sexuality provides a meaningful way to demonstrate you're aware of the cultural chaos, your heart for families, and the relevance and importance of God's Word and principles. While most parents in your church will appreciate your boldness and practical help, others may not. Anxiety about sexual ethics abounds, and pushback could be redirected toward you and other leaders.

Inform parents and ministry staff about what's illegal in your state. Include information about parental control tools to monitor children's technology use and prevent them from visiting certain websites.[19] At the same time, emphasize the importance of teaching children why and how to protect their hearts because these systems don't always work and may not be in place everywhere. Encourage parents to teach children about their family values for bodies and sexuality so children can begin to determine what's good for them and what isn't. Teach critical reasoning skills, media literacy, and discernment. You can also teach children to bounce their eyes quickly from what they wish they wouldn't have seen rather than staring at it.

WHAT IF TEENS ARE SEARCHING OUT OR ADDICTED TO PORN?

Pastors and parents need to do what they can to prevent future exposure to porn at home, church, their children's schools, and friends' houses—which is true for anything unhealthy or unwise that children may seek. Parents will want to check in regularly without making every visit to a teen's bedroom about porn. Parents and youth pastors need to stay alert to changes in teens' moods, which may be telltale indicators of porn use.

---

[19]For example, see these websites: Circle (https://meetcircle.com/); Bark (www.bark.us/); Canopy (www.canopy.us/); SecureTeen (https://secureteen.com/); Bumpers (www.bumpers.app); Wisephones (https://techless.com/).

Consequences might include new limits on devices and platforms. For instance, you can consider the amount of time they're allowed to use devices, what they do on them, with whom they share, and where they use them. Not allowing device use after bedtime is an important parental control. It's usually not effective to ban their use at any time. Children will feel punished, which may mean they won't be honest with you in the future. They may get around this policy by hacking passwords and borrowing other people's devices.

Accountability is helpful. Parents can model the benefits of having accountability partners in their own lives by sharing how they approach accountability relationships and for what reasons. If adults have struggled with porn or have their own accountability for blocking it, sharing that honestly will usually help their teens. Emphasize that accountability is helpful to reinforce godliness and is not punitive. When teens understand this, it may be easier to be honest about their challenges. Make wise accountability plans together, and get children's buy-in.

If porn usage escalates, counseling is something to consider. Counseling may help uncover abuse the child has experienced, anxiety or depression, or family dynamics contributing to porn use. Sometimes porn use is a canary in the family coal mine that can illuminate more significant problems, so the desire for porn can be reduced once they're addressed. Professional therapists can help uncover underlying issues and respond to the unmet needs the child is trying to meet through using porn.

Teaching truth is vital. It can inspire teens to stop their viewing habits (or never begin if you offer preventative teaching). Teens can be equipped to teach peers. For example, one young teen I respect stumbled on porn when a friend worked past a supposedly effective preventive system on his device. Thankfully, he was disgusted by what he saw and was open with his parents, which allowed him and his dad to talk. He now understands the ideas described below, which he regularly shares with his peers.

Porn does not line up with a biblical worldview for several reasons. First, sex is to occur within a committed marital relationship between a man and a woman. Porn does not portray sex the way healthy married couples enjoy it. Porn makes sex seem consequence-free and only about immediate pleasure. Because porn teaches an unrealistic expectation for sex in marriage, porn viewers who try to replicate something they saw or felt may feel like failures in marriage.

Second, porn dehumanizes men and women and everyone involved in the industry, including viewers, those featured in porn, and those who produce it. Porn has led many women to be trafficked and forced to "act." Depending on what teens tell you about their addiction, you may want to point out that producers intentionally escalate the porn. Porn producers understand the porn addiction cycle, namely that those who watch porn need more and more and rougher and rougher sex to get the same reaction.

These disturbing details shouldn't be shared lightly. But communicating with teens at the right time can radically help them understand that porn is an industry designed to trap and change them. It might be one of the best examples of the opposite of holiness we can think of. It dishonors God and his ways.

Dishonoring God is an understatement. Youth may be interested to learn and motivated to stop viewing porn when you tell them that 43% of male college students and 20% of female college students report that pornography worsened their relationship with Christ. There's more. Increased porn use "is significantly related to reduced church attendance, diminished faith, lessened prayer frequency, and diminished feelings of closeness to God. At the same time, porn use increased religious doubts."[20]

SPIRITUAL FORMATION: A POSITIVE CONCLUSION

Let's end the chapter on a positive note! Used wisely and under the careful eye of God-discerning pastoral leaders and God-honoring parents, technology can be used to grow children's faith. Praise God that not all children will want to view porn or risk getting into trouble through the misuse of technology. Instead, they may use Bible verses and a movie clip when talking to a friend about why they love God. They may use an alarm to remind them to set the table for dinner, walk their dog, or start their homework. They can FaceTime with grandparents and easily stay in touch with others. Podcasts, apps, and internet sites can encourage

---

[20]Sam Black, *The Healing Church: What Churches Get Wrong About Pornography and How to Fix It* (New York: Morgan James, 2023), 8.

personal and spiritual growth. Teaching mature, positive technology use can be an important antidote to the negative influences of media.

Most significantly, as a pastoral leader, you can work with parents to teach children the truths to combat the four lies identified above.

- God is the center of the universe (to counter Lie #1: "I am the center of my own universe"). I serve Him; He doesn't serve me.
- Prioritizing happiness isn't wise (to counter Lie #2: "I deserve to be happy all the time"). Consistent joy because of my dynamic relationship with Jesus is available no matter my circumstances.
- Choices are a privilege, not our right (to counter Lie #3: "I must have choices"). With God's help, we can make God-honoring, wise choices.
- Believing we are our own authority is dangerous and foolish (to counter Lie #4: "I am my own authority"). I need to respect and learn from God-given authority exercised in love and grace. God's authority is best.

Technology is here to stay, with more advances coming in the future. Knowing how these digital technologies affect children and families will make you a more relevant and effective ministry leader. Always keep learning![21]

---

[21] For example: Black, *The Healing Church*; Amy Crouch and Andy Crouch, *My Tech-Wise Life* (Grand Rapids, MI: Baker Books, 2020); Andy Crouch, *The Tech-Wise Family: Everyday Steps for Putting Technology in Its Proper Place* (Grand Rapids, MI: Baker Books, 2017); Frances E. Jensen and Amy Ellis Nutt, *The Teenage Brain: A Neuroscientist's Survival Guide to Raising Adolescents and Young Adults* (New York: Harper, 2016); Jean M. Twenge, *iGen: Why Today's Super-Connected Kids Are Growing up Less Rebellious, More Tolerant, Less Happy—and Completely Unprepared for Adulthood—and What That Means for the Rest of Us* (New York: Atria Books, 2017).

11

ADULTS AND SCREENS

Preventing Crisis Through Digital Discipleship

ARLENE PELLICANE

A self-employed father of three, Russell is constantly on his phone. There are jobs to check on and future business to secure. He also volunteers at his church and does a great job keeping men informed of events by calling and texting. But to his kids, he seems forever occupied with his phone.

Russell's wife, Nancy isn't doing much better. Her family gave her the nickname "Twitter Queen" because she is constantly checking her social media. Her obsession began innocently as a way to reach out to women in the church and share encouraging quotes and photos. Over time, she was constantly communicating on social media, even on date nights with her husband. Being digitally connected became a habit, and she didn't know how to stop.

Russell and Nancy aren't the only parents having trouble balancing their screen time and family time in your congregation. How helpful it would be to engage in regular "tech checks" to determine how screen time infringes on family life.

Russell and Nancy go to lunch with Todd and Carla, the family ministry leaders at their local church. Russell and Nancy complain about each other and how their kids are always getting in trouble. While the family is struggling, nothing seems terribly wrong. There's no abuse, chronic illness, or mental health disorder. They seem like a typical American family. The family seems to be digitally over-connected, but isn't everyone in America today? Perhaps excessive screen time is the culprit, not only for Russell and Nancy but also for many other families. Here's a quick quiz to gauge how you and the adults you minister to are doing with device use.

QUIZ: IS IT WELL WITH YOUR PHONE?

Answer the questions either yes or no as you reflect on your screentime.

1. Do you lose track of time when scrolling through social media or websites or watching TV?
2. Do others in your life complain about the amount of time you spend on digital devices?
3. Do you check your phone first thing in the morning?
4. Have you ever spent time at home watching TV, playing video games, or answering emails instead of going out with family members?
5. Do you find yourself answering texts even if it means interrupting what you are doing?
6. Do you think your use of technology decreases your productivity?
7. Do you watch videos, use the computer, or check your phone late at night?
8. Do you use the phone during meals or eat in front of a screen?
9. Have you ever changed vacation plans because of Wi-Fi availability?
10. Do you correspond with some online-only friends more than people you actually see in real life?
11. Do you have three or more active social media accounts you use daily?
12. If someone asks to have a talk, do you keep your phone close in case it vibrates?
13. Do you have your phone next to your bed or pillow when you sleep?

14. Do you check your email more than twenty times a day?
15. Excluding time at work, do you spend more than four hours a day using electronic media such as TV, video games, phones, or tablets?
16. Do you feel behind and overwhelmed on most days with all you have to do?
17. When you have free time, do you use the phone or another device to relax?
18. Do you ever regret something you watched online, on TV, or something you posted on social media?
19. Do you find it difficult to sit through church without touching your phone?
20. On your day off, would it be hard for you to refrain from all electronic media?

If you answer YES to 3 questions or less, you are *Calm, Cool, and Connected*. You have a remarkable ability to balance technology and being fully present.

If you answer YES to 4-9 questions, you are *Almost Calm, Cool and Connected*. You haven't gone overboard with technology, but you can get swept away by screen madness. Work on building a few positive habits by setting limits on your screen time. Your relationships will be healthier, and you'll be much happier.

If you answer YES to 10-14 questions, you are *Barely Calm, Cool and Connected*. Warning lights are flashing. You are spending too much time looking at a screen. There are more important things to do like being with loved ones, getting a good night's sleep, and having fun without the help of technology. Make the decision to scale back your screen time before it dominates your life.

If you answer YES to 15-20 questions, you are *Nowhere Near Calm, Cool and Connected*. Red alert! Your phone is in your pocket or within three feet at all times because you love that thing. Without the constant stimulus of your phone and other screens, you'd feel anxious.[1]

---

[1] This quiz is for self-exploration and reflection, not a validated research instrument. It was adapted from Arlene Pellicane, *Calm, Cool, and Connected: 5 Digital Habits for a More Balanced Life* (Chicago: Moody, 2017), 52.

As you can probably tell, kids and teenagers aren't the only ones spending too much time on devices. The whole family needs guiding principles and wisdom when it comes to screen consumption. Unfortunately, families of faith are struggling with tech overuse just like the families outside of the church. How might family ministers respond to this ubiquitous overconsumption of the online world?

THE PROBLEM AT HAND: DIGITAL THREATS TO PARENTING AND MARRIAGES

In a study of fifty-five parents and caregivers eating at fast-food restaurants with children, researchers found that forty used a mobile device during the meal. Sixteen of those adults used their phones throughout the entire meal. No wonder some children acted out by singing or getting up to gain attention. Other children just looked straight at their parents, but their gaze was never returned.[2]

Granted this research study had a small sample size. But you can probably attest that you've seen that scene played out over and over in your experience. In a more extensive survey of six thousand children from different countries, researchers found that:

- 54% of kids felt their parents check their phones too often.
- 36% of kids said their parents' worst habit was getting distracted by their phones in the middle of a conversation.
- 32% of kids said this behavior made them feel unimportant.

Respondents from Brazil reported being the unhappiest, as 87% of kids said their parents used their phones too often.[3] Local cultural norms can pull the most loving parents both inside and outside the church into bad habits. This bad habit has been called *technoference*, a term coined by Brandon McDaniel, PhD, of Illinois State University. Technoference refers to the interruptions in interpersonal communication caused by the

---

[2] Brian Alexander, "Put Down That Cellphone! Study Finds Parents Distracted by Devices," NBC News, March 9, 2014, www.nbcnews.com/health/parenting/put-down-cellphone-study-finds-parents-distracted-devices-n47431.

[3] "Kids Resent Parents Who Are Glued to Their Phones, Study Finds," Advocate Aurora Health, accessed April 26, 2024, www.ahchealthnews.com/2015/09/29/kids-resent-parents-who-are-glued-to-their-phones/.

attention paid to devices instead. It is happening when your church member is looking at his phone, and he doesn't hear the question his child asks, even though he is supposedly listening. McDaniel and his team of researchers studied 170 families with children ages five years or younger. They found parents who had a more challenging time managing their own phone use were more likely to experience technoference with their children, which was linked to worse behavior in the kids.[4]

Our culture's obsession with digital devices threatens to erode the quality of our closest relationships. Instead of the families we minister to attaching to each other, they are attaching to devices. It's said that beauty is found in the *eye* of the beholder, not the posts or likes of the beholder. Eye contact is a key ingredient in any healthy relationship, and yet it's lacking in many Christian homes.

Digital screens not only threaten parenting relationships, but they also threaten marriage relationships in your congregation. I remember when my husband James and I were first dating. We could spend hours sitting on the couch, just talking, and looking at each other. Although the hours of affection displayed during courtship are hardly sustainable, daily eye contact and warm physical touch are necessary for couples to thrive. Are we now in danger of finding our metal phones more suitable for companionship than our flesh and blood spouses? It's a drift that happens subtly over time. One husband told me he and his wife used to read together in bed, cuddle, and talk before bedtime. Now his wife holds her phone, eyes glued to the screen, as he turns off her light. Another woman tells me her husband plays video games nonstop in his free time. She must constantly compete for his attention. Many married couples around us are vying for each other's attention but, in many cases, to no avail.

With a twinkle in your eyes, you can coach your church members to ask this question: Is my spouse more interesting than my phone? Be honest. In the dating days, the answer was easy . . . absolutely! But now that you've grown accustomed to your spouse and the phone offers so much novelty and excitement, would you admit that your phone is more interesting? Researchers found that smartphone users touch, tap, or

---

[4] "Technoference?," Positive Parenting, January 24, 2018, https://positiveparentingnews.org/news-reports/technoference/.

swipe their devices an average of 2,617 times a day. Users spent an average of 145 minutes on their smartphones, divided into an average of 76 sessions. That would be roughly 34 touches per smartphone session, which seems very plausible.[5]

Now just think what would happen in the marriages in your church if spouses would just spend 15 minutes with each other and touch each other ten times a day. That could start a romantic revolution! I don't think any of us decide, "I'm going to ruin my marriage by giving too much attention to my phone, tablet, or TV." However, it's a slow slide of gradually reinforcing harmful screen habits. It happens as easily for a pastor as for a layperson. We must all put boundaries on our screen time by answering some critical questions:

- What will we create with our devices?
- What will we allow on our devices?
- When screen time is hurting a relationship, will we sacrifice the screen time or the relationship?

It is unfair and unreasonable to expect a child to regulate screen time if parents can't do it. As the late Howard Hendricks said so well, "You cannot impart what you do not possess."[6] The most effective teaching takes place when a parent shows a child how to manage the digital world wisely out of his or her own positive experience with technology. This principle especially shines brightly in the marriage relationship as an exemplar of family relationship for children and others who are watching. Church staff can lead the way.

THE ADDICTIVE POWER OF TECHNOLOGY

Are you aware that the device in your hand is not neutral? This truth is something you can drill into the parents in your ministry. Former Google design ethicist Tristan Harris says the problem isn't that people lack willpower. It's that "there are a thousand people on the other side of the

---

[5] "People Touch Their Smartphone Over 2,600 Times a Day, Research Shows," *Brussels Times*, June 3, 2022, www.brusselstimes.com/232851/people-touch-their-smartphone-over-2600-times-a-day-research-shows.

[6] "Howard Hendricks Tribute," Dallas Theological Seminary, accessed March 8, 2023, www.dts.edu/howard-hendricks-tribute/.

screen whose job it is to break down the self-regulation you have."[7] Phones and tablets are supercharged to engage you on every possible level, designed to capture attention and never let go. In his book *Irresistible: The Rise of Addictive Technology and the Business of Keeping Us Hooked*, Adam Alter explains why it's so hard for us to disengage from screen time.

There are no stopping cues. Here's how television used to work for your parents and grandparents: You watched your favorite program for thirty minutes, and then the commercials came on. You didn't like the next show, so you turned off the TV or changed the channel. You had to wait a whole week to watch it again. But now, in the world of streaming and YouTube, there are no stopping points. Nothing cues you to think, "Oh, the program is over. I should go do something else now." Instead of a stopping point, another video (or the next episode) cues up automatically and starts playing. Before Netflix introduced "post-play" in 2012, you had to choose to watch another episode. Now you have to choose *not* to watch. That little change has ushered in an age of binge-watching. Social media works the same way. You can scroll for hours, and you will never find an end. It is bottomless.

Screens provide unpredictable rewards. In 1971, psychologist Michael Zeiler conducted his now-famous experiment with pigeons about the best way to deliver rewards. Sometimes the pigeons would peck at a button, and a pellet would drop every time. Other times, the food was only delivered some of the time. The results revealed the pigeons pecked almost twice as often when the reward was given randomly. Their brains "were releasing far more dopamine when the reward was unexpected than when it was predictable."[8]

Like those pigeons, the adults you serve love receiving unpredictable and intermittent rewards during screen time. Posting on social media is like pulling the lever on a slot machine—anticipating what kind of feedback will I get? Will my friends love it? Will they ignore it? Video game designers know gamers are likely to stop playing a game that

---

[7] Adam Altar, *Irresistible: The Rise of Addictive Technology and the Business of Keeping Us Hooked* (New York: Penguin Books, 2017), 3.

[8] Adam Altar, "How Technology Gets Us Hooked," *The Guardian*, February 28, 2017, www.theguardian.com/technology/2017/feb/28/how-technology-gets-us-hooked.

doesn't quickly deliver a dose of small, intermittent rewards. Those rewards could be as basic as a "ding" sound or a flash of light.

Screens tap into the power of goals. Exercise apps track steps, heart rates, and fitness goals. Social media tells us how many followers we are accruing. Snapchat leverages our innate desire to reach goals with the creation of the "streak." A streak means you and one of your Snapchat friends have both snapped each other a picture or video within a twenty-four-hour period for at least three consecutive days. The idea is that you and your friend keep this streak going for as long as possible. Some super goal-oriented Snapchatters have kept their streak going for more than 1,400 days. That's every day for almost four years! If the focus of that screen-tapping is personal or spiritual growth and warm connection to people we love, that might be healthy. But it can easily become digital "candy" which at daily levels is unhealthy. As spiritual leaders, we aren't immune to this temptation in our work and personal lives. We must be on guard against the screen's ability to hijack godly goals by giving us artificial and inferior goals. When families we minister to understand these three persuasive technology tactics and teach them to their children, it will help them recognize when their attention is being manipulated.

SPEAKING THE TRUTH IN LOVE IN A DIGITAL ENVIRONMENT

Church leaders can be resources to families to create a spiritual response to digital media temptations. When we post something unkind or untrue, we can join the disciples and pray, "Forgive us our debts, as we also have forgiven our debtors. And lead us not into temptation, but deliver us from the evil one" (Mt 6:12-13). Because of the blood of Jesus, we can live forgiven with a clean conscience. But we all must be aware of the modern obstacles that can easily ensnare us all, including ministry leaders. Our mobile phones, computers, tablets, and flat screens can lead us down subtle, unsavory paths—even while doing the work of the ministry.

DISRESPECT IN DIGITAL ENVIRONMENTS

The online world is a dangerous place for the soul. Adults are fed sensational panic-ridden news that fights against the biblical instruction "do not worry" (Mt 6:34). Scantily clad models and porn sites tempt us to forgo the instruction "flee from sexual immorality" (1 Cor 6:18). Perhaps we have systems in place to avoid these pitfalls but allow ourselves to get pulled into angry and disrespectful social media exchanges. We can show our love for God by being courteous in a crass and contentious world. Just scroll through comments on YouTube or other social media for proof that society badly needs a filter. Even on Christian-based websites, comments can be very harsh, hurtful, and combative. I've read comments like: "I'm sorry, but you are so wrong!" "You must be an ATHEIST!" "How dare you call yourself a Christian?" Perhaps you have even seen church members, or leaders, engaging in this harsh online behavior. It's important to consider that online behavior is similar to public behavior, and emotional immaturity like this is part of discipleship training. If someone from your church was saying something like this at a restaurant where you were also there at the table, how would you respond?

Christians in our congregations should be discipled that their social media be constructive and not destructive. Romans 12:17-18 states, "Do not repay anyone evil for evil. Be careful to do what is right in the eyes of everyone. If it is possible, as far as it depends on you, live at peace with everyone." Author and Christian apologist Sean McDowell says, "Remember, the goal of a conversation is not to sound smart. It's not to be right. The point is to love someone. Love certainly requires speaking the truth at the right time and in the right manner, but our greatest goal in engaging others must always be to love them. Period."[9]

One teaching you might include in a class, sermon, or pastoral care discussion could ask, "Is what we post in the privacy of our home good enough to proclaim in public? Would we post the exact same words about someone or to someone if he or she were in the room with us?" Jesus' command to love our neighbor includes exercising self-control before posting a comment or photo. If they don't care about keeping a clean conscience before God when they are online, moral plaque can begin to form imperceptibly in their hearts and minds. Don't wait for

---

[9] Sean McDowell, *A Rebel's Manifesto* (Carol Stream, IL: Tyndale Momentum, 2022), 229.

catastrophic problems that will necessitate counseling and reconciliation. It's much easier to remind your church family to brush their hearts regularly and keep soft, humble hearts before God. As a church minister, teach the people you counsel to heed the words found in Proverbs 4:23, "Above all else, guard your heart, for everything you do flows from it."

DIGITAL HABITS FOR CHRISTIANS

When my son Ethan was in middle school camping with his Royal Rangers group, he went a few days without brushing his teeth. It wasn't that he forgot his toothbrush. He had it in a little plastic bag, but he was distracted with other alluring activities like eating s'mores. He neglected his mouth while roughing it, but when he got back home, he returned to brushing as usual.

Even more important than clean teeth is a clean heart. Just like Ethan was tempted to skip his dental hygiene in the woods, we can face all sorts of temptations online that take us away from the healthy routines prescribed in God's Word. Wouldn't it be beneficial to our souls if we automatically checked our conscience at the end of the day? What if we paired a ritual—like brushing teeth—with a quick heart check? You can suggest something like this (called an examen in certain ancient Christian traditions) for the families of your church. They might write Psalm 17:3 (NIRV) on an index card and put it on the bathroom mirror: "Look deep down into my heart. Study me carefully at night and test me. You won't find anything wrong. I have planned nothing evil. My mouth has not said sinful things."

Technology can be used for the glory of God and to advance the cause of Christ in the family. That's one legitimate reason your church members bought a phone or computer in the first place. They might listen to Bible teachings, use a Bible app, or learn a language online for an upcoming mission trip. These are what I like to refer to as digital vegetables.

But adults, not just kids, waste many hours on digital candy–amusing distractions that help us cope and keep us from the real work at hand. So, before we pick up a phone or sit down at the computer, ask this clarifying, powerful question: *What am I here to do?* Teach your community to be able to give a concrete answer. It may be something like: "I am going to text my friend about lunch," "I will answer my work emails," or "I'm completing my report." This is what intentional technology looks like.

When church members use their devices without being intentional, they end up doing things like browsing Amazon for something new, checking how much round-trip airfare would be to the next travel destination, scrolling through Instagram, clicking on that sale ad, or going on a news site. Do they tend to dabble in this and that online, not really finishing the things they start? Research shows every time they become distracted, it takes an average of 15 minutes to regain complete focus. Fifteen minutes . . . and that's just to get back into the zone they wandered away from in the first place![10] These constant activities are keeping adults from doing the work of godly parenting and discipleship.

A study by Adobe showed that adults reported spending an average of 209 minutes checking their work email and 143 minutes checking their personal email, for a total of 352 minutes (almost six hours) each day.[11] Author Peter Bregman observes there's a reason email management has grown so much in one generation. "Email is such a seductress in terms of distraction because it poses as valid work."[12] When you don't feel like correcting a child or reading a book with a daughter, it's much easier to keep checking email.

A WISE RESPONSE TO DIGITAL TIME-WASTING

Here's some advice you can share with the tired mom or dad who feels like they just don't have enough time to spend with their kids. To fight the urge to waste time online, they can try different methods, such as the Pomodoro Technique,[13] to get things done. This method, created in the 1980s by Francesco Cirillo, uses a Pomodoro tomato-shaped timer, but any timer will do. Here's how it works. Choose a task, either big or small,

---

[10] Joshua Leatherman, "How to Use Batching to Become More Productive," Full Focus, accessed April 30, 2024, https://fullfocus.co/how-to-use-batching-to-become-more-productive/.
[11] Abigail Johnson Hess, "Here's How Many Hours American Workers Spend on Email Each Day," CNBC, September 22, 2019, www.cnbc.com/2019/09/22/heres-how-many-hours-american-workers-spend-on-email-each-day.html.
[12] Laura Vanderkam, "Stop Checking Your Email, Now," *Fortune*, October 8, 2012, https://fortune.com/2012/10/08/stop-checking-your-email-now/.
[13] Francesco Cirillo, "What Is the Pomodoro Technique?," The Pomodoro Technique, accessed April 23, 2024, www.pomodorotechnique.com/what-is-the-pomodoro-technique.php.

that you have been putting off. Set the timer for 25 minutes. Work on the task until the timer rings. If you think of a different task needing attention during those 25 minutes, jot it down on paper, then continue with your main task. When the timer rings, put a checkmark on a piece of paper. Take a short break, such as getting coffee or taking a quick walk. After completing four Pomodoros (equaling 100 minutes of productive work), you can take a longer break of 20-30 minutes.

Others may find 25 minutes to be limiting, preferring to work in longer chunks toward a lunch break or a dinner break. The key is finding a system that works for your church members to get tasks not just started but done. Minimizing online interruptions, having a clean workspace, and building momentum will help them be more focused and productive. What activities can they batch together on an average workday? When they learn how to use time wisely and can account for actual work being done, this will build confidence and character in the area of technology.

Here are five suggestions you can give to your community members to be wise online:

- Use a timer and put it next to your computer. Work in chunks of time with short breaks in between.
- Keep a daily updated list of things to do and stick to the list.
- Program your computer to shut off at a certain time each evening.
- Make your computer desktop clean and organized. Use wallpaper you find inspiring and motivational.
- Listen to music that works best while working.

THE USUAL SUSPECTS: FIVE TYPES OF PROBLEMATIC SCREEN TIME

All screen time isn't created equal. Dr. Dimitri Christakis, a pediatrician and director of the Center for Child Health, Behavior and Development at Seattle Children's Research Institute states that the total amount of screen time isn't as important as the breakdown of how it is spent. He notes, "We can't simply count all screen time as the same. Look at the things you think of as being entirely recreational or entirely a waste of your time, and ask yourself, is there a way that time could have been better spent?"[14]

If you are looking for something to teach your congregation, we offer ideas here for your next class or sermon relevant to families and screentime. Here are five types of screen time that usually rob time from families:

1. Social media. Social media is marketed as a platform to connect us. After all, a strong correlation exists between social interaction, health, and well-being.[15] But social media is an oxymoron like jumbo shrimp. There is nothing social about sitting alone to post selfies or scroll through celebrity feeds.

Many experts have found that time spent on social media apps is not only troublesome for kids and teens; it also spells trouble for adults. In his *Wall Street Journal* article, Geoffrey Fowler writes that "mindlessly checking Facebook makes you an awful lot like a lab rat habitually pressing a lever hoping for a pellet . . . but you're no rat. Human brains can resist the ways apps hijack our brains if we learn a few coping skills."[16] The creators of social media have capitalized on social psychology research on attention to tailor the media to the human brain to increase engagement, specially tailored to younger brains.[17]

God has created us with more sophisticated brains than lab rats, but we are susceptible to the weaknesses that social media companies exploit. In response to the overwhelming pressures to overuse social media, church leaders can encourage and model balanced digital habits that bring positive changes to the home environment. One step is to delete certain social media apps from phones. Think of it as removing the slot machines from our living rooms. The Bible instructs us many times to

---

[14] Jamie Friedlander Serrano, "Experts Can't Agree on How Much Screen Time is Too Much for Adults," *Time*, May 9, 2022, https://time.com/6174510/how-much-screen-time-is-too-much/.

[15] "How Does Social Connectedness Affect Health?," CDC, March 30, 2023, www.cdc.gov/emotional-wellbeing/social-connectedness/affect-health.htm.

[16] Geoffrey A. Fowler, "Take Back Your Brain from Social Media," *The Wall Street Journal*, February 1, 2017, www.wsj.com/articles/take-back-your-brain-from-social-media-1485968678?mod=ST1.

[17] Bobby Allyn, "Here are 4 Key Points from the Facebook Whistleblower's Testimony on Capitol Hill," NPR, October 5, 2021, www.npr.org/2021/10/05/1043377310/facebook-whistleblower-frances-haugen-congress.

examine our ways and test them (Lam 3:40; 2 Cor 13:5; Gal 6:4). We must be honest in evaluating how our time on social media is impacting us spiritually and in our closest relationships.

Here are specific ways the people you minister to can put boundaries around social media overuse:

- *Allot a certain amount of time for social media.* Do they use social media for personal reasons? Fifteen minutes a day may be plenty. Need to use social media to promote a business? Maybe one hour a day will do the trick. Determine how much time per day they'll spend on social media and stick with it. Track the time for one week if they have a hard time getting off.
- *Eliminate social media during mealtimes.* Dinner is not the time to scroll through social media posts, even when their party is waiting for a table at a restaurant.
- *Don't look at social media first thing in the morning or at bedtime.* If they greet the day with text messages and notifications, they will feel behind before breakfast. Instead, spend the first minutes nourishing the soul in prayer and reading God's Word, which is a much better way to frame the day. Likewise, drift off to sleep by counting blessings instead of counting all the likes friends are getting. Consider keeping the smartphone outside of the bedroom to help increase bedtime peace and quiet.
- *Participate in social media fasts.* If they would be anxious about missing out on social media for one week, they are a good candidate for a fast. Researchers are finding chemical changes in certain pleasure areas of the brain when they get that "social media hit." If it's becoming addictive and disruptive to the rest of life, a time of detox can be very healthy. They can also take one day a week off or have social media-free weeknights.
- *Use social media to stay connected with a handful of friends.* Many adults use social media to share photos with family members in other states or overseas. When they use social media to stay in touch with just a few people, it can enhance relationships versus scrolling through news feeds to check in on the masses.

Social media is especially tricky because you can use it to communicate with your families about upcoming church events. Teaching your families to be intentional with social media will help them use it for specific purposes instead of scrolling mindlessly.

2. Video gaming. As a family minister, it's only a matter of time until you are called on to intervene when video games are interfering and wreaking havoc on home life. You can share this story I heard from a pediatrician about a young, sleep-deprived couple bringing in their brand-new baby for an exam. The father sat in a chair next to the mother and baby, physically present but mentally far away. He was playing video games on his phone. At that moment, the pediatrician decided to say something. "You have a responsibility to your wife and baby, so please put away your phone and learn how you can help." That same call to action applies whether a child is a baby or approaching young adulthood.

Video gaming can be a source of tension in a marriage or with kids and teenagers. Men tend to play video games competitively for long stretches of time, and women tend to play shorter games on the go as they have free time. Dr. Andrew Doan, a Johns Hopkins–educated MD with a PhD in neuroscience, is also a recovering video game addict. He played fifty to a hundred hours a week while attending medical school on a full-ride scholarship at Johns Hopkins. He was a "functional addict," but he was constantly sleep-deprived and chronically angry. His wife left with the kids and filed a restraining order. Today, Dr. Doan has restored his relationship with his family, but only after hitting bottom and dramatically changing his ways.[18] You can learn more about video game addiction in his book *Hooked on Games: The Lure and Cost of Video Game and Internet Addiction*. It's a cautionary tale that could really wake up some families while there is still time.

You can alert the families under your care about the addictive nature of video games through hosting guest speakers, recommending reading materials, organizing small groups around the topic, and having conversations about the role of video gaming in the home.

---

[18] Andrew P. Doan and Brooke Strickland, *Hooked on Games: The Lure and Cost of Video Game and Internet Addiction* (Coralville, IA: F.E.P. International, 2012), 18.

3. Pornography. The stigma once associated with going to a seedy adult store to view pornography no longer exists. Porn can be accessed by anyone in the privacy of one's home or anywhere with a mobile device or tablet. John Foubert, PhD, has studied sexual violence and the harms of pornography for more than 30 years. He wrote:

> Today's internet porn is nothing like your father's *Playboy* magazine. The endless supply of novel images that can be clicked through in seconds have fused the concepts of sex and violence. . . . Research of popular pornography films found that in 88% of the scenes—not just the movies, but the scenes in these movies—there was verbal or physical aggression, usually toward a woman. The more interesting finding is that 95% of the time when someone is violent with another person in porn, usually a man toward a woman, the recipient is shown as either liking that violence or having no objection.[19]

You can begin to understand how sobering and harmful pornography use is in today's marriage relationship. According to the clinical experience of Dr. Victor Cline, professor emeritus in psychology at the University of Utah, there are four steps of pornography use:

1. *Addiction*—Porn consumers get hooked. They keep coming back for more. Pornography provides very exciting and powerful imagery. For many, addiction involves an anxiety that is resolved by use of porn, creating a feedback loop. Addiction also tends to include problematic behaviors that affect work productivity, relationships, sexual, personal, or spiritual functioning of the person.

2. *Escalation*—With the passage of time, the addicted require rougher, more explicit, more deviant sexual material to experience pleasure.

3. *Desensitization*—Material that was originally thought of as shocking, taboo, illegal, repulsive, or immoral in time is seen as acceptable and commonplace. The sexual activity depicted becomes legitimized.

---

[19]John D. Foubert, "The Public Health Harms of Pornography: The Brain, Erectile Dysfunction, and Sexual Violence," *Dignity* 2, no. 3 (July 2017), www.johnfoubert.com/_files/ugd/3caeed_34 f57e3b84b041e0b459f3db95e4976a.pdf.

4. *Acting Out*—Some will try to act out the behaviors viewed in the pornography.[20]

Remember that the porn industry is a business that wants to get more business. Worldwide pornography revenues are $100 billion annually. This is more than the combined revenues of Microsoft, Google, Amazon, eBay, Yahoo, Apple, and Netflix. In the United States alone, the porn industry makes $13 billion each year. That's more than the National Football League, Major League Baseball, and the National Basketball Association combined.[21]

Porn is an evil business that preys on the young, contributes to human trafficking, and ruins meaningful romantic relationships. Lynn Marie Cherry understands the deep pain of betrayal. A few days after she delivered their second child, she discovered her spouse was addicted to pornography. She and her husband have walked down the road to recovery. Here's what Lynn writes about using the internet accountability and filtering service Covenant Eyes, an app that uses an accountability partner who is given access to user history and filters porn websites from devices or computers:

> We were crunching numbers, trying to make room in the budget for something I can't quite recall, when I asked my husband if we still needed to pay for Covenant Eyes. We were years down this recovery road. He hadn't acted out online in a long time. I figured maybe all was well, and we could eliminate this vestige of our past pain from the spending plan. I was wrong. My husband responded quite adamantly that we still needed Covenant Eyes and would be using it for life because it helped him not give in when he was tempted. *When* he was tempted? It was disconcerting to hear my husband talk about being tempted. I would like to believe that temptation was dead and buried right along with that secret life he once lived. "So, you're still tempted?" I asked. "I thought you were walking in freedom." "Freedom is not the absence of temptation," my husband replied. I walked away from the conversation evaluating my safety. And here's . . . why I'm on board with

---
[20]Victor Cline, *Pornography's Effects on Adults and Children* (New York: Morality in Media, 2001), www.dropbox.com/s/10sfmazkwsxmazb/Dr-Victor-Cline-Pornography-s-Effects-on-Adults-and-Children.pdf?e=1&dl=0.
[21]John Foubert, "How Much Do Pornographers Make?," accessed March 9, 2023, www.johnfoubert.com/how-much-do-pornographers-make.

using Covenant Eyes for life: . . . After forty-eight weeks of group therapy and watching the pain I walked through, my husband does not want to see that again. He knows I'll receive the weekly accountability report, and he doesn't want to hurt me. He also doesn't want to answer . . . his friend, that is sure to follow up on anything that doesn't look right. . . . Even though it may not make sense at first glance, I am safer when my husband embraces his weakness than if he is over confident in his own strength. He tried for many years to find freedom on his own. We know that white-knuckling it doesn't work.[22]

As a family ministry leader, you can cast light into this dark, shamed-filled world of pornography by making it a topic discussed in the church. Tough conversations are needed to truly help adults, both men and women, overcome any harmful habits with pornography.

4. Shopping. Compared to porn or posting insults, going online to shop appears harmless, right? My husband routinely has some kind of exercise equipment, air filter, book, or battery in our online shopping cart. Whether your church members are ordering books, jewelry, tools, or home decor, online retailers have made shopping easy, fun, and hassle-free. One study found three key factors, which make people especially prone to an online shopping addiction:

- People like to buy anonymously and avoid social interaction.
- People enjoy a wide variety and constant availability of items.
- People like instant gratification.

I like shopping in the comfort of my home without fighting for a parking spot. I also like the wide variety of items and getting my order delivered magically to my doorstep. Does that mean I have a shopping addiction? Maybe, maybe not. If your people have an unhealthy addiction to online shopping, they will feel preoccupied with shopping and feel like they have no control over it. Look for these five signs to determine whether they have a serious problem with online shopping:

1. They feel like they can't stop online shopping even if they want to and/or have tried to stop without being able to.

---

[22]Lynn Marie Cherry, "Why We Will Be Using Covenant Eyes for Life," Covenant Eyes, July 29, 2021, www.covenanteyes.com/2016/10/20/why-we-will-be-using-covenant-eyes-for-life/.

2. Online shopping has hurt their relationships, work, or financial situation.
3. Their family members or friends are concerned about their online shopping. They end up in arguments with their loved ones over it.
4. They get grumpy or upset if they can't shop online.
5. They often feel guilty after they go online shopping.

If those you minister to struggle with keeping online shopping in balance, these suggestions can bolster the resolve to live with more financial responsibly:

- Write shopping lists and stick to them.
- Avoid things like TV shopping channels and online stores when you are just browsing.
- Unsubscribe from sale emails from retailers.
- Only purchase things online on a certain day of the week.
- Don't leave your credit card information online as a default. Make it harder to make a purchase by requiring the manual labor of typing in the numbers each time.
- Don't go to a favorite shopping website during downtime. Stretch, go outside, write a note, or read a book instead.

Money is a source of friction for many couples. As you help your community recognize the common pitfall of overspending and online shopping, you can strengthen marriages in your church.

5. News and entertainment. According to a University of Nevada study, "cyberloafing" (which is basically wasting time online) costs US businesses as much as $85 billion a year. People in another study admitted to cyberloafing from 60-80% of their time online at work.[23] Whether your congregation members work for a traditional employer or for themselves, the reality is we're all vulnerable to digital distractions like news, sports, and entertainment.

---

[23]Cat Zakrzewski, "The Key to Getting Workers to Stop Wasting Time Online," *The Wall Street Journal*, March 13, 2016, www.wsj.com/articles/the-key-to-getting-workers-to-stop-wasting-time-online-1457921545.

News can seem like a legitimate use of time. But there are downsides to living in the era of the 24-hour news cycle, which is fast-paced, panic-inducing, and always changing. Consider the newspaper of yesteryear. It was not only more content rich than television or online news; it was confined to the breakfast table or a favorite chair. Catching up on the news had a beginning and an end. News is now everywhere, carried conveniently in their pockets.

You can advise church members to try a different system to save time. They might try to go back to an actual newspaper. Any current event that's really important will be there. Or plan to check the news just once a day online, preferably not the first thing. A brain is freshest as it starts the day on your computer. People might try to use that time for more challenging work and leave the news for an afternoon break or later in the day.

Encourage the families in your church to inspect their digital diet from time to time. Maybe it's time for a news or entertainment fast.

HELP YOUR CHURCH KNOW TO GROW

The amount of knowledge available today through the internet would be unfathomable to someone just two generations ago. Pandora's box has been kicked wide open with ChatGPT and other artificial intelligence (AI) tools that can seemingly answer questions, tell stories, compose essays, create art and music, and write code. ChatGPT was trained using text databases from the internet which included books, articles, and other pieces of writing online. Three hundred billion words were fed into the system. It's a bottomless pit of information.[24]

The wired world is a behemoth of knowledge. How will the families in your congregation use it? Encourage people to go online not just to *know* more but to *grow* more. There's a world of difference between possessing knowledge and putting it into practice. Encourage those in your church to assess their technology use with questions like:

- Are you learning about new tools to do your job better?
- Do your Bible study apps add depth to your reading?

---

[24] Alex Hughes, "ChatGPT: Everything You Need to Know About OpenAI's GPT-4 Tool," *BBC Science Focus*, September 25, 2023, www.sciencefocus.com/future-technology/gpt-3.

- Are you learning new biblical ways to communicate effectively with your spouse? With your kids?

You can help the adults in your church by providing needed education and inspiration regarding screen time and the family. Ideas include:

- Hosting a parenting workshop or conference (also serves as a great ministry outreach).
- Planning a question-and-answer time with a mentor couple who has navigated screen time successfully.
- Reading technology books as a small group, such as my book co-authored with Dr. Gary Chapman, *Screen Kids: 5 Skills Every Child Needs in a Tech-Driven World* (video course available), or Molly DeFrank's book, *Digital Detox: The Two-Week Reset for Kids*.
- Introducing concepts like "the pivot" and a "digital sabbath" in church teachings and discussions.

You can challenge your church group to employ the pivot or digital sabbath as part of your discipleship across age groups. The pivot simply means that when you are looking down at your device and someone walks into the room or near you, you pivot away from your screen and give that person eye contact. If you're sitting down looking at the computer, you turn your chair away from the screen toward the incoming person. People are more important than computers. Pivoting away from your device communicates with your body language that you are listening and present.

A digital sabbath is a screen-free time you create in your home to take a break. You might unplug the modem for an entire day or have a certain weeknight to be screen-free. You even set aside the whole weekend to unplug to reset your home. This would be an excellent church-wide campaign one weekend.

Author William Powers decided to unplug their home modem from Friday at bedtime until Monday morning. At first, it was incredibly hard for Powers, his wife, and their son. They realized how hooked they were to digital platforms.[25] After two months of dark computer screens on

---

[25] I recognize that digital platforms get more complex as phones are not dependent on modems or Wi-Fi. Smart homes make unplugging increasingly more difficult. Like Powers, a thoughtful

weekends, it started to get easier, and after four or five months, they began to actually enjoy the benefits. They noticed that things didn't change overnight:

> We'd peeled our minds away from the screens where they'd been stuck. We were really there with one another and nobody else, and we could all feel it. . . . There was an atmospheric change in our minds, a shift to a slower, less restless, more relaxed way of thinking. We could just be in one place, doing one particular thing, and enjoy it. . . . The digital medium allows everything to be stored for later use. It was still out there; it was just a little further away. The notion that we could put the crowd, and the crowded part of our life, at a distance like this was empowering in a subtle but significant way. It was a reminder that it was ours to put at a distance.[26]

NEW HABITS AWAIT

English writer Samuel Johnson (1709–1784) said it well, "The chains of habit are too weak to be felt until they are too strong to be broken."[27] That's true of bad habits, but it's also true of good ones. Your church members may not instantly feel a difference when pivoting away from the phone to look into a daughter's eyes or when taking a quick break outside instead of scrolling through social media. But small changes pave the way for bigger changes. Small wins (they got through lunch without touching their phones) lead to big wins (they're talking to their teenagers again). Help your congregation members see the power of these small changes and encourage them with hearty praise along the way. When adults are able to overcome digital addictions, unhealthy practices, or bad habits, kids will be empowered to do the same.

Psalm 18:19 speaks of how God delivered David from his enemies to a spacious place. God can do the same for the families you minister to. The enemy of our souls would love to keep us all chasing notifications, posting comments, and using the bulk of our free time for entertainment.

---

review and decision-making of each new technology with the family's needs, stage, and humility will be necessary.
[26]William Powers, *Hamlet's Blackberry: A Practical Philosophy for Building a Good Life in the Digital Age* (New York: Harper, 2010), 228-31.
[27]Samuel Johnson quotes, *Brainy Quote*, accessed March 9, 2023, www.brainyquote.com/authors/samuel-johnson-quotes.

Technology can certainly be used to advance the kingdom of God, but many times, it's simply used to eat up valuable time.

Notice the personal pronouns as David continues in verses 20-22: "The LORD has dealt with *me* according to *my* righteousness; according to the cleanness of *my* hands he has rewarded *me*. For *I* have kept the ways of the LORD; *I* am not guilty of turning from *my* God. All his laws are before *me*; *I* have not turned away from his decrees."

Like David, we can live righteously in an ungodly age. It starts with one person, with one family in your church. It doesn't matter if "everyone is doing it." Help your congregation dethrone the phone from guiding their lives and filling each day with empty and harmful content. A collective of families that support each other in digital limits is an important service to the families in your congregation. No matter what the world says, a fully charged phone with Wi-Fi can't provide what we really need. Only God can do that. As you and your church members walk humbly with God, he will lead you to regular screen-free green pastures that restore your soul. Others outside the church may notice your balanced lives and be encouraged to join you in the journey. Equip men and women to be intentional and wise about technology. By watching the examples of healthy adults in their lives, children will learn how to navigate screen time well.

12

RACE, DISCRIMINATION, AND STRESS IN THE FAMILY

Cassandra D. Page and Eric M. Brown

Ministry leaders often navigate the stormy waters caused by racial stress, discrimination, and trauma. These two scenarios offer cases in point. Pastor Deal had prepared what he thought was a good biblical sermon about racism and discrimination. He had clear Scriptures and concepts to share with a strong focus on Acts and Pauline teaching on how people within a church should treat each other. He was shocked at the complaining and defensive emails in his inbox on Sunday night. His office staffer, a biracial woman who screened his emails, came to him in tears. The discipleship coordinator, Gayla, dropped in the office to rant about how several church members had complained to her about the sermon being too "woke." The church had been making good progress on race relations and had even had good engagement in a community walk against racism just three years ago. This tension slowly subsided over time with some one-on-one meetings between church leaders and defensive members (and a few members moved on from the congregation). Six months later, two families came to the discipleship coordinator with new pain over race-based stress and discrimination they had experienced. The pain was still in the water, so

Pastor Deal and Gayla sat down to discern the best way to respond to their pain.

Pastor Jones leads a primarily African American church in suburban Buffalo, New York. He loves the congregation and the work they are doing as a community to grow in the Lord, disciple others, and be a blessing in the community. However, the lasting effects of the Buffalo grocery store shooting and its aftermath were causing ripple effects in the church. Recently, racist graffiti tags had been posted in their neighborhood. A wise elder in the church came to Pastor Jones to ask the best way to respond to the pain and trauma he was observing in the congregation. Teenagers were becoming more insulated and withdrawn, even in church gatherings. Families seemed to have more mental health problems. The pain of the community appeared as graffiti on the church walls, and Pastor Jones and the elder sat down to discern the best way to respond to their pain.

Addressing racism and discrimination in the families in your church community requires the ability to sail through storms. We know sailors do not typically aim to set sail during storms, but storms may transpire while sailing. Likewise, those entering church leadership ten or more years ago may not have anticipated the socio-political waters to be as turbulent as they are now. Yet, you are still positioned to lead your congregation through the storm. Perhaps you have been called to courageously enter into difficult conversations and create space for both dissent and understanding. The presidential elections of Obama and Trump; protests over the killing of Black people such as George Floyd, Brianna Taylor, and Ahmaud Arbery; the January 6 insurrection; and responses to Covid-19 have deepened fissures within the evangelical church around race and politics for which most church leaders were unprepared.

Timothy Dalrymple, the CEO of *Christianity Today*, stated, "New fractures are forming within the American evangelical movement, fractures that do not run along the usual regional, denominational, ethnic, or political lines. Couples, families, friends, and congregations once united in their commitment to Christ are now dividing over seemingly irreconcilable views of the world. They are not merely dividing but becoming incomprehensible to one another."[1] Views on politics and racism have been the main drivers of the deep fissures within congregations.[2]

Congregants who are racial minorities come to church seeking respite from the racial stress they experience daily. Yet, some people of color are leaving some churches due to experiencing either racism within the congregation or an absence of pastoral care related to racial wounds.[3] Paul speaks directly to ethnic divisions in the church and reminds us that Christ is our peace and that he has demolished any barriers and walls of hostility (Eph 2:14). The spirit of reconciliation is a result of the grace we have received from Jesus. As we grow in our felt need for the forgiving work of Christ, we are emboldened to confess our sins to one another, based on humility and the motivation to seek peace and unity with believers from other racial backgrounds.[4] This unity across racial and socio-political lines where it exists is a vivid witness to the gospel of Jesus.

Our aim in this chapter is to equip church leaders to minister courageously and compassionately to families and individuals experiencing racial stress in their daily lives, both within and outside the church. Thanks be to God! The good news of the kingdom of God provides several pastoral resources to draw on for those affected by racism. This chapter offers guidance on developing desirable skills when talking about race, racism, and its components first among yourselves as a leadership team (e.g., church leaders, clergy members) and then with your congregation.

THE INTERSECTION OF FAITH AND RACE

Having the proper tools and shared end goal for the journey helps us navigate these stormy waters, especially when sailing with a team (like

---

[1] Timothy Dalrymple, "The Splintering of the Evangelical Soul," *Christianity Today*, April 16, 2021, www.christianitytoday.com/ct/2021/april-web-only/splintering-of-evangelical-soul.html.
[2] Michael Graham, "The Six Way Fracturing of Evangelicalism," *Mere Orthodoxy*, June 7, 2021, https://mereorthodoxy.com/six-way-fracturing-evangelicalism/.
[3] Campbell Robertson, "A Quiet Exodus: Why Black Worshipers Are Leaving White Evangelical Churches," *The New York Times*, March 9, 2018, www.nytimes.com/2018/03/09/us/blacks-evangelical-churches.html.
[4] John Perkins, *One Blood: Parting Words to the Church on Race and Love* (Chicago: Moody, 2018), 47.

you and your pastoral staff or congregation). To that end, using shared terminology as a compass through these challenging conversations is paramount.

Defining race, race-based trauma, and discrimination. To prepare for conversations about race, racism, race-related stress, and racial trauma, we define these terms so you are more than prepared, vocabulary-wise, for such interactions. Society uses *race* to categorize people based on perceived shared physical traits. Sometimes this categorization can create behaviors, thoughts, or feelings called *racism*: "behavior . . . based on the belief in the superiority of one group of people and the inferiority of another."[5] We know commonly and spiritually that we have all fallen short of the glory of God. One result of our fallen nature is *discrimination*.[6] Discrimination occurs when groups are seen as or treated as inferior compared to others based on distinctive characteristics (e.g., race, gender, age, sexual orientation). Stress experienced from this different, less-than, inferior treatment can result in negative psychological consequences (i.e., soul pain). *Race-related stress* is one such consequence.[7] A form of race-related stress, a reaction to dangerous events, and real or perceived experiences of racial discrimination, is called *racial trauma*.[8] Discrimination compounded as race-based trauma is a scenario you will often encounter in conversations centered around negative experiences due to race, as this is bound to explore not just one singular incident of pain, but many multiplied over a lifetime. Sometimes, being told of the pain inflicted on a brother or sister in Christ (whether you or a stranger is the offender) becomes a heavy burden. How do you address these racial wounds?

---

[5] Equity, Diversity, and Inclusion Office, *Equity, Diversity, and Inclusion Framework* (Washington, DC: American Psychological Association, 2021), 12, www.apa.org/about/apa/equity-diversity-inclusion/equity-division-inclusion-framework.pdf.
[6] Equity, Diversity, and Inclusion Office, *Equity, Diversity, and Inclusion Framework*, 12.
[7] Alex L. Pierterse and Robert T. Carter, "An Examination of the Relationship Between General Life Stress, Racism-related Stress, and Psychological Health among Black Men," *Journal of Counseling Psychology*, 54, no. 1 (2007): 101-9.
[8] Della V. Mosley et al., "Critical Consciousness of Anti-Black Racism: A Practical Model to Prevent and Resist Racial Trauma," *Journal of Counseling Psychology* 68, no. 1 (2021): 1-16, https://doi.org/10.1037/cou0000430.

HELPING CHURCH LEADERS ADDRESS CONGREGANTS' EXPERIENCES OF RACE-BASED DISCRIMINATION AND TRAUMA

Most often, when families from racial minority groups seek help from church leaders, they do so for the same reasons White families seek pastoral care: financial stressors, marital troubles, or conflicts with adolescent children. Ministry leaders should know that although family members may not explicitly bring up topics of racism, racial stress, and discrimination, they are often a perpetual undercurrent that compounds whatever issue they bring to the church leader. So, an immigrant family that comes and wants to talk to the pastor about their teenage daughter who is acting out, is not likely to bring up the racism their daughter experiences at school as a part of the issue. They also may not bring up the discrimination they experience at work, affecting their ability to speak calmly and patiently with their daughter when upset. The church leader needs to recognize that race-based stress or trauma may be an underlying factor in their familial conflict. Ministry leaders should engage in conversations that allow family members to express their struggles with racism and how this may impact how they relate to each other, similar to what Pastor Deal hoped to achieve in his sermon on racism recounted in the opening vignette.

PASTORAL RESPONSE: JAMES 1:9

Feeling unprepared. Some pastors do not feel prepared to discuss race and racism, particularly if the congregants do not share their racial identity. But pastors should be reassured that topics such as race and ethnicity appear throughout the biblical narrative.[9] From Abraham and his descendants' encounters with non-Jewish nations to the great vision of every nation, tribe, and people coming before the throne and the Lamb of God in the book of Revelation, we read of the ongoing significance of race. Although our identity in Christ is central to who we are as disciples, our race significantly shapes how we experience the world. Yet, many ministry leaders feel ill-equipped and fearful of discussing race and racism.[10]

---

[9] David Swanson, *Rediscipling the White Church* (Downers Grove, IL: InterVarsity Press, 2020), 13.
[10] Rich Villodas, *The Deeply Formed Life* (Colorado Springs, CO: Waterbrook, 2020), 56.

Pastors and ministry leaders may need to remind themselves that the Spirit of God in Christ dwells in them and their congregants. Therefore, the effectiveness of the pastoral work to be done is not based solely on the education or intelligence of the minister. Ministers can trust the Spirit to guide their work in discussions around racism and racial trauma to assist church families as they navigate the rough waters of racism, like Pastor Jones did when responding to a racially motivated killing spree in his city. To better access the work of the Spirit, ministers will need to practice humility around issues of race and culture.

Cultural humility as spiritual formation. Cultural humility is a tool I needed when responding to families seeking help because they have experienced discrimination. Cultural humility is a term that describes engagement with another person that honors and values their unique constellation of identities such as ethnicity, race, gender, and socioeconomic status. Jesus modeled this way of relating to others by being other-oriented rather than self-focused.[11] He was interested in and open to exploring the cultural background of those with whom He was interacting. For example, Jesus related to the woman at the well by recognizing her cultural heritage and being willing to talk with her despite any scandal that could have resulted when speaking to her by herself without others present. Cultural humility contrasts with color blindness. Where the latter claims to ignore the racial identity of others, cultural humility recognizes and appreciates the unique strengths and struggles that people of various ethnicities and races experience.

How to respond effectively. Trying to engage sensitively and with humility can prove overwhelming. Maybe someone shares an experience with you where they are obviously hurt, but you cannot understand why. Different types of responses (not reactions) are essential to further invite people into sharing versus dismissing their experience. Three particular skills that add to the foundation of cultural humility are discussed below.

Listen to hear, not respond. The first pastoral task around responding to race-based stress and trauma issues is to listen to hear, not respond prematurely. Many of us have already formed our opinions on such issues and

---

[11] Joshua Hook, Don Davis, Jesse Owen, and Cirleen DeBlaere, *Cultural Humility: Engaging Diverse Identities in Therapy* (Washington, DC: American Psychological Association, 2017), 8.

are likely to listen to those we minister to through our own filter. Therefore, it will be essential for us to remember to listen and listen thoroughly. When I (Eric) was pastoring, my general rule was that the congregant or the family should do most of the talking. As a preacher, it was easy for me to talk and give my Holy Spirit-endowed two cents. Over time, I recognized that I was underappreciating the ministry of presence, which sets the tone for a relationship where family members could be upfront and honest about their pain. James 1:19 reminds us, "Everyone should be quick to listen, slow to speak and slow to become angry." This is undoubtedly true for pastoral care around race-induced stress and trauma and provides a framework for building trust with families that have encountered bigotry. In contrast, the ministry leader who does not listen to learn may be unable to empathize with others' racial experiences.

Empathize well. The second pastoral task is to empathize deeply, which means not minimizing a person or family's experiences or moving too quickly toward forgiveness. *Empathy* describes the ability to enter into another person's experience, feel what they may feel, imagine what they may be going through, and then articulate their pain back to them so they feel understood. This means we must be able and willing to sit with someone else's pain, which is why listening to hear and not responding too quickly is so important when doing any kind of pastoral work, especially when racial experiences differ from their ministry leaders. Far too often, ministry leaders avoid sitting in the pain of others by speaking "biblical truth." In psychology, we use the term "spiritual bypass" to describe the avoidance of painful emotions and psychological realities by jumping straight to spirituality or religion. As a pastor, I (Eric) often remind myself that a faithful cross-shaped ministry means I must be willing to sit in the grave with a person for at least a little while before jumping too quickly to the resurrection.

One way ministry leaders have failed to empathize with persons suffering from racial stress and discrimination is by moving too quickly to instruct those in pain to forgive. Although we, as Christians, are commanded to forgive by Jesus, it is important to be clear on what forgiveness is not.[12] Forgiveness is not denying that what others have done is harmful or

---

[12]Worthington Touissaint and David Williams, *Forgiveness and Health: Scientific Evidence and Theories Relating Forgiveness to Better Health* (New York: Springer, 2015), 18.

minimizing one's pain. Forgiveness is not the same as forgetting; it is not acting as if everything is okay. Forgiveness also does not mean that we do not pursue justice. Martin Luther King Jr. and other Christian civil rights activists often spoke of forgiveness as freeing one's spirit from bitterness to continue the fight for justice unhampered by hatred. Authentic forgiveness is best engaged when the feelings of pain have been fully acknowledged and experienced. God's forgiveness of our sins by no means entails denying or minimizing our transgressions and their effects on recipients of racial trauma.

Focus on the wounded, not the offender. A third way ministry leaders fail to empathize with people suffering from race-related stress and race-related trauma is by focusing more on the offender rather than those impacted by the offense. Our quickness to forgive sometimes unintentionally elevates the person who offended us and forces them to repent. Consider this. Reggie, a Black man states to his Hispanic friend Marcos, "I am so frustrated with the number of Mexican immigrants coming to this country and taking our jobs." A ministry leader overhears this conversation and swiftly tells Reggie to apologize to Marcos and repent for his words. Once Reggie has done so, the ministry leader walks away pleased. Instead of checking in with Marcos, the offended, about how the conversation made him feel, asking him to share his experience and how he might be concerned Reggie sees him as "just another immigrant taking jobs from Americans," the focus stayed on Reggie, the offender. However, when the offender has fully acknowledged the feelings of hurt and pain experienced by the offended through empathy, the offender can apologize for both the act and the impact of the action. If Marcos was encouraged to share his hurt and Reggie empathized with the pain he caused to Marcos, Reggie could apologize for his words and their negative impact on Marcos and their friendship. This process allows the offended person to say how he or she was hurt and why, for the transgressor to be held accountable, and for a path forward to be constructed.

CONGREGATIONAL RESPONSE COVERS A SPECTRUM

We have covered responses from ministry leaders regarding addressing the pain of congregants. We now shift to discussing how congregants may respond. They may feel supported, unsupported, or anything in between. The congregational response is unpredictable, just as surprising as the tides turning in a storm. However, a spectrum exists within this unpredictability. Here we discuss two ends of the spectrum: separation/disharmony and unity.

Separation/disharmony. Albeit unpredictable, a response of separation or disharmony should be expected as a significant portion of the stormy weather, mainly if your congregants or staff are inexperienced sailors (i.e., avoid talking about race and racism, fear the wrong thing might be said, or have a more homogeneous racial church makeup). This problem is characterized by the complaining emails that Pastor Deal received in the opening scenario. Often, fingers are pointed at who is at fault for racism or who continues to perpetuate racism. Sometimes, speculation circulates that some chose to enter the conversation about racism to cause shame and guilt intentionally. Yet other times, some describe the storms of racism, discrimination, and race-related stress as minor compared to more pressing matters. When disharmony erupts because of fear, it can feel safer to retreat and self-protect with whatever shelter you may find. However, a leader should courageously demonstrate empathy, listen to the grumblings, and strive to understand. Find a common link. Take things piece by piece. Return to navigational strategies that will weather the storm until the waves cease and the turmoil subsides. A path forward will result. It might not be clear and smooth (or even straight), but you will move forward.

Unity. We liken moving forward to a unifying experience founded on a commitment to move through difficult conversations instead of succumbing to them. Most people tend to avoid tension and work quickly to make amends. Sometimes, this comes at the cost of minimizing hurt or forcing forgiveness. Acknowledging pain or wrong done and sitting in the tension of hearing another's pain can be incredibly uncomfortable. Trust us; we know! It is human and helpful to acknowledge the discomfort of seeing a brother or sister in Christ and not having the words to say to make their pain go away. The choice to listen communicates empathy. The choice to enter into pain and carry the burden of another family member in Christ is the path forward.

Current crises. As mentioned, sailing may not be smooth. The church is experiencing a crisis of mistrust, anger, and misunderstanding due to racial upheaval, which can easily morph into an us versus them mentality. This reality often results in viewing the "other" as deserving of punishment, regardless of the side they occupy. This church fragmentation results from an inability to empathize with someone in pain, reinforcing a dark squall in our church's racial history. You might explore your local area, reading about what race-based historical events have affected your city or interviewing local people who carry the ethnic and racial stories of your community. As church leaders, it is your responsibility to understand the backbone of the current crisis as well as the history of its foundation.[13] Recognizing the outrage *then* will provide a stronger understanding of the outrage *now*. This will assist you in preparing for these conversations, engaging with them, and providing a factual foundation for the emotions you will encounter. This is the act of Jesus choosing to sit at the table and seeking to understand; this is Jesus leaning out of avoidance and into discomfort.

LEANING OUT OF AVOIDANCE AND INTO DISCOMFORT

Given the stress that ministry leaders have faced due to the effects of Covid-19 and the social upheaval of the past several years due to political polarization, many ministers report feeling burned out and have considered leaving the pastorate. These stressors may contribute to church leaders avoiding racial conversations, regardless of whether or not they are paid in ministry. It may be helpful to know that avoidance is a coping mechanism that can minimize stress in the short-term but can ultimately prolong suffering—both for ministry leaders and congregants.

Church leaders mainly avoid the pain of racial stress in two ways. The first way is through passive avoidance, characterized by not talking about racism and its effects on individuals and families, as if racism no longer exists. The second way is a more active avoidance by pre-emptively telling others their views of race relations, perhaps even what the Bible says about how we should relate to one another, without taking the time to listen deeply and empathizing with the pain of those suffering from racism. To be able to sit with the pain of others requires spiritual and emotional maturity, along with patience. Just as Peter, James, and John

---

[13]Ken Wystma, *The Myth of Equality: Uncovering the Roots of Injustice and Privilege* (Downers Grove, IL: InterVarsity Press, 2019), 25.

were unable to stay awake with Jesus in the Garden of Gethsemane, our weariness in ministry can often hinder our ability to be fully present with others who are suffering.

PRACTICAL AND EFFECTIVE MINISTRY RESPONSES

Self-preparation. To sit and empathize with the pain of others in these courageous and difficult conversations can be challenging and at times draining, especially for those who are uncomfortable sitting with others' pain. The first practice we suggest to ministry leaders is learning to engage in spiritual disciplines that enable you to sit with your discomfort. The book of Psalms contains several prayers and songs of lament that get very little attention within our church services or popular Christian literature. We suggest meditating on a psalm of lament, such as Psalm 10 or 22, as a prayer on behalf of oneself and others who are hurting. Jeremiah recorded an excruciatingly painful lament, where he described his feeling forsaken by God to such an extent that he wishes he had not been born (Jer 20:7-18). Meditating on these painful passages of Scripture reminds us that we can fully experience our pain while holding on to our faith, knowing God is present. One of the most significant markers of spiritual maturity is sitting with one's pain and the pain of others. By doing so, we can give the ministry of presence through which a congregant can sense the Holy Spirit working through us despite their current turmoil.

Recognize spiritual warfare. As ministry leaders, we must also remind ourselves that Satan is alive and well and seeks to destroy all human beings' peace; indeed, this is true for those who have given their lives to Jesus. Some Christian traditions use the term spiritual warfare to describe the reality of what Paul states in Ephesians 6:12: "For our struggle is not against flesh and blood, but against the rulers, against the authorities, against the powers of this dark world and against the spiritual forces of evil in the heavenly realms." We may forget that the armor of God described in Ephesians 6:13-17 enables believers to fortify themselves to withstand the enemy's devices. As we recognize that racism and bigotry are a part of the devil's schemes to hurt and divide humanity and the church, we are emboldened to enter into discussions with prayer and intention.

Develop the fruit of the Spirit. Ministering to families experiencing race-based stress in our present age of political polarization, incivility, and contentiousness will require a degree of spiritual maturity and wisdom only possible through God's grace. As we become more aware of the devil's schemes, we appreciate how our spiritual formation into Christlikeness, or the lack thereof, will significantly impact our ability to minister effectively to families experiencing racial stress and trauma. In Galatians, Paul writes that the fruit of the Spirit is characterized by love, joy, peace, forbearance, kindness, goodness, faithfulness, gentleness, and self-control (Gal 5:22-23). Paul describes these qualities as the fruit of the Spirit—singular not plural. The fruit of the Spirit, embodied by ministry leaders, can provide families the comfort they need. As ministry leaders embody all aspects of the Spirit's fruit, we are better able to sit with the pain of people suffering from racism in a way that is healing and affirming. The ministry of presence is central to caring for individuals and families affected by racism. The fruit of the Spirit empowers us to be a healing presence for those wounded by racism.

Turn to wise and supportive others. Finally, ministry leaders must be relationally connected to those who are wise, supportive, and knowledgeable about current and past racial issues. These connections will greatly improve ministry leaders' ability to engage in courageous dialogues and adeptly respond to racial tensions in the church. During our current moment of social and political upheaval, it is all the more critical for ministry leaders to be in fellowship with others who understand the unique stressors that ministry leaders face. Moreover, it is essential to connect with others on the journey of learning how to best serve those suffering the consequences of racism. This will be especially true for leaders within multiethnic ministries, primarily-minority churches with many members struggling with race-based stress or discrimination, or those with changing neighborhood demographics, where political tensions and racial protests may have already resulted in divisions. Consider exploring citywide church networks or your denomination's efforts, as many cities or denominations have racial justice or reconciliation groups with resources available.[14]

---

[14]Some parachurch organizations that attempt to address the issues of racism in churches include Arrabon, Redeemer City to City ministry, or books by Christian publishers such as InterVarsity Press on the subject of social justice.

CONCLUSION: NAVIGATING THE STORM

Validate, externalize, celebrate, re-narrate. When sitting with a person or family suffering from racial stress or trauma, we suggest a four-step process. First, the person's feelings and emotions should be validated and honored. We do this by empathizing with their pain and appreciating how the long history of racism and bigotry manifests in our current day. Second, we externalize the racial stressors that the family is facing. In other words, we help families understand that the racial discrimination they are experiencing is a result of the sickness and sinfulness of our society. By doing so, we seek to help each family member empathize with the other by appreciating that their spouse, child, parent, or sibling also faces daily challenges due to being a racial minority. Third, we use cultural humility to celebrate the unique strengths and assets of a family's cultural heritage. Racial stress and trauma can too quickly become internalized and cause persons and families to hold negative views of their own racial and ethnic groups. We must help families appreciate the beauty of their ethnic community. Finally, we help families re-narrate their stories. We do this by assisting them in placing their story within the larger biblical narrative of how God is redeeming a broken world and viewing their family's story as one of strength and resilience despite the demonic influence of racism.

A Call to Action. We leave you, as a ministry leader, emboldened with the Spirit of God, positioned to help others navigate these difficult storms. Joshua was encouraged to be bold and courageous as he prepared for battle, to approach his enemies without fear, knowing the Lord would be with him wherever he went (Joshua 1:9). As we close our chapter, my (Cassandra) final encouragement on how to approach race, discrimination, and race-based stress from a faith lens is fourfold. First, step boldly into this stormy journey with applicable tools that we have provided. Second, enter difficult dialogues courageously. Third, embrace discomfort without fear. Fourth, trust that the Lord your God, who entrusted your congregation to you and placed you as their leader, will be with you on this journey in calm or stormy seas.

13

MINISTERING TO FAMILIES IN POVERTY AND FINANCIAL CRISIS

Kristen Kansiewicz

Poverty has many faces. It would be impossible to give one illustration of a family in poverty or financial crisis. Hence, I offer four fictional stories based on real-life examples from my ministry to impoverished individuals and families. Their stories will weave throughout this chapter to illuminate some of the challenges you may face in your ministry. While this approach is not exhaustive, it aims to be representative.

FOUR STORIES OF POVERTY

The case of Sam. Sam is a homeless, 24-year-old White man whom you met outside the church as a recovery meeting was wrapping up. You said hello and invited him to come to a Sunday service. Since then, Sam has come to your church sporadically. You learn that he has a pattern of using methamphetamines. His homelessness and drug use frequently led to brief stints in jail. During the periods that he is clean, he shows significant anxiety, and you understand this to be part of why he turns back to using. He has asked if he can stay at the church at night because his belongings are stolen when he stays in the local shelter. You've said "no," but now that the weather is getting colder, you are unsure if this is the Christlike thing to do.

The case of Vanessa. Vanessa is a 35-year-old African American mother of two who has attended your church faithfully for several years. She is active in ministry and holds a full-time job. You have not thought of her as "poor," but during a pastoral meeting, you learn that she lives in government-subsidized housing and relies on food stamps. She shares that her salary as a certified nurse's assistant is enough to cover utilities, car insurance, gas, and basic household needs for herself and her two children, but rent costs are over half of her monthly salary. The father of her children is in jail and has not paid the child support he owes for many years, even before his incarceration. When he is released in a few months, he has promised two things: first, that he will help out financially, and second, that he wants to spend time with the children. Vanessa worries that if he pays child support, he may become entitled to demand parental visitation. She does not want his influence in her children's lives and asks you if that is the wrong way to think.

The case of Bob. A family of five has attended your church for the past year. You have engaged in several pastoral counseling meetings with the father, Bob, after you saw some unemployment patterns and became concerned. Bob told you that he had started several small businesses over the years. and none of them have ever taken off "due to the economy." Most recently, he has been running a used car business, "flipping cars" from the family's garage. The money from each "flip" is never as much as he anticipates. During his last meeting with you, he said his family may lose their home as they have fallen behind on the mortgage. A friend offered Bob a commission-based job in insurance sales, and he is considering taking it. He asks for your advice on whether to take the job after telling you that his friend makes six figures working fewer than 40 hours per week. Bob is also worried that his wife is thinking of leaving him.

The case of Camilla. Camilla is a 46-year-old Latina living in a mobile home about 20 minutes outside town. She has been on disability income for the past fifteen years due to chronic pain. She has also struggled with depression, as it is hard for her to get out, and she is often unable to come to church. The pandemic created the opportunity to watch church services on YouTube. She hasn't returned post-Covid. She continues to feel isolated and lonely. She would like to work. She was a good secretary with clerical skills and worked successfully for over ten years. However, with her chronic pain flares, she cannot predict her good days or bad days. You wish you could do more for her, but you aren't sure what you can offer besides a monthly visit by the women's ministry leader.

SYSTEMIC ISSUES IN POVERTY

Defining poverty. As is evident from the vignettes, individual depictions of material poverty can vary widely. The focus of this chapter will be on the United States population. This writing will not address international poverty, but good resources exist elsewhere.[1] According to the US Census in 2021, approximately 11.6% of the nation's population lived in poverty.[2] That's almost 38 million people whose income fell below the federal poverty line (i.e., for a family of four, that's just under $28,000 per year as of 2021). To put that in perspective, a person earning $15/hour and working 40 hours per week would make about $30,000 working 50 weeks per year. The actual take-home pay may be considerably less after any additional health insurance premiums and taxes. If that worker is the primary wage earner for the household, that could quickly put a family in the poverty category. Of course, many have income even lower than United States poverty thresholds, and many who have income above these federal guidelines struggle to make ends meet due to rising housing costs and inflation.[3] For those receiving disability income from the Social Security Administration, as of 2022, the average monthly payment was $1,358, or $16,296 per year.[4] These numbers provided for the United

---

[1] Anne Rathbone Bradley and Arthur Lindsley, *For the Least of These: A Biblical Answer to Poverty* (Grand Rapids, MI: Zondervan, 2014); Brian Fikkert, *From Dependence to Dignity* (Grand Rapids, MI: Zondervan, 2015); and Ronald J. Sider, *Rich Christians in an Age of Hunger* (Nashville: Thomas Nelson, 2015).
[2] John Creamer et al., "Poverty in the United States: 2021," United States Census Bureau, September 13, 2022, www.census.gov/library/publications/2022/demo/p60-277.html.
[3] Laurence M. Ball, Daniel Leigh, and Prachi Mishra, "Understanding U.S. Inflation during the COVID Era," International Monetary Fund, October 28, 2022, www.imf.org/en/Publications/WP/Issues/2022/10/28/Understanding-U-S-525200.
[4] "Fact Sheet: 2022 Social Security Changes," Social Security Administration (2022), www.ssa.gov/news/press/factsheets/colafacts2022.pdf.

States do not account for variance in location, where access to public services and living costs can shift the look and feel of poverty as well.

As we consider ministering to families in financial crisis, we need to consider those that may not appear to be experiencing poverty right now. They may own a home or have expensive possessions and may not even realize their impending financial crisis. Bob's vignette offers an example of a family that may appear suburban and share a middle to upper middle-class lifestyle like other congregants. Still, the actual financial picture is very different. Adjustable-rate mortgages, credit card debt, college debt, medical debt, unemployment, and even addiction can be hidden underneath a temporary picture of stability. Yet, unseen drains to monthly income can leave families with dwindling financial resources. Some families in your congregation may be close to losing their homes or declaring bankruptcy. But their lifestyle does not yet reflect this reality. It is important not to make assumptions about a person's financial stability or instability simply based on how they outwardly appear.

Family structure. Families facing poverty may not fit into a neat mold. When thinking about ministering to families, you might picture an idealized family from the 1950s with a father, a mother, and two or three children. The reality is that there are complex systemic factors that contribute to poverty. Those to whom you minister are likely to have messy lives. Even outside the scope of poverty, family structures are changing across American culture, with fewer marrying and more cohabitating.[5] The data on families indicates more children live apart from at least one biological parent and have more half-siblings than in previous eras.[6] As of 2021, about 28% of those who live in poverty are single mothers.[7] That statistic might fit a growing narrative: single motherhood = poverty. However, the same data indicate that 72% of those who live in poverty are not single mothers. In our four vignettes, we see a single young man,

---

[5] Marcia J. Carlson, Christopher Wimer, and Ron Haskins, "Changing Work, Changing Families, and Public Policies toward Low-Income Families," *RSF* 8, no. 5 (August 2022): 1-22, https://doi.org/10.7758/rsf.2022.8.5.01.

[6] Carlson, Wimer, and Haskins, "Changing Work," 5-6.

[7] Melissa Radey and Lenore M. McWey, "Safety Nets, Maternal Mental Health, and Child Mental Health Outcomes among Mothers Living in Poverty," *Journal of Child and Family Studies* 30, no. 3 (March 2021): 687-98, https://doi.org/10.1007/s10826-021-01909-3.

a single mother of two, a family of five with a married mother and father, and a single middle-aged woman with chronic pain. When we ask ourselves, "What does it mean to minister to families in a financial crisis?" the answer usually lies in the reality that you minister to those who present themselves to you in whatever form they may arrive. Be prepared for circumstances and situations that don't fit the pattern.

Generational patterns: What's their contribution? Many families have generational patterns that contribute to ongoing poverty. Education level is a leading predictor of poverty. Someone living in a low-income area starts with fewer options for quality education and fewer hours with their primary caregivers.[8] This educational pathway may end early and limit future educational opportunities, leading to unemployment or underemployment. Obstacles from ethnicity, immigrant status, disability, addiction, and criminal involvement added to the picture, and you have significant risk factors for generational poverty.[9] It is important to consider both the macro- (i.e., neighborhood, schools, community resources) and micro-systems (i.e., individuals, families) involved in material poverty to not oversimplify our responses.

Mental health and chronic illness: Understanding the connection. Research has shown a direct correlation between poverty and illness.[10] This link exists for those with chronic or acute illness, as well as for those with mental illness, although there is more yet to be understood about the nature of these relationships.[11] We cannot say that poverty causes illnesses or that having an illness leads to poverty. However, the association between poverty and illness helps us understand that we need to consider the complexities of poverty and health when working with a low-income population.

Churches can play an important role in addressing belonging for those living on the margins of society. According to Clark and her team, "Poverty

---

[8]Carlson, Wimer, and Haskins, "Changing Work," 8-9.
[9]Jeremy K. Everett, *I Was Hungry* (Grand Rapids, MI: Brazos, 2019).
[10]Carolyn B. Swope and Diana Hernández, "Housing as a Determinant of Health Equity: A Conceptual Model," *Social Science & Medicine* 243 (December 2019): 112571, https://doi.org/10.1016/j.socscimed.2019.112571.
[11]China Mills, "The Psychiatrization of Poverty: Rethinking the Mental Health-Poverty Nexus," *Social and Personality Psychology Compass* 9, no. 5 (May 2015): 213-22, https://doi.org/10.1111/spc3.12168.

experiences increase the risks of ill-health and mental illness that are often caused by social and economic barriers associated with poverty, such as limited access to food, housing, employment, education, healthcare, and mental health care."[12] You can understand this with the case of Sam, who is chronically homeless, which contributes to his anxiety. His anxiety likely also contributes to being homeless, creating a feedback loop. When working with those who are experiencing poverty resulting from an illness, it is important to focus on their need for belonging. They are often marginalized by society in many other ways.[13] In considering spiritual needs, some studies have determined that those with chronic illnesses' most significant spiritual needs are a sense of inner peace and being able to give to others actively.[14] As you minister to this population, remember that their financial needs may not be the most important need to them, and your congregation can address loneliness and a sense of belonging for many members.

Cultural and regional factors: Hindrance and resource. Poverty is multifaceted. Some people's experience of poverty is influenced by culture and geography. Poverty can be quite different across regions, with urban poverty experienced more by people of color and rural poverty impacting a higher percentage of people of European descent.[15] In rural areas, those in poverty have lower access to resources, including health care and mental health care. Research indicates that those who experience rural poverty are less likely to use resources due to cultural attitudes that value independence.[16] In both urban and rural areas, women

---

[12] Madeline Clark et al., "Best Practices for Counseling Clients Experiencing Poverty: A Grounded Theory," *Journal of Counseling & Development* 98, no. 3 (July 2020): 283-94, https://doi.org/10.1002/jcad.12323.

[13] You might also refer congregants with chronic illness to the online community at https://chronic-joy.org/

[14] A. Büssing, H. J. Balzat, and P. Heusser, "Spiritual Needs of Patients with Chronic Pain Diseases and Cancer: Validation of the Spiritual Needs Questionnaire," *European Journal of Medical Research* 15, no. 6 (June 2010): 266-73, https://doi.org/10.1186/2047-783x-15-6-266; Maciej Klimasiński et al., "Spiritual Distress and Spiritual Needs of Chronically Ill Patients in Poland: A Cross-Sectional Study," *International Journal of Environmental Research and Public Health* 19, no. 9 (May 2022): 5512, https://doi.org/10.3390/ijerph19095512.

[15] Adele N. Norris, Anna Zajicek, and Yvette Murphy-Erby, "Intersectional Perspective and Rural Poverty Research: Benefits, Challenges and Policy Implications," *Journal of Poverty* 14, no. 1 (January 2010): 55-75, https://doi.org/10.1080/10875540903489413.

[16] Addie Weaver et al., "Depressive Symptoms, Material Hardship, Barriers to Care, and Receptivity to Church-Based Treatment among Food Bank Service Recipients in Rural Michigan," *Social Work in Mental Health* 18, no. 5 (August 2020): 515-35, https://doi.org/10.1080/15332985.2020.1799907.

are more likely to be in poverty than men, in part due to wage inequality. In contrast, African American women are twice as likely as women in general to be the head of a household.[17] Overall, minority groups have a poverty rate twice that of their White neighbors.[18]

Local culture and regional factors can be a resource of relationships or institutions, with many accessing long-held friend and family connections as extremely important for those who struggle with poverty. Your church can be a significant resource to those who have little. Local and regional factors can also further isolate your parishioners due to a broken local system of care for those experiencing poverty. Knowing the resources and networks for those in poverty in your community can be extremely helpful for your church leadership.

Subsidized living: Compassion for all. You may find working with individuals and families living in material poverty challenging or frustrating because of views regarding government programs. Most of us have opinions about the role of government in aiding the poor and may think it is not doing enough or is doing too much. While working with this population, it is important to recognize any biases or feelings you may have. Considering the factors we have discussed, situations of poverty are complex. While we can work toward empowerment to help people rise out of poverty, some in your congregation may not be able to sustain living without government assistance, and others may choose not to. Research has shown that those who live in subsidized housing programs lack opportunities to advance their education and frequently struggle with unemployment.[19] Some argue that these programs foster dependence on government assistance and perpetuate a cycle of generational poverty.[20] Research results, however, have been inconclusive on the long-term

---

[17] Brenda A. Randle and Sandra L. Combs, "The Other America: African American Women Living in Poverty," *Race, Gender & Class* 23, no. 1–2 (January 1, 2016): 108-17.

[18] U.S. Census Bureau, "Table 2. Poverty Status of People by Family Relationship, Race, and Hispanic Origin," 2022, https://www.census.gov/data/tables/time-series/demo/income-poverty/historical-poverty-people.html.

[19] Mi Hee Shin, "The Race to Get In, and the Struggle to Get Out: The Problem of Inter-Generational Poverty in Federal Housing Programs," *Washington University Journal of Law and Policy* 40, no. 1 (January 2012): 337-64.

[20] Sandra J. Newman and Joseph M. Harkness, "The Long-Term Effects of Public Housing on Self-Sufficiency," *Journal of Policy Analysis and Management* 21, no. 1 (Winter 2002): 21-43.

outcomes for children growing up in these environments.[21] The lack of clarity in research suggests that both government assistance and self-reliance have validity, making awareness of personal bias more important. Housing and income benefits come with regulations, and these realities can impact decision-making and have moral implications.

For example, a couple may choose to marry to receive better benefits or live together without marrying to not disrupt their government assistance. Some cannot have more than a certain amount in a savings account without losing food assistance. Others have limits on how many hours they can work before they lose supplemental income.[22] These decisions directly impact the daily lives of congregants, and you may be asked to advise from moral and spiritual perspectives. Compassionate responses from you and those in church leadership with you are important. Those depending on subsidies have fewer choices than most people and may prioritize survival and retaining a home over other values, such as marriage. A gentle, supportive response may help parishioners consider all options.

Food insecurity: Trends and resources. According to data from 2018,[23] 12.3% of people are experiencing food insecurity. The US Department of Agriculture defines this term as households with limited or uncertain access to food sources.[24] Churches have an opportunity to play a role in addressing food insecurity in the short- and long-term. Later in the chapter, we will explore some long-term, systemic strategies that churches can use to reduce the overall problem of food insecurity. In the short term, when someone is in a situation where they may not have enough food or access to quality food, churches can operate food pantries or create food baskets to distribute in communities of need. If these ideas are unsustainable, consider a ministry in which some of your congregants donate gift cards for local grocery stores. Pastors or

---

[21] Swope and Hernández, "Housing as a Determinant."
[22] Shin, "The Race to Get In," 337-64.
[23] Carley Ward et al., "Attitudes toward Food Insecurity in the United States," *Analyses of Social Issues and Public Policy* 18, no. 1 (December 2018): 400-424, https://doi.org/10.1111/asap.12168.
[24] "Definitions of Food Security," October 25, 2023, Economic Research Service, US Department of Agriculture, www.ers.usda.gov/topics/food-nutrition-assistance/food-security-in-the-u-s/definitions-of-food-security/.

benevolence ministry groups can have these on hand to distribute when needed.

A THEOLOGY OF POVERTY

When we explore systemic factors that surround poverty, we may be left with further confusion. To what degree do we blame these systems versus acknowledging personal responsibility? What does a theology of poverty look like? How do we come to terms with the suffering that poverty brings? To what degree are we helping versus enabling when pastors and churches get involved? What is the church's role in responding to and engaging with poverty? These are important theological questions because our answers will guide our ministry decisions and directly impact our view of persons as we minister.

A view of persons. Pause for a moment and imagine that you are sitting with any one of the four people in the cases from the start of the chapter. What do they look like? What feelings arise as you sit across from them? What is the cause of their problems? Do you blame some of them for their situation while others you see as victims of circumstance? What makes the difference for you in their stories? Taking this moment to reflect and even write your personal observations can help identify your view of persons and the potential biases you may carry. How might developing Christlike humility assist in ministry to the poor? Such an exercise is useful in your private study rather than when faced with a congregant at your door.

In addition to general stereotypes and personal biases, let's examine the range of human emotions that can arise when engaging a person experiencing material poverty. Commonly known as the "empathy continuum,"[25] we can range from feelings like apathy or indifference to pity, sympathy, empathy, and compassion. When we are apathetic, we do not emotionally care about people or their experiences of poverty. We may not even be aware of their existence or their struggle. Other negative emotions may arise, such as anger or discrimination. Next comes pity, in which we look down on someone in a difficult situation and feel better

---

[25] Ross Smith, "Blog: The Empathy Continuum," The RSA, December 8, 2015, www.thersa.org/blog/2015/12/the-empathy-continuum.

about ourselves for not being in that situation. Sympathy moves us toward feeling bad or regretful for that person's situation, while empathy enables us to put ourselves in the other person's shoes. Compassion leads us to action as we step toward helping the person in need.

Most people stop at compassion. However, let's add one more step: empowerment. While we may act to help when we feel compassion, empowerment allows us to offer support and positive belief in the person to rise from their current position. Empowerment focuses on the person's strengths and removes the savior complex that helpers can sometimes feel when they view the person as in need of rescue. It is a humble attitude, treating those in poverty as equals. God has given us all the power to make choices, even when a risk of potentially disastrous consequences exists. He supports and partners with us even when he can fix, solve, or do it for us. As we minister to those experiencing poverty, we have the opportunity to follow God's example.

The Bible offers examples of how God views the poor and how he expects us to treat them. James 2 paints a picture of a wealthy and poor man entering the church and warns against favoritism. Dishonoring the poor is called evil and judgmental (Jas 2:1-4). In Exodus 23, Deuteronomy 24, and Micah 6, we are told to act justly toward the poor. We read in 1 Samuel 2:8 that God "raises the poor from the dust and lifts the needy from the ash heap; he seats them with princes and has them inherit a throne of honor." Psalm 68 states that God provides for the poor, and Psalm 69:32 describes the gladness of the poor in seeking God. Jesus fulfilled Isaiah 61:1 in bringing good news to the poor (Lk 4:18), and he encourages generosity in Luke 12:32-34. Finally, in Matthew 26:11 and Mark 14:7, Jesus told his disciples that the poor would always be with them. In this broken world, poverty will not be eradicated, yet we have a mission as the church to be generous and just to the poor.

A THICK THEODICY FOR POVERTY

How can we make sense of all these Scriptures when we face a challenging ministry situation? What are we to do with the reality of suffering that accompanies poverty? Where is God in these situations? When people cry out for provision, yet it does not seem to come, how do we speak into that moment? Proverbs is filled with wisdom on avoiding poverty with hard work. Does this mean that those who experience material poverty are lazy or to blame for their situation? Even if they did bear some responsibility, should that change our response? A thick theodicy for poverty offers church leaders a complex and wise understanding of the suffering of people in poverty.

Ultimately, we must acknowledge that we all live in an unjust and oppressive world. We bear personal responsibility for our choices. However, many experience oppression and injustice that limit their capacity or options to make confident choices.[26] While American culture is individualistic, and we often look solely through this lens, systemic evil permeates our world and leads to all kinds of suffering. Our theology is built on the knowledge that Jesus is working to build a new kingdom and is raising the poor for "a throne of honor" (1 Sam 2:8). Despite the admonitions of Proverbs, God seems far more interested in holding oppressors of the poor accountable than holding those in poverty responsible.

THE CHURCH'S ROLE IN RESPONDING TO POVERTY

So, precisely what is the church's role in responding to poverty? Is the church a social service agency or a philanthropic entity? What does discipling and shepherding a flock with mixed income levels mean? Are we all called to engage with those in material poverty? Are you off the hook by ministering in a wealthier environment?

In his book *I Was Hungry*, Jeremy Everett cites Jesus' challenge in Matthew 25:40, "Whatever you did for one of the least of these brothers and sisters of mine, you did for me."[27] Jesus' parable in Matthew and examples of the early church in the book of Acts suggest that giving and sharing generously are priorities for the global and local church. The first ministry team created by the twelve apostles described in Acts 6:1-7 was formed in response to injustice in delivering a food distribution program. The assumption is that feeding, clothing, housing, and visiting the poor are not only an assumed role of the church but also a heavenly evaluation measure of our love of Jesus. James 2:17 suggests that our faith is dead if

---

[26]David P. Gushee, *Toward a Just and Caring Society* (Grand Rapids, MI: Baker, 1999).
[27]Everett, *I Was Hungry*, 35.

we are not engaging in these ways. Such a theology is a challenge to all of us individually and as the body of Christ.

ENGAGING WITH INDIVIDUALS AND FAMILIES IN POVERTY

If caring for the poor is the church's role, how are we going about it? What would you do if one of the vignettes were real and the person was sitting in your office?

To minister to those experiencing chronic poverty, it is important to realize that these needs are unlikely to resolve quickly. These church members may need ongoing support. Sometimes, church members can become disgruntled when they repeatedly see the same person receiving help. You can model acceptance and compassion in this area by creating non-judgmental systems that allow for repeated access. One example would be having pre-packaged food on hand to quickly give to someone who comes to a welcome desk needing breakfast or lunch. Another ministry in the church may offer to provide and pack these ready-made meals. Keep an eye on expiration dates and choose items that do not require heating or can openers. Choose items that you would want to eat rather than unappetizing items. You may also want to have a few gluten- or nut-free options to prepare for those with allergies.

Kids' ministry staff needs to think through how to engage in situations of material poverty. It is essential to get to know the families and guardians as well. A well-meaning volunteer might get a child a new shirt, thinking the one they came in was dirty or ripped, only to offend the family who did not view their clothing as a problem. You can prevent this type of interaction by running a winter coat drive or having a sign that offers clothing of various sizes to anyone who comes. Most people do not want to receive help—even help they would wish for—if it will single them out as different or needy.

Beyond the specifics of the types of systems you might create in your church, it is important to be clear on what you can and cannot provide. If your church cannot create a benevolence fund to assist with rent or monthly bills, simply be clear that this is not something you can help with and connect your congregants to other community resources. If you do not have someone to lead a ministry team that addresses material needs, consider partnering with a sister church or inviting a local social service agency to present a workshop. Before implementing any new ministry, pause to ask, "Is this sustainable long-term? Does this fit our community's needs? Are there many individuals in the congregation passionate about this ministry?" You will likely do more harm than good if your efforts are unsustainable.

LEADING A CHURCH THAT WELCOMES THE POOR

One of the challenges in creating a church system that welcomes the poor is that "crisis" is not a tidy word. In generational poverty, for example, a baseline of stability to which an individual or family can return is untenable. When we think of ministering to those in financial crisis, we might imagine a single scenario and how to navigate it. If you truly lead a church that welcomes the poor, crisis becomes a way of life. Simply putting out fires as they occur will not help in the long run. In situations that have multiple systemic factors contributing to poverty, think marathon over sprint.

If you are going to address systemic issues of poverty, you need to do so as a church system. When someone like Sam enters your door, does he see a social service agency? Does he see a family? Does he see a place to learn about Christ and be discipled? Different congregations have different missions; he might feel any of those things or all three. How does welcoming the poor work with your mission as you consider your setting? If your sign says, "All are welcome," but conformity is required to really find belonging, your system is not genuinely welcoming to the marginalized.

SPIRITUAL FORMATION AND DISCIPLESHIP FOR THOSE FACING POVERTY

Let's dive back into our vignettes from the start of the chapter. Imagine that you are trying to help each one of them. What strategies might you try, considering everything we have discussed so far? What would spiritual formation and discipleship look like for each of them? How might you help them physically, emotionally, and spiritually without enabling them? How would you move from pity to empowerment? I'd encourage you to pause here to think about each case to compare your notes with the following recommendations.

The case of Sam. Sam is young. He hopefully has a lot of life in front of him, yet we know that he is at serious risk for relapse and even death by overdose if he does not get the right kind of help. He has asked if he can sleep at the church due to problems at the local shelter. Considering this request, the first question is whether or not the church has systems to do so. Providing overnight housing can require local zoning approval. If your church is not set up to be a temporary shelter, you may have problems with your city government. If sheltering systems are not in place, then it is also likely that you do not have overnight staff who can ensure the safety of Sam or the church property. While it is difficult to consider someone sleeping on the street while you have a warm building available, it is likely to cause more harm than good without the correct systems in place.

Because we are unlikely to be able to say "yes" to Sam's request, let's consider alternatives:

1. He doesn't like the local shelter, and we can agree with him. Sam needs more than a shelter can provide. He needs treatment for his addiction and likely his underlying anxiety that seems to fuel his drug use. A Christian substance use program would be the ideal setting for him. For example, Adult and Teen Challenge is a nationwide residential treatment program that would help Sam get clean and provide a discipleship pathway. If that is not available, look for a listing of sober homes in your area, and be sure to find out about their reputation before recommending any to Sam.

2. Depending on where Sam is in his addiction cycle, he may need to go to a detox program and, from there, into a sober house.

3. At the same time, you can help Sam connect with outpatient mental health and substance use services by making phone calls with him in your office. A local hospital, community health center, or mental health agency can help guide you to the right services, particularly if Sam is uninsured or needs help applying for a government health plan.

4. The church could consider employing Sam as a part-time janitor or landscaper or connect him to other local employment resources or a vocational rehabilitation office. Find out Sam's highest level of education and talk to him about any goals to further his education. State and local programs are periodically available to pay for education or job training for low-income people.

5. In addition to all these practical resources, you could identify a strong male leader in the church to serve as a mentor who could lead him in prayer and Bible study. This mentor would have to understand the realities of addiction and the potential for manipulation to maintain clear boundaries. Use the church systems, like Bible studies, to help Sam find a sense of purpose and belonging. Growing in his faith and being a part of the body of Christ have the power to transform Sam if his other physical needs are also being met.

The approach described here considers Sam's housing situation, health, employment, and spiritual needs. When we do not become limited in our thinking by his initial request, we can think holistically about how to empower him to be well. You have a unique role in Sam's life that no other community organization can provide, so focus on what you can do instead of what you cannot offer.

Of course, Sam may not be ready for these steps. He may simply become angry at you for saying "no" to his request to sleep at the church and may even lash out at you. You may not hear from him for a while. No amount of effort can override a person's ability to choose their path to wellness, and this is not your burden to carry. Even Jesus asked those who sought help from him, "Do you want to get well?" (John 5:6). They had the choice to listen and follow. Part of empowering Sam is respecting his right to continue to live in addiction after offering him a pathway out.

The case of Vanessa. Unlike Sam, Vanessa has not asked you or the church for direct assistance. She is hard-working and a good provider for her children. The government subsidizes her housing, and she does not want to stop receiving this benefit. She appreciates receiving food stamps, but they limit her long-term ability to save more than $2,000. Her primary pastoral concern surrounds the father of her children and her desire to protect her children from him. While her request is not financial, it is an example of the concern that can come with past or present poverty. Here are a few possible action steps:

1. In this vignette, the father of Vanessa's children is in jail, but his release is not imminent. Because you have some time, you may want to recommend a good therapist who could work with Vanessa on various underlying issues to ensure that she has had time to process, heal, and determine what boundaries can and should be set.
2. Vanessa also may need legal assistance to advocate for the safety of her and her children. You want to avoid giving mental health or legal advice and ensure she has the appropriate resources for these needs.
3. Pastorally, she is looking to you to determine whether her thinking is Christlike. She doesn't want the father to negatively influence her children, which he may try to do if he demands visitation in exchange for child support. You can encourage Vanessa that her desire to protect her children is appropriate, yet she can do so while maintaining an openness to the deeper work of forgiveness. You could explore her concerns with her and help her distinguish between forgiveness and reconciliation.
4. You could ask Vanessa if she would like you to try to reach out to the father while he is in jail to offer spiritual help and resources. She may appreciate your help knowing that you are also willing to pastor him (while not talking about or involving her or the children). You are staying within your calling of pastoral care and extending yourself to the father if he is willing. If she does not want this help or it is impossible, you could simply pray with her for wisdom to wait for God's leading in future decisions.
5. Encourage her to utilize the church's resources, such as a Bible study or small group that could share this burden with her in prayer.

Even though she is not seeking financial help, there are several additional considerations to consider as you pastor Vanessa. First, consider her strengths. She is a spiritual leader and has a lot to offer the congregation when it comes to resilience. Her testimony and example may inspire others. Second, consider her wider family system. Depending on the health or unhealth of Vanessa's family relationships, she can either lean on them or set boundaries to continue to move forward. A third consideration is Vanessa's education. She works as a certified nursing assistant, but she could obtain a higher-paying job with increased education. You can help her identify scholarship opportunities and provide mentorship, spiritual guidance, and educational resources for her children to help them rise out of poverty long-term.

The case of Bob. This vignette might be more typical of a suburban context where you do not have as much direct connection with those who are homeless or supported by government assistance. Bob is married with three children and owns a home. On the outside, Bob and his family may not seem different from other church members. However, given his employment patterns and the current financial crisis, significant credit card debt may keep the family afloat.

Signing Bob up for a Christian financial wellness course or focusing on helping him spiritually lead his family may be tempting. These are possible steps, but if we miss the root issues of the problem, we are likely to watch the patterns repeat. Bob's pattern and presentation in the pastoral meeting indicate some concerns. He seems to want to take frequent risks and has a grandiose vision of possible (but unlikely) positive outcomes. His business choices reflect that he believes he can receive a big payout for little work. Indeed, spiritual principles speak directly to these concerns, but he is unlikely to be able to apply them without additional help.

Bob would benefit from a more holistic set of choices:

1. You could encourage him to meet with a therapist who could evaluate his mental health. He could have a variety of diagnoses, including bipolar disorder, attention deficit hyperactivity disorder, or even a gambling disorder. If these symptoms of risk-taking and grandiose thinking go unaddressed, your biblical and pastoral guidance will not work in the long run.

2. In the pastoral meeting described in the vignette, Bob has allowed you to speak into his life. He has presented this new job in insurance and claims that his friend makes a lot of money with little work. You can point out your concerns that Bob wants to "make it big" and explore the spiritual principles of hard work. You can explore Bob's worries that his wife may leave him and directly ask about the patterns that have led to her frustration. Being direct with Bob is most likely the best way to cut through his denial (or oblivion).

3. While a referral to couple's counseling may be useful, this is likely a secondary step after Bob has pursued his own individual counseling. Otherwise, he may be able to deflect the problems and avoid taking personal responsibility.

4. Financially speaking, the primary focus should be to ensure that Bob's wife and children have what they need if Bob continues his behavior patterns. You might want to have an individual meeting with Bob's wife to hear from her what her needs and concerns are. Helping empower her to have her financial provision, including exploring educational and work options, would reduce her dependence on Bob. If the pattern is chronic and unhealthy, encourage her to have separate bank accounts and potentially take control of the family's finances. She may also benefit from counseling or a meeting with a financial adviser. Spiritually, you can help her grow in a way that is not dependent on how Bob is doing. A mentor or women's Bible study may help her in this area. When you think of "empowerment," you want to consider ways in which both Bob and his wife can live empowered lives.

The case of Camilla. Our final vignette paints a picture of a middle-aged Latina woman suffering from chronic pain. On the surface, because of her age and the nature of her illness, you or some in your congregation may struggle with Camilla. Much of the time, she may seem like she would be perfectly capable of work. Her loneliness may seem like her own choice to isolate. Her financial limitations may seem solvable. Throughout this chapter, we have sought to become aware of potential biases, and our internal responses to chronic illness are important to notice. We can connect with compassion when we see the word *illness* in writing. When we see someone actively talking about an invisible disability over years or decades, it can be a lot harder to stay connected to compassion.

In this vignette, Camilla is asking for companionship and understanding. Camilla is culturally from a very connected system. However, her family may have negative biases toward her as well, exacerbating her feelings of loneliness. She's asking for the church to accommodate her needs, whether directly or not. She may struggle to be part of a ministry team because she must cancel at the last minute on certain Sundays. Others may perceive her as unreliable or making excuses. If Camilla perceives this resistance from others, she may fade into the background and further limit her possibility of connection. Unlike our other vignettes, additional work or educational opportunities are not a focus because Camilla cannot consistently work or attend school. Camilla could become a lifelong learner and use these resources if she desired various free online options. However, this type of learning is for her personal benefit and enjoyment and will not result in her being able to improve her financial situation.

As you consider her situation, you need to think long-term. Camilla is only 46 years old, and her circumstances are unlikely to change dramatically unless she were to experience supernatural healing. If she would like this type of prayer for recovery, it is undoubtedly an option to provide while at the same time committing a congregation to walk alongside her as she lives a life of chronic illness. What would this look like?

1. Create a team of people who can visit Camilla and others like her who need visitation and additional care. Having multiple people involved helps share the load and creates a mechanism for people to bring her meals or help clean her house. Be careful not to presume what Camilla wants or needs, but give a list of what the care team can provide, and she can select from a list of options. Her needs are likely to vary based on the day or the week, so having a system in place for her to communicate those needs to the right person is helpful.

2. You can also accommodate Camilla by relaxing some of the rules for serving at your church. Are there roles that could be fulfilled

without advanced planning? Perhaps Camilla can come any Sunday, and she has a spot at the door where she can greet people as they come. She may even be able to do so while sitting down. Camilla herself could be a part of the care team even as she receives care by calling others who cannot get out of the house throughout the week. She may also be able to write cards or do some administrative tasks from home as she is able, given that she has a background in secretarial work. When the church can provide opportunities like these, it helps increase a person's sense of belonging.

3. Consider what spiritual growth and discipleship look like for Camilla. She is experiencing suffering—does she connect this with her spiritual journey? As cited earlier, Camilla's most important spiritual needs are to find a sense of inner peace and to be able to continue to give to others actively. Helping her find purpose and peace amid suffering is the key to her ongoing spiritual growth and well-being.

MAKING LONG-TERM IMPACTS IN YOUR COMMUNITY

While the church can offer short-term, informal safety nets to help those in immediate need,[28] you can also consider long-term and prevention strategies to change the generational trajectory of poverty for those in your community. An excellent example is Pastor Wayne Gordon's work in the Lawndale neighborhood of Chicago. Through the trusting relationships built as he led Lawndale Community Church in the 1980s, they established a community health center and, later, a community development organization focused on creating low-income housing opportunities. They ultimately built on this work to create employment opportunities, and through their efforts, they saw a major community transformation.[29] Another example is the Jobs For Life 8-week curriculum that many churches use to increase job and life skills.[30]

---

[28] Radey and McWey, "Safety Nets," 687-98.
[29] Sean Zielenbach and Inc Netlibrary, *The Art of Revitalization: Improving Conditions in Distressed Inner-City Neighborhoods* (New York: Garland, 2000).
[30] "Take the Class," Jobs for Life, accessed May 3, 2024, https://jobsforlife.org/take-the-class/.

Depending on your neighborhood or regional context, you may find other types of needs in your community. Generally, long-term strategic efforts involve increasing educational and employment opportunities, creating home ownership or affordable housing pathways, and offering mentoring relationships to at-risk youth. A great way to start is to conduct a community needs assessment, and the Centers for Disease Control and Prevention provides some helpful tools on their website.[31] The Substance Abuse and Mental Health Service Administration (SAMHSA) also offers useful resources for addressing poverty and homelessness that may give you a guide on how to get started.[32]

BUILDING RELATIONSHIPS IN YOUR COMMUNITY

As you consider possible long-term impacts that your church could make in your community, it is important not to approach that as a solo effort. Individuals, groups, agencies, politicians, and businesses seek to make a long-term difference in every community. For example, Atchison describes several effective partnerships between churches and community law enforcement.[33] Such partnerships have been shown to reduce violence and improve outcomes for adolescents who were at risk for gang activity by providing mentorship. Other examples include social services, mental health agencies, hospitals and community health centers, the Rotary Club, and community action corporations. Reach out to these local groups and offer to meet with key leaders for lunch or coffee. Learn about their efforts and ask how the church might be able to help and support what they are doing. You may find that none of these organizations work directly together as you network. You may be able to function as a connection point and bring several community efforts together.

---

[31]"Assess Needs and Resources," CDC, October 19, 2022, https://archive.cdc.gov/#/details?url= https://www.cdc.gov/chinav/tools/assess.html.
[32]Lynne Walsh, "Homelessness Programs and Resources," SAMHSA, January 21, 2016, www.samhsa .gov/homelessness-programs-resources.
[33]Samuel K. Atchison, "Flashpoint: The Church and Law Enforcement in Poor Black and White Communities," *Journal of Hate Studies* 15, no. 1 (September 2019): 203, https://doi.org/10.33972 /jhs.168.

CONCLUSION

Through the cases and exploration of short- and long-term ways to alleviate poverty in your community, along with the discussion of a theology of poverty, I hope this chapter has given you a spark of passion for doing this work. Your role is not easy, and much of what you are called to do is not in the seminary or Bible school curriculum. Take the time to read the references in this chapter, including some of the book titles you and your congregation may use to spark further dialogue. I leave you with this challenge: Do something, no matter how small it may seem. From there, God will lead you where he has work for you to do.

14

THE CHALLENGE OF HELPING COUPLES IN CONFLICT

David C. Olsen

One of the significant challenges of pastoral care ministry is supporting and helping couples. Watching couples move from the bliss of premarital counseling, where often couples are so "in love" that they do not anticipate problems, to the sacred beauty of the wedding and reception, to the reality that about 50 percent of marriages will fail can be discouraging. Watching discouraged couples in pain, and feeling unprepared to help, becomes painful and discouraging for you!

During premarital counseling sessions, Christian counselors and ministers help couples understand that the idealization they hold for their partner can rapidly become disillusioned when the reality of being married and living together begins to set in. That disillusionment, while usual, can be shocking and painful and begin the downward spiral of a relationship. Unfortunately, most couples in premarital counseling do not believe that will happen to them but rather that their love will conquer all.

It is difficult to watch the pain and deep emotional distress as this occurs, not to mention the impact on their children. Too often, as it occurs, it is easy for the church leader to feel helpless once the spiral of pain picks up speed. Today, despite these couples' spirituality and participation in Bible study groups, worship, and community, they still struggle painfully in their marital relationships.

While church leaders are not trained to be marital therapists, nor do they have the time to devote to time-consuming marital therapy, practical principles in the Bowen family systems theory can be helpful in their ministry.[1] Among a small number of early originators, Murray Bowen was one of the creators of family therapy. He helped create a shift in the way therapists think about problems. Rather than seeing problems as occurring within individuals, he suggested we consider how problems exist and are maintained with family systems, literally between not within people. In an era when adolescents and children were seen alone for therapy, he suggested that therapists work with the whole family since the child's behavior was often connected to what was happening in the family.

Many church leaders are aware of Bowen's work through the writings of Ron Richardson,[2] Peter Steinke,[3] Roberta Gilbert,[4] and Edwin Friedman.[5] Unfortunately, many are not aware of the practical implications of his research for helping couples.[6] These family systems principles, when adopted, can help clergy immensely. They can be used for premarital counseling, workshops, integrated into sermons, or applied directly to ministry with couples. The following three principles, if applied by church leaders, can benefit the couples you have grown to know in your church community.

PRINCIPLE 1: THE ONLY PERSON YOU CAN CHANGE IS YOURSELF!

The first Bowenian principle sounds simple, but in actuality is quite complicated. The principle states that the only person you can change is

---

[1] Michael Kerr and Murry Bowen, *Family Evaluation: An Approach Based on Bowen Theory* (New York: Norton, 2018).
[2] Ronald Richardson, *Becoming a Healthier Pastor: Family Systems Theory and the Pastor's Own Family* (Philadelphia: Fortress, 2004).
[3] Peter Steinke, *Healthy Congregations: A Systems Approach* (Herndon, VA: Alban Institute, 2006).
[4] Roberta Gilbert, *The Eight Concepts of Bowen Theory* (Pompano Beach, FL: Leading Systems, 2018).
[5] Edwin Friedman, *Generation to Generation: Family Process in Church and Synagogue* (New York: Guilford, 1985).
[6] David Olsen and Erin Belanger-Free, *Renewing your Relationship: Five Necessary Steps* (Parker, CO: Outskirts, 2017).

yourself! While the principle sounds obvious and simplistic, it is at the heart of most couple conflicts. Most couples think they know their problems' source: their partner. They believe that if only their partner would change, get some therapy, figure out their family of origin issues, be less critical, and learn to communicate, the marital issues would be solved. Their focus is on their partner, how they are the source of the problems, and how they need to change! They are convinced that the source of their marital distress is their partner, and too often begin to believe they may have married the wrong person and that perhaps their real "soulmate" is out there somewhere. Sadly, their contribution to the problem is largely overlooked, and they are frequently blind to the way their own behavior also contributes to arguments and marital pain.

According to Bowen's theory, change comes when individuals focus less on their partner, explore how they themselves contribute to marital problems, and attempt to change their own behavior. Ministers will notice while listening to couples argue that each spouse is primarily focused on their partner's deficits or problems, and continue to hope they can change their partner. While couples are frequently told in premarital counseling that "what you see is what you get," they secretly hope, too often, that they can change their partner. In reality, personality does not change much with time. What can change is the interactions between partners; despite this, most continue to attempt to change their partners.

This is a profound spiritual principle. Jesus' words in Matthew 7:1-5 speak powerfully to this principle. "Do not judge, or you too will be judged. For in the same way you judge others, you will be judged.... Why do you look at the speck of sawdust in your brother's eye and pay no attention to the plank in your own eye? ... You hypocrite, first take the plank out of your own eye, and then you will see clearly to remove the speck from your brother's eye."

Jesus touches powerfully on what marital therapists call *projection*. Rather than looking at oneself, it is much easier to project problems onto the partner and see them as the source of all marital difficulties. While Jesus' words above are quoted often and most are well aware of the statement, it is rarely applied in marital counseling. Ironically, couples focus on the "specks" in their partner while ignoring the "logs" in their eye. Even a speck in one's own eye can be incredibly annoying and blur vision, making it difficult to see oneself.

At the same time, marital therapists recognize hope and potential for change when both partners begin to recognize how they are hurting their partner and attempt to change themselves rather than their partner. Without this type of self-awareness and introspection, there is, in fact, very little hope of change.

On a practical level, church leaders can focus on this Matthew 7:1-5 principle in sermons and study groups and apply it in working with couples. While it is a complicated principle that people would prefer not to hear, applying this principle is the key to spiritual and relational maturity. Couples who have successful, long-term marriages will be the first to acknowledge that they have been unable to change their partners but have focused on changing themselves.

PRINCIPLE 2: COUPLE CONFLICT MAKES SENSE IF YOU UNDERSTAND THE DANCE

While couples often feel overwhelmed and lost in their conflict and cannot see a pattern, in reality, they are almost always caught in a predictable choreographed dance that takes on a life of its own. This pattern can be explained, however, so that hope for change increases, especially if it is combined with focusing on changing one's role in the dance.

To illustrate, Sarah complains that her husband Fred frequently watches ESPN while she desperately wants to talk. She constantly pursues him, asking for more conversation. The more she pursues, the more her husband distances himself. Furthermore, the more he distances, asking for space, the more she pursues. They have co-created a powerful dance which, not surprisingly, is referred to as the pursue-distance dance. In reality, their dance is so powerful that they inadvertently create the very thing they dislike in others. Fishing for connection will influence the partner to withdraw, and withdrawing from a connection will influence the partner to pursue them. A pursuer creates distance in her husband, while his distancing creates more pursuit. They blame each other rather than understand their roles in maintaining the weak interaction.

Couples often talk to their minister or therapist about a particular problem, such as money, sex, parenting, how to handle in-laws, or even their partner's lack of interest in spiritual things. Unfortunately, they fail to realize that the real problem is the interaction they create around their complaint. Partners who constantly push their partner to be more involved in church or Bible study do not realize that their solution to the problem has a paradoxical effect, creating the opposite of what they hoped for. The interactional pattern is the problem. While their intent might be positive, their interactional style ensures they will not get the desired result.

These dances or interactional patterns make it impossible to solve the presenting problem or complaint and make it difficult to see one's role in the problem. Over time, these dances take on their own life and become very difficult to change. These dances fall into two categories: (1) complementary and (2) symmetrical.[7]

Complementary dances. In complementary dances, partners take on complementary roles which reinforce each other. Several examples of these are the pursue-distance dance, the over/under-responsible dance, the dominant-submissive dance, and the fight-flight dance. They are complementary in creating a circular pattern where each reinforces the other.

For example, as mentioned, the pursuer creates their partner's distance, while the distancer reinforces the partner's pursuit. The over-functioner creates under-functioning in the partner, while the partner's under-functioning seems to force the over-functioner to take on too much. They complain about the other without realizing they are trapped in a reciprocal dance, which Murray Bowen calls "reciprocal functioning."[8] The over-functioner complains that they must do too much and often see their partner as a child. The under-functioner, on the other hand, often complains that no matter how hard they try, their partner will inevitably redo their work. Charles and Diane illustrate the point. Diane complains about doing everything and states how she is exhausted constantly. Charles agrees to manage the kids' homework to give her a break, only to find that Diane checks up on the homework anyway, leaving him

---

[7] Olsen and Belanger-Free, *Renewing Your Relationship*.
[8] Kerr and Bowen, *Family Evaluation*.

exasperated and feeling there is no reason to try. They are caught in a vicious cycle, leaving them distant and frustrated.

These complementary dances are challenging to disrupt for several reasons. First, couples are often unaware of what is happening and the pattern they are trapped in. Second, they constantly reinforce the problem with their reciprocal functioning, complicating even the most straightforward problem. Take money, for example. In reality, financial issues are not all that difficult to resolve. It does not take exceptional intelligence to create a budget that lines up income with expenses and then allocates spending based on those figures. However, in an over/under-functioning dance, this becomes incredibly complicated. The over-functioner does not believe their partner is financially responsible and does not trust their partner with money. Under-functioners then resent and see their partner as controlling or cheap. They may see themselves as entitled to make spending decisions, so they buy things, maybe even essential things. This affirms the view by the spouse that the spender is irresponsible and in need of greater control. The couple's dance becomes self-sustaining and difficult to alter. The real problem is not money but rather their dance around money. Unless the dance is recognized, the problem will never be solved.

Symmetrical dances. On the other hand, symmetrical dances are equally challenging to resolve. In symmetrical dances, partners each take on the same role. Two examples of this are the rapid escalation dance and the conflict-avoidant dance. In the first, couples rapidly escalate their conflicts, beginning with discussing a typical conflict such as money or parenting. Then, they rapidly escalate the argument by jumping from one issue to the next until they are exhausted and hopeless. They cannot stay on point with any one topic and quickly pile on multiple topics.

Conflict-avoidant couples are the opposite. They bury and avoid conflict and stay clear of complicated issues. While polite, they frequently lack intimacy and passion, and they complain about feeling distant, like they are simply living as roommates.

Recognizing the pattern. Whether complementary or symmetrical, the dance or interactional pattern is the problem. Church leaders can help couples look more broadly at their dance and recognize the pattern they are caught in. Rather than getting caught in the trap of attempting to make suggestions or come up with solutions for the presenting problem, the goal is to watch for the interactional dance. One of the most helpful interventions is to help couples recognize their patterns, which can create hope as they recognize patterns and are more likely to find hope for change.

As church leaders listen to couples complain about their issues, they can learn to listen for patterns that, interpreted, can lead to change. This can be done in pastoral counseling, workshops, or groups for couples in a more psycho-educational format using workbooks. In these group formats, light bulbs often go on as couples can understand these larger patterns and see themselves in them. They begin to smile when they realize they are caught up in dances bigger than themselves and that they are not alone. When combined with the principle that the only person we can change is ourselves, couples can examine their position in the dance and try to shift it.

A helpful technique is to ask couples to pretend that one of their dances or arguments was caught on film, and then ask them to pretend they are watching the dance in slow motion. The goal is not to focus on what their partner is doing wrong but rather on their role in the argument/discussion, and play with how they could do something different to confuse the dance. Quite often, while one partner is talking, the other is already rehearsing his or her response rather than listening. Instead, simply saying, "I want to make sure I understand what you are saying . . ." and then summarizing what they hear to ensure they have adequately understood will slow down and potentially shift the pattern and constructively confuse the dance. Shifting patterns is the key to change, which requires understanding the dance and shifting one's role in it.

In this sense, church leaders can combine these two principles: the principle of self-focus and the principle of understanding the pattern. Both are wise, mature responses that a Christian would aspire to. Thus, when a couple recognizes the particular dance they are caught in and begins exploring their role in the maintenance of that dance, they can experiment with changing their role, which may positively impact the dance.

PRINCIPLE 3: THE ROLE OF ANXIETY IN COUPLE CONFLICT

While these principles are fundamental and can be pretty helpful, they are made more complicated by anxiety. One of the central tenets of Bowen's family systems theory is that of chronic anxiety. Anxiety builds, and it powerfully drives dances and couples' interactions in very unhealthy ways. Think of anxiety as putting predictable interactions on steroids. For example, if one spouse pursues their partner, their pursuit will intensify if they are highly anxious. As that anxiety-filled pursuit intensifies, the anxiety in the partner grows, and they may become even more distant. This is the same as the anxiety of the over-functioner. The normally over-functioning person becomes very anxious, and they can quickly become hypervigilant and over-function even more, feeling that if they do not manage everything in the world, or at least in their world, they will fall apart.

Anxiety dampens the capacity for creative thinking, and chronic anxiety makes people even more reactive and agitated. They become less creative and more reactive, often more primitive in their functioning. Watch a highly anxious couple: their dance intensifies to the point where they can both feel helpless. In the same way during Covid, church leaders watched as chronic congregational anxiety built, and typically bright, logical people became more and more reactive. People caught in an anxiety-fueled dance can engage in highly uncharacteristic behaviors never witnessed in non-anxious moments.

Neuroscience has helped further explain this concept. During low anxiety, people are far more capable of logical non-reactive thinking, where the prefrontal cortex region of the brain is in charge. However, after periods of chronic anxiety and cluster stress, the brain can shift, leading to an amygdala hijacking. The brain's amygdala region is incapable of logical thinking and reverts to fight, flight, or freeze. Watch a couple in prolonged chronic stress. As they become more and more hijacked and the amygdala kicks in, they become even more reactive, and their typical dance looks like it is on steroids! It can look crazy and irritating because their usual dance is hijacked by high anxiety, creating a powerful fuel.

To better illustrate this principle, consider the case study of Abraham and Sarah. Abraham and Sarah have a promise from God to live out a great covenant. They were to be the seed for a great nation (Gen 12:2). Unfortunately, they were aging, and Sarah was infertile. Understandably, their anxiety built as they aged, leading them to try to contain it through an alternate path. Their anxiety led to a crisis of faith and trust, resulting in Abraham using Sarah's servant Hagar to produce a child. This solution in reality creates more anxiety, as now Abraham has two women in his life, and Sarah faces the prospect of raising a child that is not hers. The situation becomes even more complicated when Sarah becomes pregnant, and now there are two sons, two women, and a very anxious Abraham! In Bowen's theory, chronic anxiety leads to reactive decision-making, creating more anxiety and complicated interactions. Things heat up to a point where Abraham, driven by his and Sarah's anxiety, makes the decision to send Hagar and Ishmael away. The reality is that this "cut off" (to use another Bowen term) has ramifications for generations to come as the descendants of Isaac and the descendants of Ishmael have had a more than complicated relationship with long-term generational conflict.

This biblical family is a powerful example of how even a family of faith can become overwhelmed by anxiety leading to difficult and painful marriage and family choices, which impact future generations. Their children and grandchildren, to some extent, replicated some of the same anxiety-based decisions. Jacob and Esau become estranged due to Rebecca's anxiety, leading to another cut off where Jacob had to flee for his life. Then Jacob's children attempt to (literally) cut off their brother Joseph. The implications of Bowen's theory of chronic anxiety are profound. Chronic anxiety impacts marital functioning, but it can powerfully impact future generations too.

PASTORAL CARE IMPLICATIONS

So, what are the practical ministry implications? The implications are significant for the three principles to (1) change oneself, (2) recognize one's own role, and (3) reduce anxiety in the couple's relationship. Unfortunately, people rarely realize that they are in a state of chronic anxiety and, therefore, cannot think and problem-solve creatively. Effective church leadership understands this concept on multiple levels. For example, leaders may sense underlying anxiety and agitation building when leading a board or committee meeting. Naming the anxiety and allowing people to talk about it helps them reduce anxiety. Church leaders can use educational opportunities in ministry, such as couples groups or workshops, to explain this concept. Most of the popular workbooks or famous couples' material do not adequately address this issue of how anxiety exacerbates marital conflict. As a result, it can be futile to attempt to implement strategies such as improved couple communication without explaining the concept of chronic anxiety. It is helpful for couples to understand that anxiety is fuel for couple interactions, making change almost impossible. Helping couples learn to listen to their bodies and understand when they are being hijacked by anxiety can significantly slow down escalating interactions.

THE COMPLICATED NATURE OF COUPLE PICTURES

Part of helping couples also involves understanding that as these anxiety-driven dances become more predictable and frequent, couples begin to see each other in more destructive ways. The over-functioning spouse begins to see their partner as lazy or as a child and responds accordingly, while the under-functioning spouse sees their partner as a control freak. These negative pictures begin to be cemented in place by repetitive interactions. As a result, partners begin to think they know their partners. They lose all sense of nuance and balance and form a black-and-white picture. They have lost sight of what initially attracted them and now hold a negative picture of their partner.

Unfortunately, these destructive patterns can spiral down quickly. Negative pictures of partners form, self-focus decreases, and it becomes easier not to understand one's contribution to the problem once a negative view of a partner is formed. The dance becomes intense once this negative picture becomes locked in place. This spiral becomes destructive. Interactions are driven by the negative pictures formed. Let's return to Diane and Charles. When Diane sees Charles as irresponsible and immature, she becomes the over-functioner. On the other hand, Charles sees her as controlling and critical, and as a result, he shuts down and withdraws, strengthening Diane's negative picture of Charles. They reinforce each other's negative pictures, resulting in a more negative spiral. Without intervention, this will end badly.

One of the vital leadership roles is to help reframe pictures before they become too damaging. For example, a counselor could help Diane understand that Charles is not simply withdrawn and spiteful but instead hurt. The counselor would also help Charles see that Diane is exhausted and overwhelmed and needs help. Then, they can see each other with more nuance, and their view can soften, perhaps leading to more empathic understanding.

A key ingredient in helping to create change is to confuse the pictures couples have of each other and see a more complex, nuanced picture that creates hope and healing. Fortunately, when a couple is in the downward spiral, their pictures of each other can become locked into the negative and they cannot see anything else. While this is very complicated to disrupt, it is integral to pastoral care. Often one party will come to talk to you complaining about their partner with a very negative picture, and of course, not seeing any of their own contribution to the problem. They are the "saint," while their partner is the "sinner." It is, of course, a dangerous "triangle," to use another Bowen concept. A triangle involves three people, where two align against the other. In this example, the person who sees themselves as the "saint" hopes they can persuade their minister that the other is fully to blame. Church leaders must be very careful not to get drawn into this dynamic. Even being too empathic with the person bringing the complaint can leave the person believing that their church leader is on their side, supporting them with their challenging spouse. Instead, you need to look for ways of gently reframing the picture and attempting to confuse the couple's perceptions of each other to shift away from black-and-white thinking. We, in theory, stress that there are equal sides, meaning that both contribute equally. The leader needs to remember that no matter how convincing someone's story is, there is always another side of the story.

The truth is complex. Part of family ministry care is helping couples see the truth more accurately. It is very much in keeping with the Gospel accounts. Often in the Gospels, people see incorrectly. For example, in the story of the healing of the blind man (John 9), the wrong questions are being asked by both disciples and the Pharisees. Their questions focus on blame and why he was blind. Is the blindness the result of his sin or his family's? They were attempting to see from a particular frame of reference, which missed the point. Jesus drives home the point by saying, "For judgment I have come into this world, so that blind will see and those who see will become blind" (Jn 9:39). Jesus flipped the question upside down from one of blame to one that was loving and healing to the blind man and his family. Seeing is complicated!

Martin Buber referred to *I-It* relationships vs. *I-Thou* relationships. In I-It relationships,[9] others are reduced to an "it"—meaning they are placed in a category such as "immature," "angry," or "unfeeling," which then limits what can be seen. The blind man was in a category of "outsider" and "beggar." In an I-Thou relationship, a sense of mystery and a more expansive view is taken. The "thou" is someone who is complex in motives, emotions, and meanings. The blind man's response is refreshing. It does not look for categories but instead says, "I was blind but now I see!" (Jn 9:25). This exhibits much more of an I-Thou relationship. Because of his encounter and relationship with Jesus, he no longer feels reduced to an "It" but has been seen as a "thou," changing his view of himself.

In healthy marriages, couples keep discovering each other and keep seeing more and more of their partner, leading to more of an I-Thou relationship. They avoid rigid black-and-white categories or reducing their partner to an "It," and instead they keep growing and learning to see more expansively. Church leaders can encourage families to see each other in complex ways.

Church leaders can help couples by continuing to talk about this more expansive way of seeing versus the destructive, reductionistic style used too often by distressed couples. Furthermore, this can be part of pastoral counseling, workshops, or even biblical preaching and teaching.

The longing for redemption. Finally, church leaders can listen to the deep longing for redemption on the part of couples, which is frequently unconscious.[10] During premarital counseling, most couples think they

---

[9]Martin Buber, *I and Thou*, trans. Ronald Gregor Smith (New York: Scribner Classics, 2000).
[10]David C. Olsen, *The Spiritual Work of Marriage* (New York: Routledge, 2008).

understand the unwritten rules that guide their relationship. They confidently talk about how many children they hope to have or how they will handle money and their roles. At this stage, they are incredibly optimistic about their future together and are still mainly in a state of idealization. But they don't know what they don't yet know. Their ideals have yet to be tested and challenged.

As idealization turns to disillusionment, their dances become more predictable, and their pictures of each other become increasingly hostile. Underneath negative pictures are often unresolved family-of-origin issues. Most people emerge from their family of origin with some wounds. These include not being seen accurately, lack of nurture or support, or sometimes significant levels of abuse. These unresolved issues become part of the marital dynamic, and couples hope (usually unconsciously) marriage will heal them. When healing does not occur (due to the interactional dances already discussed), the pain becomes intense, and the pictures of the partner become even more damaging, setting up an even more negative interaction.

Miguel and Susan illustrate this dynamic. Susan complains that she is exhausted by Miguel's demands. When she is not in the mood for sex, Miguel sulks and becomes angry and withdrawn, leaving her resentful and even less in the mood to be intimate. As she begins to think of sex as Miguel's drug of choice, she becomes even more distant, leaving him even more angry. The interactional sequence leaves them both frustrated, and, of course, each sees the other through a very negative lens, creating even more distance and resentment. What is missing in their discussion is their unresolved family of origin material. Miguel's father was angry, rejecting and criticizing everything Miguel did, while at times becoming quite violent. Miguel received very little nurture. Like many men, he sees sex as the ultimate nurture without understanding how deprived of nurture he has always been. On the other hand, Susan was repeatedly told that it was a woman's duty to satisfy her husband.

Without this couple talking about their family of origin material, it is unlikely that they will be able to shift both their negative interactions and extremely harmful pictures of each other. On the other hand, as Miguel is helped to understand the profound injury of his family of origin,

Susan's view of him shifts, and she can feel more empathy. When Susan can talk more about her family of origin's messages about sex, Miguel can become more understanding. While this is anything but easy, understanding family of origin material and the longing for redemption leads to more empathy, understanding, and potential healing. When couples are helped to understand that they are helping heal each other and changing history, they build hope.

Typically, when couples talk more honestly about the pain in their history, their partner's empathy grows, and the negative picture they held can soften. It is surprising how often spouses do not understand the pain of their partner's childhood and its effect on their functioning in the present. A child with an addicted or a mentally ill parent can grow up reactive to conflict. Similarly, growing up in deprivation where their emotional needs were not met can create a distancing response. This could set off a chain reaction leading their partner to become more critical without understanding the effects of early pain still at work. Childhoods are full of painful events that shape us. Partners see the current behavior, never the pain from childhood underneath. This promotes misunderstanding or negative judgment.

It is not always easy to help couples move to this type of healing depth. However, through workshops, discussion groups on marriage, or even teachings on family of origin material, church leaders can set the stage for these discussions. Probing couples about where their pictures of their partner come from can also sometimes elicit this material. Previously, this was complicated work, but it is the beginning of potential redemption.

Putting it all together. Helping couples navigate the journey of a long-term marriage is anything but simple. It is a vital part of church ministry. While it is easy to describe and diagnose the problem, it is another thing to provide help. At the same time, church leaders see couples through several life phases and can be extremely helpful along the way. Like traditional couple counseling, church leaders have the unique opportunity to assist in the developmental cycles of marriage. From performing a marriage, to the birth of a first child, to coping with school-age children, to launching college and career, to the empty nest, to the final chapter of life, church leaders have the unique opportunity to provide guidance, feedback, and support for couples. Normalizing the developmental challenges, focusing on moving away from self-focus to complexity and empathy, tracking interactional sequences, and helping reframe pictures, there are numerous opportunities to shepherd couples' growth.

Utilizing the principles of Bowen family systems theory can ground couples to a way to think and understand themselves and their families. Bowen's systems theory implies a way of thinking and understanding the human condition, and it can inform multiple ministries and pastoral care levels. These principles can be worked into preaching and teaching, can impact how boards or committees are run, and can be enormously helpful for the leader's own marriage and family life. When people in relationships begin to see their role in problems, learn how to hold onto their reactivity, and shift their interaction style, change and even redemption can occur.

PRACTICAL STEPS FOR HANDLING COUPLES IN CRISIS

These Bowen-based principles provide a framework for ministers helping couples in their congregation as they seek to build quality marriages amid multiple stressors. While these general principles can inform pastoral ministry, some practical suggestions for helping couples in crisis might provide further guidance.

Imagine a couple in crisis calling for an emergency session and announcing that they will arrive in an hour. The urgency of the crisis is apparent in the phone call, and all indications are that it will be a challenging and emotional hour. The following are some practical steps to follow.

First, the minister must regulate their own anxiety. When sitting with a couple in crisis, it is easy to catch the anxiety and feel an enormous pressure to fix the problem. Avoid the pressure to feel like there has to be an answer that will immediately solve the problem. By regulating personal anxiety, the minister can better listen to the process instead of getting lost in the content and detail and struggling to provide answers. Typically, in crisis, couples talk rapidly with high anxiety and flood the room with anxious and angry descriptions of the problem. It is way too easy to make the mistake of responding to a crisis by trying to solve the problem prematurely. When anxiety goes up, there can be a tendency to try to solve the immediate problem, which rarely works. The goal here is to listen to how the couple talks rather than what they discuss.

Second, after listening to the content, typically it is easy to see the dance pattern. Is one partner over-functioning and angry that they are doing all the heavy lifting? Is one partner anxiously pursuing while the other is distancing themselves? Listening to the process rather than the content makes the dance easier to understand. While the couple might want a magic solution (usually meaning they want you to take their side), their dance makes the problem impossible to solve and keeps them trapped in an endless cycle of despair. This is a delicate step. The couple is in crisis and, thereby, wants answers. But the answers are not a simple word of advice. The church leader can assure the couple that they understand the urgency while firmly pointing out the interactional pattern and asking them if they agree that the pattern is pervasive in their marriage.

Third, provide the couple with concrete feedback about their dance pattern and ask if that resonates. Explain briefly that when anxious, the dance intensifies and that they are creating the very thing they do not like in the other person. For example, the pursuer creates distance in their partner, and the distancing partner creates pursuit. The overfunctioner trains their partner to under-function; by under-functioning, the other teaches their partner to over-function. This is a critical concept; if the couple can recognize it, there is hope for change in the patterns. During a crisis and high anxiety, if the couple can see their pattern, they feel hopeful. A helpful question is to ask the couple, if their arguments were recorded on video so they could watch it in slow motion, would they observe the pattern, and more specifically, what would they notice about themselves in that pattern?

Fourth, and perhaps the most challenging part, help each person understand their role in the dance and help them understand that the only person they can change is themself. This concept is not easy since they are often hijacked and can only see what their partner is doing wrong. Coach them to prayerfully ask to reveal what they can do to change their role in the dance and then see what happens if they change. This can be framed as a spiritual practice, since most spouses secretly hope that their partner will be the one to start changing. Furthermore, if one person changes their role in a dance, the dance, by definition, must be altered. Many church leaders will need to refer many couples at this point for more time and in-depth counseling than a church leader usually has available. You can be encouraged that if you have been able to get the couple to recognize the dance, their couples counselor will thank you as they work through the process of change in the coming months of counseling.

Finally, the church leader should offer hope! In an emotional hijack, couples often feel hopelessness and despair. Christianity offers great hope, which you can convey in your prayers and by listening to the family. By clarifying the interactional dance pattern and beginning to help each partner see their part in that dance, you have offered hope for change. In this initial session, the essential task is to help make sense of the despair that the couple is experiencing by clarifying patterns, helping them see that their problem has a clear pattern to it, and as a result offering hope that the problem can be solved.

15

TRAUMA IN FAMILIES

Ministering When the Unimaginable Happens

FRED C. GINGRICH AND HEATHER DAVEDIUK GINGRICH

How can you help families deal with trauma? What distinguishes trauma from crises? Reading this chapter will help you answer these questions and give you some practical ideas as to how you and your church can minister to families where an individual member or the entire family has experienced trauma. The case of the Albright family will be used throughout to illustrate the potential difficulties of working with complex situations as well as some possible ways forward.[1]

THE ALBRIGHT FAMILY

The Albrights were a multigenerational, multi-racial family with school-aged children living with a mom, her boyfriend, the boyfriend's adult brother, and their parents. It was a busy household where something was always happening.

---

[1] This chapter is based in part on Heather Davediuk Gingrich, *Restoring the Shattered Self*, 2nd ed. (Downers Grove, IL: IVP Academic, 2020), and chap. 8 of Heather Davediuk Gingrich and Fred Gingrich, eds., *Treating Trauma in Christian Counseling* (Downers Grove, IL: IVP Academic, 2017).

Six-year-old Sammy opened the garage door one day to look for his soccer ball. The light popped on, and there, to his shock and terror, was his mother's boyfriend, Zeke, hanging from the ceiling, still moving. Sammy screamed, bringing his mother, Tonya, running, who, upon witnessing the unbelievable, also began screaming. Tonya was torn between protecting her son and saving her boyfriend, unable to do either. Hearing the commotion, Zeke's older brother, knowing that something had to be drastically wrong, raced to the scene and, with considerable poise and quick thinking, figured out how to get his brother down and checked to see if he was still breathing (he was), called 911, and contacted their parents who met them at the ER.

This was a complicated family relationally, all living together in a single-family home. The older parents, their two young adult sons, Zeke's girlfriend, and her two young children from previous relationships were trying to make life work, but the relational and emotional complications for everyone leaked out in extreme ways. Drugs and alcohol were part of the story for the young couple. But the suicide attempt primarily was borne out of the emotional toll it was taking on 19-year-old Zeke in his desperate attempts to rescue the woman he loved and the children he was hoping to adopt someday. Despite the help that Zeke's parents were providing in the form of housing, food, and emotional support, the ongoing external stressors, as well as exacerbating conflict with his girlfriend, became too much for him to handle.

In the aftermath of the suicide attempt, Zeke was hospitalized for several days but did not receive appropriate and ongoing mental health treatment. Social services investigated possible risks for the children, resulting in Zeke and Tonya splitting up and the girlfriend and her children having to find another place to live.

Where was the church in this? Zeke's parents were members of a solid, caring church where Zeke and his brother had attended a vibrant youth group. Although Zeke was no longer associated with the church, his girlfriend's children regularly attended with his parents, so the congregation was soon aware of the family crisis. Usually quite responsive to pastoral care needs when someone was sick or dying, church members and staff seemed overwhelmed by the complexity of this family situation, in particular the mental health issues. Just as Tonya was paralyzed in the moment of crisis, so, too, the church seemed paralyzed.

CRISIS VERSUS TRAUMA

While related concepts, *crisis* and *trauma* are different. Both begin with an event that, at a minimum, is experienced as stressful. In his book *Stress without Distress,* Hans Selye, the father of stress research, stated that stress is a necessary part of life.[2] Therefore, the key to healthy functioning is not to avoid stress but rather to develop the ability to cope with the stresses that come our way without inordinate anxiety or distress. Selye likens a healthy degree of stress to the strings on a guitar that have the perfect amount of tension on them to enable the instrument to be played in perfect tune. Too little tension means pleasant music cannot happen, while if too much tension is applied to the strings, they snap. If we humans are under so much stress that we do not have the tools to cope with what is perceived to be the problem (whether or not our perception accurately reflects reality), we, too, can "snap," that is, experience a crisis. If we fairly quickly remember how to use the coping tools we already have, we can develop new coping skills or find external resources to help. Generally, the crisis is resolved. If none of the above happens, the crisis can become trauma. In other words, all traumas begin as crises, but not all crises become traumas.

In what ways did the Albright family experience crisis? Certainly, every member of this family experienced the crisis of having one of their loved ones attempt suicide that was close to being successful. No one was prepared for that. It created a crisis for every family member that initially challenged the coping mechanisms of each one, but then became traumatic for Zeke, Tonya, and Sammy as long-term and serious consequences emerged, such as homelessness, posttraumatic symptoms, continued suicidology, depression, and anxiety. While shaken up, Zeke's parents were healthy emotionally, and they had the psychological and spiritual resources to cope with the immediate situation effectively. Dealing with the aftermath was very stressful for them, but it was not experienced as traumatic in the long term.

---

[2]Hans Selye, *Stress Without Distress* (New York: New American Library, 1974).

"BIG T" VS. "LITTLE T" TRAUMAS

Cataclysmic events such as natural disasters or terrorist attacks can be called "Big T" traumas. Similarly, sexual assault and other types of abuse perpetrated on adults or children can easily be seen as potentially "Big T" traumas, as can be other sudden, uncontrollable events such as being in a bad car accident or witnessing an unexpected death. Trauma is primarily subjective in nature. "No trauma is so severe that almost everyone exposed to the experience develops PTSD."[3] Only 25-35% of people who are exposed to a traumatic experience develop PTSD.[4] As the statistics tell us, to an extent, trauma is in the eye of the beholder. While it may seem totally overwhelming, a traumatic experience might not be that way for someone else. Conversely, what does not seem devastating to us might be world-shattering for someone else. Other events, however, may not as readily be perceived as traumatic to an outside observer yet be experienced as traumatic by an individual. For example, a comment about her developing body made by a father to his pubescent daughter might be deemed inappropriate but not necessarily viewed as sexual abuse by many. To the daughter, however, that comment may feel as intrusive as if he had fondled her or raped her. For example, for some missionaries, the daily, stressful challenges of living cross-culturally may accumulate over the months to the point of feeling traumatic.

PTSD VERSUS COMPLEX PTSD

Posttraumatic Stress Disorder (PTSD) can result from even one traumatic event, such as a natural disaster, car accident, combat, or sexual assault. Complex PTSD (C-PTSD), on the other hand, is chronic, relational, and is most often the result of abuse in childhood. While posttraumatic symptoms (see the section on "Identify Trauma Symptoms" below) will be seen in both, the normal process of child development is thwarted for survivors of C-PTSD, resulting in psychological and relational deficits. For example, C-PTSD survivors usually struggle with

---

[3] Alexander C. McFarlane and Giovanni de Girolamo, "The Nature of Traumatic Stressors and the Epidemiology of Posttraumatic Reactions," in Bessel A. van der Kolk, Alexander C. McFarlane, and Lars Weisaeth, eds., *Traumatic Stress: The Effects of Overwhelming Experience on Mind, Body, and Society* (New York: Guilford, 1996), 148.

[4] Eve B. Carlson, *Trauma Assessments: A Clinician's Guide* (New York: Guilford, 1997), 4.

emotional regulation and often do not have an integrated sense of self. Since they suffered trauma at the hands of another person, often by someone who was supposed to protect them (such as their mother, father, uncle, teacher, youth pastor, or camp counselor), individuals with C-PTSD often do not feel safe in relationships, have difficulty connecting with others, and usually have little sense of what comprises a healthy relationship. Therefore, if you notice that C-PTSD survivors within your congregation seem to have deep difficulty connecting with the people at your church or that they have frequent misunderstandings in relationships, you can understand this as a natural response to the chronic relational trauma they have experienced.

Complex PTSD is not an official diagnostic category, which means that it is sometimes missed, even by counselors who consider themselves trauma experts. Treatment, however, is much more multi-faceted with complex trauma survivors, usually requiring years rather than months or weeks.

HOW CAN YOU DETERMINE WHAT IS TRAUMATIC AND WHAT IS NOT?

Unless you are a licensed mental health professional, you will not be able to make a diagnosis of PTSD or C-PTSD. You can, however, look for indicators that an individual in your congregation has experienced or is experiencing trauma. Noticing the presence of possible posttraumatic symptoms can alert you to the possibility that this crisis has become a trauma, which will help you determine the next steps, including possible referrals to appropriate mental health providers. In crisis and trauma situations, two courses of action can assist pastoral leaders in discerning how to come alongside a church member who may need help: (1) ask about the subjective experience, and (2) identify the trauma symptoms. Both are described below.

Ask about the subjective experience. Whether or not the stressor looks like trauma to you, find out how the individual perceives it. Do they use the word *trauma* (frequently used these days and perhaps overused) to describe their experience? Perhaps they use intensely negative emotional words while talking about their emotional reactions (e.g., "horrific," "terrifying," "overwhelming"). It is also possible that individuals are not honest with you (or even themselves) when they tell you they are fine. Their emotional reactions could also be blocked. While you cannot totally rely on self-report for these reasons, asking can still be helpful to understand how you might minister to the person.

Identify the trauma symptoms. Posttraumatic symptoms can serve as clues that a crisis has become a trauma. The individuals affected may not necessarily make that connection, though, so asking questions related to potential symptoms can be helpful.

Be on the lookout for the common posttraumatic symptoms:

- Intrusion
- Avoidance
- Alterations in arousal and reactivity—hyper- or hypo-vigilance
- Negative alterations in cognition and mood
- Dissociative symptoms

Posttraumatic symptoms are listed in The *Diagnostic and Statistical Manual of Mental Disorders (DSM-5-TR)*, which mental health professionals use to diagnose mental disorders.[5] They include the following:

Intrusive, reexperiencing symptoms. As the name implies, these symptoms involve reliving some aspect of the event. Flashbacks may be so vivid that the individual believes the trauma is happening here and now. Someone could also have a partial flashback where they are experiencing terror, for example, or physical pain but not understand why. For months, both Sammy and his mother were plagued with nightmares and flashbacks of seeing Zack hanging in the garage while also reexperiencing the associated fear and horror.

Avoidance. Traumatized individuals attempt to avoid anything that could potentially trigger an intrusive symptom. For some, experiencing amnesia associated with the traumatic event or showing no feelings when describing the trauma can also be evidence of avoidance. Sammy and Tonya did not want to go into the garage after the traumatic incident, using a different entrance to the house. Breaking up with Zeke may also

---

[5] American Psychiatric Association, *Diagnostic and Statistical Manual of Mental Disorders*, 5th ed. text revision (Washington, DC: American Psychiatric Association Publishing, 2022), https://doi.org/10.1176/appi.books.9780890425787.

have been an unconscious avoidance mechanism. For a few weeks after the event, the parents buried themselves in their work to avoid being at home and seemed emotionally numb when asked about it.

Alterations in arousal and reactivity. Hypervigilance for danger, increased startle response, irritability, and risk-taking all fit this category. Zeke's already anxious girlfriend became even more jittery after this incident and startled more easily. Sammy, whose agitated behavior had settled down after a few months in this (formerly) safe housing situation, once more exhibited hyperactive behavior, and the elementary school grew concerned.

Negative alterations in cognitions and mood. Trauma survivors tend to blame themselves for the trauma, whatever the circumstances. Self-esteem may tank, and their view of the world around them becomes distorted. This view can also affect a person's spiritual worldview, frequently showing up as becoming cynical or angry. Increased anxiety or depression are also common. Tonya's anxiety increased, as did her sense of helplessness and hopelessness. Sammy's symptoms took the form of decreased ability to concentrate.

Dissociation and dissociative subtype. According to the *DSM-5-TR*, dissociation involves disconnection from some aspect of self or experience. That disconnection can take the form of total amnesia for specific traumatic events or memory gaps of entire months or years. It is possible, therefore, that you know someone whose past has been trauma-ridden without them even knowing it. So, when they deny having experienced trauma, they think they are telling the truth. It is also possible that an individual has disconnected from their emotions to the extent that they deny the experience was traumatic, even if they have cognitive knowledge of the event. Memory loss can be total or partial. The incident may be remembered, but the related emotions, physical sensations, and behaviors may be cut off from the cognitive knowledge of the memory.

The *DSM-5-TR* includes a dissociative subtype of PTSD that is applicable when dissociative symptoms of depersonalization or derealization are present. Depersonalization is a sense of disconnection from one's body, while derealization is the sense that the environment or other people are strange or unfamiliar. When Tonya found Zeke hanging, she not only felt immobilized, but she described feeling as though she was looking at herself from the external vantage point of ten feet away rather than inhabiting her own body (depersonalization). The child, Sammy, talked about only being aware of Zeke and the rope; he was not even initially aware that his mother had entered the garage. Such feelings of detachment from self or distortion in the environment can potentially last for moments, days, weeks, months, or even years, particularly when there are reminders of the traumatic event.

While posttraumatic symptoms can serve as more direct indicators that family members have been traumatized, dissociative symptoms can serve as indirect clues. For example, take notice of large or small gaps in memory or when someone does not seem to be experiencing emotions that would be considered normal under the circumstances. Pastoral care workers may mistake dissociation for a sense of God's peace, thereby missing an opportunity to help.

> **Quick Tips**
>
> It may be a trauma response if the family/family member:
> * is still not coping well after several days;
> * uses the term *trauma* or *traumatic* to describe their experience;
> * shows prolonged expression of intense, negative emotional language or no emotional response; and/or
> * exhibits some posttraumatic symptoms.

THE IMPACT OF HISTORICAL TRAUMA

Past traumas can serve to inoculate against the negative effects of subsequent trauma, or they can result in exacerbated symptoms. Particularly salient may be the presence of family secrets or family skeletons, for example, alcoholism, mental illness, or abuse within the family system. Trauma histories of individual family members, particularly those that involve child abuse or sexual assault, can be particularly influential. Research is clear, for example, that individuals in the military who have been abused as children are at much higher risk of developing combat-related PTSD.

Tonya had suffered multiple traumas over her twenty-five years of life. She had experienced neglect and emotional abandonment at the hands of her parents, had been raped multiple times, had witnessed violence to others, and had been incarcerated as both an adolescent and an adult. Clearly, the current situation with Zeke had triggered memories and emotions related to these previous traumas. For example, not only was she having nightmares about Zeke's suicide attempt, but she was also having nightmares and experiencing flashbacks related to the prior incidents.

Similarly, her son Sammy had experienced other terrifying events. For example, a former neighbor who was high on drugs once burst into the apartment where his mom and he were living, wielding a knife and yelling threats. The 911 call made by his mom asking for help ironically resulted in more trauma for them both. The police involved child protective services, who determined that Sammy was not living in a safe environment and temporarily placed him in foster care. Similar to his mom, the situation with Zeke just heightened posttraumatic symptoms that were already there for Sammy.

HOW THE CHURCH CAN HELP

While pastors and church members do not have the time, energy, or skills to meet all a family's needs amid the crisis or help the family fully heal from trauma, there are many ways that church leaders and the congregation can help. Families and their individual members are unique, so what is beneficial for one will not necessarily be useful for others. Nonetheless, the same general principles will apply. We will discuss three broad categories of help: (1) pastoral care in the immediate crisis, (2) longer-term intervention, and (3) prevention.

Pastoral care in the immediate crisis. How to help in the immediate crisis is the main focus of many chapters in this book. We will not spend much time on this topic since much of what the other authors have suggested will also apply here. We do, however, provide a quick overview of helpful tips.

Show up! Reach out to family members, preferably in person. Do not be fooled by superficial appearances that they are coping well; that may or may not be true. Where trauma has been experienced, a sense of safety is of the essence, so pastoral care providers who have relationships with specific family members should be the ones to reach out. In the case of the Albrights, Zeke's parents had the closest relationship with the senior pastor, so it would make the most sense for him to offer help even though pastoral care was the primary responsibility of an associate pastor. While Zeke had not been attending church in recent years, the layperson who had led his small group when Zeke was attending youth group would potentially be well received. Sammy had only known the children's pastor for a few months, and they did not have a close relationship, so Sammy would not likely feel comfortable with a lot of contact, but a hand-delivered gift with an age-appropriate expression of care (e.g., "I hear you had a really scary time, Sammy. I just wanted you to know that I'm sorry to hear about that. Here is a little gift to remind you that I am praying for you, and I hope to see you back in Sunday school soon.") could be received well.

Offer resources. Make family members aware of any services the church could provide or are available in the community. You should have referral sources readily available, preferably of people or organizations you have already vetted. Your list should include trauma counselors with the types of trauma each one is trained to deal with. If possible, trauma counselors skilled in the needs of people of various races, ethnicities, and genders can help make the initial connection easier. Try always to have at least two, preferably three, options for them to choose from. Do not assume the family has the financial resources to enlist professional help. Find out what the counseling fees are, whether the family can pay for them, and, if not, find a way for the church to subsidize counseling, at least in the short term.

Normalize symptoms. People often assume that trauma symptoms will abate over time, and sometimes they do, but often they do not. You can help by educating family members that the posttraumatic symptoms they may be experiencing are normal while also letting them know that they may need further help if symptoms do not decrease within a couple of weeks.

Check in over time. Churches often do well in the first days or weeks of a crisis but not so well in the longer aftermath. Put in your calendar reminders to follow up with family members. You may need to involve others in the congregation if longer-term support is required. Natural friendships and community support go a long way in the months of recovery ahead for a family like the Albrights. Isolation is a common but unhealthy response to trauma.

Longer-term intervention. Depending on the trauma, healing can take months, years, or even decades. Churches should have systems to help their members wherever they are in the healing process. Following are some suggestions:[6]

Formal care. Churches can develop programs and resources to help. These include offering groups, developing a lay counseling program, and making mentors, spiritual directors, and life coaches available to their congregants.

Groups. Support groups, if volunteer leaders are properly trained, can be helpful. Knowing that other people are struggling, too, can provide relief and some release from guilt and shame. Celebrate Recovery, a church-based program that was developed primarily for those struggling with addictive behaviors, can be helpful for some trauma survivors. Twelve-step groups, such as Alcoholics Anonymous, have been adapted for use in churches. Adult Children of Alcoholics groups can be particularly helpful for a broader range of individuals who are struggling emotionally, including trauma survivors.

> **The Horrifying Case of Child Abuse in a Church**
>
> Many of us act as if child abuse does not really happen or happens only rarely in church and church-related organizations and programs (e.g., camps). However, the statistics do not support this perception. In any mid-sized church or larger, child abuse is likely currently happening. Stories abound of congregations that have tried to handle such situations internally. Rarely does that work out well for the victim, the perpetrator, or either of their families.
>
> In addition, at least in the United States and Canada, not reporting child abuse is illegal. Whether or not the church has faith in the local Child Protective Services to handle such a situation well, making a report of even suspected child abuse to the local authorities is mandatory. This is not a situation in which civil disobedience is

---

[6]Heather Davediuk Gingrich, "How the Church Can Help," in *Restoring the Shattered Self*, 2nd ed. (Downers Grove, IL: IVP Academic, 2020), chap. 10.

> defensible. So, report it and then to the degree those involved allow, walk with them through the long, complicated, divisive, emotionally tumultuous, legally complex, and at times seemingly unfair process. Be careful of sharing premature opinions. Even if it is unclear whether abuse has actually been perpetrated, it is important to consistently advocate for the safety and healing of the alleged victim. Much more could be said on this issue, but suffice it to say that this is perhaps the most difficult and horrendous form of family trauma anyone can experience.
>
> What does your state require in such situations? Does your congregation have a planned response? What policies do you have in place to help prevent child abuse? If not, you might consult with your church insurance company, denominational leadership, or local churches for recommendations.

Trauma survivors often struggle in their relationship with God, wondering why a loving God would allow them (or their loved ones) to suffer so much. Diane Langberg's book, among others, is a wonderful, readable resource.[7] Regular church programming does not generally address the depth of such questions, with the result that they are sometimes minimally helpful to church members experiencing trauma. There are, however, group curricula available for wounded individuals, including trauma survivors, who have cognitive distortions about who God is. One example is Lydia Discipleship Ministries, which has a manual that contains everything needed to train lay leaders to facilitate a weekly, one-year group and offers many other resources.[8] Another option is The Trauma Healing Institute, offered through the American Bible Society with materials available in sixteen languages.[9] They offer several levels of training and supervision to pastors and lay leaders to prepare them to run intensive church-based, biblically oriented, psychoeducational groups that research has shown to be effective locally and globally.

---

[7] Diane Langberg, *Suffering and the Heart of God: How Trauma Destroys and Christ Restores* (Greensboro, NC: New Growth, 2015).
[8] Lydia Discipleship Ministries (www.lydiadm.org/).
[9] Trauma Healing Institute (https://traumahealinginstitute.org/).

The groups discussed so far have as their focus trauma survivors in general or ministry to wounded people, which includes some trauma survivors. It can also be beneficial to offer groups for specific populations of survivors (e.g., child sexual abuse or veterans with PTSD). Parents of traumatized children can benefit from a support group too. For example, a church we attended offered a monthly group for parents who had taken in foster children or who had adopted children. Every meeting began with a meal that included the parents and their children, after which adults with some training in dealing with traumatized children provided safe childcare. While the children were cared for, parents gave each other support, and shared resources, and leaders or invited guests provided education about children and trauma. Zeke's parents could have taken advantage of such a group when they "fostered" Tonya and her children.

Lay counseling. While lay counselors are not equipped to do therapy with traumatized individuals, they can be trained in trauma-informed spiritual care and offer much-needed support to survivors. Inner healing prayer can be effective provided the prayer ministers/lay counselors are supervised by a professional counselor who can help them decide who might be a good candidate for such ministry and what it should involve. An error we have seen far too often is that of prayer ministers unintentionally opening up a Pandora's box of trauma memories with the accompanying symptoms and then not knowing how to help survivors stabilize. In the worst of these cases, church members who are already traumatized have been revictimized by those who are supposedly helping by being told that they do not have enough faith or that they have not prayed hard enough. Even good lay leaders can become overwhelmed and frustrated with the stuck nature of trauma and respond in harmful or unhelpful ways. This amounts to spiritual abuse and must be carefully guarded against.

Mentoring, spiritual direction, and life coaching. Trauma-informed mentors, spiritual directors, and life coaches can also have a positive influence. These helpers usually will not be equipped to enable survivors to process their trauma. They can, however, help survivors wrestle with spiritual issues, grow in their relationship with Christ, and provide a safe place to risk making new life choices (e.g., jobs, education, and relationships) that the trauma has directly or indirectly prevented them from making.

Informal care. A church can provide emotional and spiritual support in both formal and informal ways. For example, if a survivor is already a part of a small group, members of that group are in a great position to ramp up their support during a crisis. A danger comes from well-intentioned but uninformed leaders or group members offering simplistic solutions, for example, suggesting that they must pray more or spend more time meditating on specific Scripture passages. While prayer and Bible reading certainly have their place, if healing does not happen quickly, the victims can sometimes be blamed for not being spiritual enough. While this cannot be totally prevented, small group leaders can be trained in trauma-informed care and hopefully recognize when spiritual resources are being misused. Another danger of groups comes from members and leaders not respecting the survivor's need for privacy and confidentiality, especially when the survivor shares detailed information at a moment of vulnerability. Mental health professionals emphasize this in their training, but it is not automatically practiced in church contexts.

Trauma survivors do not want to always talk about their trauma; they also need to be around healthy people and families just doing life. Eating, laughing, playing games, and just enjoying each other's company can heal traumatized individuals and families. Fostering a congregation-wide culture of friendliness and hospitality where hurting people are accepted as they are can make a big difference. Unfortunately, our busy lifestyles can make it hard to include others in our plans unless encouraged.

Prevention. While it may not be possible or ethically advisable for many churches to provide intensive therapeutic intervention, churches can build a culture that anticipates crises and traumatic experiences. But this does not happen easily and requires intentionality. A range of prevention activities will help raise awareness, allow people to connect the events of their weekly lives to the relatively brief time they spend at church, and may put teeth into the gospel—that God is interested in the nitty-gritty difficult experiences of our lives.

Education. Preachers and teachers have an opportunity to educate about trauma from the pulpit and in other teaching contexts. Including trauma-related topics such as intimate partner violence, sexual abuse, and PTSD in sermons, Bible studies, and small group formats can help survivors recognize that they are not alone and that they are not to blame. Including Bible passages such as those that describe tragic war narratives, Jonah, Job, shipwrecks, and so on, can help to show that Scripture is relevant to their situations.[10] Some of these even include descriptions of posttraumatic symptoms. For example, the biblical narrative describing the rape of Tamar by her half brother Amnon provides an excellent illustration of both the impact of the trauma on Tamar herself as well as the impact on her family (2 Sam 13).

When Tamar's pleas for Amnon to refrain from sexually assaulting her and then to not send her away afterward fell on deaf ears, she went into mourning, putting ashes on her head and tearing her robe "weeping aloud as she went" and then continuing to living "in her brother Absalom's house, a desolate woman" (vv. 19-20). This kind of dramatic change in emotional state is a common posttraumatic symptom.

In their misguided attempts to comfort their loved ones, family members often end up minimizing the victim's pain, and Absalom was no exception when he said (author's paraphrase), "at least it was your brother who raped you and not someone outside the family" (v. 20). But witnessing Tamar's continued pain must have eaten away at Absalom because two years after the rape, he murdered Amnon in revenge, which had further negative consequences for the family.[11]

Examining the intense emotions expressed by the psalmist (e.g., Psalm 88) can help normalize strong emotions and God's acceptance of even those often viewed as more negative (e.g., anger, rejection, desolation). Those fortunate enough to have not experienced trauma themselves may be less quick to judge survivors or say something inappropriate to them as a result of being more scripturally informed.

Educational opportunities related to understanding trauma and the process of healing from trauma can also be offered to caregivers such as

---

[10] For additional biblical and theological reflections on trauma, see Langberg, *Suffering and the Heart of God*; Gerald W. Peterman and Andrew J, Schmutzer, *Between Pain & Grace: A Biblical Theology of Suffering* (Chicago: Moody, 2016).

[11] For example, David's other sons were distraught, and the household servants were upset (v. 36), so Absalom fled, and David felt Absalom's loss keenly (v. 39).

pastoral staff and lay helpers, as well as to general members of the congregation. Churches can avail themselves of outside resources such as conferences, seminars, webinars, and podcasts or bring experts from the outside into the church to discuss these experiences and the healing process.

Building family resilience. Especially in contemporary society, there is a broad range of what is considered a normal family. In addition, there is considerable discussion about how dysfunctional families occur. The church tends to focus on healthy Christian families. Given the amount of trauma and the number of people impacted by trauma, it may be more helpful to think in terms of resilient families. We talk a lot about resilient individuals, but what does a resilient family look like?

Resilient families can bounce back in the aftermath of stress and trauma.[12] They acknowledge that trauma can occur at any time and are not surprised when difficult things happen. They realize they are not immune from the pain life can bring. They understand and can anticipate that family processes can be learned and practiced that will help in challenging times. They recognize that avoiding all stress is not realistic, and they develop patterns that can respond effectively to traumatic experiences. In times of stress, these families need targeted support and education and are receptive to others' efforts to help.

In the Albright family, it is clear that while some family members were more resilient than others, overall, individuals could talk through the experiences. They were available to each other, responsive to each other, and had the flexibility in work and commitments to follow through with each family member. The parents also had the resources to take advantage of medical and community services, such as hospitalization for Zeke and counseling for Sammy and his brother, and offered to help Tonya process what happened. A strong, supportive church would have helped even more by creating communities where each individual could be supported and through which the grace of God could be experienced.

---

[12]Fred Gingrich, "Strengthening Family Resilience to Trauma," in Heather Davediuk Gingrich and Fred Gingrich, *Treating Trauma in Christian Counseling* (Downers Grove, IL: IVP Academic, 2017), 163-87.

A family resilience model. The table below describes what Froma Walsh, a family therapist, has described as the key components of resilient families.[13] These concepts have relevance to how churches can respond.

PROCESSES AND ACTIVITIES FOR RESILIENT FAMILIES

FAMILY PROCESSES	SPECIFIC ACTIVITIES
Belief Systems	• Making meaning of adversity • Positive outlook • Transcendence and spirituality
Organizational Patterns	• Flexibility • Connectedness • Social and economic resources
Communication and Problem-solving	• Clear, consistent messages • Open emotional expression • Collaborative problem solving

Of the nine specific activities related to the three processes proposed by Walsh, all are readily available in most congregations. The first three activities under the category belief systems (Process 1) are at the core of our faith perspective, given the biblical emphasis on salvation, healing, and hope in a fallen world. Making meaning is a tricky one since imposing our meaning on those while experiencing trauma is usually not helpful. For example, saying to young parents whose baby has died that all things work together for good (Rom 8:28) may not connect with their beliefs, which are clouded by their loss. But pointing to biblical and other resources to help a family make sense of the suffering can be valuable. A positive outlook, while not denying the pain and turmoil, is the hope of the gospel. Recognizing that there is more to life than this present suffering and that there are spiritual resources we all have access to is the gift that Scripture and the church have to offer.

Regarding organizational patterns (Process 2), the church can model flexibility rather than rigidity or chaos in how they interact and assist in planning a response. The church must provide some structure and stability. Of course, the church provides connection and should do so even

---

[13]Froma Walsh, *Strengthening Family Resilience,* 2nd ed. (New York: Guilford, 2006), 131.

more in times of trauma. Despite the chronic economic stress many churches live with, earmarking some funds for use by members who need financial help can be considered.

Communication and problem-solving (Process 3) can be especially difficult to remember in the long aftermath of a complicated trauma, especially when things appear to be going well and returning to "normal." Continuing to communicate is, however, necessary. For instance, after the death of a family member, the remaining family members are potentially at risk around the time of the first anniversary of the death—that is a long time after the event is over. The church can offer a context for emotional expression, even extreme, out-of-control expression. Counselors and people in ministry often face emotionally distraught people. Still, perhaps the individuals in the congregation could benefit from getting more comfortable with intense expressions of emotion, including anger, anxiety, and fear. It can also be helpful for people to learn to recognize the opposite, which is avoidance, denial of emotion, or emotional or behavioral cut off that can arise out of fear.

The ninth specific activity in the list, collaborative problem-solving, is an important reminder that problems need to be solved, and problem-solving is frequently our favorite form of helping. But notice the essential word *collaborative* in this activity. Problem-solving is not done well from a position of misplaced and insensitive authority or with any semblance of coercion. This takes much more communication than many of us are comfortable with. Sometimes, we just want them to get on with it, making the needed decisions so we can move on. But what does the family experiencing trauma actually need to move on? Maybe it is to remain paralyzed for now, or a while longer, before solutions are decided on and implemented.

> ### Dos and Don'ts for Church Caregivers of Families with Trauma
>
> **DO:** reach out, listen, empathize, be emotionally present, coordinate responses, provide resources, refer, set boundaries, take care of yourself.

> **DON'T:** offer simplistic solutions and problem-solve, have an agenda or timeline, touch without full consent, try to do it all yourself, move on too quickly, let your anxiety get in the way of being thoughtful, clear, and empathic.

Our chapter on family resilience previously referenced takes a detailed look at two types of families (military and missionary families) that are particularly vulnerable to trauma.[14] In each case, geographical factors may make it difficult for a home church to respond. We would now add refugee and immigrant families to the list of those that are particularly susceptible, both because of migration stress as well as to possible racial trauma for which those of minority cultures are at high risk.[15] While these types of families may have access to other social and economic resources through their umbrella organizations, one of our observations is that families in crisis do better when there is a home church that is available to assist and be the place they can come home to if things fall apart, as described in the story of the missionary family below.

Story of a Missionary Family in Crisis

I (Fred) always knew that if something ever happened to Mom and Dad, my sister and I would go to live with my aunt and my cousins. As a missionary kid, it helped to know what would happen if a crisis occurred to our family. Decades later, when I was a missionary counselor, a family met with me, sharing their devastating story. I knew that they had to quickly make some decisions. They needed a place to go and a place to be safe and to heal, but they were not sure they knew where that place would be.

Their son, Tom, mature and big for his age, had sneaked out of the house and taken a taxi to downtown in their megacity, gone to a night club, and picked up a girl. He was fourteen. His parents had no idea that anything like this was happening until friends

---
[14] Fred Gingrich, "Strengthening Family Resilience to Trauma," 163-87.
[15] Sheila Wise Rowe, *Healing Racial Trauma: The Road to Resilience* (Downers Grove, IL: InterVarsity Press, 2020).

> revealed that they had seen a description of the event that Tom had posted online.
>
> Is this a family crisis? Definitely, yes, since in this city there was no 911 emergency system—only a limited and often corrupt police presence—and as an expatriate family, they were potential targets of kidnapping and crime. Perhaps of even greater concern was that Tom was not remorseful. He denied that he was in any danger and refused to commit to being careful. All of this was in addition to difficulties with Tom's involvement with alcohol and drugs. Tom's parents quickly and devastatingly made the decision that they had to leave the country after 15 years of ministry and return to their home country.
>
> What would you do if you were their home "sending" church, and you received their call for assistance? Would they perceive your church to be a safe place for them to heal?

The process of strengthening family resilience and healing. Facing a crisis like this missionary family's can be confusing. Sometimes, a roadmap (fig. 15.1) describing the healing process is helpful to keep church leaders on a positive course.[16] What appears below is not the only way healing can happen. Other elements can be included and could happen in a different order. But we particularly want to highlight the first two elements every church can provide to traumatized families.

First, while not the primary intention behind churches as sanctuaries, every church needs to be a safe place, a haven, and a protective environment from further harm. Second, every church should instill hope amid sorrow and suffering. It is also good to realize how many families that have gone through a major trauma often undergo significant shifts in family involvement and commitment. Hence, such families may not stay connected to the congregation throughout their entire healing process, so the church might not be a part of the final healing steps. Nonetheless, the church is essential in helping families in the short term and sometimes in the long term.

---

[16] Walsh, *Strengthening Family Resilience*, 162. Graphic created by Jennifer Ripley.

Strengthening Family Resilience

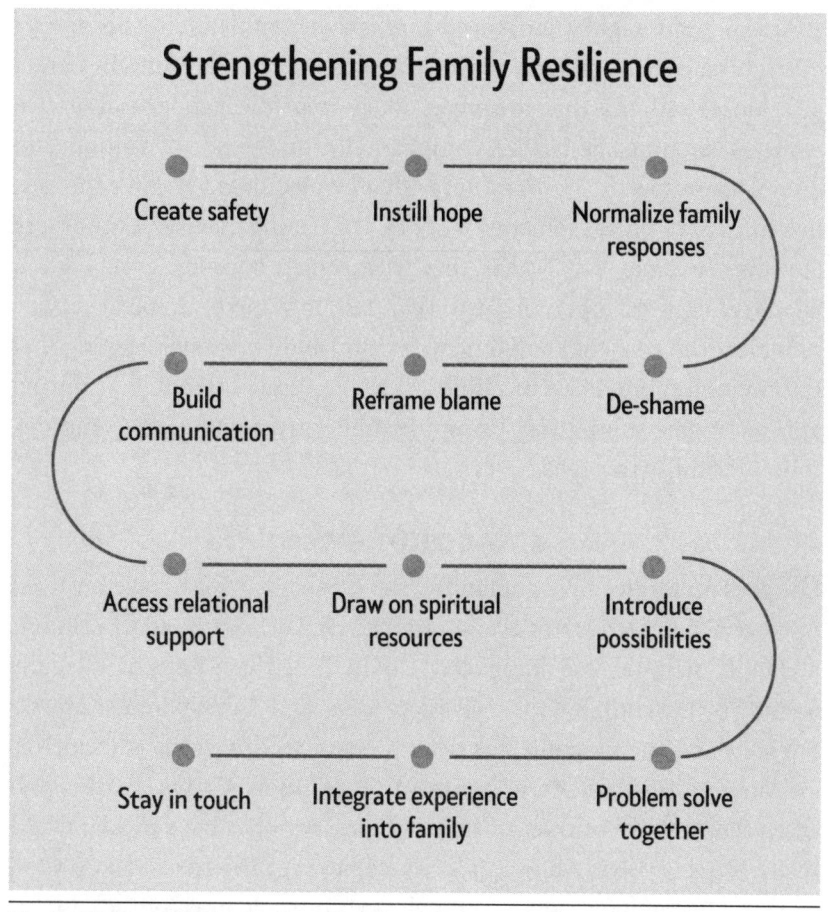

- Create safety
- Instill hope
- Normalize family responses
- Build communication
- Reframe blame
- De-shame
- Access relational support
- Draw on spiritual resources
- Introduce possibilities
- Stay in touch
- Integrate experience into family
- Problem solve together

Figure 15.1. Strengthening family resilience

MAKING A VALUABLE REFERRAL

A positive recommendation for community services can be immensely helpful for a family in crisis. Researching, contacting, and beating the bushes to find the right people to assist is worth a lot to an overwhelmed family that is barely functioning and for whom phone calls are overwhelming.

For the Albright family, while the church was not a major resource, the parents could advocate for their family members and find the right people to help. We talk these days of a mental health crisis, and Covid-19 stretched mental health services to the max. But a church can be of immense support if you know the right people, can make the contacts, and can help navigate the medical and social systems.

One point to highlight in this regard is that confidentiality becomes a critical issue with multiple players involved. Typically, churches are a little looser with this than are professionals in medical and social service contexts who must be HIPAA compliant. Err on the side of caution, and do not share specific information with anyone unless you have the family's consent or unless someone is at risk of harming themselves or others. However, we may not realize that with signed consent, even a good friend, church member, or pastor can talk to a medical/social service provider. The consent should be in writing and two-way, meaning that information can be shared. While it is a complicated step to take during a crisis, it goes a long way toward instilling trust and clear communication for those involved.

FINAL THOUGHTS

Life goes on for the Albright family. The subsequent years have involved other crises, but while not everyone is thriving or connected to a church, all family members are doing okay. Could things have been handled differently by the church, the service providers, and Zeke's parents? Maybe, but we think the outcome has been pretty good given the extreme circumstances, and we see glimpses of redemption. Crises, particularly when they involve trauma, change families. Families have to adapt, and relationships evolve. All we can do is step toward the crisis and do what we can at the moment, follow through as we can, and pray for the wisdom to know how to effectively and courageously respond to those who are hurting. Fortunately, as Christians, we have the body of Christ to reach out to and rely on when the unimaginable intrudes on our lives or impacts those we contact.

16

MINISTRY TO BLENDED FAMILIES

DAVID P. MIKKELSON AND SUZANNE E. MIKKELSON

Counseling blended families is among the most challenging ministry tasks. Stepfamilies, as they have been called in the past, have often been ignored or neglected. Churches have been slow to understand them and to offer them wise assistance.[1] Blended families, whether formed through death, divorce, or abandonment, often involve complex challenges, and the stigma they face of being "less than" is pervasive. The best place for hurting people to address these life wounds and challenges is in the church, where healing is offered through God's redemption and grace. Perhaps God will use you, a ministry leader, to raise your church's awareness of blended family challenges and be part of developing effective ministry to them.

The number of blended families is increasing, with no indication of slowing down. Over 40% of all families in America have a step-relationship of some kind,[2] and at least 30% of all weddings in America

---

[1] Ron L. Deal, "A Message to the Church: Ministering to Stepfamilies," Smart Stepfamilies, accessed May 3, 2024, www.smartstepfamilies.com/smart-help/learn/the-smart-stepfamily-bonus-material-deleted-chapters/a-message-to-the-church-ministering-to-stepfamilies.

[2] Patricia L. Papernow, "Clinical Guidelines for Working with Stepfamilies: What Family, Couple, Individual, and Child Therapists Need to Know," *Family Processes* 57, no. 1 (2018): 26.

will include children of one or both new spouses.[3] A 2015 Pew Foundation report noted that 15% of children live in a stepfamily with married parents, while another 7% of children live in a stepfamily where the current parents are unmarried.[4]

A church minister will likely be asked to help a blended family or a member of a blended family work through confusion or distress. Abundant research indicates that blended families face significant challenges that are fundamentally different from first families, which places them at higher risk for negative outcomes.[5]

Working with any family in distress can be a daunting task, as the number of participants with different goals for seeking help and the complicated relationship dynamics can leave the ministry leader feeling uncertain of where to start or how to help. When the family seeking help is a blended unit from two or more original families, complexity compounds. This chapter provides a fresh theological perspective on blended families that will motivate church leaders to embrace this ministry, lays out practical information about the typical challenges and needs of blended families that are different from first families, and offers realistic methods to engage with and help blended families in need.

FAMILY TERMS

It will be helpful to understand important terms used in this chapter. A first family is any family composed of adults in their first marriage and the biological children of these adults. The word *first* is used chronologically, as all members are in their first (and only) family thus far; first does not suggest a morally preferred or superior family structure. In these families, only two parents of all the children live in the same home. Although it is the least complex family structure, any spouse or parent can attest that simplicity of structure does not mean a problem-free home.

---

[3] Deal, "A Message to the Church."
[4] Pew Research Center, "The American Family Today," December 17, 2015, www.pewresearch.org/social-trends/2015/12/17/1-the-american-family-today/.
[5] This chapter will cite with frequency the works of Emily and John Visher, Ron Deal, and Patricia Papernow. For ministry contexts, we suggest Ron Deal's website: https://rondeal.org/.

A blended family occurs when at least one parent-child relationship in the present home predates the adult couple relationship.[6] The word *blended* is preferred over the earlier term stepfamily, although stepdad and stepmom are still commonly used to distinguish the current spouse of a biological parent. Blended not only describes the type of family structure, but it also represents a dynamic process whereby two previous family structures are now continuously integrating into a new one without the old ones being negated or ignored. Members of previous family structures, both adults and children, whether that structure was a first family or another blended family, remain a part of the lives of current family members, even if they are separated, incarcerated, deceased, or their location is unknown.

Blended families come in many forms and levels of complexity, with the number of parental figures, siblings, grandparents, and beloved extended family members interwoven. One can imagine how overwhelmed a school-age child might feel trying to navigate these complex family relationships with much less life experience, less cognitive development, less emotional maturity, and less power or influence in the process. Elizabeth Marquardt documents the complexity of children's experiences in her qualitative analysis of blended family experiences called *Between Two Worlds*.[7]

The purpose of this chapter is to inspire ministry leaders to accept the challenge of providing God's love and care to blended families. Every blended family is a unique combination of possibilities, joy, and new beginnings that exist alongside loss, hurt, and confusion. As ministry leaders offer hope, encouragement, and challenge to these families, the ideas in this chapter can serve as a guide for how to connect with, minister to, and support with greater effectiveness.

A BIBLICAL REFLECTION ON BLENDED FAMILIES

Churches can communicate a bias toward nuclear or first families and against blended families. This may arise because blended families are

---

[6]Papernow, "Clinical Guidelines," 27.
[7]Elizabeth Marquardt, *Between Two Worlds: The Inner Lives of Children of Divorce* (New York: Three Rivers, 2005).

most often the product of divorce. The colloquial term used for families of divorce is that they are *broken*. This stigma can result in members of blended families avoiding church involvement. Ministry leaders often feel unprepared to address the complex needs of these families, adding a sense of isolation or neglect to the stigma. This section will present biblical evidence and a fresh biblical perspective, demonstrating that blended families were common in the Bible, are in the center of God's redemptive plan, and are worthy of our best ministry effort to help them be healthy and successful.

It is easy to miss the reality that Jesus was born into a blended family, as Joseph was not his biological parent. Of course, he had no other human parent to complicate the relationship between Joseph and Mary. Yet, his parents were aware of his unique status, and his sinless childhood would have undoubtedly set him apart from his half-siblings.

In the Old Testament, the patriarchs and prominent leaders of God's people often lived within blended families. Abraham was 75 years old, married to Sarah, and childless when they enter the biblical story in Genesis 12:1. In Genesis 16, we see that Ishmael was Abraham's only son for fourteen years before Isaac was born, creating half brothers in the same home and adding to the family's complexity and rivalries. Jacob's family was complexly blended with four wives and twelve sons, and was full of violent rivalry. David first married Michal and then added seven more wives, and the resulting family strife would plague David's reign over Israel. Solomon is said to have had 700 wives (1 Kgs 11:3), many of them politically motivated unions as he consolidated rule over his vast kingdom. One also encounters Levirate marriages where Israelite men were required to marry a brother's wife and father children through her if the brother had died without heirs so that his brother's family and name would continue within the tribe (Gen 38:8; Deut 25:7). This practice, strange to us and resulting in blended families, was an ancient plan to provide protection for women and preserve the tribes.

Theologically, God's Old Testament instructions for his chosen people to be generous toward foreigners in their midst (Lev 19:33-34; Deut 24:19-20) and to include them in religious festivals such as Passover as equal participants (Ex 12:48-49; Num 9:14) foreshadowed the eventual inclusion of the Gentiles in the New Testament church. Paul extends this critical doctrine when he states that all believers are adopted into God's family (Rom 8:15, 23; 9:4; Gal 4:5; Eph 1:5), thus characterizing the church as a blended family with no rights of membership by birth. Indeed, blended families provide a human picture of the complex relationships that exist within every local church, collections of adoptees parented by leaders with no blood family authority.

FIRST FAMILY DEVELOPMENT

It is helpful to recognize the significant ways that first families develop differently from blended families. As Patricia Papernow creatively points out, "Using a first-time family map to navigate stepfamily relationships is a bit like trying to drive around Los Angeles with a map of Boise, Idaho. You and your clients will make many wrong turns, frustration levels will rise precipitously, and accident rates will increase significantly."[8] An accurate map of the terrain we are traveling is critical.

In a first marriage, spouses go through a transition period in which their identity shifts from being a child in their family of origin to creating a new family system. This process of leaving, cleaving, and becoming one flesh (Gen 2:24) reflects not only the depth of intimate joy and safety in marriage that God designed for us but also the new union as image bearers of God (Gen 1:27). The wedding is the formal transition point where the primary allegiance shifts from the family of origin to this new family of two, though relational adjustments often continue for several years.

The new spouses will continue to strengthen their love and attachment to each other, build trust, and form a shared identity as a new family. Each spouse must make their own decisions about what values and behaviors to continue from their own family of origin and what values and behaviors to reject. Indeed, one not only marries an individual with a certain personality, but each person brings with them an array of values, rules, rituals, norms, roles, and expectations about how families should operate. Marriage becomes the integration of two family systems, a process that requires patience, humility, and negotiation.

---

[8] Papernow, "Clinical Guidelines," 27.

When the first family expands through the addition of biological children, those children will typically attach to both parents hopefully equally, although personalities, availability, and parental roles will influence the depth and strength of closeness. The children will assimilate into the family culture expressed through values, rules, rituals, and roles. Values may be generosity, humor, and loyalty, while rules may include children never arguing with parents, dad is always right, or children never spending the night in other people's houses. Rituals are behaviors repeated around important events such as birthdays and holidays, or even regular events, such as eating dinner together. Assigned roles—like men taking out the trash, teenagers mowing the grass, or mothers disciplining the kids—also develop. The efficiency and peacefulness of any family are largely determined by how well the members cooperate in this family system.

BLENDED FAMILY DEVELOPMENT

Blended families, however, develop very differently. Perhaps most dramatically, the parent-child(ren) relationship(s) existed before the current married couple solidified their relationship. This means that the parent-child relationships not only came chronologically before the marriage, but the attachment bonds, closeness, and trust in these parent-child relationships are often deeper and compete for priority with the current marriage. Additionally, while first-family children often attach firmly to both parents, children in blended families may not attach at all to their new stepparent, creating significant rifts in the family network of closeness. Especially when older children enter the new family, stepparents may take on a role more like an aunt or uncle, and biological parents assume primary obligations to maintain the solid bond and priorities of their children that they brought into marriage.

Taken a step further, if both spouses in the new blended family brought children with them, the family formation process now involves integrating not only the spouses' two families of origin but also the previous families that were in various stages of development before they ended. If there were multiple previous marriages, the number of family identities expressed through values, rules, rituals, and roles only increases and adds complexity.

When one or more families were cohabiting, the additional uncertainty also makes the formation of family identity very challenging.

Given these complexities of blended family formation and development, we recognize six specific challenges that blended families face that often underlie their reason for seeking help. While some complaints are part of every family's development, such as communication struggles, eroding marital closeness, and teenage exploration, blended families often face additional challenges. Consider the blended families you minister to and how they may be facing these challenges.

SIX BLENDED FAMILY DIFFERENCES AND CHALLENGES

1. Loss and adjustment. While first families typically begin with eagerness and joyful expectation, blended families are often formed amid loss and anxious uncertainty. One parent and one or more siblings have left the family system through divorce, abandonment, or death, and that loss will likely be a strong source of sadness, confusion, or anger. In addition, the new stepparents and stepsiblings may bring uncertainty and annoyance or threaten family identity, forcing significant adjustments to function.

The blended family you see is often the third (or more) family system and structure that members have been navigating. After the first family was divided through divorce, abandonment, or death, the remaining parent and child(ren) must adjust to new household responsibilities, process emotions around loss, and develop new styles of discipline and nurturance in the now single-parent household. Important questions are inevitably raised, such as why it happened, who is responsible, and what the future holds. Some single-parent families adjust better and more quickly than others, but in most cases, it is a difficult struggle that few people are prepared to navigate, even if getting away from a toxic situation also feels like a relief. The sense of loss can feel overwhelming, whether the complete physical loss of a spouse through death or the loss of a family dream, social status, a familiar home or neighborhood, school, friends, grandparents, or other extended family.

Church leaders should note how soon after the previous family(ies) ended, the new blended family was formed. After working through the adjustments and losses to become a functional single-parent home, the joining families must go through the major adjustment of blending. While the adults have developed a trusting relationship to the point of marriage, the children may not be nearly as ready to enter into a new family system, and they often have little say in the matter. The second round of changes and adjustments can be quite challenging for children, as they often feel that life is out of control, unpredictable, or threatening. Further, if they don't like the new stepparent or stepsiblings, or they regard the new stepparent as a rival to their biological parent's love and time, then resentment and hostility may quickly follow.

2. Loyalty struggles inside the home. In first families, the marriage is the first relationship to form, develops without the competition and resource drain of needy children, and typically strengthens over time into familiar habits and rhythms of connection and intimacy. Even when children are added to a first family, the primary loyalty of spouses remains to each other, which forms a strong foundation for the whole family.

In blended families, the parent-child relationship(s) predate the current marriage, and the older the children, the longer the history of attachment than the current marriage. Parents and children often develop even stronger bonds as they navigate the transition from a first family to a single-parent home, and adding a new marriage to one or two existing parental systems is very different from how first families develop. The resulting struggle between sets of parent-child systems for primary loyalty is common and can be very distressing in the new home. Parents in blended families sometimes agree implicitly or explicitly that their biological children come first, threatening the couple's bond with the new spouses.

Papernow offers a brief example of Jake and Eva being married for one year: "Jake has two children, Emma (12) and Josh (10). The children's stepmother, Eva, says to Jake, 'Whenever your kids show up, it's like I'm invisible.' Jake responds, 'But they're my kids. What do you expect?' Eva strikes back: 'But I'm your wife! When do I ever get to come first?' Jake says desperately, 'Eva. Please. Don't make me choose.' Eva dissolves in tears."[9]

---

[9] Papernow, "Clinical Guidelines," 29.

This blended family is clearly struggling, as Jake feels trapped and forced to choose between his kids and his new wife of one year. While first families can also feel the strain of attention diverted from spouses to children, blended families feel this much more intensely since the parent-child relationships predate the current marriage. Blended families must figure out how to balance the needs of the children while still forming a healthy bond as a married couple.

3. Loyalty struggles outside the home. In addition, loyalty struggles often exist outside the home between children and their non-residential biological parents. Most often, this other parent is involved in the child's life on a regular basis, depending on the child custody arrangement. While the biological parents have divorced and chosen to live separately, the children usually long to maintain a loving connection with both parents. In other words, while spouses can divorce and choose to live apart, children cannot divorce their parents. The children must learn to live with both parents across divided households, perhaps during ongoing parental conflict. This dynamic is an immense emotional and relational challenge that many people underestimate. When visiting the part-time custodial parent who has remarried or is cohabiting, the child must also navigate a relationship with this part-time stepparent, who may simply be tolerated or more overtly ignored.

4. Parenting roles and power struggles. Blended families can face two common challenges regarding power struggles in parenting. The first is the conflict between blended family parents as they each strive to have their values, methods, and expectations preserved. Parents can become emphatic about their preferences when drawing on a previous marriage that ended in divorce and their insistence that they know how to prevent it from happening again.

Even if an adult with no children marries for the first time into a blended family, he/she has entered an existing family system that the new stepparent was not a part of forming. These power struggles often revolve around topics such as what chores are appropriate for which child, how often and where the family eats meals together, bedroom assignments, use of technology rules and limits, dating, how money is provided to kids, and how many activities or sports they can choose. While first-family parents often develop these rules over time and accept adjustments along the way, blended-family parents can clash, and children may feel upset and resentful when their previous patterns or privileges are significantly changed.

Sometimes, children do not accept the power or authority of the new stepparent. This may be especially true of children in high school who have their own growing sense of autonomy and power to make increasing daily decisions in life, with little interest in coming under the authority of the new stepparent. These children also may believe that their time in the home is limited and that investing in the new relationship may just not be worth the effort. Instead of power and authority resting with both parents in the home, blended families must creatively navigate the roles of both biological and stepparents. Encouraging biological parents to "step up" or take the lead in parenting decisions provides secure parental leadership for the teen and often reduces the frequency of conflict between the teen and the new stepparent. Biological parents who prioritize a collaborative parenting style despite their own relational conflict help shepherd the teen through this difficult transition to a new adult in the home. Strong leadership from the biological parents also frees the stepparent and teen to create a more amenable relationship without the pressure of constant navigation of changing rules and routines.

5. *Family life cycle differences.* The marriage and family therapy community has long described the common life cycle that families go through. The family cycle starts with marriage or cohabitation. While much should be said regarding cohabitation as the initiation for family formation, we advise pastors not to engage in that discussion at this point. The fact remains that families have beginnings, whether formally through marriage or non-formally through cohabitation. The next life cycle stages are adding new children, transitioning to parenting teens and then launching children, learning to parent adult children, and then a major shift in releasing children into their own marriages, becoming grandparents, and finally determining a family legacy. This family life cycle can be difficult for many first families to successfully navigate, as each stage has new challenges and key relational tasks to accomplish.

When a blended family forms, it may involve two family systems joining at different stages of the family life cycle. For example, an adult with no children suddenly becomes a stepparent without the benefit of slowly learning the role from the child's birth. A family with teenagers or even adult children is in a different life cycle stage than those with preschoolers or young elementary children. Blended family spouses may also step back to an earlier stage if they choose to have their own children, which creates a third (or more) biological sub-system in the home. Suddenly navigating across life cycle stages can be a major challenge for blended families.

6. Shifting sibling position. The formation of a blended family often creates changes in sibling positions, which in turn can significantly shift the family dynamics and can lead to unhappy children who resent the changes. For example, a 13-year-old daughter with two younger siblings has enjoyed the status of oldest child her entire life, but the marriage of her parent may add older children, suddenly shuffling the oldest child into a middle child position of a much larger family. Such shifts can be hard for kids to manage and can lead to significant behavior issues.

When working with children of blended families, help them identify the reason for their complaints or misbehavior. Children who are upset about a shifted sibling position and act out in rebellion to the change may be interpreted as rejecting the new stepparent when, in fact, their distress is with a new stepsibling, or they may be upset over being shuffled into a new place in the family. Parents and ministers should value the child's input rather than just searching for new ways to apply discipline. Younger children, especially, do not have the cognitive maturity or emotional vocabulary to process and verbalize their hurt or complaints effectively. They let their actions do the talking. Discerning whether misbehavior is a message to be heard and valued or is a deliberate act of rebellion that should be disciplined is one of the hardest parental tasks in any family structure.

Explore creative ways to help children find new roles and responsibilities within the family. Perhaps an older child could help coach a younger stepsibling in a family chore or learn a new skill like building with Legos or hitting a baseball. Parents can help their children feel significant and valuable within the new structure, even if their sibling's position or role has changed.

MINISTRY TO BLENDED FAMILIES

Years ago, we drove our RV along the entire length of the Oregon Trail. This massive voluntary migration of people across the continent in the mid-1800s has always fascinated us, from understanding the myriad reasons that led migrants to leave civilization behind and venture into the vast unknown to exploring what it was like to plod endlessly across boring flatlands and then navigate treacherous mountain slopes and wild rivers. In several sections of the trail, entrepreneurs realized that people would pay for expert help to navigate a dangerous river or steep slope as the migrant's normal skills, experience, or equipment proved insufficient. This is a wonderful picture of effective helping, whether by a church-based ministry leader or trained mental health professional. The person or people in need must navigate life with the family and friends they have chosen. While success depends mostly on their own determination and resources, they will sometimes need the help of trained people along the way to inform, help, equip, and point them to the next horizon on their journey.

The foundation for helping blended families, whether as a ministry leader or pastoral counselor, is to focus on understanding the challenges the family is facing. It is not helpful to view blended families as failed or deficient. Questioning how the family formed or why they are struggling is neither respectful nor helpful. Biological parents may be absent due to incredibly heroic stories of death during military action, first responder duties, or missionary service. Conversely, their story may be one of life-long incarceration, sudden abandonment, drug overdose, or suicide. It is best to approach each blended family with a sense of curious compassion and a gentle eagerness to hear the story of how God has brought them to this point on their journey and how they presently need help.

In his excellent book on helping others, Everett Worthington urges ministry leaders not to give advice to the blended family unless the ministry helper understands:

- "the person's understanding of the problem;
- what alternatives the person has already considered and rejected, and the reasons why;
- what alternatives the person is now considering; and
- what will happen if each alternative is tried."[10]

This general approach to begin with understanding can be utilized by any ministry leader, regardless of the level of formal training. Not only can it fit smoothly and logically in a conversation, but it also keeps responsibility for changes on the side of the person seeking help and minimizes the pressure for the ministry leader to generate clever advice to remedy the identified problem. In other words, the minister can feel released from any pressure to tell the family what to do and instead focus on how the person or family can engage in healthier ways to define and explore the problem.

PRACTICAL STRATEGIES FOR HELPING BLENDED FAMILIES

The final section offers a menu of options available to those ministering to blended families. The effectiveness of each of these strategies will rely on the foundation of good active listening skills, including being quick (and patient) to listen and slow to speak (Jas 1:19) and maintaining a stance of humility and respect at all times, even as the family struggles right in front of you.

The authors have drawn on a number of books, articles, presentations, and over 30 years of experience in counseling conversations as a pastor (David) and as marriage and family therapists (David and Suzanne) to develop the list of strategies below. None of these practical suggestions for helping blended families requires formal counseling training. Most of them can be done in one meeting or perhaps spread out over two to four meetings. The minister will not be able to fully resolve the multilayered issues that blended families face in just a few sessions, as that may take months or years. However, the ministry leader can help them get

---

[10] Everett L. Worthington, *When Someone Asks for Help* (Downers Grove, IL: InterVarsity Press, 1982), 92.

unstuck, better equipped, and reoriented so they can continue their journey west. It is vital that any helper rests securely in this label or role of temporary helper and does not attempt to be a fixer or solver of all their issues. No reader should feel compelled to use all of the strategies below, but rather, the list is offered as a menu of useful options from which the ministry leader can choose based on their own comfort level, training, experience, and the family's needs.

1. Employ active listening skills. The ministry leader should employ effective listening skills such as appropriate eye contact and briefly paraphrasing the person's story every minute or two to communicate that the minister grasps the story accurately. Intentionally reflecting on the person's expressed emotions is critical as it lets them know you hear and grasp more than just information, but what it is like to be them in this situation. Offer empathy through both appropriate facial expressions and statements such as, "I hear how hard this has been for you," "I can feel your sadness as you share this," or "It breaks my heart to see how lonely you feel." Good pastoral care takes the experiences of the parishioner seriously through active and effective listening. If the church minister has not been taught these skills, he/she might seek appropriate training or coaching to improve these skills and apply them naturally and consistently. Empathetic listening is critical to communicating the unspoken messages: "I care about you, I respect your story, I am here for you, you are not alone."

2. Normalize the difficulty, which increases hope. While the blended family was formed with high hopes of love, connection, joy, and fulfillment, the complex dynamics discussed in this chapter can leave family members feeling disappointed and frustrated. A beneficial response is to normalize the fact that forming strong and healthy blended families is a complex process that often takes several years for the family to find its identity, rhythms, and comfortable attachment. This strategy often provides great relief and shifts the family away from feeling broken, deficient, or hopeless, helping them create hope that they can make it.

A normalizing statement might be, "As I have listened to your story and the struggles you are facing, it strikes me that you are pretty much right where I expect you to be. These are common and difficult issues that every blended family must navigate, and you are not broken or crazy or falling apart, although it feels that way sometimes." Two of the more common concerns brought into counseling, whether stated overtly or implied in subtle ways, are "I think I am going crazy" and "This is hopeless, and I am doomed." Whenever we see blended families facing any of the six common challenges listed above, we normalize their struggles and assure them they are neither crazy nor doomed to fail when they reach out for God's help. Normalizing can be immensely helpful in other situations as well, such as working with confused teens, helping young couples as they realize how hard marriage can be, or helping an elderly person struggling with whether their lives have made a difference. This response is a powerful way to lower anxiety and instill hope that, though hard work remains, they can make it.

3. Explore losses. Blended families are often born in the midst of loss, not just of actual people but also of hopes, expectations, and life dreams of growing old together.[11] It is often easier to explore losses if the ministry leader encounters the family as the first family is breaking up or soon after the first family becomes a single-parent family, as these are often difficult and painful times. Once a blended family is formed, everyone may feel spoken or unspoken pressure to be a happy family again, and losses that may not have been fully identified and grieved may linger and emerge as anger or reluctance to embrace the new blended family. Some losses just won't go away, such as every time teenagers are forced to visit a parent they don't like or who treats them poorly, the loss of emotional safety and control is reintroduced or reinforced.

The ministry leader who detects this dynamic can normalize it: blended families are most often a strange and confusing combination of joy and sadness, of gain and loss. The minister can lead a conversation with all family members present and make a list of losses each family member has felt over the period of time the blended family has been formed. The key is for the helper not to become anxious as the list of losses grows, and the conversation feels negative or heavy. If the family members are talking about it, the losses are an important part of their

---

[11]Ron L. Deal, *The Smart Stepfamily* (Minneapolis: Bethany House, 2014).

lives, and they deserve the minister's patience and respect. By verbalizing the losses, perhaps writing them on a list, and having them validated by the ministry leader and other family members, the grieving process can move forward.

4. Promote one-on-one special time. Blended families can feel confused or overwhelmed with so many different relationships, activities, and priorities in the home. Ministers can explore what kind of one-on-one special time the blended family is currently employing to help build relationships in a quieter, more focused, and undistracted way. This strategy can help restore the special time a parent and biological child had before it joined a large, blended family with so many distractions, and it can help stepparents get to know and then express value and appreciation for stepchildren.

If a blended family already engages in this practice, the ministry leader can ask how this habit has been most helpful for them or what changes they want to make in how these special times are planned or carried out. In this case, the minister is not responsible for convincing the family to take this time but rather for exploring how they can do it more effectively in the future.

5. Improve partnership parenting. A common blended family challenge is how the adults navigate parenting each other's biological children, as well as how each parent navigates how to partner with the other non-residential biological parent. These complex negotiations and the resulting challenges for children who may be dealing with four parents can be quite distressing. What are the behavior rules and relationship expectations in each household, who will guide and enforce the standards, and how will this be done? Again, the ministry leader should feel completely free from any responsibility to referee arguments about a particular method or quantity of discipline, a specific number of hours of screen time per day, or the age at which kids should get a smartphone or a TV in their room. Effective parenting in any family includes the twin pillars of *consistency* from parent to parent (mom and dad have the same standard) and *reliability* across time (what was allowed or rejected yesterday will also be true today). The result is family predictability and safety, even when the kids do not agree with all the limits or consequences.

Partnership parenting promotes the well-researched and commonsense idea that family success is greatly improved when parents work together. The ministry leader could assist the parents in having a more structured conversation about the needs of their biological kids and how the other spouse can be most helpful and supportive. Remind them of the number one principle of negotiation: no one gets everything they want. Without parental teamwork, the entire family will likely follow the parent's example and divide into biological subsystems. If the couple is asking for your help, they have not been able to have these conversations in a healthy way. So, the ministry leader may need to interrupt the usual conversation and gently insist on using new ways to talk and listen.

Deal refers to this kind of partnership parenting as a parenting coalition.[12] Biological parents will need to step up and be strong parents themselves and not relax or defer parenting to the new adult in the home. They will also need to visibly honor the stepparent's role in the family and pass the power that is needed for them to function as a partner. Monthly or quarterly meetings can help keep communication open about how things are going in the home. Common topics that often need to be addressed more than once include bedtimes, responses to violating family rules or standards, cell phone privileges, dating, managing money, or saving for college.

Scaling questions can be a very helpful method to increase partnership parenting. The minister would ask each adult to rate from 0–10 their sense of how well they are currently functioning as parenting partners. Ask each of them to briefly elaborate on their identified number, exploring what it is like for them to be in that situation and steering the conversation away from accusation and blame. Finally, within a few minutes, ask each of them how they could increase their rating by one point. Alternatively, the minister could ask each spouse what they would need to do differently to increase their parenting partnership by one point, not what their spouse needs to do differently. Whatever they identified, the parents just identified their own action plan going forward, and the minister did not have to suggest the ideas, only ask a few key questions.

---

[12] Deal, *The Smart Stepfamily*, 175-88.

6. Establish new rituals. When blended families have a hard time finding a shared identity or a sense of belonging, ministry leaders can suggest finding new rituals that everyone can do together. Rituals are repeated actions that bring a sense of predictability, comfort, and safety to our lives—like picking out a Christmas tree, having grandma's sweet potato casserole at Thanksgiving, or going to the lake on July 4. Weekly rituals might be having pancakes every Saturday morning or family game night on Thursdays. Even daily rituals can be very important, like having toast with jam for breakfast, walking the dog with a parent, or a child taking a lunch to school that was prepared by mom. If the word *ritual* is difficult for them to embrace, suggest family habits or special events in their family.

Ministry leaders can involve the whole family in making a list of rituals that are important to them and dividing them into daily, weekly, or annual events. Be sure to ask the kids which ones are important to them. The leader can then ask how well the family has been safeguarding their rituals, which ones need to be restored, which ones may need to be retired because kids have grown up, and what new rituals may need to be developed. Applying this strategy with an entire family can be a very empowering experience for children and increase family cohesion.

7. Hold family discovery sessions. A healthy way for families to explore the issues and challenges they are facing is to hold family discovery sessions. As the term implies, these are not problem-solving sessions that inevitably and quickly devolve into power struggles as family members compete for the preferred solution. Instead, discovery sessions are more like educational documentaries where the family learns about the current joys, disappointments, and wishes of each family member around a certain topic while avoiding any fix-it responses. Relational communication is all about understanding, accepting, and respecting the views, feelings, and hopes of others, all essential for the development of connection and trust. Helping families embrace a safe and open communication environment establishes the trust, connection, and loyalty that form the basis for effective negotiation.

On a practical level, a small talking stick that gets passed from person to person helps promote good listening and respect for each speaker.

While the decision-making power of the adults supersedes the kids, showing respect, kindness, and value toward each family member is essential. Another practical technique is to have each member write a topic for discussion on an index card and place it in a basket or box to be drawn at random during a discovery session, leading to brief input from every family member.

One technique is to let each family member have the talking stick for 3-5 minutes, depending on family size. The first time around the circle, each person shares observations, thoughts, feelings, or wants about the topic, with no judgments or criticisms allowed of others' statements. The second time around the circle, each person gets 2 minutes to comment on something positive or encouraging that another person said. In other words, the helper is changing the style of communication in the family to be equitable, respectful, and encouraging. This is an extremely valuable intervention that prompts talking across parent-child lines and promotes positive interaction.

8. Create age-appropriate anger expression. A common oversight in any home is parents not providing children with age-appropriate spaces and methods for expressing anger. Adults get angry on a regular basis, often for appropriate reasons, but most adults have learned socially appropriate and relationally safe methods for expressing that anger without harming people or things. Children have far less emotional and relational maturity and strategies for managing anger, yet they, too, get angry on a regular basis, starting in the first hour of life when they are hungry, cold, or scared. When anger and the powerful emotions behind anger, like hurt, rejection, invalidation, shame, and others, get suppressed, they go underground, fester, and then re-emerge at inappropriate times and places.

Ministry leaders who see that anger is being quickly shut down in the home can encourage parents to determine age-appropriate spaces and methods for anger expression. Choices such as expressing frustration with words, punching a bean bag chair, taking a walk, drawing it out, slowing breathing, or taking a time out can help children learn to regulate anger and leave room for the underlying emotions to be discovered and addressed. As in other strategies, the ministry leader is not responsible for offering answers for the family but rather for helping them address key issues and promote healthy family conversation.

9. Dual family citizenship. Just as becoming a Christ-follower involves dual citizenship in the physical world and in heaven, living in a blended family is also like having dual citizenship in two cultures. Each of these family cultures has important differences, such as different vocabularies, food preferences, values, and customs. Sometimes, it can be helpful for older children to take this dual citizenship approach to the two homes they visit and the two families of which they are a part. It is not possible for them to combine the two homes back into a single happy family with a single, simplified culture. Instead, they might take their passport with them when they switch homes, reminding them that each home has a right to its own culture and ways of doing things. They can be strong enough to switch back and forth without becoming angry or bitter while appreciating the differences.

10. No kid messengers. A common mistake that divorced parents make is to use their children as messengers between the two households. Worse, parents sometimes turn the kids into spies, pumping them for information about the other parent's behaviors, financial decisions, or new friends. While the parent may feel justified in having the information, it is damaging to put the children in a position of providing information they recognize can harm the other parent whom they also love. Children can feel deeply distressed, as though they are traitors, being placed in the emotionally impossible position of choosing which parent to favor.

When this situation is encountered, ministry leaders can both coach and challenge the adults to be adults in these situations. Even if they are still annoyed with their ex-spouse, they can learn to communicate directly with them when needed and exercise self-discipline to not ask their children for information about the other household.

CONCLUSION

As we conclude this chapter, we encourage pastors and church leaders to consider employing corporate responses for the effective care of blended families. Ron Deal offers several helpful ideas for how local churches can train lay-people and staff in family ministry and provide support to blended families:

- educate and sensitize teachers and leaders about blended families,
- be ready to communicate hope and determination,
- offer competent pastoral counseling for longer-term care, including referrals, and
- reach out to them intentionally with small groups or Bible studies specifically for these families. These small groups provide a setting for them to experience fellowship and connection with others who "get their story."[13]

Working with blended families is inevitable for any ministry leader or counselor in the local church. However, blended families are not failed, or problem families. Rather, they function as complex systems of combined expectations, rules, rituals, and roles. It is inevitable, even expected that some blended families will need a trail guide to help them at some points on their journey. Blended families need redemption and grace just like everyone else to overcome obstacles and mistakes, and their higher risk for conflict and divorce makes them an especially valuable ministry focus. Hopefully, this chapter has better equipped you to embrace effective and practical short-term ministry to the blended families in your church and community, even as believers also live and worship in blended families of faith.

---

[13]Deal, "Message to the Church," in *The Smart Stepfamily*.

17

FAMILIES AND ADDICTIONS

Megan M. Cannedy and James N. Sells

In the sport of track and field, starters are essential. From middle school to the Olympics, starters create order amid the chaos. Starters inform and remind the athletes of the rules and place them at the starting line. They get them set and send them off in their respective lanes. That last phrase is important: "in their respective lanes."

When a family contacts you regarding an addiction, turmoil is usually present. Sometimes, you will be the starter. The encounter will likely include words of disarray, frustration, and blame. You will hear phrases and descriptions such as:

"I don't have a problem. It's not like I drink every night or stumble out of a bar, not knowing who I am or where I live."

"I'm not going to a hospital. I had a friend who went because of cocaine use, and he said it was the worst week of his life, and it didn't even help."

Maybe a parent says, "I don't think it is that bad, really. It's something he can handle at home." But the other parent says, "No, we have to all agree to insist on hospitalization."

"No, we don't . . ."

"Yes, we do!"

At a track meet, the starter will be the one dressed in a bright color with a bullhorn. Attention is required. A leader is at work. While the sporting event may be focused on the athletes, the starter is in charge. Starters make for a successful race. One might hear the bullhorn of one wearing a red coat and fedora hat exclaiming, "Runners, focus your attention on me! I will tell you where and when to line up. For now, everyone must stand behind their starting blocks in the assigned lane. I will call your name." Starters take charge. Church leaders don't usually wear a plaid sports coat or blow a loud whistle to exercise authority. However, the strength of personality is still required to create order. The fedora is optional.

Without trusted and informed leadership, families with addicted loved ones remain disorganized and in disarray. If the substances and self-harming behaviors are at work, families cannot function. In caring for families with an addicted family member (AFM), starters are needed. An essential idea contained in this metaphor of the Track and Field starter, which is central to working with families and addiction, is this: Starters and pastors are not in the race! They are not the athletes. They are not in the event. They are not responsible for how the runner runs the race. They organize; they launch. The rest is up to the athletes!

When families first address addiction, everyone has an opinion. Often, misinformation is everywhere. Confusion reigns. Enter the starter or the church leader. This entrance is often the first action step taken by the family. Order, direction, and organization are sought. They are vital in coordinating the family, garnering resources, and helping them make essential decisions. This chapter offers guidance to church leaders in aiding families facing addiction. Be it chemical or behavioral addiction, common tasks must be met. It is common for families to become stuck before they begin to understand how to proceed. The church leader is called. The pastor assists them in getting to the starting line.

This chapter also describes the process of family addiction in four themes. The first theme is to know the science of addiction. Families have near-sighted explanations for complex issues. Church leaders can translate complex information about addiction, the brain, and how healing occurs to family members. Because addictions are dangerous, being the first person to observe and know the first steps is essential. Providing meaningful and correct information to families is vital.

The second theme is to understand addictive patterns within individuals and factors that contribute to addiction formation and sustainment. This assessment process will need to be explained to families. Church leaders serve as important detailers to reduce resistance when words like detox, family treatment, inpatient/outpatient services, codependency, or others are used.

The third theme asks the essential question, "What do I do to help?" Church leaders can play a crucial role in helping everyone get in their starting spots without becoming addiction specialists. With elegant, sensitive leadership, church leaders unify families toward achieving a common goal. This theme will provide instruction as you prepare to meet with any family member seeking your support to address addiction.

Finally, we offer suggestions to understand, instruct, and minister to families that are theologically grounded and central to your mission to "teach and admonish one another" (Col 3:16). Your church has incredible potential to render collaborative care with medical and mental health professions to restore families.

THE SCIENCE OF ADDICTION

Families facing addiction often enter a pastor's office in chaos and distress. They likely have a limited understanding of how addiction forms and usually do not know treatments. Your expertise regarding addiction treatments and resources available in your community is needed to help those seeking help to understand what they are facing and how to respond going forward. Historically, messages surrounding addiction cast those with destructive chemical and behavioral habits as weak-willed or lacking in moral character. Today, we know addictions involve many factors, but weakness is not one of them. Addictions involve personality, brain functioning, and experiences that encompass unique and compounding contributors to everyone's story. We also know addiction is connected to brain cycles of impulses, rewards, and memory. If left unaddressed, chemical and behavioral dependence can cause destructive effects on a person's relational, physical, emotional, professional, and spiritual life.

Chemical addiction. Chemical addiction refers to chronic and compulsive use of a substance. It can develop in two forms: psychological and physical. Psychological addiction presents as a need to fill a previously reinforced reward, meaning the brain comes to expect the habitual pleasure that the behavior provides. Physical addiction is when the body becomes dependent on the chemical for daily functioning and expects the chemical molecules to be present. When the chemical substance is not present, the body reacts by experiencing withdrawal symptoms. Many reading this might be familiar with a headache if you skip that morning coffee. The body is used to the expected caffeine hit and reacts when it is not present. The list of substances with the potential for addiction ranges from illegal drugs to prescribed drugs or even legal and recreational importance.

Alcohol is one of the most common substances available. The National Institute for Alcohol Abuse and Alcoholism reported that 86.5% of Americans 12 years and older drank alcohol in the last year, and 14.5 million individuals reported an alcohol use disorder.[1] Marijuana is another recreational, medicinal, or legal drug in most states. The Substance Abuse and Mental Health Services Administration (SAMHSA) reports that approximately one in ten users will develop marijuana dependence.[2] In addition, cocaine and methamphetamines are illegal stimulants that are highly addictive and widely available in the United States. Finally, the current opioid crisis highlights the tragic loss that chemical addiction can cause. Opioids are rampant illegal and legal depressant drugs that include heroin, the synthetic opioid fentanyl, and prescription painkillers. They are not only addictive but also can be highly deadly. The CDC reported 75,673 opioid deaths in the United States from April 2020 to April 2021.[3] Herbal drugs such as kratom and cava can be misused.[4] It is confusing that they

---

[1] "Alcohol Facts and Statistics," National Institute on Alcohol Abuse and Alcoholism (NIAAA), 2023, www.niaaa.nih.gov/alcohols-effects-health/alcohol-topics/alcohol-facts-and-statistics.
[2] "Know the Risks of Marijuana," SAMHSA, February 27, 2023, www.samhsa.gov/marijuana#:~:text=Approximately%201%20in%2010%20people.
[3] "Drug Overdose Deaths in the U.S. Top 100,000 Annually," CDC, November 17, 2021, www.cdc.gov/nchs/pressroom/nchs_press_releases/2021/20211117.htm.
[4] "Kratom," National Institute on Drug Abuse, March 2022, https://nida.nih.gov/research-topics/kratom.

are currently legal in the United States, with many users unaware of potential dangers. Although the chemicals discussed in this section reflect a primary but not comprehensive list, a diverse number of substances have the potential for addiction and, when unchecked, can cause harm to individuals and their families. Addiction to any substance that alters behavior is dangerous. Death and severe injury occur frequently, and the need for serious attention is critical and cannot be overstressed.

Behavioral addiction. Addictions rooted within behaviors have similarities with chemical addictions. Jon Grant and colleagues write, "A growing body of literature implicates multiple neurotransmitter systems (e.g., serotonergic, dopaminergic, noradrenergic) in the pathophysiology of behavioral addictions and substance use disorders."[5] This statement means that while behavioral addictions are different from chemical addictions, the human brain engages in some of the same patterns for both.

Behaviors with high intensities produce sharp spikes in pleasure-producing neurotransmitters. These serve as emotional payouts. People can come to crave and become obsessed with the blasts of pleasure, mainly to ward off other painful emotions like anxiety, depression, or loneliness. A person desires and compulsively acts for this reinforced reward. While not involving a substance, these behavioral dependencies are psychological addictions, and like chemical addictions, they can negatively impact an individual in all facets of their life. Some individuals may partake in behaviors without any symptoms of addiction. But in commonality with substances, addictive behaviors have the potential for dependence in combination with other compounding considerations. Examples of common behavioral addictions visible within our culture include activities involving gambling, the internet, gaming, and pornography. These can develop as compulsory habits despite negatively impacting a person's life. It's important to note that, as with chemicals, our youth are also very susceptible to addictions, such as the internet, gaming culture, and pornography, due to access to modern technology and their developmental risks.[6]

---

[5] Jon Grant et al., "Introduction to Behavioral Addictions," *The American Journal of Drug and Alcohol Abuse* 36, no. 5 (2010): 233-41, https://doi.org/10.3109/00952990.2010.491884.
[6] Katie Mackinnon and Leslie Regan Shade, "'God Only Knows What It's Doing to Our Children's Brains': A Closer Look at Internet Addiction Discourse," *Jeunesse: Young People, Texts, Cultures* 12, no. 1 (June 2020): 16-38, https://doi.org/10.3138/jeunesse.12.1.16.

Distinctions between use, misuse/abuse, and dependence. Within the addiction conversation, it is essential to distinguish between use, misuse/abuse, and dependence. First, chemical use and addictive behaviors can be wise or counterproductive and may be aligned with or against general Christian convictions. Examples of use include the morning coffee, wine at dinner, a rare cigar on the golf course, and participating in the office Final Four basketball pool. Each of these, by themselves, are harmless. Individuals, couples, and families will make choices regarding their use and will model these choices to children. Evidence suggests that legalistic rigidity against all behavior can backfire and promote substance or behavior misuse.[7] Families must model healthy life patterns around substance use and behavior.

Second, some substances and behaviors can be employed by individuals in ways that are unwise and problematic, as in misuse, yet do not rise to the level of addiction. The most obvious example of this in American culture is food. Binge or chronic overeating are demonstrations of misuse. A binge consumption of alcohol at a New Year's Eve or Super Bowl party that produces a hangover the next day is another example of substance misuse. Your body tells you the next morning— "Hey, don't do that to me!" In these areas, it is helpful to discuss whether such use is a beneficial habit, considering the physical, spiritual, and emotional factors that contribute to such an assessment. Parents who discover their adolescent made a wrong decision and got drunk after a football game should address alcohol consumption as a poor decision. They should closely observe future behavior and decision-making. However, an occurrence of substance misuse is not abuse or addiction.

The third distinction relates to abuse, which ups the ante. This pattern is defined by what it implies: a chemical or behavior that is wrongly used and harmful. Abuse often has holistic (i.e., social, emotional, spiritual, and physical) contributors that may motivate the substance or behavioral habit. Individuals abusing drugs or behaviors are not technically considered biologically addicted. They may be

---

[7]Terence McCann and Dan Lubman, "Help-Seeking Barriers and Facilitators for Affected Family Members of a Relative with Alcohol and Other Drug Misuse: A Qualitative Study," *Journal of Substance Abuse Treatment* 93 (October 2018): 7-14, https://doi.org/10.1016/j.jsat.2018.07.005.

psychologically or physically able to stop. However, the engagement with the substance or the behavior is causing harmful patterns. Marital conflicts occur more frequently and are more caustic after a few beers. People can't meet their monthly credit card debt, but they habitually purchase more things rationalized by the phrase "I need it." Frustration with sexual contact correlates with late-night access to pornography and masturbation. Abuse can be dangerous. Besides the damage to themselves (and possibly others), the overuse of chemicals or behaviors can lead to dependence. While the average person doesn't intend to become hooked, chronic abuse can alter brain chemistry and create a continual and usually escalating need. Over time, this reinforced desire becomes an addiction and an integral and destructive component in the person's life.[8]

Fourth, a dependence addiction occurs neurologically because the brain follows its created design: to remember and to keep the body balanced. As substance use or behavior becomes repetitive, it makes a heightened pleasure response in the brain, in other words, a "high" of endorphins. This is called intoxication, when the brain develops new pathways of remembered reward for the specific high. In reaction, the brain also completes its God-given task of directing balancing chemicals to bring the whole body back to homeostasis, known as "withdrawal," as the pleasure in the brain decreases. Withdrawal can trigger physical and emotional reactions, including anxiety, depression, and shaking. With the neural memory, the brain (and with physical dependence, the body) once again craves that euphoric experience and screams out an obsessive yearning to use the chemical or behavior again to recreate the same feelings. Over time, tolerance can develop within the brain and body as more substance is needed to return to the remembered neural pleasure. Thus, a cycle of addiction continues.[9] Particularly with chemical dependence, medical oversight is essential when seeking to break free from its grasp, especially when managing initial

---

[8] Debesh Mallik et al., "Examining the Role of Craving, Mindfulness, and Psychological Flexibility in a Sample of Individuals with Substance Use Disorder," *Substance Use & Misuse* 56, no. 6 (March 2021): 782-86, https://doi.org/10.1080/10826084.2021.1899220.

[9] Henrietta N. Barnes, *Hijacked Brains: The Experience and Science of Chronic Addiction* (Hanover, NH: Dartmouth College Press, 2015).

withdrawal symptoms. Because withdrawal from addiction may range from minor to deadly, leaders must refer their congregation members to their medical professional as an initial step within the assessment and treatment process. Withdrawal and detoxification must be monitored by medical professionals.

ASSESSMENT: IDENTIFYING ADDICTION AND THE FAMILY PROCESS

As starters, church leaders are often called to supply information about the race the family is about to run. They need to participate in the process of assessment. Assessment is the term used to determine what occurs on multiple levels. Assessment in clinical addiction involves a behavioral history, testing, and learning the context around which the addiction occurs. As a church leader, your assessment will not be clinical. Still, it is extremely important to understand the depth, breadth, and context of all that has occurred so you can effectively minister to the whole family. God is a multi-faceted being, displaying different components of his identity throughout Scripture. He defines the spiritual, demonstrates emotion, exists in relationships, and, through Jesus, embodies the physical nature. The creation account reflects how God intentionally fashioned humankind according to his likeness: "Let us make mankind in our image" (Gen 1:26). Therefore, it's no surprise we need to assess the multi-faceted and holistic aspect of our being.

An assessment includes various dimensions of our identity: (1) the physical (our bodies), (2) the emotional (our affective well-being or mental health), (3) the spiritual (our beliefs about and experiences of the eternal), and (4) the social (our relationships, family, friends, and environment).[10] It also includes history—the healthy and unhealthy developmental contributors to our identity. As a pastoral leader, exploring this back story with families of addicted loved ones provides a richer insight into who they are, which parts of their world are thriving, and which ones need further care.

---

[10]For a holistic approach to formation in these dimensions, see Diane J. Chandler, *Christian Spiritual Formation: An Integrated Approach to Personal and Relational Wholeness* (Downers Grove, IL: IVP Academic, 2014).

Church leaders are often the first to make this needed assessment. "What is going on?" and "What must be done?" are the two fundamental questions to be addressed. When an individual, couple, or family enters your office for support, direction, and problem-solving, they need to understand the multi-component context of addiction. You need to ask the initial questions to understand the needs and offer responses from a scripturally based and spiritually minded perspective. However, there are more assessments and decisions to be made by authorities and experts in the medical and mental health fields. Church leaders will prepare families for the assessment experience as part of "lining them up and starting them off."

ASSESSMENT RESPONSE STEPS

Jerry Juhnke and Bryce Hagedorn describe seven essential steps, or tasks, in the assessment experience that families might anticipate.[11] The first step is the *Identification Phase*, identifying family members who should participate and the addicted family member (AFM) in treatment. Age, proximity, and contribution to family stress must be considered. Inclusion should not be based solely on who wants or doesn't want to. Instead, the question becomes, "Who can contribute to the healing process?" It is common for families to minimize the participation of others, engaging the fewest as possible. We intend to employ the most significant number, all of those who can stand together in the healing process. Ideally, this would be all the adults and older adolescents who have ongoing involvement in the regular activities of the home. In this first phase, the pastor or counselor will decide who needs to be present to create order and a plan of action.

The second task is to reduce anxiety, worry, avoidance, and denial of the AFM and the family. Juhnke and Hagedorn refer to this as the *Introductory Phase*. Church leaders can initiate this task with information, prayer, and presence. Your primary mission is to transmit hope and to offer an immediate strategy to establish safety and prompt care. This is where the leadership of the caregiver is to rule. Confusion, shame, anger,

---

[11] Gerald A. Juhnke and W. Bryce Hagedorn, *Counseling Addicted Families* (New York: Routledge, 2013).

irritation, and denial—worded in statements of unrealistic hope, such as "it will all be fine, no problem"—usually reign in the family discussion or the avoidance of a debate. Resistance is reduced when there is perceived to be someone who stands for the family. The whole family. Not parts. It cannot be projected that the leader exists to help the parents get their young adult son or daughter help or to assist the addicted spouse in keeping employment and social status. The leader stands to assist the whole family by being an advocate, resource, and guiding support as they face the addiction as a family.

The third phase is the *Strength Assessment*. The task is to identify resources evident in the AFM and the family. Such strengths include ways that the family has navigated challenges in the past, which led to positive outcomes. The Strength Assessment reminds the family that they have already addressed many other difficult things before what they are facing now, and they can come through this as they have before. The church leader should acknowledge that this circumstance is challenging, but the family possesses the strength to address the difficulty. The assessment might start with this type of observation by the church leader: "When you face addiction as a family, it is easy to only see blame, only feel shame, and only express anger. But each of you is showing courage and commitment by being here right now. This is not the only time you have seen each other stand up to challenge, individually, as a couple, or as a family unit. What are the other times you have acted with courage?"

The fourth phase, or the *History Phase*, requires the team of caregivers to understand the AFM's use of substances and behaviors without minimization or avoidance. Psychological patterns of mood and coping are included in this phase. The church leader can recall with the family the details that influence the addictive behavior and how the family has coped, both successfully and poorly, in the past. The leader can ask each participant about their observations regarding the factors that brought the AFM toward addiction.

In the fifth *Reestablishing Phase*, the professionals will compare notes. They will integrate the information generated from the AFM, individuals, and the family to form a treatment plan. This phase often exposes family secrets or avoidances that have contributed to the addictive patterns. Here, the church leader can bring everyone together to identify the most important responsibilities, limitations, and boundaries. Everyone must commit to doing his or her job. Three goals comprise this phase: (1) determine from the family that the whole story is expressed, (2) model the skill of asking for help, and (3) affirm the family's commitment to health—as a family.

This leads the AFM and the family to enter the sixth phase, *Asking for Help*. Here, the AFM can set goals for treatment outcomes toward which the family can participate. Pastors often are called to assist, encourage, and support families as they work with professionals to set goals and set a path for healing.

Finally, in the seventh *Commitment Phase*, the AFM asks the family to participate in the care relevant to the AFM's progress. Pastors are not usually central to this part of treatment. However, their supportive role is significant for success. Juhnke and Hagedorn's description of these steps aims to create a pathway of anticipation. Church leaders can provide direction, which reduces family reactions and resistance. Knowing what to expect is redemptive by itself. Families experience addictions as chaotic. Clarity creates cooperation.

CHURCH LEADER AS EDUCATOR

Church leaders can coach the family in preparation for their involvement with the AFM toward treatment. Being informed of the general process of entering treatment for addictions can help you be more effective as you educate the family on what they might see in the coming days or weeks. Church leaders and family members can be crucial in providing appropriate help. You might coach a family member to say something like this: "Alcohol is not my problem; it is yours. I cannot solve it or prevent it. But, with your invitation, I can help you. I would value collaborating."

Addictions are complicated, containing many sides, angles, and surfaces, demonstrated in their history, current impact, and needed treatment for those struggling with dependence. It is most common for the issue to be defined as resting on a person and with the family, marriage, or group system.[12] This idea is usually not understood. Addiction is not an individual experience found in one or more family members. Instead, the addiction is typically found and sustained within an entire family context. Addictions are addressed individually and relationally.

Previous trauma or grief can affect someone's desire to use or develop unhealthy coping behaviors. Emotional issues such as anxiety and depression can equally affect chemical and behavioral addiction. Socially, an unhealthy environment can facilitate and perpetuate addictive dependence. Most central to your calling as a church leader is a robust spiritual life that can provide resiliency, hope, and support for addicted individuals and family members. However, traumatic spiritual experiences or faith wounds can alternatively feed dependence. As a church leader, you might discuss with the person the effects of spiritual experiences on their substance use and, conversely, the impact of their substance use on their spiritual growth. This comprehensive assessment conducted before treatment assists clinicians and healthcare professionals as they tailor the best course of care and appropriate treatment plans.[13] Each plan must be uniquely tailored to meet the specific needs of a person facing addiction.

LEVELS OF TREATMENT FOR SUBSTANCE ABUSE: PREVENTION, SUPPORT, AND EDUCATION INTERVENTIONS

Once assessed, several tiers of professional chemical and behavioral responses exist based on the level of need the family would expect to receive once in treatment. Early intervention and support groups are the lowest level of intervention for milder problems or prevention of serious issues. A family with a teen caught with marijuana or a spouse who binge drinks a few times a year might be a good match for this. This includes teaching by offering readings, direct instruction, and guidance on ending chemical and behavioral dependence, focusing on a generalized approach

---

[12]Anne Schanche Selbekk, Hildegunn Sagvaag, and Halvor Fauske, "Addiction, Families and Treatment: A Critical Realist Search for Theories That Can Improve Practice," *Addiction Research & Theory* 23, no. 3 (2015): 196-204, https://doi.org/10.3109/16066359.2014.954555.

[13]Jack J. Tawil, "Trauma and Addiction," *Psychiatry* 82, no. 3 (September 2019): 291-93, https://doi.org/10.1080/00332747.2019.1653147.

vs. tailored care, and providing in-person or virtual support and accountability to people confronting similar issues. The goal of these initial responses is to prevent substance or behavioral abuse or misuse or early signs of addiction from escalating further. Hopefully, individuals referred to this lower level of care are physically capable of stopping their behaviors with minimal intervention. With early intervention, individuals choose how long to be in treatment and can come and go.

Outpatient treatment interventions. The next level of treatment response utilizes outpatient services. In outpatient treatment, individuals attend a program part time and have the flexibility to continue in their personal and professional lives. This option benefits persons with a high level of support within their social circles who demonstrate personal motivation for change.[14] Outpatient treatment is recommended for mild addictions and includes more specialized treatment than early intervention and support groups. The programs include drug or behavioral education, individual and group counseling, and building life tools to cope without the substance or habit. Medication consultation can also be offered when needed. Treatment facility or medical checkups may be warranted during the program to assess the mental health and physical progress of individuals during the detox process.

Inpatient detox and rehabilitation. The highest levels of response and treatment include inpatient detox and rehabilitation. These are 24-hour-a-day residential programs in response to high addiction needs without the usual routines of everyday life. Inpatient programs tend to have more medical intervention and monitoring while providing psychoeducation on addiction and both individual and family counseling. A specialized individual plan is tailored to each person's needs, and a full-time staff of psychologists, counselors, and psychiatrists are on-site to administer full-time care. The following section provides an example of how you, as a church leader, might respond when approached for help regarding a family intervention.

---

[14]Vincent Wagner, Didier Acier, and Jean-Eric Dietlin, "Outpatient Addiction Treatment for Problematic Alcohol Use: What Makes Patients Who Dropped out Different from Those Who Did Not?," *Substance Use & Misuse* 53, no. 11 (February 2018): 1893-1906, https://doi.org/10.1080/10826084.2018.1441310.

FAMILY INTERVENTION: WHEN A FAMILY NEEDS HELP INVOLVING ADDICTION

They just arrived and are seated outside your office. A family. Husband and wife. Adult children. You can see them through your door window. They appear tense. The email requesting an appointment said that Fred, the father who serves as a church deacon, had finally agreed to get help for his drinking problem. You have known him for years and didn't even know he drank, let alone had a problem. A prayer flashes through your mind as you walk to the door, "Lord, help me help this family." And the healing begins.

We offer four tasks that can be your guide and direction for the meeting with the family. Overall, remain focused on being the starter. It is highly unlikely you will run the race of recovery as the counselor. You are to help them create initial boundaries, prompt their thought processes, assist them in organizing a plan, and encourage them on their journey.

The first task: Define boundaries. As a church leader, you are in a position to abundantly bless and empower families as they seek and receive help. You are the addiction treatment starter. The family will take their positions and understand the basic rules through your leadership. Then, you will send them to their lanes and start them down the track toward the finish line. Your job's essential components are necessary for a smooth and successful start.

The first task you will encounter is to highlight the reality of boundary confusion. You will be helping them answer the question, "Who has what job, and when does that job need to be performed?" Clarity among church leaders and counselors regarding boundaries in your role with the family enhances success or contributes to failure. As a church leader, you will want to retain and remain in the shepherding role. As Tom Nelson and Chris Brooks note regarding the art of pastoral shepherding, you are the spiritual support and faithful presence in the family's journey.[15] Not a physician, therapist, or even a family friend. You are to direct and guide, not negotiate or coach. Neither is it your responsibility to do the follow through or addiction healing work for the AFM and family. Just

---

[15] Tom Nelson and Chris Brooks, *The Flourishing Pastor: Recovering the Lost Art of Shepherd Leadership* (Downers Grove, IL: InterVarsity Press, 2021).

as a free choice is given in accepting or rejecting the gift of Christ, AFMs and family members have a choice in receiving treatment and support. You are the leader and the trusted starter. You are not the finisher. You help the family organize and launch them into their race. They have trusted you to initiate and faithfully guide them well.

As the starter, you are facilitating the introduction of addiction care to the AFM and the family. Nowinski describes this facilitation process with two goals. You will introduce a new support culture and community to the AFM to promote, engage, involve, identify, and connect them in their recovery process. "The primary goals of early recovery, namely, acceptance and surrender, are achieved not only through dialogue with the facilitator but also through action on the part of the patient."[16] You are encouraging acceptance of a new way of life.

The second task: Receiving the chaos and not joining it. It is common for families to respond to the need for addiction interventions with disorder, disagreement, and denial, exhibited by intense and diverse emotions and behaviors. Chaos is usually rampant in addicted families. Markéta Rusnáková suggests that "the members of a family of an alcohol-addicted member are experiencing reality differently."[17] With that different reality comes a chaotic form of family rules. The primary rule of order in the chaotic family rulebook is to pull anyone who seeks to bring about change into the chaotic fray. Change is hard. But if the one seeking change is pulled and embroiled into the conflict, that one can be rendered powerless. This pulling is experienced as the raising of the helper's emotions. Someone will provoke the church leader to anger, agitation, withdrawal, or hopeless frustration. Once that happens, that leader is no longer leading.

In the face of this chaos, your primary task is to create order and thus facilitate a predictable process. Your calm presence, with a degree of emotional insulation from the family response, is powerful. The family reaction to addiction, usually a pain response to cover shame, embarrassment,

---

[16] Joseph Nowinski, "Facilitating 12-Step Recovery from Substance Abuse and Addiction," in *Treating Substance Abuse: Theory and Technique*, ed. Frederick Rotgers, Joe Morgenstern, and Scott T. Walters, 2nd ed. (New York: Guilford, 2003), 39.

[17] Markéta Rusnáková, "Codependency of the Members of a Family of an Alcohol Addict," *Procedia* 132 (May 2014): 647-53, https://doi.org/10.1016/j.sbspro.2014.04.367.

discouragement, anger, fear, and many other intense emotions, creates confusion and maintains the family "stuckness." Wherever you see such turmoil and chaos, you want to become a leader directing them toward peace, calm, and thoughtfulness in their situation. By thoughtfulness, we refer to families who are literally "full of thought." They are not acting out of fear, panic, anger, or shame. Instead, they are poised, deliberate, and intelligent in their decisions. Pastoral leaders represent such strength to the family.

The disorder often found in families facing addiction has reinforced dysfunctional patterns and roles of rescuers or judges to maintain the family system. For example, parents or a spouse might take on too much control, all in the name of protecting and wanting to be helpful. They address the responsibilities of the addicted to give them a better chance of succeeding, but the result is like the helicopter parent prone to overprotect and rescue.

Then, in the other extreme, family members could obstruct the addicted from getting help, stating that addiction is merely poor moral choices, laziness, lack of discipline, poor friend and life choices, and personal faults, which can be overcome by determination, self-restraint, prayer, and submission to God. The perception created is one of judgment, guilt, and shame. Often, the roles of the rescuer and the judge operate within the same family system. Recognizing these patterns can help you avoid encouraging these rescuer or judge roles in the family system and aim to reinforce peace and calm within the family.

The third task: Stay focused and avoid the ditches. Family members facing addictions are experiencing pain. When in pain, people pull, influence, sometimes demand, throw tantrums, withdraw, become helpless, complain, or present a host of other responses to reduce their pain and protect those they love. Like when everyone sings a different song in a different key with his or her own rhythm, chaos results.

Families often display this chaos by presenting two extreme attitudes: judgment and codependency. Both perspectives contain partial truths magnified into absolutes and laced with unclaimed falsehoods, quickly creating failure. The judgmental attitude assumes addiction is a matter of poor choices stemming from laziness, lack of discipline, the wrong friends, bad life decisions, and personal faults, which can be overcome by determination, self-restraint, prayer, and submission to God.

Church leaders, counselors, the addicted, and their families must avoid the ditch of moral superiority. It is experienced with declarations such as "life is hard... be strong... like me." Admonitions declaring that addictions are conquered by discipline and self-management will likely carry the effect opposite of the desired intent. Identification, humility, collaboration, and humble declarations of truth-telling steer one away from this ditch. It is no accident that the first step in the AA tradition is that people understand they are powerless over their addiction. It is central to orthodox Christianity that sin is more powerful than human will, and we cannot, by our strength, overcome it. Assistance is needed.

The second attitude develops from excessive empathy and care, often called codependency. Here, you might find family members describing addiction as a disease, and one cannot control the behavioral impulses. They might say things like, "Let's not be too hard or harsh here, the poor thing," and, "We know you just can't help it, dear. But we love you and will do everything we can to help you stand on your own two feet."

The codependency ditch is helplessness and perpetual disappointment. Often, the codependency ditch is dug by shame for personal failure. There is identification with the addiction on the part of the family member. The unhelpful label leads them to think, "If I hadn't failed, you wouldn't have to do this hard thing. I must relieve my guilt by helping you."

You will feel the pull toward each extreme. Be careful not to join them. If they are open to awareness, you can even provide biblical truth to ground them to avoid extremes. Be kind to them. Please support them. Just don't believe them or follow them. Each extreme is a trap resulting in a simplistic understanding and response to complicated family needs.

The fourth task: Bring community resources to the family. The pastoral leader is the ultimate care broker. They will connect the AFM and the full family to the resources needed to address the addictive need. These include (1) medical resources—their PCP, the ER if needed, (2) specialty inpatient and outpatient medical care for addiction in your community, (3) AA groups, and (4) Celebrate Recovery meetings. Families come to you so you can direct them to where they must go.

Residential treatment facilities exist in almost all communities. Church leaders might be more inclined toward using Christian resources, but consider that the best treatment for an individual's higher needs may be residential and Christian residential options may not exist in your community. Most residential facilities have access to chaplains or Christian support groups within their facility that you could engage. A clergy member, such as yourself, can offer hospital visits to residential care and will likely find the administration open to your pastoral care.

Community support groups are essential to treatment for those working toward sobriety. There are Christian support groups in most large or moderate-sized cities, such as Celebrate Recovery. Family members often benefit from AA or similar support groups for education and support. Learning about the resources in your community through your network of pastors or denominational leadership can be extremely helpful to families.

SPIRITUAL CARE TO FAMILIES FACING ADDICTION

In response to families seeking guidance regarding addiction, how do church leaders conceptualize the role of spirituality in recovery? Equally important, what is the role of church leaders in assisting families with this process? As mentioned previously, the causes of addiction and its healing process are multi-faceted. However, the beauty of human complexity is that it mirrors the integrated components of our Creator's identity. We are not merely our spiritual selves in bodily form, nor are we reduced to conditioned physical responses. We were made as holistic, multidimensional beings in the image of God. Similarly, God's mission for the church body and his restorative work is holistic, utilizing all people and resources.[18] Therefore, as God created people holistically, addiction treatment is, in response, designed to meet, heal, and restore all parts of the person to his or her God-given purpose. Restoration encompasses awareness and attention to a person's physical health, mental wellness, social support, and spiritual peace, which in the mental health field is referred to as the bio-psycho-social-spiritual focus. As you

---

[18] Sherron George, "God's Holistic Mission: Fullness of Parts, Participants, and Places," *Missiology* 41, no. 3 (March 2013): 286-99, https://doi.org/10.1177/0091829613480625.

similarly encourage each member, you holistically minister to the whole family system and the way they will heal and be restored as a family.

As spiritual leaders, you play a vital role in this recovery process. Pastoral care is greatly needed in ministering to families suffering from addiction.[19] Families can receive three-tiered support when they come to church leaders for help with addiction. Think of it as three legs to a stool on which anyone in the family may be seated.

1. The first leg is to provide direct spiritual intervention in leading individuals and families to Christ's compassion and care, given the addiction.
2. The second leg may include prayer or modeling unconditional love for the addicted person and corresponding family members navigating pain.
3. The third leg may also include identifying wounds and inviting the Lord into spiritual healing and restoration in individual and family relationships.

Remember that the church leader's role will include these components in ministering to the family. Addictions emerge in relational contexts. Maintaining the focus of treatment solely on the person who exhibits addictive patterns sets the family up for future recidivism. Whenever invited, the church leader assists the whole family with comprehensive behavioral, psychological, and spiritual renewal. Recovery is magnified when it is *our* recovery, not *yours*.

AN OUNCE OF PREVENTION: BEFORE THE FAMILY COMES TO YOUR OFFICE

We have come to this chapter with the model of the church as hospitality, not the hospital, and can provide the connection to resources for treatment that support the spiritual. There are also preventative measures. Ministry leaders can also systemically develop preventive measures to strengthen the resilient armor of their flock to guard against addiction.

---

[19]Tracy Anderson, "Review of the Recovery-Minded Church: Loving and Ministering to People with Addiction, by Jonathon Benz with Kristina Robb-Dover," *Journal of Applied Christian Leadership* 13, no. 2 (2019): 113-15, https://digitalcommons.andrews.edu/jacl/vol13/iss2/11.

Churches can take a plurality of steps to address addictions before they happen. We propose a few of the most important that are within easy reach.

Preach on addiction. First, preach on addiction. Addiction is the language of human sinfulness. Addiction is the surrender and loss of self, with powerful similarities to Paul's teaching to the church in Ephesus, where he writes:

> As for you, you were dead in your transgressions and sins, in which you used to live when you followed the ways of this world and of the ruler of the kingdom of the air, the spirit who is now at work in those who are disobedient. All of us also lived among them at one time, gratifying the cravings of our flesh and following its desires and thoughts. Like the rest, we were by nature deserving of wrath. But because of his great love for us, God, who is rich in mercy, made us alive with Christ even when we were dead in transgressions— it is by grace you have been saved. (Eph 2:1-5)

Pastors can preach that addiction—the sinful nature that has captured us all and is seen obviously through controlling substances and behaviors—also insidiously exists in our pride, possessions, and perspectives. Indeed, we are addicted to ourselves as saviors and lords. Then, churches can be open to the healing culture of self, couples, and families. When communicating the sinful nature and the commensurate power of divine grace seen through addiction lenses, the tone goes far in creating a culture of safety to confront and support.

Create addiction ministries. Second, create ministries focused on addictions. There are many to choose from, or you can start your own. AA chapters are the most obvious. The need for meeting space is always a challenge. However, because AA has adopted a spiritual rather than an explicit Christian language, it may not suit your church. So, find something that is, such as Celebrate Recovery or Regeneration, or create your own. Mental health providers need referrals of addicted families coming to us from churches and faith communities who can understand and offer care. If no daily meeting ministry program is available in your area, start one. It is common to have someone in every church who has the passion to help the addicted family as they were helped. Find that person or persons.

Church as a culture of care. Third, support a culture of care in all ministries, including men's, women's, couples', and youth ministries. We propose making the church the community of those in a process toward reconciliation and restoration. The church's goal is to reduce the shame of sin, which is certainly fading compared to the joy of honest, truthful existence with self and others.

CONCLUSION: DON'T CONCLUDE—CLARIFY AND ENCOURAGE AS THE RACE CONTINUES

The nature of family ministry is to walk alongside individuals, couples, and families as they glorify God with their lives and learn to live faithfully through the days God has awarded life to each. Church leaders are in the long-term care ministry. Addicted families in recovery can become the church's most mature, stable, insightful, honest, authentic, and righteous people. Families who pursue recovery from addiction create unintended parallels to the essence of the Christian faith by modeling sacrificial love and long-suffering.

Church leaders start families on the race toward understanding and experiencing the grace of restoration. Running the race as a family is challenging. Church leaders can help stabilize, organize, and send. Because church leaders are known, trusted, and interested in the best for the family, couple, and individual, they frequently are the first point of contact and continue in consulting, counseling, and shepherding roles with the family. Families that face addictions can experience powerful transformation. Robert Warfield and Marc Goldstein note the potential families face as they consider the race before them: "Positive spiritual growth is tested in the humble acceptance of responsibility for wrongs done to others. Making amends or being willing to do so increases self-esteem as it erodes egocentricity and constructs positive spiritual connections with others."[20]

The formula for addiction recovery for human recovery is a life-long journey. We have used the metaphor of a competitive race and described you as the starter. Your role as a shepherd will likely continue long after

---

[20]Robert Dodd and Marc B. Goldstein, "Spirituality: The Key to Recovery from Alcoholism," *Counseling and Values* 40, no. 3 (1996): 196-205.

the initial family discussion. You will continue to consult, encourage, confront, comfort, and counsel. The initial conversation with families is just the beginning. We believe that Jennifer Payne summarized the role of the church leader well: "When pastors accept a call to the ministry, a call to teach and preach is given . . . some pastors may need to assess their definitions of 'calling' and to view calling differently."[21]

We believe that a significant component of that calling is that of the starter. Church leaders carry incredible authority in organizing families who experience confusion about substance or behavioral addiction. The focus is not to conduct treatment but to inform, resource, and organize the family to enter the recovery race. "Runners, take your mark!"

---

[21]Jennifer Shepard Payne, "'It's Kind of a Dichotomy': Thoughts Related to Calling and Purpose from Pastors Working and Counseling in Urban Resource-Poor Communities," *Journal of Religion and Health* 56, no. 4 (February 2017): 1419-35, https://doi.org/10.1007/s10943-017-0363-7.

18

FAMILIES, AGING, AND CAREGIVING

Terry D. Hargrave and Paul Flores

The vortex of caregiving for the aged has become the most difficult and sometimes longest stage of life for the 21st-century family. According to the National Alliance for Caregiving (NAC) and AARP, as of 2015, about 45 million caregivers in the United States provide unpaid care for a family member. Of these, at least 35 million provide care for an adult family member over the age of 65. What we know is that this number, approximately 10% of the population in the United States, is providing care for predominantly older family members for most of their emotional, physical, and mental health needs. Additionally, aging family members provide an increasing amount of care for their elderly loved ones.[1]

Put in other terms, if you look at your ministry group or congregation, the people who are 65 and older are more likely than not to care for an elderly parent or family member in some capacity. When you would expect this group to be gliding into their final work years and spending time with grandchildren and relaxing, they are having to work much longer and hold onto jobs that require more of them. They provide care

---

[1] Terry Hargrave, *Loving Your Parents When They Can No Longer Love You* (Grand Rapids, MI: Zondervan, 2004), 68.

and concern for their adult children and their grandchildren, as well as cope with the stress of negotiating a caregiving role with a family elder with various levels of need and willingness to cooperate and receive care. In addition, they must deal with the eventual death and dying of that elder, which might be the most complicated and stressful than any other for the family. As of 2009, female caregivers, who make up 82% of the caregiving population to the elderly, find this to be especially true.

How do these caregivers survive such stress? Mostly on their own. As the caregiving population is required to attend to the needs of the elderly at increasing levels, they tend to attend church and ministry activities less and less. They become a silent group that leaders are only vaguely aware of, and fewer still have outreach and care available to assist them.

In this chapter, we confront this issue by offering helpful suggestions. First, we spell out the specifics of how Western countries have found themselves in this quandary and identify the needs of the aged and caregiving family. Second, we focus on the essential role of the caregiver in the family and the likely support, education, and needs that ministry leaders can help address. Finally, we offer encouragement to those who care for the caregivers as a worthy task of building intergenerational health in and for the family.[2]

HOW DID WE GET HERE?

There is a real and profound temptation to rationalize and spiritualize the process of aging. Like the Scripture referring to the patriarchs around their deaths, "old and full of years," we tend to forget that older people are indeed real people who are not just full of years; they are full of emotions, thoughts, problems, ailments and, yes, even resources. We suggest that aging is one of the primary factors that God uses to shape the intergenerational family, particularly in making interdependence and teamwork more necessary. Westernized cultures tend to focus on individuality and independence more than interdependence. For the most part, especially in more affluent communities and groups, this independence works quite well. For instance, most elders relate life satisfaction and the quality of their lives based on their ability to maintain independence in their daily

---

[2]Hargrave, *Loving Your Parents*, 222.

activities.[3] The aging process, as well as poverty, however, forces the family to cope differently. We define the aging process not as some arbitrary age but rather the time of life when an individual becomes unable to care for oneself independently or can only do so in a progressively deteriorating manner. In other words, because aging results in deterioration, a person *must* be interdependent with the people who provide care.[4]

Most people in the Western world think of this time when aging family members truly are old and in need of care as being relatively short. But just as medical technology and better community health have expanded the average lifespan to beyond 77 years, it has also expanded the ability of societies to keep elders alive for a very long time. Only one-third of caregivers attend to an aging member for less than a year, and a full quarter of caregivers do their jobs for five years or more, making the average caregiving experience four years (National Alliance for Caregiving 2009). Family elders live much longer and also increasingly lose their health. Caregiving used to be applied to seniors in cases of terminal illnesses, such as heart disease and cancer, which would end life quickly. Because of medical advances, however, approximately 85% of older adults have at least one chronic illness, and 65% have two or more. At the time of this writing, according to the National Institute on Aging website, it is not unusual for an aging member who has a terminal condition such as heart disease or cancer to live for ten years or more with the condition as a chronic ailment.[5] When caregiving becomes necessary for an aging member, it is complicated and is usually more long-term than people imagine. In turn, this reality forces caregivers—especially family caregivers—to sacrifice their time, energy, and resources to care for someone who is most assuredly headed toward more deterioration and eventual death.

This idea carries more than a hint of Romans 5:7-8 in suggesting that while someone might give their lives for a good person, God in Christ demonstrates his love for us in giving himself to those who are sinners and

---

[3] Luis Garcia and Jose Navarro, "The Impact of Quality of Life on the Health of Older People from a Multidimensional Perspective," *Journal of Aging Research* (May 2018): 1-7.
[4] Hargrave, *Loving Your Parents*, 18.
[5] Aruna Muthukumar, "How Do We Overcome the Burden of Chronic Disease for Older Adults?," *The Pursuit*, University of Michigan School of Public Health, January 30, 2019, sph.umich.edu/pursuit/2019posts/chronic-disease-older-adults-013019.html.

the least of humanity. Caregiving for elders changes the intergenerational family because it challenges the family caregiver to the sacrificial love of Christ by giving themselves to the least of our family members who possess the least ability to contribute and have the shortest time to live. Learning how the aging person in need can accept the love of the caregiver and how the caregiver can grow a heart of sacrificial love changes the nature of familial relationships. This exchange provides the opportunity for caregivers to love and give sacrificially like Christ, which is the legacy that changes us as individuals and changes our intergenerational families.[6]

As a local church leader, you might have found that when elders need substantial caregiving, they seem to simply disappear from your church body. Of course, they don't disappear at all. Instead, they and their caregivers are simply out of sight. It is as if the church believes that elders have little to nothing to offer the church. Elders often have a rich history and wisdom to share about many things, including investing one's life in things that last, seeing and gaining virtuous life lessons through difficult times, and recognizing the value of life, along with lessons on death and dying.[7] When we as the church ignore this part of the body of Christ (frail elders and caregivers), we suffer through the loss of their gifts, talents, and contributions, and the whole church is diminished. But even more, the church misses the opportunity to experience love in a pure and undefiled manner in giving to those who in no way can give back in like kind (cf., Jas 1:27). Aging church members and caregivers are real and substantial parts of the body of Christ. Helping them negotiate this difficult and long-lasting stage of life is perhaps one of the most lacking ministries of the church. How does the local church respond in a manner that is inclusive, loving, and realistic?

WHAT SHOULD WE DO WITH THE ELDERS?

There are multiple things that almost any church community can do to respond to the needs of families with caregiving needs. The first step in this process is to orient ourselves and our congregations toward the

---

[6]Hargrave, *Loving Your Parents*, 249-50.
[7]Terry Hargrave and William Anderson, *Finishing Well: Aging and Reparation in the Intergenerational Family* (New York: Routledge, 2013), 110.

ministry of caregiving. This orientation, more than anything else, is a process of education and application that must be supported by the leadership of the church. Leaders can invite church members or community specialists with elder care expertise to offer seminars in the church on elder care and caregiving. We can also suggest that this education must embrace three principles: (1) take responsibility, (2) be openhanded, and (3) understand evenness in caregiving.

Take responsibility. The first principle is to take responsibility. The command of Exodus 20:12 that we honor our fathers and mothers so that we may live long in the land is clear, namely that we indeed need a caregiving perspective for our elders. However, the command is not pointed backward in terms of fulfilling some obligation or debt to elders, but rather it is forward-looking: "that you may live long in the land." This command points toward the fact that it is healthy for a church body to not only help the elders finish out their lives with dignity and respect but also help them integrate and tell their stories of life lessons to others. Again, elders have much to contribute if we pay attention. Caregiving and honoring elders teach people the temporality of life, the importance of relational connection, and the strength and power of endurance and faith. When we embrace the responsibility of caregiving for the good of our congregation, we embrace the virtues of living the truths that life is fleeting, relationships are essential, and faith and love are best realized in the face of hard times. Taking on this responsibility is so much deeper than simply caring for elders out of obligation or indebtedness—it teaches our congregations how we survive and endure in hard places.[8]

Be openhanded. The second principle in teaching our congregations how to embrace caregiving and elders is that of being openhanded. Deuteronomy 15:7-8 states that when we encounter those who are poor and needy in our midst, we should not be hard-hearted and tight-fisted with our help and support, but instead be openhanded with a desire to meet their needs. We realize that responding to the needs of the elderly is a difficult issue to confront as there is so much overwhelming need in all parts of a congregation—both financial and emotional. Simply stated,

---

[8]Terry Hargrave, *Boomers on the Edge* (Grand Rapids, MI: Zondervan, 2008), 45.

however, the needs of the elderly often go unnoticed because we see the group as so unable to ever contribute to the body as a whole. In many ways, they are the least of these.

It is not exactly that our churches are anti-elderly or selfish. Rather, as congregations, we have simply grown out of touch with seeing this group as needy. Why have we, as the church, grown tightfisted with our support of caregivers and frail elderly members? Could it be because of our financial and time stresses within our immediate families? Or perhaps because we fear that we will not have enough financial or emotional resources to care for the overwhelming need of this group? Or maybe the thought is that this group of frail elders did little to care for the previous generation themselves? Since church resources are often scarce, needs always outstrip resources, and very seldom is life fair in terms of what we receive versus what we give. The point is that there is an enduring virtue gained in being openhanded instead of tightfisted because it trains us to be giving and open. Caregiving and eldercare generally are some of the few places where we learn these virtues.[9]

Understanding evenness in caregiving. Responsibility and openhandedness may seem to be overwhelming, particularly in the context of the church, where many times we do not have these caregiving and frail elderly issues on our ministry radars. This is why it is essential to remember the third principle of caregiving, namely evenness. We often see Christ amid overwhelming need, withdrawing to pray by himself (Lk 5:15-16), and calling attention to the need to "let the dead bury their own dead" in preference to focusing on proclaiming the kingdom of God (Lk 9:60). The point is that loving and caring for one another in the church does not take precedence over loving God and focusing on spirituality. We are meant to care for and give to elders and caregivers, but it is not an exclusive command. It is important to remember that all elders—as well as the rest of us—will eventually deteriorate and die. While we should train ourselves to care for and meet needs, it is also important to remember that we can never fix the issue of continuing deterioration and death. This reality teaches us something inherent in the balance of life

---

[9]Hargrave, *Boomers on the Edge*, 50-53.

while we care for others, namely that we ultimately give ourselves to God. Caring for the least among us may be an expression of our spiritual service to God, but it should never take the place of our dedication to God. A desire for sanctified balance teaches us to meet the needs we can meet by giving ourselves to God and others.[10]

CAREGIVING FOR THE WHOLE FAMILY

Educating members in family caregiving as Christian love. Caregivers and frail elderly members of congregations are inextricably linked to one another, so ministering to one means that we also will be ministering to the other. One way for the church to take on this issue and resource members is to actively teach congregants who are likely caregivers the essentials of preparing for the task. As we have discussed earlier, most caregivers of the frail elderly are family members, and the overwhelming majority of those caregivers will be between the ages of 60 and 75. One of the frustrating surprises of this age group is the reality they run into when they expect the ease of retirement but find an overwhelming caregiving responsibility for aging parents or family members. It is helpful for the church to target these age groups with caregiving resources and short-term classes on practical caregiving but also preparing for the family dynamics that will require change.

For instance, teaching a short-term class that helps them recognize and assess how an elder is doing in activities of daily living (i.e., eating, dressing, and toileting) and instrumental activities of daily living (i.e., cleaning, driving, washing clothes, and keeping finances) would be helpful. This class could also provide perspective on how to talk to an elder about eventual caregiving needs, developing a plan of eventual caregiving that designates options of caregiving for the elder, locating realistic services that will be accepted and who the primary caregiver will eventually be, and finally considering the practical aspects of emotionally preparing oneself to take on the stress and demands of caregiving for an elder.[11]

From a ministry perspective, it often is a knee-jerk reaction to assume that the responsibility for caregiving for an elder should be shared by all

---

[10]Hargrave, *Boomers on the Edge*, 58-59.
[11]Hargrave, *Loving Your Parents*, 94-98.

family members. While this may sound fair, the reality of the demands of the job usually means the caregiving job is vested in one primary caregiver. There are reasons this happens. First, families of the elder are often spread out geographically and are unable to effectively be present and coordinate care. Second, the elder often has one person with whom he or she is most comfortable and prefers as the caregiver. But third and most importantly, caregiving is a demanding job, requiring decisiveness and close connection with the elder. Housing, services, and financial decisions often need to be made quickly and effectively and cannot be done by a family committee. As a result, we often recommend the model of care for an elder demands a designated caregiver in the family.[12]

In our view, therefore, it is essential for the church in its education role for family caregivers to have these conversations early before the caregiving of an elder is essential or forced by some health crisis. In addition, ministering to the nuclear family of the elder means being supportive of therapy services for these families as they work out the details of eventual caregiving or perhaps training members of the church to effectively facilitate conversations between family members, caregivers, and elders. Preparing the family for this one primary caregiver model for elder care is one of the most helpful ministry strategies the church can have, and we believe it can be implemented in a three-to-four-week study, targeting the described age group once or twice a year. We often say to families of elders, "Talk early about caregiving and talk often." The church is an excellent place to facilitate this conversation.

Extended family support for caregivers. This kind of discussion does not mean that the rest of the family cannot and should not be involved with the elder or the caregiving task. Indeed, it is helpful for the church not only to educate the family of the elder on the same issues of caregiving but also to mobilize the family and orient them toward the primary focus of caring for the caregiver. Efficiency and effectiveness often demand an elder have one primary caregiver, but the caregiver, in turn, needs essential support through help, respite, and emotional commitment. Church leaders must teach the caregiver and family of the caregiver to be

---

[12]Hargrave, *Boomers on the Edge*, 167.

a part of providing the caregiver with listening sessions, financial backing, and needed time off for the caregiver to be able to survive the long-term effects and detrimental physical and emotional tolls of caregiving.[13] Because of this reality, we advocate for the rest of the family, friends, and church to mobilize themselves as a support group for the one primary caregiver model. Again, the church can effectively mobilize this education and training to help friends and family who are not primary caregivers learn how they can be most effective and supportive.

Church family support for caregivers. In the larger sense, the church itself should be a supporter, advocate, and participant in this primary caregiver support group. In most cases, the church is not equipped to do the essentials of elder care (e.g., supervision, medication distribution, and meal provisions), but it should be equipped to resource the family with support group help for the caregiver, counseling and therapy services, and financial help in cases of extraordinary needs. We have already mentioned how the church can be of help in introducing, educating, and facilitating movement in the family toward caregiving. However, ministry help for the caregiver and elder aiming at the general emotional well-being of the intergenerational family is vital.

Emotional support for the caregiver and elder. It is safe to say that every church has members, staff, or pastors who know the stress and strains of caregiving. Given the number of people who have experiences in this developmental period of life, it is surprising that most churches do not see this phase of life as a serious ministry and educational opportunity similar to divorce support groups, parenting classes, and addiction support meetings. Emotional support groups for caregivers can be an essential connection point for people in need in the community. When these support groups are led by those who have been through the caregiving process before, members can share their experiences, frustrations, and stresses and be heard and prayed for in the immediate moment. As well these groups may also have the function of educating and encouraging each other as people who walk out of the caregiving experience and share their knowledge and experiences that have been beneficial. For instance,

---

[13]Richard Schulz and Paula Sherwood, "Physical and Mental Health Effects of Family Caregiving," *American Journal of Nursing* 108, no. 9 (September 2008): 23-27.

many churches have Alzheimer's or dementia support groups where members stretch across various stages of the disease or elder incapacity. These types of groups give the participant not only support but also hands-on help in determining new ways of coping and caring for their elder. Churches also have natural means of emotional support in regular spiritual practices such as prayer or bringing food to those who are ill.

Another modification of a support group is for the elder. While not held in a group format, per se, a few churches have elder care teams that visit frail elders. Along with more traditional visits and thoughtful gifts of flowers, these teams are also trained in techniques of life validation and life review which help the elder and team member consolidate the life story of the elder as well as focus on lessons learned and maturity gained through the experiences.[14] A few of these teams even take the time to further consolidate the stories into memory books or videos that can be reassuring to the frail elder but also a treasured touchstone for the family of the elder. While the frail elder may not be able to be a physical part of the group, the elder's story and life become a more ingrained part of the family and congregation through the teams that work with the elder.

Caregiving and aging are isolating tasks. Death and dying are hard work. At the same time, death is one of the great unifiers of humanity. When we refuse to share our common experiences that are tough and unpleasant, we contribute to the isolation and loneliness we and others may feel. When we walk together and tell our stories, we still have a tough process to go through, but we do not have to go through the process alone. This shared reality, in the end, contributes to our sense of belonging and safety.[15] This kind of support is essential for the church to offer as we seek to help the intergenerational family negotiate this life stage of aging and caregiving.

Respite care for caregivers. Caregiving for an elder and parenting have at least one thing in common. Both expressions of caregiving never stop in terms of being emotionally taxing and always on call. Many churches and ministries have the idea of giving families a "parent night out" in

---

[14] Hargrave and Anderson, *Finishing Well*, 110-18.
[15] Terry Hargrave, Nicole Zasowski, and Miyoung Yoon Hammer, *Advances and Techniques in Restoration Therapy* (New York: Routledge, 2019), 123-30.

support of marriages, but seldom do the same churches have the focus of a "caregiver night out" to support the emotional health of these individuals. Activating this idea could easily begin with a group of caregiver support members from a church who are willing to visit with a frail elder for two hours, bring a meal, and share a video or book. The value of such a group providing this kind of service becomes clearer when it enables the regular caregiver a break to go to an exercise class, see a movie, go to a church service, or simply grab a coffee with a friend. Imagine the emotional impact this kind of respite could have on a group of caregivers if they were able to provide that respite regularly, once or twice a week.

Caregivers and the elders they care for may be reluctant to accept this kind of respite care. Remember, these frail elders have substantial and serious health issues, and caregivers often develop a fear that something will happen when they are away or take time for themselves. We have found that this is one of the places the church can exert some gentle pressure to acclimate both the caregiver and elder to new people who can offer the gift of space and time, which often results in more emotional and physical grounding for the caregiver.

Emotional care for the overwhelmed. As the church, we tend to forget just how fragile things can be emotionally for both the caregiver and the frail elder in terms of physical, mental, and emotional well-being. Many elders have experiences ranging from psychosis, delusions, and misuse of medications.[16] Of all the psychological issues that caregivers and frail elders face most often, depression is the greatest. Current research tells us that the frailer the elder is, the more likely the caregiver is to be depressed. Up to 15% of caregivers for elders suffer from chronic depression, which seems to be substantially on the rise within this group.[17] Although depression among the elderly seems to be lower than among the younger population, the consequences of that depression are much more dangerous and consequential. As many as 20% of suicides in the United States occur among the elderly, with elderly men being most at risk.[18]

---

[16] Hargrave, *Loving Your Parents*, 103-4.
[17] Abdullelah Alfakhri et al., "Depression Among Caregivers of Patients with Dementia," *Inquiry* 55 (January 2018): 1-6.
[18] Amy Fiske, Julie Wetherell, and Margaret Gatz, "Depression in Older Adults," *Annual Review of Clinical Psychology* 5 (2009): 363-89.

This reality confirms what we already know: aging, death, and caregiving comprise an emotionally taxing job. Not all churches, but many have acknowledged the need to offer counseling and therapy for families and church members of the aged. In some cases, this help can be provided through church counseling services housed within the church or through professional services available in the community, especially when serious psychological issues present. We advocate for churches and leaders to at least consider the tremendous need that exists for psychological services for members who carry tremendous emotional burdens and problems. Church advocacy for professional help, as well as community support, are essential for a wide range of issues that exist in congregations, but particularly needed for caregivers and frail elders in the church.

One ministry churches can provide is to procure resources for members of their church body, even if they are a very small church with only one or two families in this life stage at once. Such resources might also supplement a large, robust ministry to elders and their families. The following resources can support the families:

1. DVD Video Seminar by Terry Hargrave on *How to Love Your Parents When They Can No Longer Love You*
2. *Boomers on the Edge* book by Terry Hargrave
3. National Alliance for Caregiving Website: www.caregiving.org/
4. Podcasts: *The Caring Generation, Happy Healthy Caregiver Podcast, The Caregiver Community*

THINKING RIGHTLY ABOUT AGING

Imagine standing on a bridge that seems to go infinitely from you in both directions. In many ways, this accurately represents how intergenerational families work. They reach backward for many generations to people they do not know or relate to. Yet, these past generations are responsible for our whole genetic makeup and a good part of our emotional and psychological strengths and weaknesses. We likely think, act, and believe much more like these former family members than we do anyone else in our current context. Our family past is our intergenerational lineage and heritage—for better or for worse.

But the bridge also goes in the other direction. From where we stand, generations will come from us into the future as we give our genetic and psychological messages to that family group, for better or for worse. And here we stand on the bridge of the intergenerational family as well as the intergenerational church, deciding how we will do the important work of loving our God and loving others in such a way that strengthens the bridge. We hope not to weaken the bridge. What have we done with the legacy handed to us, and what will we do for the generations to come?

As authors who deal with aging families and see the important impact of this stage on the family and individual, we can speak to the idea of how the past and future are connected. The faithfulness of people who care for elders well and help them on the path of aging contributes to their strength and character, as well as their genetic characteristics to family members they will never see but will love and treasure just the same. It is this dance of caregiving at the end of life that says so much about the value of a single soul—regardless of whether they are cognitively "all there" or able to physically contribute—that tests our mettle concerning love and trustworthiness. Honoring the past generation at the end of life somehow provides the clarity and character of how to be loving and trustworthy in the current generation and into the future. William Faulkner famously once said, "The past is not dead. It's not even past."[19] We would add that what we do with our frail elderly does much to either strengthen or deplete the intergenerational lineage that comes from us in terms of love and trustworthiness. We will either strengthen or weaken the family as a result of what we do with our elders. The church can play a much more strategic role in this process.

Certainly, the intergenerational family is an accurate picture of how the church works from legacy to legacy, from generation to generation. It behooves us, therefore, as people who minister in the church to look at the whole of the family life cycle and choose to minister in responsible, openhanded, and even ways to care for caregivers and elders.

---

[19]William Faulkner, *Requiem for a Nun* (New York: Vintage Books, 2012).

LIST OF CONTRIBUTORS

Anna Brose, MA, is a doctoral student in the PhD program in clinical psychology at Wheaton College, where she works as a teaching and research assistant in the Sexual and Gender Identity Institute.

Eric M. Brown, PhD, is assistant professor in the mental health counseling and behavioral medicine program at the Chobanian & Avedisian School of Medicine, Boston University. He is a licensed mental health counselor and publishes in the area of trauma and burnout-resilience of therapists and church leaders.

Megan M. Cannedy, PhD, is a professor at Colorado Christian University's School of Counseling. She is a licensed marriage and family therapist in two jurisdictions and publishes on the psychology of religion, family development, and multiculturalism.

Diane J. Chandler, PhD, is associate professor of Christian formation and leadership at Regent University School of Divinity in Virginia Beach, Virginia. She is the author of *Christian Spiritual Formation: An Integrated Approach for Personal and Relational Wholeness*, along with numerous articles and book chapters on spiritual formation and leadership themes.

Janet B. Dean, MDiv, PhD, is professor of pastoral counseling at Asbury Theological Seminary. She is a licensed clinical psychologist and an ordained elder in the Church of the Nazarene. She publishes in the intersection of sexual and gender identity and faith.

J. P. De Gance is the founder and president of Communio, a ministry the equips the local church to share the gospel through marriage and relationship ministry. He designed and oversaw the largest privately funded community-based marriage initiative in the nation's history, which led to a 24 percent decline in divorce across Jacksonville, Florida, from 2016 to 2018.

Paul Flores, PhD, is a licensed clinical psychologist. He serves military veterans through assessment as they seek compensation for mental health disabilities incurred by service. He has taught variously in undergraduate, masters, and doctoral programs in psychology and marriage and family therapy.

Heather Davediuk Gingrich, PhD, developed and coordinates the five-course Graduate Certificate in Trauma Therapy at Toccoa Falls College School of Graduate Studies. Her books *Restoring the Shattered Self* and *Shattered No More!* are descriptions of the healing process for survivors of complex trauma.

Fred C. Gingrich, PhD, is program director of the marriage and family therapy MA program at Toccoa Falls College. Together Heather and Fred coedited *Treating Trauma in Christian Counseling* and coauthored *Skills for Effective Counseling: A Faith-Based Integration*. Heather and Fred have taught and practiced in Canada, the Philippines, and the United States, with a call to serve and respond to the mental health needs of the global church. They have three biracial, adopted sons.

Stephen Grcevich, MD, is president and founder of Key Ministry and serves as associate professor of psychiatry at Northeast Ohio Medical University. He is known for his work as a practicing child and adolescent psychiatrist and his publications on church-based disability outreach and inclusion.

Terry D. Hargrave, PhD, is the Evelyn and Frank Freed Professor of Marriage and Family Therapy at Fuller Theological Seminary and is president of and in practice at Amarillo Family Institute, Inc. He has authored over forty professional articles and fifteen books.

Kristen Kansiewicz, PhD, LPC, is assistant professor and graduate counseling program director at Evangel University in Springfield, Missouri. She is a Licensed Professional Counselor who served with her husband in urban pastoral ministry for twenty years.

Kathy Koch, PhD, empowers parents, educators, and pastors to celebrate kids as Jesus did. A renowned speaker, author of seven books with Moody Publishers, and frequent guest on *Focus on the Family*, she explains identity and faith formation in keynotes, breakouts, and special addresses. She earned her PhD in reading and educational psychology from Purdue University.

Lynne Marie Kohm, JD, is the John Brown McCarty Professor of Family Law at Regent University School of Law in Virginia Beach, Virginia. She is licensed to practice law in five jurisdictions and is known for her research and publications on family law in the context of family restoration.

David P. Mikkelson, MDiv, PhD, is a retired US Army Chaplain with over thirty years of experience working with blended families in a variety of settings. He is currently a Licensed Marriage and Family Therapist and AAMFT Approved Supervisor focused on training therapists at Hill City Counseling in Lynchburg, Virginia.

Suzanne E. Mikkelson, PhD, is clinical director of Hill City Counseling, a clinical training center preparing the next generation of Christian counselors and therapists. She is licensed as a marriage and family therapist with expertise in trauma recovery. She is an AAMFT Approved Supervisor and a national trainer in EMDR therapy.

David C. Olsen, PhD, LMFT, is executive director of the Samaritan Counseling Center of the Capital Region and coauthor of *Saying No to Say Yes: Everyday Boundaries and Pastoral Excellence* and *The Couple's Survival Workbook*.

Cassandra D. Page, PsyD, is assistant dean and associate professor for the College of Health and Behavioral Sciences at Regent University. She is a licensed clinical psychologist and publishes in the areas of psychology and social justice.

Arlene Pellicane, MA, is an author, speaker, and host of the *Happy Home Podcast*. Her books include *Screen Kids* (coauthored with Gary Chapman) and *Parents Rising*. She has appeared on media outlets such as the *Today Show*, the *Wall Street Journal*, and *Focus on the Family*.

Jennifer S. Ripley, PhD, is professor and the Rosemarie Scotti Hughes Professor of

Integration at Regent University School of Psychology and Counseling and codirector of the Charis Institute. She is licensed as a psychologist and publishes in psychology of religion and family.

James N. Sells, PhD, a licensed clinical psychologist, serves as professor of counseling and the Rosemarie Scotti Hughes Professor of Integration at Regent University School of Psychology and Counseling and as codirector of the Charis Institute. His area of research and publication focus on couples, clinical supervision, family reconciliation, Christian integration of faith and clinical practice, and church mental health collaboration.

Stephen P. Stratton, PhD, is professor of counseling and pastoral care at Asbury Theological Seminary and codirector of the Van Tatenhove Center for Counseling at Asbury. He is a fellow in the Sexual and Gender Identity Institute at Wheaton and is licensed as a psychologist in Kentucky.

Darby A. Strickland, MDiv, is a counselor and faculty member for the Christian Counseling & Educational Foundation. She is the author of *Is It Abuse? A Biblical Guide to Identifying Domestic Abuse and Helping Victims* and *Trauma: Caring for Survivors*. She regularly trains churches in abuse care and contributed to the free curriculum *Becoming a Church That Cares Well for the Abused*.

John Van Epp, PhD, is founder and president of Love Thinks, LLC, and author of *How to Avoid Falling in Love with a Jerk* and *Endgame: The Church's Strategic Move to Save Faith and Family*. He has developed relationship programs that have been taught to over one million people and previously has been a pastor, an adjunct seminary professor, and a clinical counselor in private practice.

Ryan Wolfe is the president and executive director of Ability Ministry. He is a respected leader, author, and speaker in the field of disability ministry. He has twenty years of experience both at the local church level and leading a national religious nonprofit.

Mark A. Yarhouse, PsyD, is the Dr. Arthur P. Rech and Mrs. Jean May Rech Professor of psychology at Wheaton College, where he also directs the Sexual and Gender Identity Institute.